Does God Truly Exist?

The Most Rev. Peter J. Akinola. DD, CON., *Archbishop Metropolitan and Primate of All Nigeria (Anglican Communion) and National President, Christian Association of Nigeria.* February 2006.:-

"This is a result of a commendable study of the Holy Scriptures by someone who is in a relationship with God. Temitope brings to fore the many questions faced by Christians world over as they try to stand up for their belief in God and their reliance upon the time-tested Holy Bible to guide their new life in the revealed begotten Son of God - Jesus the Christ. This book is a valuable material for anyone who is tired of dodging the questions our modern society keeps propping up in attempts to make man ignore the Almighty Creator."

The Rev. Olugbenga Olagunju M.Th., *Chaplain, The Chapel of Faith, Federal University of Technology, Akure, Nigeria.* March 2006.:-

"This is a book for every inquisitive mind. The book is apologetic, theological, philosophical, scientific and spiritual in content. It answers questions about the existence of God, creation, sin, atonement, redemption and many more. This is a book we've all been waiting for. It is a valuable material for anyone who wants to know more about the existence of God. I recommend it to all people no matter their religious persuasions."

Does God Truly Exist?

WHY YOU SHOULD OPTIMISE YOUR PERSONAL RELATIONSHIP WITH GOD – AND HOW YOU CAN DO SO – IF HE TRULY EXISTS!

Temitope O. Oyetomi

Baal Hamon Publishers
Akure, NIGERIA.

The first edition of this book was published in 2004 on behalf of the author by Pleasant Word, Enumclaw, WA, United States. The author reserves all rights in all editions.

This repackaged edition is published by Baal Hamon Publishers, P. O. Box 2338, Akure, Ondo State, Nigeria.

www.baalhamon.com/publishers/

publishers@baalhamon.com

ISBN-10:   978-075-682-5
ISBN-13:   978-978-075-682-6
EAN: 9789780756826

DEDICATION

Dedicated affectionately to the **God of Abraham, Isaac, and Jacob** - "***The Eternal Mystery***".

Now to the King eternal, immortal, invisible, the only God, be honor and glory for ever and ever. Amen.

(1 Timothy 1: 17)

Also dedicated to the loving memory of **Uncle Feyi, Aunt Ibidun and Aunt Aduke** who passed on in an automobile crash on the 27th of May, 2006.

If people die, can they come back to life? . . ..

(Job 14: 14, Good News Bible)

CONTENTS

ACKNOWLEDGEMENTS

To all who have helped me in life and faith until now.

I thank every one of you who has contributed in one way or another to my life and faith until this moment; especially in the writing and publishing of this book. I wish I could list the names of all of you here but, for several reasons, I cannot. However, I am delighted to say, "**Thank you very much and God bless you**". God sees your labours of love, and he would surely reward you.

FOREWORD

This book, **"*Does God Truly Exist?*"**, is radical. The author no doubt had the influence of the unusual when he was writing it. A reflection of deep personal experience has been brought to bear upon various scientific, theological and philosophical positions. It is like the battle of the minds, starting of course from the obvious religious experience.

Writing from the position of a believer, it is naturally most unlikely that Darwin's evolutionary theory would have been an asset to the author who has raised a fathom of questions thereby. The type of raging questions which could have troubled Christian physicists and scientists like Isaac Newton, Michael Faraday or Albert Einstein as they set to make a meaning out of life are the same type of imageries that reflect in this book. Essentially, it is to prove something: the existence of a Supreme Being, an Uncaused Cause, an Unmoved Mover who has been identified as God.

However, a lot of issues have been raised and no reader will be left without being provoked. Yet many questions will be left unanswered with a lot of statements which are personal expressions rather than globally acceptable phenomena.

Nevertheless, this book forms a good reading that will plausibly challenge every mind.

The Rt. Revd. G. L. Lasebikan, *Ph.D.*
Bishop of Ondo Diocese,
Church of Nigeria (Anglican Communion)
April 2006.

PREFACE

While **two billion of the** world's six and half billion individuals identify with Christianity, and just less than four billion others identify with myriads of other religions, ***there are yet so many people who strongly believe that God does not exist.***

Atheists [people who believe that God does not exist] put forth several reasons – **logical** and illogical – for their beliefs; and the fact, that among avowed atheists there are *very influential personalities*, makes it impossible to simply ignore the reasons put forth by atheists. Moreover, there is an ever-increasing tendency in the modern secular world to uphold as authoritative only what can be scientifically proved. But there is a big issue with the fact that a large number of the world's most respected scientists believe that God does NOT exist. And therefore one should question how logical it is to believe in God and how rational are the doctrines of the world's many religions.

It is a fact that almost every person respects the views of prominent scientists and professors on many issues – health, weather, earthquakes, space, *et cetera*. But when the same professors whose views are respected on these issues say that *"God does not exist"*, most people that are religious simply ignore the scientific opinions and stick to their religious convictions all the same.

The most interesting part of it all is that there is no religion that does not hold that the world was created – yet most of the world's best researchers and scientists maintain that the world was not created. And the non-creationists seem to be winning – at least in schools and in the minds of young people; because in secular schools and to many young people, it is taught that religious beliefs and creation stories are no more than *"myths"* [unfounded beliefs] while atheistic conclusions and evolution theories are often upheld as *"facts"* [proven and logical inferences]. Therefore, there is the strong challenge to inquire (in a scientific manner) whether indeed the existence of a Creator, or God, is a myth or perhaps it is a fact that scientists have erroneously denied.

"There is strength in numbers", people say. But might we as well conclude that the world's five billion, nine hundred and ninety million creationists cannot be wrong at the expense of the few million atheists? Of course, such a conclusion would appear too simplistic – because creationists, in fact, are multiply divided on what creation is or is not. Moreover, there are endless incompatible descriptions of the (assumed) Creator, or creators. With these listless incompatibilities, religious beliefs would indeed continually be regarded in the secular world as *"myths"* rather than *"facts"*. On the other hand, suppose there are major evidences that the world's prominent scientists and professors have mistakenly ignored; suppose there is a single evidence that is enough to establish the fact (scientifically) that creation is undeniably the origin of the world; why should we not give that evidence at least a thought? And if, by any means, we find that creation is *"a fact"* and not *"myth"*, can we successfully segregate rational theories on creation from the irrational concepts on it? Most importantly, can we by any means determine the unquestionably right among the myriads of creation *"concepts"* in the world? Can we prove (in a manner that is amenable to science) that a supreme creator, God, truly exists?

> *Can we prove (in a manner that is amenable to science) that a supreme creator, God, truly exists?*

Just before we go on to answer these questions, and several related others, let us go through a short but necessary overview of the **importance** of discussions about God's existence. We should begin by examining these few points:

- How important is the subject of this book?
- Why has the author written the book?
- How does the book differ from other books of the same category?
- Why must we **be free and fair** in our approach to the issues raised in this book?

How important is the subject of this book?

Existence after death is an idea common to most religions. Most religions teach that in one form or another, you and I would continue to exist after we die physically. Invariably, it is taught that what we do in our earthly lifetime plays a significant role in determining the conditions of our existence after death. "***That's all trash***", I could have loved to say, except for the part that implies "*what we do in our earthly lifetime determines the conditions of our existence after death*". Really, nothing could be better than being nonchalant and damn whatever lies after death IF ONLY we are certain that there is nothing dangerous ahead. But are we so "***certain***"? Have we examined **ALL** possibilities and ruled out with full assurance the eternal torments about which several religions warn us? That is the point – the modern secular world has not examined **ALL** possibilities – yet many of us would say, "*I don't give a damn about life after death*". This appears quite imprudent – we would all give a damn if CNN's Breaking News were:

FIFTY-TWO TERRORISTS THREATENING TO DESTROY THE WORLD WITH BIOLOGICAL WEAPONS ARE AT LARGE IN THE UNITED STATES! NO ONE YET IS ABLE TO IDENTIFY THEM OR THEIR PRECISE LOCATIONS BUT AMPOULES CONTAINING A NEW KIND OF VIRUS WERE RECEIVED IN THE MAIL AT THE WHITE HOUSE THIS MORNING – TOGETHER WITH A THREAT LETTER. THE TERRORISTS CLAIM TO HAVE A GLOBAL NETWORK ALREADY DEPLOYED. THEY DEFY ALLEGIANCE TO ANY STATE, RELIGIOUS OR POLITICAL FORMATION.

I really think you would give a damn wherever you are in the world. You would at least consider whatever "*relevant information*" or "*possible precautions*" are announced. So, what is wrong with giving consideration to whatever "*relevant information*" or "*possible precautions*" are preached by religions about torments in existence after death? What is wrong with examining every ***possibility*** and concluding once for all whether God truly exists?

That is the primary concern of this book. It is about your **safety**; your eternal safety. Some provable evidences may establish after all that torments after death cannot be ruled out; and could be averted by simply taking a few *"possible precautions"* – so to say. This book calls you to consider those "provable evidences" and precautions.

Why was this book written?

Librarians classify this book primarily as *"Christian apologetics"*. Christian apologetics is the branch of knowledge that deals in the defence and clarifications of the fundamental principles of Christianity. It is typical that books in the Christian apologetics genre set to show the reader proofs upholding the rationality of being a practicing Christian.

Christianity accounts for the religious beliefs of more than one-third of the world's population and its doctrines on the existence of humans after death are quite impressive, if not threatening. Most threatening is the Christian doctrine that ALL non-Christians would be tormented eternally in the existence after death. Unto many of us, anyway, that sounds like mere propaganda. But is it really propaganda? Is it not possible that we have, perhaps (just perhaps), overlooked some very important evidences that authenticate the Christian doctrine on existence after death? I think, therefore, that I have found impeccable reasons for writing this book, which primarily are:

i)	To make known the fundamental principles of Christianity, as comprehensively as possible;
ii)	To re-examine the rationality of being a practicing Christian and the dangers of being otherwise;
iii)	To clarify as much as possible the many difficult fundamental doctrines and beliefs of Christianity; and
iv)	To help people make well-informed decisions about existence after death.

How is this book different from other apologetics?

There are already so many books of Christian apologetics and they all seem to debate the same points. Ordinarily, a debate could be much fun if it unravels the facts that we have always wanted to know. However, most Christian apologetics often fall short of the game spirit of friendly debates and at once they avoid the most difficult questions. In fact, many of them express sentiments that appear imbalanced and offensive to non-Christians, because the arguments are built with rather faulty logics and "facts" [so-called] that are easily disproved. This book is intended to be different from all such. Of course, like them, it is classified into the apologetics genre because it essentially sets out to defend and clarify the seemingly *"outrageous"* claims of the Christian faith, yet, unlike them, its approach and the premises of its facts are such that might even upset the typical Christian apologist. For instance, while the other books mainly employ theology, this one applies not only theology but also the other spheres of knowledge – science, general philosophy, metaphysics, and above all, logic and common sense in fairness to all. The need to be fair to all was a major challenge I faced while writing this book. Traditionally, apologetics tend to be partisans in their approach and judgments. But as work on this book progressed, it became increasing imperative to put as many people as possible into consideration. I reckon that there is little or no point in enforcing the fundamental principles of Christianity on a person who does not believe in Christ (or even that God exists) in the first instance. There is little or no point in thrusting the Bible upon people who not only disbelieve, but also detest, the Bible. But if a person first observes the undeniable evidences of God's existence and how the Bible justifiably embraces many of these evidences, then the person would understand and appreciate fundamental Christian doctrines better.

> *There is little or no point in thrusting the Bible upon people who not only disbelieve, but also detest, the Bible.*

However, it is not only non-Christians who have problems with the fundamental principles of Christianity, many Christians also (several of whom are leaders and pastors) have difficulties with some Christian doctrines. Therefore, in this book there is as much consideration for the atheist as for the *"chief apostles"* of Christianity. But I might thus have assumed an apparently fence-sitting position, which could make the discourse more approachable for many non-Christians, but somewhat poignant to some categories of Christians who are more likely to take the seemingly fence-sitting position as being *"lukewarm"* rather than being *"fair to all"*. Yet, even if it seems so, I do not intend to sit on the fence: there are well researched facts that I must uphold but in doing that, I must as much as possible be fair to everyone concerned.

Indeed, if I was writing solely on subjects that are essentially internal to the Christendom such as faith, prayer, *"spirit-filled lifestyle"*, *et cetera*, I might sound to several Christians as *"anointed"* or *"spiritual"*. But because apologetics as I have come to see it concerns not only Christians but non-Christians as well, I have decided to write in a language and tone that should be approachable to a very wide audience. Nevertheless, I have an imperative to give non-Christians the **deserved** opportunity to hear and understand the gospel of the Jesus in an impartial voice.

> *There is no genuine thing that lacks proof. Proofs cannot be overlooked when it comes to verifying the actuality of controversial claims.*

The discourse in this book begins and ends in that impartial voice of which several authors of Christian apologetics have deprived non-Christians. I think it is good that while seeking to make known the principles of Christianity to ALL, I should not insist on speaking *"Christianese"*, or else only Christians would understand me. Now, however, for the sake of non-Christians, I might well imitate Apostle Paul, who *spoke to Romans as a Roman, that he might make the doctrines of Christ known to the Romans, and for the same purpose spoke to the Jews as a Jew, eventually becoming all things to all men for the sake of the gospel.* [1 Corinthians 9: 20 – 22].

Thus, in this book, I am:

i) **Reasoning like an atheist,** so that I might make the atheist consider more evidences that prove the existence of God;

ii) **Reasoning like a non-Christian,** so that I might show the non-Christian why Christians uphold that Jesus is the Christ and Lord;

i) **Reasoning like "a babe in Christ",** so that I might wean the *"babe"* from *"milk"* unto *"strong meat"*; and

ii) **Reasoning like an apostle,** so that I might remind the *"chief pillars"* of the *"church"* today that *"he who would be the greatest among you, should be the servant of all"*.

Where my task becomes quite difficult is that all these diverse, seemingly incompatible, levels of reasoning must be blended into one singular discourse because many people actually pass through all these four levels of reasoning at various stages of their individual lives and with particular difficulties at each level. As certain individuals progress from one of these levels of reasoning to another, they are compelled to seek understanding of specific issues per time. Blending these four levels of reasoning into one piece would supply such people with a perennial reference source from which they could continually find answers to their questions. Of course, to some people several portions of the long discourse would appear to state the obvious – but common sense is in reality not common to all. I would, therefore, solicit your tolerance of other peoples' levels of reasoning as inculcated into this book, for the benefit of all, that we may be free and fair as much as possible in examining the issues concerned.

Why must we be free and fair in our approach to the issues raised in this book?

There is no genuine thing that lacks proof. Proofs cannot be overlooked when it comes to verifying the actuality of controversial claims. We should reckon that if the proofs are genuine which are presented by those who believe that spirituality and eternity are not real, then every religious mind is misguided and religion is of little benefit. But if the proofs are genuine which are presented by those who believe in spirituality and eternity, then there is a great disadvantage, if not danger, for everyone who is not religious. This danger cannot be avoided by simply turning down discussions about spirituality. The safest way, therefore, would be to re-examine the proofs presented by both sides and judge the proofs by yourself – taking the judgments of other people into consideration but not relying entirely on them since you are most accountable for your own thoughts and beliefs, after all.

for any book of this nature, it is the conclusion that ultimately matters. But . . . we pursue such a sensitive and far flung conclusion that we cannot afford to rush towards

However, in judging the proofs presented by both sides [the religious and non-religious] – and within the sides – you must first make sure that you have the *competence and sincerity* required to weigh the evidences. It is naturally common to every one of us, human beings, to disregard the virtues of others and to defend even our own vices. Anyone who aspires to sincerity would first strive to overcome this natural prejudicial tendency, and acquire a sense of impartiality. If we want to discover the real truths, we must be prepared to accept rightful criticisms and recognize that every virtue is good, even if it is not "ours", and every vice is bad, even if "we" are the perpetrators of it. The discussion in this book will progress in this spirit of selfless sincerity. In reasoning at the discourse, therefore, **YOU** must be objective and accommodating as much as possible and patiently work out (through facts and evidences) a logical conclusion on the proofs of spirituality and the fundamental principles of Christianity.

Now, with a mind set for fairness, objectivity, and truth, let us earnestly begin our discussion and examination of the proofs and facts of spirituality and the fundamental principles of Christianity. And while we do this, let us remain cognisant of the fact that for any book of this nature, it is the conclusion that ultimately matters. But in this present book, we pursue such a sensitive and far flung conclusion that we cannot afford to rush towards, neither indeed can we jump to it.

PART I

THE ROOT OF SIN

This section of the book, *Does God Truly Exist?*, has eight chapters. The first chapter is an introduction examining the importance of the different theories on the origin of the world and their implications for Christian beliefs. It is taken for granted that the reader is already familiar with the different theories [creation and evolution] examined and therefore details of the widely known theories are avoided.

The second chapter re-examines the biblical account of the origin of the world with particular focus on the popular *"Garden of Eden"* story.

Chapter Three examines the significance of biblical principles in the modern world. If the Bible's teachings about the nature of humankind and the world are not authentic, why is it then that people do things that seemingly reiterate biblical principles?

From the fourth chapter to the eighth, much of this part of the book is theological, with Chapter Four examining the nature of a popular evil entity, Satan. Is Satan a person, or just a figurative identity used to represent the force behind evils; if he is a person, what does he look like, where does he live, and how does he work?

Chapter Five examines the existence of evil spirits and the different magical arts, witchcraft and occultism. Are magic and witchery real, or are they just farces? Are spirit beings real? What about horoscopes, *et cetera?*

Chapter Six examines the Christendom and denominational Christianity. Evidence from the Christian New Testament suggests that the foundation fathers of Christianity emphasized the importance of oneness and unity of faith; but today, the Christendom is far from being united; and what is believed and preached varies so widely. Is there any link between the ideal form of Christianity and the denominational Christianity practiced today?

Certain people have crossed the carpet from genuine Christianity to other faiths, or even to atheism. Why did they quit and what are the implications? Does the fact that several people defect from Christianity not imply that Christianity fails to satisfy their quests for spirituality? These are some of the questions to examine in the seventh Chapter.

Chapter Eight, the last chapter in this part, re-examines the question of the existence after death, particularly the eternal lake of fire foretold at the close of the Christian holy book, the Bible. Is eternity in *"hell"* real? Would there indeed be a burning lake of fire? Would non-Christians be indeed tormented forever in that lake? How reasonable is such a belief?

Chapter One

THE BIBLE TELLS ME SO

"In The Beginning God Created".

The Bible Tells Me So

God made the entire universe. The Bible tells me so. But you may rightly wonder why a person should hold a belief, and keep on re-affirming it, just because the Bible teaches that belief. And like you, I too might have at least several causes to wonder.

What is it that distinguishes the Bible from any other book in the world? Is it the fact that it is the widest read book (read and/or believed by above two billion people)? Is it the fact that it is the most translated (available in all the world's major languages and with several parts of it available in over 1000 languages and dialects)? Is it the fact that it is the most debated book (with millions of people contending its relevance and meanings everyday)? Is it the fact that it is the unrivalled perpetual worldwide Number One bestseller (with up to 100 million copies produced every year)? Well, these reasons should not be enough for anyone to believe whatever is found in the Bible without further verifications. So, why should I just believe and declare that God made the world simply because the Bible says so?

The Bible essentially belongs to Christians. In Christian homes, people are brought up with the idea that *"the Bible is the Word of God"*. Therefore, Christians are prone to believing that an idea is *"right"*, or *"good"*, or *"true"*, if the Bible says it is. However, many Christians become confused when they discover that what they have always believed to be true has been proved otherwise by science. Sadly, this had led the Christendom into several blunders in the ages past – such as forcing the notable scientist, Galileo, to admit that he was *"heretical and false"* in regard of the movements of the earth and the sun.

The tendency to write off scientists' opinions as *"heretic and false"* has not departed from the Christendom. Science says one thing and the Bible says another; and then there comes a conflict of ideas for the science-inclined Christian. For instance, I once asked a Christian friend who is an engineer to give me his opinion about the origin of the earth and I half-expected a direct answer. But he answered with a question – *"do you want a biblical or scientific answer?"* I believe this engineer ought to have given me the answer that he knows to be absolutely true without bothering whether it is scientific or biblical. But he probably felt that as an engineer, he would be wrong to give me an answer that is *"not right according to science"* or as a Christian to seemingly *"deny his faith"* by giving an answer that is *"not right according to the Bible"*. However, if what is right according to the Bible is different from what is right according to science, then which should be upheld? The Bible and science cannot both be right and yet contradict each other. Nevertheless, we know that while science seeks to base its conclusions on observable phenomena, religions generally uphold *"believing without having observed"*. And then again, there is a conflict between what is reckoned as "right" in one religion and what is "right" in another religion.

The difficulty affects the word "right" itself. It is one word that is so often misapplied today. One people would assert to the last drop of their blood, that an idea is "right" or is "the truth"; while another people would likewise assert that a contrary idea is the "truth". Yet, logically, "truth" can never contradict itself.

If it is stated, *"the entire universe was made by God"* it can only be **either** true or false. It cannot be **both** true and false. Therefore, if God made the entire universe, it cannot be at once biblically true and scientifically false. If it is true, then it must be both biblically and scientifically true. Otherwise, if it is false, then it must be both biblically and scientifically false. If it is *"the truth"*, the question of biblical-versus-scientific answer should not arise at all because truth cannot contradict itself. Either the Bible or science is wrong about the origin of the world.

In fairness, we should reckon that if the Bible is proven wrong on a particular point, Bible-believing people should admit it and at the same time, if science is proven wrong about a particular issue then scientists should admit it. That is the principle of fairness, objectivity, and truth – *whoever is wrong should admit it.* There is no cause for blind adherence to partisanship – if we are sure that the Bible can never be wrong, then let us prove it and if we are also sure that science can never be wrong, let us prove it as well. This way, we would discover the actual nature of the world and especially the truths about the existence of God.

Is it a (scientifically) provable TRUTH that God created the world?

The Bible opens with a very impressive statement:

In the beginning **God created** *the heavens and the earth.*

(Genesis 1: 1)

And as if this does not already raise so many questions, the Bible adds:

For by him all things were created: *things in heaven and on earth, visible and invisible, whether thrones or powers or rulers or authorities; all things were created by him and for him. He is before all things, and in him all things hold together.*

(Colossians 1: 16 – 17)

Both visible and invisible, the Bible says, all things were created by God who pre-existed all things and holds all things together. However, the modern scientific theories disagree – causing an unbridgeable rift between science and the Bible. While religion says that "*all (natural) things were created*"; science says that "*all (natural) things evolved*". Which should we rule out?

Certainly, the world has a definite origin.

Whether or not religion and science agree, one thing is **certain** – the world must have begun at a definite moment. This is confirmed by the nature of the very things that make up the world.

The world is everything put together. If **the entire** constituent parts all have their individual origins, then it is reasonable to reckon that the world as a whole began from somewhere, some time ago, when the very first constituent of the world had its own origin. That point in time – what happened then, how it happened, and why – is an issue of perennial interest and debates for humankind. Various "*myths, fables and theories*" have been formed over the ages. These are categorized into three – creation, evolution, and steady state theories.

Some creationists believe that a supreme Creator (God) made the world and everything in it at once or one after another in close sequences. Other creationists believe that some lesser creators [gods] helped an "*Overall Deity*" in the creation work by individually specialising in the creation of specific things. Evolutionists believe that every matter [living and nonliving] came from a previously existing and more primitive matter. While those who believe in the steady state theory maintain that there was never a beginning of species but that all things have always existed. Fortunately, we can (by reasoning at facts and evidences) discover how true to actuality each of these positions is, IF we already understood two basic phenomena – time and space – without which nothing could exist. Understanding the true nature of time and space would enable us maintain an impartial and safe position between science and religion.

There is always a time.

Time is infinite. Time has always been and will always be. Of course, "*there is a time for everything*" but there is no time for time itself. We know some things that are happening now. We know some things that happened yesterday. We may not know what might have happened in "*prehistoric periods*". But we know that today will be tomorrow's "*yesterday*", and that **every** "yesterday" had its own "yesterday" such that, as inconceivably as it may seem, there has always been a "*yesterday*" and time never really began.

Recently, certain scientists have tried to prove that time in fact does not exist and cannot be measured. And this opinion is based on the fact that unlike places, we cannot shuffle between times (except in our memories). Time is regarded by these scientists as just the present moment that coincides with our consciousness. But if we view time this way, how do we account for moments of unconsciousness – when we are fast asleep (and not dreaming)? Does time cease at such moments? Of course, not: at least, because other minds elsewhere are conscious at such moments when ours are not. And even if there were absolutely no conscious person in the universe, time would not cease. In fact, the same scientists who believe that time is *"only the moments that coincide with our consciousness"* also believe in evolution, which purports that very long ago, there were no conscious beings on earth. So, time is not limited to that which coincides with our consciousness – time exists, always. When you are not conscious, someone else is. And time is also not determined by activities. When we are all active, time goes on. When we are all inactive, time does not wait. When nothing happens, time goes on. When something happens, time does not wait. Thus, time is perpetual, infinitely. It never ceases and there was **never** a time at which there was no time.

> *"eternity" simply means "the infinity of time". . . Infinity is one concept people have failed to come to terms with*

Eternity – the infinity of time.

"Eternity" is a word that many people find difficult to comprehend, and many more even detest the word because it is more often used in religious discussions than otherwise. But the question should not be whether or not there is an eternal past and an eternal future; the question should be *"shall humans (both living and dead) exist in eternity?"* This is because *"eternity"* simply means *"the infinity of time"*.

We would not have much to debate on the concept of eternity if we peer into space and see the concept of infinity demonstrated. Infinity is one concept people have failed to come to terms with. But just count and multiply figures, then you approach infinity: it goes this way – 10 times 10 make 100; 100 times 100 make 10 000; 10 000 times 10 000 make 100 million; and on and on it goes. When you have reached 100 million in 100 million places, you would find that you were just beginning. *As long as you can keep counting, there would be a figure to name. It goes on infinitely.* And so is time – when something happens, time goes on; when nothing happens, time goes on. That is why it is possible to say *"sixty billion years ago"*, *"one hundred trillion years ago"*, *et cetera*. It is a universally irrefutable fact therefore, that *"eternity"* is real – because time is infinite, just as well as space.

The infinity of space.

Long has gone the cliché *"the sky is the limit"*; humankind has conquered the immediate skies, progressing from jet-powered airplanes to rocket-propelled spacecrafts. Man walked physically on the moon! The moon is not a stone's throw away – that was quite a great distance conquered. But humans have recently found that the moon is just in fact *"a stone's throw away"* – that is, when compared to other heavenly bodies – stars, planets, the sun, *et cetera*.

Space studies have revealed that our planet, the earth, is just one among several planets that court the sun – forming our own heliocentric stellar system. Our solar system is just one among a great many stellar systems that make up our galaxy, *"the Milky Way"*. The Milky Way is just one galaxy among **many billion** others making up the universe. And in fact, certain scientists are now beginning to think that there are probably so many billion *"universes"* – both dark and illuminated – such that the world could be a *"multiverse"*, and not a *universe*. Whether this new notion is right or not, one thing is certain: the world is such a vast place. But also in-between all these planets and galaxies, there are large dark *"empty voids"* where the collection of gases is too thin and insignificant to be called *"air"*.

Although space travel has not taken humans too far into the very distant places of the world, men have peered into what is so far away with the aid of powerful telescopes. However, no one has seen *"the ends of the world"*, because in the first place, no such *"ends"* [boundaries] exist.

Whether the world is a universe or a multiverse, there cannot be any material thing existing besides the material world since the word *"world"* stands for *"the collection of everything that exists"*. And if we have put all things (visible and invisible, known and unknown) together, then we have left nothing out. It follows therefore that the material world is either itself infinite or surrounded by an infinite vacuum. And the latter is more probable because the material world, as modern space studies have revealed, is constantly expanding. If the world were itself already infinite then it would not be possible for it to expand; for then there would be no space for it to expand into. But the material world expands because there is an empty space surrounding it into which it expands.

The empty space into which the world expands must be infinite or else space must be surrounded by matter. But as much as we have put together all matter that exists as *"the material world"*, then there can be no other material thing outside the material world. Thus, we could reckon that the *"constantly-expanding"* material world is **finite** but surrounded by an **infinite** vacuum, the void and empty *"space"*.

The dimensions of space are infinite and unlimited. It is impossible to reach the ends of space because, like time, the absolute quality of space is infinity. If it were possible for a spacecraft to navigate beyond the edges of the material world and escape from the magnetic pull of the universe (or universes), such a craft, if it could keep propelling itself, would only travel infinitely; it shall never discover the boundaries of space, because no such boundaries exist.

The material world has a definite beginning.

At the end of December 1999, there were global celebrations for the end of a millennium and the beginning of another. One millennium ago, so many things that we have today did not exist – and these are not limited to the sphere of artificial things. Over the centuries, mountains have sprung up, deserts have emerged, and climates have changed – bringing several plant and animal species to extinction, while agriculture has brought in hybrid animals and plants and new *"subspecies"* have also emerged in the wild. Thus, it is obvious that things are never in a steady state, there certainly must have been a time when there were no species at all, when the earth itself did not exist.

If anything is constant, that thing must be change itself. Change is ever taking place and for the simple reason that things change, the steady state theory cannot hold. The universe itself is constantly expanding, rapidly; this observation has led scientists to believe that there was certainly a time at which everything stood compacted together: a time at which there were no distinct galaxies, much less solar systems, or planets. And again for this demonstrable cause, the steady state theories cannot hold. Thus, we are left with evolution on the one hand and creation on the other hand.

Evolution, Big Bang, and the remote origin of the universe.

While pursuing evolution, modern sciences give ages to rocks and planets, asserting that the earth on which we live did not exist some six billion years ago. The sun is claimed to be slightly older, (in Planetology six billion years is a slight difference). However, not only the sun but also the entire solar system itself could be given some birthdates by science. Our galaxy has its own estimated probable birth date; everything has its own beginning. And with regard to our constantly expanding universe, scientists have found good reasons, based on evidences, to believe that there was a time when everything was compounded together in only one singular mass. But then questions arise about the origin of the *"singular-mass universe"*. And scientists have consequently presumed that the constantly expanding material world must have begun from a very small volume – *"in fact not quite the size of the proton of an atom"*. The present settings of the material world is scientifically thought to have developed when that remote extremely minute mass of matter continually expanded and eventually exploded in a Big Bang to form the present billions of revolving *"pieces"* or *"galaxies"* which nevertheless hold and spin together. However, it appears that science fails to give a rational basis for how that minute mass of matter (which we could name *Matter* for now) came into existence. Science only maintains that *Matter* came into existence when *"a certain particle not quite the size of the proton of an atom suddenly appeared in space and continued to expand rapidly until it eventually exploded"*. The problem with this theory is that it **fails** to satisfactorily account for the origin of that tiny sub-proton-sized particle, yet the theory seems to hold true up to the point that the entire universe banged out from only one remote material source.

If we assume that science studies things factually, then it means we assume as well that the evolution theory and the Big Bang theory are true. Nevertheless, if this were the case, then nothing would actually be in existence: because *Matter*, the original insignificantly small material, which evolutionists believe is the remote source of the entire universe, could not have appeared in space of its own accord. Unless there was an energy that caused such an appearance or another matter from which the tiny particle fell out, *Matter* could not have appeared in space. And thus, if *Matter*, as described in the Big Bang theory (in accordance with evolution), were the source of the material universe nothing would exist until now. There would only be an empty infinite space – with no material thing at all in it.

The Big Bang theory and its apparent imperfection.

Evolutionists, having arrived at the conclusion that species evolved and were not created could not further explain the remote origin of the entire world and therefore invented the Big Bang theory – with the rather weak apology that further inquiry into the Big Bang theory could be carried out, or a let-us-not-bother-about-that excuse. Nevertheless, to creationists, the theory looks like fraud. But we have an imperative to examine it well enough from every possible perspective before we can agree with the creationists that the big bang theory is fraud.

In the first place, the Big Bang theory appears to be inconsistent with many other proven scientific laws – for instance the Law of Inertia which upholds that a thing would remain in its state unless acted upon by some forces. According to Big Bang theorists there was nothing at all in space before the sub-proton-sized *Matter* appeared in space – no stars giving emission, no source of nuclear or electrical or whatever energy. So, why did *Matter* just appear in the empty vacuum space and how could it? However tiny that particle was, its appearance was an occurrence, an action, which of course must have involved some sort of energy no matter how minute. The point is, if irrefutable scientific laws hold true, the vacuum called space that has for an infinity of time remained a vacuum should also have continued to remain a vacuum forever since (according to the theory) there was nothing at all in space from which the energy to make *Matter* appear was emanating. The "*sudden appearance*" of *Matter* in space, and hence the Big Bang Theory apparently contradicts at least the Law of Inertia among other scientific laws.

> *the Big Bang theory appears to be inconsistent with many other proven scientific laws – for instance the Law of Inertia*

Moreover, eternity is too long for such a theory as Big Bang to hold true. Prehistoric time was an eternity – time never began – the past is infinite just as well as the future. Space was existent all through the eternal past, all through the prehistoric time, and if space was completely void, something must have changed before *Matter* could appear suddenly in space.

Certainly, it cannot be supposed that *Matter* itself had existed eternally. If *Matter* were eternal and was indeed a sub-proton-sized particle that Big Bang theorists say it was, with nothing else existent beside it, then it must have needed a source from which to draw the energy to expand and change into the diverse elements and compounds of which the world now consists. However, if it did not require an external source of energy to expand and diversify, its expansion might well have been because the vacuum that surrounds it was pulling it apart – or it must have started to expand by its own internal energy. Whichever way, *Matter* must have originally had an impossibly extreme density (because expansion can only affect the **volume,** NOT the **mass,** of any material thing: the mass of an expanding matter must remain constant, or at least cannot increase – if the mass of *Matter* changed at all, it would have decreased). The scientific Laws of the Conservation of Mass imply this. It is also implied that for the Big Bang Theory to hold true, the sub-proton-sized *Matter* that expanded and eventually exploded in the Big Bang must have had the mass equivalent to, or greater than, but not by any means less than, the mass of the present universe.

To imagine that the proton of an atom could have a mass equivalent to Mount Everest alone is unthinkable, much less that a particle smaller than a proton should have the mass of the entire universe. As far as science has discovered, such densities cannot exist. A proton is so tiny that it cannot be visible under a microscope that magnifies it 200,000 times. A bunch of 200,000 protons cannot be visible to the naked eye. [Please pick up your pen and make a single dot on a piece of paper. You see, the dot you make would be much larger than 500,000 protons put together]. How then could a particle that is 500,000 times smaller than a dot of ink on paper weigh as much mass as that of the entire present universe? The density of such a matter would be scientifically impossible.

The only way that the Big Bang theory could be scientifically true is if *Matter* was so much bigger than it is thought to be. However, the question of time would pop up again: if *Matter* (irrespective of its size) indeed expanded and exploded in a Big Bang, why did it not happen trillions of years earlier? The Big Bang theory is faulted again because it fails to account for the deciding factor – what decided the appearance of *Matter* in space? What decided the particular moment that it began to expand?

Could there have been a "decision maker"?

Whatever decided the appearance of *Matter* in space must have used some energy if not material as well. But on the presumption (in line with evolution) that there was no material in space until *Matter* came, we may rule out material and stay with energy. We cannot rule out energy because energy is required for action and the appearance of *Matter* in space was an event, an action. Nevertheless, energy alone could not have been enough because the energy that formed *Matter* in space would also have to comply with the scientific laws of inertia or otherwise comply with the deciding-factor question. If there was an energy that caused the sudden appearance of *Matter* in space, then why did that energy not act some trillion years earlier? What inhibited the energy from acting earlier than the moment it acted? The only key to our quest then could be found in "**control**". The energy that produced *Matter* in space must have been under a sort of control otherwise the question of the deciding factor would not be answerable. But what sort of control could have waited for zillions upon zillions of years before finally acting (or losing control) over the void of space? What sort of energy that lacked material form could have determined the sudden appearance of *Matter* in space?

Could there have been an "eternal intelligence" in space?

Because we have ruled out a material source for *Matter*, the control over the appearance of *Matter* in space could not have been chemical, or nuclear, or whatever such form that is associated with the material world. If what delayed the appearance of *Matter* in space were chemical, nuclear or biological, or any such reactions, then such a cause must have come from a material source, thereby negating our the whole idea of *Matter* being the first material thing in space. Thus, we can only take it that whatever was in space that made *Matter* appear, and caused the expansion that eventually resulted in the Big Bang, must have had some kind of intelligence. The energy that produced *Matter* in space must have had a **mind** in which it could decide to delay or trigger the appearance of *Matter* in space. Only a mind or intelligence answers the question of the "*deciding factor*" of the Big Bang. It could only be possible that the energy that caused the appearance of *Matter* in space was not interested in the existence of *Matter* until the particular moment that the mind decided that *Matter* should exist. However, if there was a mind, or intelligence, behind the origin of *Matter*, then definitely there must have been a "*being*". However, if there was such a being, what sort of an entity could it be? The entity must be an **eternal** being with an eternal intelligence and an eternal energy; otherwise, we have not found any answer to the question of the deciding factor (in view of the timing and appearance of the *Matter*) of the Big Bang.

Evolutionists essentially reject the idea of an "*eternal intelligent being*" existent before all things and causing the existence of all things — probably because such a being would match the concept of the ("*so-called*") Creator, God. However, the difficult issue for science is that if there were no such being that fits into the Creator concept, then there could not have been a Big Bang or indeed any evolution. Therefore, whether we regard the origin of things as evolution or creation, we cannot rationally rule out the existence of an eternal intelligent being that pre-existed all things and by whose decision the material world first originated. This theory is summarily demonstrated as follows:

If there was evolution, then there was the Big Bang. If there was the Big Bang, then there must have been a source of that 'big-banging' Matter. If there was a source, then the source could be the sub-proton-sized particle that first appeared in space according to science (say, several quadrillion years ago) or so much more bigger. If such a particle (whether minute or enormous) suddenly appeared in space, then something must have triggered its appearance or delayed the appearance until the particular moment that it occurred. If that Matter did not appear in space but had always existed, then something must have delayed its expansion until the precise moment it began to take place; or otherwise something must have triggered it. If there was such a delay/triggering of the event (be it the appearance in space or the expansion), it could not be due to chemical, nuclear, biological, or any such reactions unless there was already another eternal matter in space, which the whole idea of "Matter" already rules out. If the delay/triggering was not chemical, nuclear, biological, et cetera, it could only have been intellectual. If it was intellectual, there must have been an eternal intelligent Being behind it all. Otherwise, there is a nullification of the whole Big Bang theory. Nevertheless, evolution theories in seeking to answer the questions of "what gave rise to what?" can only culminate in the Big Bang theory, which itself can only culminate in the rational submission that "an intelligence" must have existed eternally before any material thing at all could emerge in space. The scientific problem is that the idea of an "eternal intelligence" would thus be similar to creationists' belief in "the eternal God".

Does God truly exist?

To this end, a very difficult question arises – *how could a living entity be immortal, never dead and never dying?*
We know that while science studies things and draws inferences, religion believes many things without necessarily studying them. So many religions have laid claims that its deity created the world but there is no uniform picture. Several religions (especially the so-called *"indigenous myths"* of Africa and Asia) present the (supposed) Creator of the world as someone with human attributes: possessing blood, bones, flesh, *et cetera*. Some myths even say that *"the Creator lived, married, gave birth . . . died"*. But Christianity and Judaism, among a number of other monotheist religions, presents a *"God that is immortal, eternal, never dead and never dying"*. Many of those who wrote the scriptures of these religions did not make any scientific studies before reaching such conclu-

sions. So, how did they discover God (if God really exists)? But before we go on to examine this, let us first examine the picture of the God that Christianity and Judaism present and see if he fits into *"the deciding factor"* of the evolutionist's Big Bang theory (as it is demonstrated that Big Bang could only have occurred if there was an *"eternal intelligence"* behind it).

"We know what we worship".

Jesus, the central figure of Christianity and a Jew by birth is reported in the Bible to have said *"You Samaritans worship what you do not know;* **we worship what we do know"** to a woman who had challenged him on the Jewish form of worship. [John 4: 22]. And when he would go on to define *"what we worship"*, he said *"God is **Spirit** and his worshipers must worship in **spirit** and in truth"*. [John 4: 24].

"Spirit" (as described in religions) is one word that is never used in science. How do we define *spirit*? What is a spirit? How do spirits look like? Of what matter are they made up?

It could be hard to define or describe what a spirit is because in the first place a spirit is perceived relative to our material world as just the only one thing of its own kind: we can only liken it to one material thing or another but essentially a spirit is a spirit, nothing more, nothing less. The English word *"spirit"* comes from the Latin word *"spiritus"* which ordinarily means *"breath"*; and in this case *"conscious self-existent breath"*. This is a difficult concept – a picture of wind, with a definite form, and a mind, but nonetheless remaining a *"wind"* – which you do not see, but can only see the things it affects – a *"breath"* which unlike our physical breath does not mix with other breaths when it comes in contact with them. But unlike wind, or breath, which has mass and occupies space, a spirit is pictured as some form of energy (or electric current) which can find accommodation in matter without significantly adding mass or weight to the matter it occupies. A spirit is pictured as something able to pass unhindered through a metal (unlike wind, but like electric current) yet maintaining its own consciousness unlike electric current. So, how then can we describe spirit relative to our material world? To material concepts, a spirit is a noumenon. In fact, the illustration that Jesus gave the woman that challenged him about forms of worship is the term *"**living water**"*

[John 4: 10]; seeking to illustrate *"a conscious current"*. If you can capture an image in your mind of *"a fluid"* that can reason, talk and act, and would not mix with other fluids of the same type if it meets them, then you perhaps have a **faint idea** of what the Bible calls *"spirit"*.

A spirit is supposed to be an intangible entity. It is not materialistic and so is *"the God of Abraham, Isaac and Jacob"* that the Bible describes. But let us leave this issue of what a spirit is aside for a moment and instead re-examine the issue of a nonmaterial *"eternal intelligence"* in space that must have brought the Big Bang theorists' *Matter* into existence.

The Universe has a uniform code.

There is an amazing level of uniformity in the universe. The saying that *"the more things change, the more they remain essentially the same"* cannot be truer than it is in application to the universe. The universe has a basic pattern implying that it is all encoded in only one *"programming language"*. Look at it:

> *The earth and other planets (all spheres/spheroids) each rotate on its axis and at once revolve round the sun in a circular/elliptical fashion. The solar system (the sun and her planets) spins as though on a central axis and at once revolves, like other similar stellar systems, in a circular/elliptical fashion round the centre of our galaxy, the Milky Way. The Milky Way also spins as though on an axis and at once revolves along with other galaxies round the centre of the universe. The Universe itself spins as though on an axis. Everything everywhere seems to be organized in spheres and circles — spinning spheres revolving circularly round spinning spheres revolving circularly round spinning spheres . . .*

Nevertheless, that was space we just viewed; too far away if you are without telescopes. However, let us look closer, under our noses:

> *Every material thing (living and nonliving) on earth is made up of specific substances or combination of substances. A substance is made up of molecules and/or atoms of compounds and elements. The atoms themselves, which are the smallest representative units of the elements, have the same pattern with the stellar systems. In an atom, there is a central nucleus consisting of spherical/spheroid proton and neutron mass, having a number of electrons each spinning as though on an axis and at once revolving round the spherical/spheroid nucleus in seemingly circular/elliptical motions.*

Thus, the world and everything in it – whatever the shapes or size – are basically composed of spheres and circles. The universal pattern is a central sphere surrounded by smaller spheres spinning and moving round the central sphere in a circular fashion. It is the same pattern whether we talk of atoms or galaxies, or even the universe as a whole.

"*Spheres and circles*" can therefore be said to be more or less the "*programming language*" of the natural world. The pattern indicates **uniformity**, which implies that the whole world ["*all things*"] indeed "*holds together*". [Colossians 1:17]. Uniformity could imply that the whole world and everything in it has a **uni-origin**. It might as well mean more or less that there was an eternal intelligent **uni-being** behind the origination of the world –whether it is by Big Bang or otherwise.

Moreover, "*spheres and circles*" is also a language of the religious world. Prayer rosaries are used across many religions and seemingly "*for invoking spiritual powers*" that are believed to be "*the underlying powers of the universe*". People have been praying and divinising with rosaries over the ages, long before it became known that physical matter and the universe consists of "*spheres and circles*". Yet after so many years, science has now found that the universe is simply a "*rosary of rosaries of rosaries . . .*" and everything in the world is built up of strings and masses of "*atomic rosaries*". On this basis, there is an implied connection between the spiritual and the physical. Notwithstanding this implied connection based on the identical "*spheres and circles*" language, evolutionists and Big Bang theorists have unwittingly arrived at the Biblical conclusion that before any material thing at all existed in the empty and void space, there could only have been an eternal *Mind* without whom it would have been impossible for anything to come into existence. And so, for the purpose of the discourse in this book, having ruled out the steady state theory (because things change) and arrived at choosing between only evolution and creation, we can and should reckon also that neither evolution nor creation (in whatever form it is) can rationally rule out the existence of an eternal God. Yet the evolution theory is NOT the same with the creation "myths".

> *The universe has a basic pattern implying that it is all encoded in only one "programming language".*

Evolution versus creation.

Both evolution and creation seek to answer the questions regarding the origin of the world and the things in it. But whereas evolution is chiefly concerned with "***what***", "***how***" and "***when***" things began, creation is chiefly concerned with "***who*** began things, and ***why***". As far as the discourse in this book has progressed, we have found that until now, neither the evolution theory (culminating in the Big Bang theory) nor creation myths, deny the existence of a nonmaterial eternal Being. And although at the beginning of this chapter, the only Christian reason we could give for believing that God made the world is that the Bible says so, NOW we can further state explicitly as follows:

*Whether the Bible (or any other book or "holy book") says it or not, whether any "authority" consents to it or not, and whether we all believe it or not **IT IS A FACT (universally undeniable truth)** that there was an eternal Being, without whose existence and deliberate decision the universe would have failed to come into existence. Creation presupposes this fact and evolution proves it, howbeit with irreconcilable differences.*

If you do not agree with this idea, I would suggest that you close this book, try to empty your mind of whatever you have read from the book, divorce **both** evolution and creation, and then begin the book again from the preface. If you come back with a free and fair mind, with allegiance to **neither** evolution nor creation, you would almost certainly reach the stated conclusion that neither evolution nor creation could rationally deny the existence of "*God*" as "*the first and eternal Being*".

> *To grasp the concept of an "eternal Being", what we really need to understand is the simple concept of infinity.*

To grasp the concept of an "*eternal Being*", what we really need to understand is the simple concept of **infinity**. If we simply understand that both time and space are infinite, we would also understand why "*a Mind without a material body*" ("*a Spirit*"), must have existed for as long as time endures (that is, infinitely). If such a being does not exist, then no material thing (living or nonliving) could have come into existence at all; or otherwise both creation and evolution, with their respective indisputable merits, are false.

Not unless evolutionists would go back into their drawing rooms and rewrite a more credible theory than the Big Bang theory, the theory would continue to apparently affirm the existence of God. But evolution is not simply a matter of the Big Bang theory; Charles Darwin's *Origin of Species*, with the subsequent anti-creation sentiments that sprung up, maintain a position that distances itself from the Bible's creation account and indeed every other creation *"myth and fable"*. However, before we can choose which to uphold between evolution and creation, we must first separate their similarities and differences.

The similarities of evolution and creation.

With regard to the anatomical developments of present-day species, evolution lends itself a great credibility but it is important to note that religion does not conflict outright with evolution. **The Bible agrees with science that humankind is just one of the animals**:

> *I also thought, "As for men, God tests them so that they may see that they are like the animals. Man's fate is like that of the animals; the same fate awaits them both: As one dies, so dies the other. All have the same breath; man has no advantage over the animal. Everything is meaningless. All go to the same place; all come from dust, and to dust all return.*
>
> (Ecclesiastes 3: 18 – 20)

Now, the Bible does not precisely say that humans are apes but it does say, of humans, *"They themselves are beasts"* [Ecclesiastes 3: 18, King James Version]. Evolutionists say a man is an ape and to be candid the biology of man, chimpanzee and gorilla does resemble closely – at least for the *"fourth cousin"* factor. However, the Bible says that man was created as *"Man"* while evolution says man evolved from earlier apes. Both positions could be sympathized with, considering the fact that the primary concerns of creationists and evolutionists are different. But what is more important immediately is the fact that evolution and creation agree that humankind is also animal.

The second agreement between the Bible and science concerns the earth itself. Long before science discovered it, the Bible has maintained that the earth in its earliest form was not broken up into continents; the whole land was simply *"gathered together"* as a single "continent". However, religion because it was not chiefly concerned with *"what happened to what"* but *"who did what"* did not dwell much on the subject of continental drift, which science was to stumble upon after so many years.

In the Bible's creation story, there is a strong insinuation of the Pangaea (one-continent earth) idea which science now upholds:

> *And God said, "Let the water under the sky be gathered to* **one place**, *and* **let**

dry ground appear." And it was so. God called the dry ground "land," and the gathered waters he called "seas." And God saw that it was good. Then God said, "Let the land produce vegetation: seed-bearing plants and trees on the land that bear fruit with seed in it, according to their various kinds." And it was so. The land produced vegetation: plant bearing fruit with the seed in it according to their kinds. And God saw that it was good. And there was evening, and there was morning – the third day.

(Genesis 1: 9 – 13)

On a third point, evolution and the Bible agree that Pangaea was probably already habited by plants and animals **before** the *"continental drift"* began; for all the seas were yet *"one sea"* and all the continents were still together when *"the earth produced"* biological life.

On a fourth point, evolution and the Bible agree that plant life (as we now know it) came before animal life. In the Bible's Genesis, plants came on board on *"the third day"*, whereas animals came in on *"the fifth day"*.

On a fifth point, evolution and the Bible agree that avian life originated in water. According to the Bible and according to evolution, reptiles and birds originated from the **sea**.

And God said, "Let the water teem with living creatures, and let birds fly above the earth across the expanse of the sky." So God created the great creatures of the sea and every living and moving thing with which the water teems, according to their kinds, and every winged bird according to its kind. God saw that it was good."

(Genesis 1: 20 – 21)

On the sixth point, evolution and the Bible agree that humankind was the *"king of the jungle"*, *"the crown of earth's natural world"*. While science portrays that humankind is *"the greatest animal that evolved"* (when greatness is rated by the ability to take dominion), the Bible says humankind was born to rule on earth over all creatures.

Considering all the points of agreement, one may perhaps (just perhaps), accept that evolutionists and the Bible's creationists are describing the same origin of the world – although from different points of view and with different concerns. The evolutionists are curious about the sequences and design of the developments while the creationists are curious about the designer and moral import of the developments. But point of view is not the only difference between evolution and creation. Evolutionists believe that it is ridiculous to imagine that the earth could have originated in the "*six days*" that Bible claims. The age of the earth, according to evolutionists should be above four billion years, and life on earth should be as much as three billion years and the sequences between the emergences of plants, reptiles, birds, *et cetera* is scientifically calculated in millions of years rather than the Bible's "*days*". The greatest point of disagreement, however, is the belief by the Bible's creationists that humankind, apart from every other earthly creature has the "*seed [genes] of God*" within him or her.

In the second chapter of the Bible, it is stated that God took man and breathed into man's nostrils "the *breath* of life". And this is depicted (from biblical points of view) as the platform for humans' **special** relationship with God among other animal species. The Bible does not present humankind as just "*administrator of the earth*" simply on the basis that it is the "highest animal" among the "higher animals". Rather, it presents man as "*son of God*". This is a concept that evolutionists find outrageous but it is nonetheless scientifically fascinating when we consider the evidences that support this biblical viewpoint.

> *The LORD God formed the man from the dust of the ground and breathed into his nostrils the breath of life; and the man became a living being.*
>
> (Genesis 2: 7)

This so-called "*legend*" of dust becoming conscious after a creator breathed into the mould is represented in many creation stories besides the biblical one. The multiple variations of the "*myth*" have therefore undermined its possible credibility, at least in the view of historians and mythologists. However, when we look more closely at the biblical record, we see that the story described above is not intended to represent that "*Creator moulded clay, breathed into clay, and 'Mr. Clay' then began to breathe*". No, that is not what the Bible tries to convey. Otherwise, why did God not breathe into the other animals that he reportedly made from the dust and yet they are "*living creatures*"? I think we should look closer at the points of the creationists.

First, the Bible says "*so God created man in his own image*" [Genesis 1: 27], yet the Bible shows us that *man is also animal* [Ecclesiastes 3: 18] while "*God is Spirit*" [John 4: 24]. It says further that Adam (the prototype man) "*was son of God*" [Luke 3: 38] and that "*animal gives birth to animal, but the Spirit gives birth to spirit*" [John 3: 6]. So, what is the Bible's summary argument about human nature? That a Spirit gave birth to animal? Certainly not.

The Bible's argument is that God is not an animal and when it says that God made man in his own image, it does NOT mean to say that God is a huge giant with flesh, blood and bones living up beyond the skies – as some perverted version of the creation story imply.

Then God said, "Let us make man in our image, in our likeness, and let them rule over the fish of the sea and the birds of the air, over the livestock, over all the earth, and over all the creatures that move along the ground. **So God created man in his own image, in the image of God he created him; male and female he created them.** *God blessed them and said to them, "Be fruitful and increase in number; fill the earth and subdue it. Rule over the fish of the sea and the birds of the air and over every living creature that moves on the ground."*

(Genesis 1: 26 – 28)

"In his own image, in the image of God, male and female" – but the Bible does NOT tell us that God has a wife or a female form. Yet *"male and female"* were both *"created in the image of God, after his likeness"*. The words *"image"* and *"likeness"*, as used in this Bible verse, do not mean "visage" but "nature". If the words mean "visage" or "silhouette", and suppose we wish to paint God on canvass, which image do we paint? Is it the breasted non-moustached one or the non-breasted bearded one? But NO, *"God is Spirit"* and *"a spirit does not have flesh and bones"*, the Bible says. And therefore, it is not in the bodily aspects that the Bible says humankind is *"the image and likeness of God"*.

The image and likeness of God that the Bible means is the *"breath"* that God breathed into the animal called man. The translators of the Bible do their best – but they are simply not perfect, they face dilemmas in their work; they tell us *"God breathed into man's nostrils the breath of life"*. Whereas, so useful is the biblical word [in the original languages – Hebrew *"ruah"* and Greek *"Pneuma"*] translated as *"breath"* that it also translates as *"spirit"* and *"wind"*. And as such, we could say *"wind* of life" or *"spirit* of life" and still not be wrong. But translators (and readers) choose the translation that seems most rational to them between ideas *"breath* of life" and *"spirit* of life", sometimes failing to match the original author's intention. Anyway, the English word *"spirit"* also has its root in the Latin word *"spiritus"* which literarily means *"breath"*. Due to the limited knowledge of lexicography for many of us, therefore, we do not know that the words "breath" and "spirit" were perfectly interchangeable in the expression *"God breathed into his nostrils the breath of life"*. But indeed, it appears that the original author of Genesis wants us to recognize the "*spirit* of life", according to today's dictions, as distinct from "*breath* (oxygen-air) of life".

As God is not animal, his breath (even if it were simply "*breath*", according to today's dictions, and not "*spirit*") could not be the normal oxygen-rich air that we now understand "*breath*" to mean. If the Creator God in Genesis is "*a heavenly Spirit*", then it only follows that the "*air*" in his own nostrils must also be *spiritual* and not our own earthly (gaseous-material) oxygen-rich breath. The Biblical concept therefore is that God put in humankind, apart from every other beast, a nonmaterial *breath* ("*spirit*", in fact) that makes humankind able to share God's (spiritual) attributes in addition to, and together with, the attributes of animals. This belief in the spirituality of humankind (as distinct from earthly life) is the most important divide between evolutionists and biblical creationists, as well as between biblical creationists and other creationists.

Therefore, our quest for the facts of God's existence invites us to step in and search human anatomy if perhaps we can find "*the nonmaterial breath*" that creationists believe in, but evolutionists reject. After all, evolutionists and creationist readily agree that man is animal; it should therefore interest us to resolve between their disagreements on the spirituality of humankind by analyzing human anatomy.

Anatomical quest – the dissecting of cadavers.

I was at a university teaching hospital and you might well know there is normally a "*Pathological Laboratory*" in there. In this special kind of laboratory, as a medical student, one would see with one's naked eyes the "*nuts and bolts*" (if we might say) of the human body; especially the delicate organs that the skin and flesh cover. But never has it been recorded in the history of anatomy that on dissecting a cadaver, one could find a sample, however small, of human *spirit*, which the Bible tell us that God had "*breathed*" into man's nostrils.

A man dies – and an autopsy is requested. The coroner works tirelessly on the lungs and other internal organs trying to figure out what killed the man. She finds from the corpse's lungs evidences of inhaled poisonous gases; there are also residues of the dead man's breath, but what the coroner could not find is the residue of the man's *spirit*. So, where is the evidence of the (spiritual) "*breath*" which the Bible says the *Creator Spiritus* had breathed into man's nostrils? Creationists must be made to understand that there is no anatomical proof of any "*(spiritual) breath of life*" in man's nostrils. Consequently, they cannot prove it as far as anatomy and science is concerned that there is an *"image and likeness of God"* in humankind. There is no trace of it. At all.

Nevertheless, we are careful not to rush into final judgment because there may be, perhaps, something fundamentally wrong with the coroner's method. Did we not ask her to find for us traces of the *spirit* of God in a man? Is a *spirit* not supposed to be nonmaterial? How then can we reasonably expect a coroner, who searches for material things, to find a noumenon? Material search is therefore a wrong method, most inappropriate to our quest. We might as well expect to simply go out and pick up micro organisms without telescopes. Nonmaterial things cannot be materially discovered. God is Spirit, and according to the Bible, *"it is by spiritual discernment that we discover spiritual things"*. [1 Corinthians 2: 14]. Therefore, to verify if humankind truly have the *spirit* of God, we have to explore human nature *spiritually*.

Tuning in to the appropriate frequency.

Radio and magnetism are two great wonders of the world. One night, a friend and I lay down idly by a small battery-powered transistor radio. As we tuned from station to station trying to catch *"anything of interest"*, we stumbled into what we first supposed was a phone-in program. *Ring. Ring. "Hello". "Helloooo"*. . . But it turned out we were actually listening to a private conversation between two phone users! We had not bugged anything and my limited knowledge of physics does not make me understand until now what precisely was responsible for that "leak" in the phone link, much more that there was no telephone line in the house. The best that I know is that phones use *"radio waves"*; so somehow, it just happened that we could clearly hear what was intended to be an exclusive conversation between two family members. It was rather fascinating.

> *Nonmaterial things cannot be materially discovered . . . to verify if humankind truly have the spirit of God, we have to explore human nature spiritually.*

What is more fascinating is the entire telephoning system. Someone holds a small lifeless gadget, presses a series of buttons, and can immediately dialogue with another person thousands of miles away on the other part of the world. They cannot see each other, but they hear each other's voice. Just because there is a similar gadget in the hands of both of them, and there is an appropriate frequency being mutually transmitted and decoded, two minds so far apart, whisper to each other.

The marvel of the cell phone system is a bit digestible considering the fact that some tangible devises are used. What is more baffling is the prayer and prophecy channel by which people claim to have contact with God. People *"pray to God"* and *"prophesy messages from God"* just as though they have some internal voice-activated cell phones. Prayer and prophecy apparently works, although many people believe that the whole thing about prayers and prophecies is make-believe; and these invite us to re-examine the evidences that support these two practices.

Telephone to Heaven – praying and prophesying.

There is a concept called *"**coincidence**"*. Very often, one thing or another happens seemingly by mere coincidence or chance. To a reasonable extent, I believe practically in coincidence, and biblically so. At least in two instances, some most-respected biblical characters used the word "chance" or "coincidence".

> *I have seen something else under the sun: The race is not to the swift or the battle to the strong, nor does food come to the wise or wealth to the brilliant or favor to the learned; but time and **chance happen** to them all.*
>
> (Ecclesiastes 9: 11)

> *And Jesus answering said, A certain man went down from Jerusalem to Jericho, and fell among thieves, which stripped him of his raiment, and wounded him, and departed, leaving him half dead. And **by chance** there came down a certain priest that way: and when he saw him, he passed by on the other side.*
>
> (Luke 10: 30 – 31, King James Version)

Every observant or well-informed person knows that chance or coincidence obviously occurs. But not all things happen by coincidence. Most things come as effects of some causes and they in turn cause other effects. If I slap you, you would feel pain. Your pain would be caused by the slap; the pain would certainly not be by chance. Likewise, your cell phone does not usually ring by chance, and you start to hear the voice of a friend by chance. Your cell phone usually rings when someone dials your number. You hear the voice because someone at the other end speaks. Now, so many people have reported hearing God (by prophecy) over the ages and they encourage us to try speaking to God (by prayer) if we too want to hear God. In practice, this seems like giving us God's phone number. Nevertheless, many people hold the idea that answers to prayers and fulfilments of prophecies are mere coincidences.

God, we learn, is a nonmaterial being. Of course, that is the only rational way he could be *"God"*. The Bible (which is a collection of books written by men who testify that they have spoken to and heard God) tells us that there is in humankind a replica of the nature of God. Now, religion and spirituality is not just about creation myths, it is more about communicating with God.

"Cousins Chimpanzee and Gorilla" do not appear to care about God. In their own peculiar ways, they do every animalistic thing that we do – they eat, they reproduce, they sleep, they have *"survival instincts"*, trying to cling to life as much as possible. But they apparently do NOT care about God. They do NOT have observable forms of worship. It does NOT appear that they pray. It does NOT appear that they prophesy . . . Yet evolutionists believe that all human religious practices were born out of our *"psychological evolution"*. But it generates much curiosity when we consider that in comparison with our memory faculties, Chimp has well-developed *"association"* abilities; but in place of our religious tendencies, it has nothing. However, religion may be considered animalistic – when we consider people's linking of natural occurrences to deistical causes, as for instance some people might believe that *"rainfall is the tears of a god"*. And many religious persons worship the so-called *"god of sunshine"*, *"god of agriculture"*, *"god of sex"*, and *"god of fertility"* – all these make the evolutionist to consider that religion is no more than a product of people's fallacious imaginations. And rightly so, largely, because we understand today that rainfall is the *"de-condensation of frozen vapours"* and this proves there is no mysterious living being in the sky shedding down tears as rain on us.

> **God, we learn, is a nonmaterial being. Of course, that is the only rational way he could be "God".**

So, perhaps it is true after all that humans worship simply because we have an animalistic desire to *"bribe"* nature to keep working to our favour. Humankind wants to appease the sun. Humankind wants to appease thunder. Humankind wants to appease everything we could not understand but need for the fulfilment of our animalistic desires. So, religion is totally animalistic and evolution can explain it? Yes and No. *"Yes"*, because there may be pseudo-religions in which they *"do not know" what they worship*. But "NO": because some can boldly say *"we know what we worship, our God is Spirit and anyone who worships him must worship spiritually"*, without wrongly alluding a deity to every natural occurrence. [John 4: 22 – 24].

Mystic religions – they that worship God in spirit.

In Latin, there is a saying that *"abusum non tolit usum"* which roughly translates as *"the abuse does not negate the right use"*. Indeed most religions have much external forms. And God (or gods) is often more than not worshipped for the sake of food, rain, sunshine, fertility and so on. Yet these do not eliminate what is claimed to be the original meaning of religion – humankind's two-way communication with God.

In so-called pseudo-religions, the answer of a man's prayers to his God (or gods) is taken only to be the manifestation of the man's desired objectives. For instance, if an ancient Greek farmer appeased **Pan**, *"the god of herds and flocks"*, and if his flock *subsequently* prospers, he took it to mean that his flock *consequently* prospered and that *Pan* had heard him. If the flocks perished, then it meant *Pan* was angry. But the farmer had no person-to-person, two-way, audio-oral communication with *Pan*. But those who claimed to know *"the living and true (Spirit) eternal God"* derided such people as worshipped such "Gods" as *Pan* that were often represented by idols.

> *The idols of the nations are silver and gold, made by the hands of men. They have mouths, but cannot speak, eyes, but they cannot see; they have ears, but cannot hear, nor is there breath in their mouths"*.
>
> (Psalm 135: 15 – 17)

However, the men of the Bible testify that *"the living and true God"* forbade being represented by idols. This God is reported to have distinguished himself from false gods by communicating with men in various ways.

> *In the past God* **spoke** *to our forefathers through the prophets at many times and in various ways, but in these last days he has* **spoken** *to us . . .*
>
> (Hebrews 1: 1 – 2)

The *"living and true God"* is said to communicate with humankind in trances, visions, dreams, prophecies, *et cetera*. If in spite of the fact that the evolutionists' Big Bang theory implies the existence of God, we still believe that God does not exist, then we should also wonder why the predictions and dreams of "*prophets of God*" often seemingly come true. Is it by mere coincidence? I doubt much and therefore would like us to re-examine the "*spirit/breath of life*" issue and consider, whether dreams and prophecies really come true. If they really do, could they further prove God's existence?

So, perhaps you would like to take a break to think about the discourse thus far; and when you come back let us consider the "*breath*" [spirit] of God in humankind, and how the Bible says that it all began in the "*Garden of Eden*".

Chapter Two

ADAM AND LUSTS

"By One Man's Disobedience".

In His own image – after His likeness.

The Garden of Eden **story** is very popular among Bible believers and sceptics alike. It is the story about Adam and Eve, as the first human beings on earth, according to the Bible. Of course, it is a religious story and scientists largely distance themselves from it much more because it reiterates the belief that *"God made man in his own image and after his own likeness"*. But in the previous chapter of this book, we had overviewed the biblical creation story and the evolution theories, and could reckon that neither creation nor evolution denies the existence of God.

However, creationists (unlike evolutionists) more readily accept the fact of God's existence. Nevertheless, no matter how far we stretch the theories of evolution, we would always arrive at a supposed *"Eternal Intelligence"* or *"Eternal Being"* who pre-existed all things and who is the remote originator of all things; otherwise the evolution theories would cease to hold true. The only alternative explanation that can take the *Eternal Being* out of the picture is the steady state theory – which supposes that diversities of natural things have always existed and that changes do not occur. However, as we see everyday that changes occur, we can only reckon that the steady state theory is out of line.

> **neither creation nor evolution denies the existence of God.**

If steady state theorists were right, then both evolution and crea-tion – would be faulty concepts. But in the previous chapter, we con-sidered the facts of evolution (the continuous origination of new spe-cies and adaptation of present species to the constantly changing envi-ronment), and ruled out the steady state theory. And as long as the steady state theory is ruled out, there remain these questions – *"what sort of energy was responsible for the origination of the material world?" – "if that 'energy' was not intelligent, what hindered it from acting earlier on?" – "if the 'energy' was intelligent, does he match the picture of the 'Creator Spirit' depicted in the Bible and/or other holy books?".*

The Bible talks of an "Eternal Wise Being".

*Now unto the King **eternal**, immortal, invisible, the only **wise** God, be honour and glory for ever and ever. Amen.*

(1 Timothy 1: 17, King James Version)

Some people have argued that if there is indeed an eternal being, a God as magnificent as the Bible and some other "scriptures" present, *He [God] must be too great for human beings to know,* much more because human beings are so insignificant in size compared to the whole uni-verse. However, it could be equally reasoned that if God is too great for us to know, he cannot be too great to develop interest in us.

Let us examine it from this perspective: anyone could have thought that a sick, poor, African child is too insignificant to have known and related with such a dignified person as the late Princess Diana of Wales. Nevertheless, on a visit to Africa, the princess carried that sick child in her arms. Although the gap between God and humankind is supposedly wider than that between Diana and the child, yet it is not impossible that God (if he is an intelligent be-ing) should stoop down and pick up a man (also an intelligent being), if God so wishes, no matter how wide the gap is. After all, human beings have taken interests in studying insects and germs and extremely microscopic organ-isms such as viruses.

> *However, it could be equally reasoned that if God is too great for us to know, he cannot be too great to develop interest in us.*

In the way the Bible paints the picture, human beings are as signifi-cant to God as viruses are to humans – as individuals they *may* be in-significant, but as a collective group, it could be too risky to ignore them. The moral submission of the Bible's stories is that God takes special interest in humans and stoops down to reveal himself to humans. The Bible's religions do not prove that humans had found God, but rather that God sought humans out. It should be interesting to verify this claim; and we should.

Certain men claimed to have heard and seen God.

The Bible, among other books, is full of the "testimonies" of people who have reportedly seen, heard, touched . . . and spoken to God. Other holy books also lay claim to men having heard and spoken, or in some other ways, related with God.

> **That which was from the beginning**, *which* **we have heard**, *which* **we have seen** *with our eyes, which we have looked at and* **our hands have touched** – *this we proclaim concerning the Word of life. The life appeared;* **we have seen it and testify**. . .

(1 John 1: 1 – 2)

"That which was from the beginning —we have seen it, and testify". This claim calls for questions – *when in particular is* **'the beginning'**? *What is* **life**? *Did men indeed* **see** *that 'life that was from the beginning'?*

When in particular is "the beginning"?

When Darwin published his *Origin of Species*, a certain bishop who strongly disagreed calculated and submitted that the world was created on a particular week in the year 4004 BC. I would not know how the bishop came about his exact dates but whatever were the basis of his supposed facts, he did not get these dates from the Bible. The Bible's creation account, like several other *"creation myths and fables"* found in all ancient literatures worldwide, simply dates the origin of the world to *"the beginning, before anything existed"*. Of course, even if the originators of these so-called myths and fables had wished to do so, they lacked the expertise that we have today to date rocks and fossils, and planets. But even science today has not been able to fix a precise date for the origin of the world, science only estimates.

Until this moment, no one has been able to determine the precise age of the universe – therefore, whether we speak in terms of religion or science, the simplest date we can give to the origin of the universe is *"the beginning"*. However, *"the beginning"* may not be as recent as 4004

BC. If those who have studied rocks, fossils, emissions from stars and other heavenly bodies, *et cetera*, are satisfied that the universe is billions (if not trillions of years) old, we need not argue with them. Although we know that scientists put prehistoric ages of in "billions" and "hundred millions" of years much more because they fail to reckon with the factor of a possible *"Architect and Builder of the Universe"*. In any case, the age of the universe does not change the fact that there could only have been an *"Eternal Intelligence"* behind it all. The more difficult argument is whether there was certainly such a *Being* and whether the *Being* truly possesses an eternal immortality. *How can a living being be eternal — living for billions of trillions of quadrillion years without dying, and without a tendency to die?* This question brings up the related difficult question *"what is life?"*.

Life, death and immortality.

In 1980, a particular young American named John, who would later attack United States President Ronald Reagan with a gun, was seemingly in the midst of an overwhelming grief. In his confusion, John wondered whether God had died but he would only conclude that *"God could not have died, in fact, he was not alive in the first instance"*. John probably reasoned that a living being could not live eternally. *"Anything that lives must die, if a thing cannot die, then it is not alive"* — he probably imagined. Nevertheless, that is just from one perspective.

From another point of view, we see life in varying degrees. The question *"what is life?"* is such a hard knot — like the question *"what is a spirit?"* which we examined in the previous chapter. Because life is *unique* — the only one thing of its own kind — it evades a concise definition or description. Invariably life is often described by the attributes of living things — such attributes as respiration, consciousness and other vital activities.

Vital attributes vary from species to species but, for human beings, respiration and consciousness are the principal attributes of life. A completely paralyzed person is still alive. A person who cannot see, hear, talk, eat, or feel, is still regarded as a living person. But a person who has lost consciousness is said to be *"in coma"*, at death's door; and a man who has lost his breath as well as consciousness is regarded as *"dead"*. However, breath is not essentially life — it is just a principal element of life. Our physical breath is nothing more than air — what we breathe in and out is the air that surrounds us. But life is more than the coming in and going out of that air from our lungs. If breath is all that life consists of, then a machine that has an air inlet and air outlet could as well be classified as a living thing.

However, our breath does one thing for us – it enables our blood cells, our blood cells in turn enables our various activities in a complex way – from thinking to feeling (because the blood enables the brain which in turns enables our nerves), across hearing, speaking, eating, growing, *et cetera*. So, with regard to human beings and animals, life may as well be taken as the breath, blood (or whatever breath supports), and the brain – life itself is indeed represented by the working combination of the entire systems. In plants also, breath is never an end in itself; it supports other activities that determine the continual existence of the plants. Thus, breath is a principal element of life but **life** itself is the entire system of auto-activity within an organism. The essence of life therefore is that complete system [breath *plus* blood *plus* brain – in the case of humans] that supports auto-active existence; for whenever any component of the system is removed, the system collapses.

Of course, to remain alive, the complete system of auto-activity within an organism must be sustained. The method of sustaining the system varies from organism to organism – in terms of breath, life in human beings and animals depends upon a certain average amount of oxygen presence in the air breathed. The amount of oxygen absorbed from the air varies from species to species – terrestrial and aquatic breath varies. You might kill a human or a land-dwelling animal by drastically reducing the oxygen content in the surrounding air. But plants, in fact, switch off their oxygen intake at night in order to keep living. So, life is not just breath – because what is consumed by breathing varies from organism to organism – what is essential to life is the sustenance of "the auto-active system".

Sustained, reproductive auto-activity is "life".

Summarily, life may be defined as *"sustained, reproductive auto-activity"*. For a thing to be classed as a living thing, it must possess a system of continuous auto-activity that prompts it to produce a replica of itself. Consequently, a robot that is endowed with artificial intelligence to perform various activities on its own accord, and is capable of sustaining this state of auto-activity, is not a living thing if by that auto-activity it cannot produce a replica of itself beginning from within itself. Although, a living thing can be barren, and barrenness would not automatically translate as death. But the ability of a species to replicate another of its own kind is a fundamental vital quality and barrenness occurs as exception in a species – an exception that has nothing to do with the general nature of the auto-activity of that species. Thus, an auto-active robot can only be classed as a living thing if only it can be proved that the nature of its auto-activity prompts the reproduction of its own kind, whether sexually or asexually.

The Eternal Being has life.

If, in accordance with evolution and creation, there is a supposed *Eternal Being* that originated the universe in *the beginning*, that *Being* must have been capable of decisions. If it was capable of decision, then it must have possessed intelligence – as proved in the previous chapter. The ability of that *Being* to make a decision and act upon the decision is a sign of auto-activity, and hence life. Of course, in *His* own case we may not need to press the issue of replication for it is certain that *He* could not be a robot, for if *He* were a robot, then he would have needed an originator or programmer. Therefore, we take the *Eternal Be-ing*'s auto-activity, solely, as life. But we may afterwards prove *His* ability to replicate.

However, one thing should be clear – the auto-activity (or life) of the *Eternal Being* must have been itself eternal, for if the auto-activity was not eternal, the *Eternal Being* would have needed a source of activation of its auto-activity, but that source is ruled out since nothing at all except the *Eternal Being* existed before *"the beginning"*. And neither can it be reasoned that the auto-activity of the *Eternal Being* had a cause or was caused by an internal factor of the *Eternal Being* because then the question of time and deciding factor would come up again – *why did that internal factor not cause an activation of the auto-activity some trillion years earlier?* Thus, we reckon that the *Eternal Being* had remained *eternally capable of decision* and *eternally auto-active*; and hence, *eternally alive*. As per his immortality, we can reckon that since his auto-activity did not have a beginning, it could have no end. If he did not die quadrillion of years before originating the material world, he could not have suddenly died at any point in time later; his eternality rules out the possibility of death.

Could the "Eternal Being" have died?

The June 25, 2001, issue of TIME international magazine discussed from a scientific point of view how the universe could have originated. One reader whose response was published four weeks later wondered if the universe originated from *the remains of God* after God might have died. This is one possibility that is out of way for the universe is made up of tangible materials, but God is supposed to be a ***spirit*** – an ***incorporeal*** being. Relative to the material world, God may simply be described "*a sort of energy*" – though by spiritual perspectives, we might well see *His* form. But the erroneously supposed death of the eternal incorporeal being could not have resulted into the formation of tangible materials. Moreover, if God (the supposed only "intelligence" in space before the origination of the universe) had died, then there would have been no single mind left in the world that would subsequently make the world "*hold together*" as a *uni*verse.

Therefore, having reckoned first that the *Eternal Being* could only have been eternally immortal and eternally intelligent, let us return towards Adam and Eve in the Garden of Eden.

The Almighty LORD God – seeing is believing.

"*Seeing is believing*" is a popular saying, and a person might well say "*I cannot believe what I cannot see*". (As scientists, we believe in protons and electrons of atoms, though, and yet we do not normally see individual protons or electrons – not even with extremely powerful microscopes). But the God that the Bible says created the world is not supposed to be a person that has never been seen.

That which was from the beginning, which we have heard, which **we have seen with our eyes**, *which we have looked at and our hands have touched – this we proclaim concerning the Word of life. The life appeared;* **we have seen it and testify** . . . **We proclaim to you what we have seen and heard**, *so that you also may have fellowship with us* . . .

(1 John 1: 1 – 3)

How, then, can they call on the one they have not believed in? **And how can they believe in the one of whom they have not heard?** *And how can they hear without someone preaching to them? And how can they preach unless they are sent? As it is written, "How beautiful are the feet of those who bring good news!" But not all the Israelites accepted the good news. For Isaiah says, "Lord, who has believed our message?" Consequently,* **faith comes from hearing the message, and the message is heard through the word of Christ**.

(Romans 10: 14 – 15)

The moral of it all is this – those who believed in God in the Bible, believed because of what they heard either from preachers or *directly from God himself*, as asserted.

Moses, the greatest prophet in the history of Judaism, did not suddenly believe in God without the employ of his physical *senses*. He claimed to have *actually* **heard** God, before accepting to preach God. And he is reported to have seen God afterwards – though, his desire to behold the undisguised visage of God appears to be more of curiosity than doubt. Of course, he could not doubt the existence of someone to whom he had been listening and speaking for a long time. However, many of us wish to share that curiosity and/or that doubt – or whatever it really was – that made Moses hear and see God.

A strange encounter.

The first encounter Moses had with God goes thus –

Now Moses was tending the flock of Jethro his father-in-law, the priest of Midian, and he led the flock to the far side of the desert, and came to Horeb, the mountain of God. There the angel of the LORD appeared to him in flames of fire from within a bush. Moses saw that though the bush was on fire it did not burn up. So Moses thought, "I will go over and see this strange sight – why the bush does not burn up." When the LORD saw that he had gone over to look, God called to him from within the bush. "Moses! Moses!" And Moses said, "Here am I".

(Exodus 3: 1 – 4)

It is traditional in science to first take as a hypothesis an idea that we wish to verify and then subject the hypothesis to tests. It may as well follow that if the biblical account that we have just read holds true, no one in his right mind could fail to respond in the way that Moses did. If it were you, you would have done the same thing – how could there be a raging fire in the bush, without the bush being burnt up? If you were passing by and see such an unusual thing, you would certainly stop to look at it as Moses did. But in turning aside to feed his eyes, Moses ran into what he never imagined: there was a *Voice* from within the fire and yet there was no silhouette in the fire or in the bush.

*The **Lord would speak to Moses** face to face, **as a man speaks with his friend.***

(Exodus 33: 11)

In the long and short of it, Moses was to have endless encounters with that *Voice* – a principle that established his faith and those of his followers in the worship of a *Supreme Eternal Being* that Moses would forever call *"the Almighty* LORD *God"*. Thus, the moral of the biblical story of Moses is that the (supposed) *Originator* of the world took interest in humankind and stooped down to speak with humankind and to make *Himself* known to humankind. However, the other contemporary religions at that time did not preach a God that could speak audibly to humankind and the contemporary generations of Jews were to deride the other nations for serving gods that could not speak, nor hear, nor breathe.

> *The idols of the nations are silver and gold, made by the hands of men. They have mouths, but cannot speak, eyes, but they cannot see; they have ears, but cannot hear, nor is there breath in their mouths.*
>
> (Psalm 135: 15 – 17)

A God that draws near.

The literatures of the ancient Jews do not only boast of **a God that can speak and hear**, but one that also delights himself in coming close to humanity. Whereas the gods of the other lands *were sought after by their worshippers*, the God of Moses was one that *sought after his people*. The God of Moses is portrayed as one that reaches out – *a Deity in search of worshippers*, unlike the gods of the other lands in which worshippers sought for a deity. *But if the God of Moses is indeed the maker of such a magnificent universe, why should He be particularly interested in humankind? What is so special about "the animal called man"?*

David, the second King to reign in ancient Israel also wondered at this:

> **O** LORD, *our Lord, how majestic is your name in all the earth! You have set your glory above the heavens . . . When I consider your heavens, the work of your fingers, the moon and the stars, which you have set in place,* **what is man that you are mindful of him**, *the son of man that you care for him?*
>
> (Psalm 8: 1 – 4)

But before we go on to consider what could have motivated that *Voice* that spoke with Moses to reach out to humanity, we need to get *His* full picture as highlighted throughout the Bible. When we see his full picture, we would be able to decide whether, and why, God should take interest in humans.

A Jealous God.

David, King of Israel apparently knew the God that Moses preached – that un-embodied *Voice* that called out of the midst of *"the burning fire in the non-burning bush"*. Today, if we hear such a voice, how can we be sure that it is the same God? *Is it even possible, in the first place, that we hear the voice?*

However, one thing is certain, the entire Israel nation (numbering above 600,000) that was in the wilderness after fleeing Egypt could not have accepted to teach to their children the principles of an invisible God if they had not seen proofs. In fact, biblical records say that they had begun to make idols and statues to themselves when they did not see Moses who had gone into the mountains to commune with God. Of course, they had seen "miracles" in Egypt and at the Red Sea, but it was impossible for them, in spite of the miracles to hold on to a **God that they had never heard nor seen**. Therefore, they made an idol and took it for a representation of the God that brought them out of Egypt by miracles:

> *When the people saw that Moses was so long in coming down from the mountain, they gathered around Aaron and said, "Come, make us gods who will go before us. As for this fellow Moses who brought us up out of Egypt, we don't know what has happened to him". Aaron answered them, "Take off the gold earrings that your wives, your sons and your daughters are wearing, and bring them unto me". So all the people took off their earrings and brought them unto Aaron. He took what they handed him and made it into an idol cast in the shape of a calf, fashioning it with a tool. Then they said, "These are your gods, O Israel, who brought you up out of Egypt." When Aaron saw this, he built an altar in front of the calf and announced, "Tomorrow there will be a festival to the LORD." So the next day the people rose early and sacrificed burnt offerings and presented fellowship offerings. Afterward they sat down to eat and drink and got up to indulge in revelry. Then the LORD said to Moses, "Go down, because your people, whom you brought up out of Egypt have become corrupt. They have been quick to turn away from what I commanded them and have made themselves an idol cast in the shape of a calf. They have bowed down to it and sacrificed to it and have said, "These are your gods, O Israel, who brought you up out of Egypt."*

(Exodus 32: 1 – 8)

While, however, they made the idols, they forgot that the God that brought them out of Egypt was a jealous God. In fact, they probably did not know for sure that he was such a jealous person. He would not tolerate any unauthorized image or idols not even one assumed to be of *His* own self. He would not accept to be worshipped together with any other *"God"* whether equal or less. In fact, he had previously warned them against idols and statues but they were simply fed up of not hearing anything from him.

> *And God spoke all these words: "I am the* LORD *your God, who brought you out of Egypt, out of the land of slavery. You shall have no other gods before me, You shall not make for yourself an idol in form of anything in heaven above or on the earth beneath or in the waters below. You shall not bow down to worship them; for* **I, the LORD your God, am a jealous God."**
>
> (Exodus 20:1 – 5)

If the God that spoke with Moses is indeed the *Eternal Being* and the maker of the universe and humans, it is understandable that *He* should be jealous whenever the recognition and admiration due to him is diverted to (or shared with) some other gods or persons. Moreover, the Jews were a people to whom *He* had just demonstrated the limitlessness of his intelligence and energy. However, on the day that he gave them the commandment that bars them from worshiping any idol or statue, they saw only the lightening and the melting mountain, not *Him*, and they heard *"the thunder and the trumpet"*. But most importantly, they as well heard a *Voice*:

> *When the people saw the thunder and lightning and heard the trumpet and saw the mountain in smoke, they trembled with fear. They stayed at a distance and said to Moses, "Speak to us yourself and we will listen. But do not have God speak to us or we will die."*
>
> (Exodus 20: 18 – 20)

It is tempting to believe that it was by coincidence that lightning and thunder happened on the very day that Moses asked the nation to meet their God. Until then, God's messages reached them only through Moses. But on that day, they themselves heard the un-embodied *Voice* and were so terrified by the smoking and quaking mountains. Moses could not have arranged the quaking and lightning at the mountain and there was no way he could have made a fire that did not burn the bush while the fire itself raged. But if the occurrences were coincidental, how could Moses have been so sure that those occurrences would coincide with the very day he appointed? Of course, there seems to be a great level of interactivity demonstrated in the mountainside occurrence. Moses apparently *"invoked"* the lightning and thunder and the *Voice* that could hear as well as respond to Moses in the presence of all Israel. The interactivity involved strongly suggests against the possibility of coincidence.

Until that event, the ancient Israelites also had the probable doubt that the *"miracles"* of Moses until the crossing of the red sea were perhaps by coincidence. They could not be so sure (just as well as we might not be sure) that Moses had a real person-to-person encounter with God – for they had grown up in Egypt amidst fetish ideologies about gods, and the God of their progenitors had been relegated in their eyes to the class of *"imaginary beings represented by stony and wooden statues"*. Consequently, Moses' God, **Yahweh,** was in the eyes of the Egypt-fleeing Jews probably considered as simply *"just one of the gods, which we may claim peculiarly as ours"*. They believed that *Yahweh* performed miracles just as much as the Egyptian creation god, **Ptah**, *"the divine potter"*, whom the Egyptians believed *"brought forth the genders from within himself"*. Moreover, the magicians of Egypt too were believed to have performed some "miracles". The ancient Jews perhaps thought of *Yahweh*, therefore, as "our own *Ptah*" and they reasoned that like *Ptah* who probably never spoke audibly to anyone among his worshippers, *Yahweh* too would lack the speech capacity. Therefore, there might have been the inherent doubt towards whatever Moses reported to the ancient Jews as "spoken by *Yahweh*" because the prevailing traditional attitude was that *"gods do not speak audibly, they only act"*. Of course, it is possible that the ancient Jews reasoned that Moses was just a greater magician than those of Egypt (and probably had learned magic in the palace) and so could make things up about *Yahweh*, taking advantage of natural occurrences whenever the opportunity arises. But *Yahweh*, the un-embodied *Voice* that earlier spoke with Moses, also spoke to many more people afterwards. And when Moses did refer to that event repeatedly, no one (in the recorded scriptures) for once refuted him.

> *You came near and stood at the foot of the mountain while it blazed with fire to the very heavens, with black clouds and deep darkness. Then the* LORD *spoke to you out of the fire.* **You heard the sound of words but saw no form; there was only a voice.**
>
> (Deuteronomy 4: 11 – 12)

It is important to note that the people to whom Moses spoke these words did not refute his claim that they *"heard the sounds of words"*. But let us pause to doubt these records: what if the succeeding generations of the Israel nation had only made up all these things? What if there was never any *"fire burning in the bush without consuming the bush"*? What if no mountains quaked with thunders and trumpets? What if there was no such thing as an "un-embodied *Voice*" speaking to Moses and to the entire Jewish camp? What if the stories about Moses and the Jews in Egypt are simply *"myths and fables"* rather than *"histories"*? Of course, if these doubts were justified then there would be no reason for the Israel nation to maintain any affinity or reverence toward that *Voice*.

A Jealous nation.

The Israel nation has been very jealous for the LORD. Although, there is indeed a strong political undertone in the Old Testament books, and until today the Israel nation holds on to the belief that a land was promised by *"the Almighty* LORD *God"* to their progenitors. But we have to consider the fact that land and politics were not the ultimate motive of the ancient Jewish nation – they were a people very jealous for the name of *"the* LORD *God"*. If land and politics were all that the ancient Jews cared for, once they had possessed the land and established a kingdom there, then it would had sufficed them to depart from serving the invisible LORD. And the nation could have taken to themselves idols and statues like the other nations. However, religion was an essential part of the national Jewish life. They were committed to serving the *"invisible* LORD*"*, *Yahweh*, in good time and in bad time, with a king or without a king, when they were in their land or away from their land, in the wilderness, in the city, in every place; the fear and love of that un-embodied *Voice* remained with the Jewish nation. Of course, it is in their religious laws to love the ***invisible*** LORD.

> *Hear, O Israel: The* LORD *our God, the* LORD *is one. Love the* LORD *your God with all your heart and with all your soul and with all your strength.*
> (Deuteronomy 6: 4 – 5)

Thus, the biblical "history" of Israel is not just a record that protects their land and kingdom but also their religion. Without these claims to history, they had no reason to worship any *"invisible deity"*, and nothing would have hindered them from indeed making and keeping idols and statues of *Yahweh* just as the other nations kept idols of "Gods" and in spite of the fact the Jews too retained a human fetish tendency to make idols. Their persistent refusal to accept any other deity or make a physical representation of their *"living, invisible Deity"*,

Yahweh, could not have been without a cause. The ancient Jewish nation must have had an encounter that instilled in them the fear of making idols and statues, and at once endeared them to a mystic form of worship – the worship of the un-embodied *Voice*. But if that fear-and-love-instilling encounter was not the speaking out of the un-embodied *Voice* at the *"quaking and smoking mountains"*, it could not be anything less wondrous and fearful. Thus, even if we assume that the records of the Bible are fictitious with regard to the *Voice* speaking to Moses and the entire Jewish nation at the mountains, we can only rightly assume that factually there could only have been a no less *magnificent* mystic encounter.

LORD *– God of the nations.*

The most important point, moreover, is that the ancient Israel did not regard the un-embodied *Voice* as just a God for them alone. They counted *Him* as the Father of humanity – a Father that is very kindly and loving but also intolerant of error and evil. It is not impossible that the ancient Jews (as claimed by some critics) have coveted a land that did not belong to them – with houses they never built, gardens they never planted, clothes they did not sew – and they may have cunningly devised fables and myths in other to justify their covetousness. Of course, they were eager to destroy whoever was on that land that possessed these things BUT more than that, *they were ready to spare whoever would serve their "Almighty* LORD *God" with them.* Thus, they believed that God was only angry with the people that served *"false gods"* and pleased with Israel that served the **"living** *and* **true** *God"*. Their national philosophy was *"whoever ascribes the glory due to God to any other god should not live and whoever gives God the glory due to his name should not perish"*. Unlike the other nations, what gave the ancient Jews their identities was therefore not just the language or the progenitors but the also religion, most importantly. A stranger could *"join himself to the Jews"* so long as he would be circumcised and devoted to that un-embodied *Voice*, *Yahweh*; the Almighty LORD God. The stranger must thereafter be treated fairly as though he was by descent a near relation of the Jews. While the "Gods" of the nations were thirsty for the blood of strangers, the un-embodied *Voice* did not want any human sacrifice at all because human beings were considered to be *His* own children. The nation of Israel did not consider the un-embodied *Voice* as just a national Deity but a Father, *the father and God of all nations.* So, even if they were as covetous as some critics claim, for any reason, far above and more important than their covetousness was the belief that all men are children of God and brothers of one another, who must in the interest of God be treated with fairness and mercy so long as they live in obedience to the *"Almighty Father"*.

I said, 'You are "gods"; **you are all sons of the Most High**

(Psalm 82: 6)

The God who made the world and everything in it is the Lord of heaven and earth . . . **from one man he made every nation of men** *that they should inhabit the whole earth . . .* **Therefore since we are God's offspring***, we should not think that the divine being is like gold or silver or stone — an image made by man's design and skill.*

(Acts 17: 24 – 29)

The Offspring of God.

Unlike the other nations (especially the ancient Egypt that Israel served) that mercilessly exploited strangers and treated slaves and servants inhumanely, the nation of Israel was commanded to be fair to their servants and slaves and treat them with respect so long as the slaves and servants also serve the Almighty LORD God. Serving the un-embodied *Voice* was therefore the paramount ideal of the ancient Jews. For instance, they must not marry wives of other nations *so that* the wives would not make them serve *other gods*. If they conquered a land, they were not to take the wives and daughters of those nations to themselves. The gods of the other nations allowed taking women as spoils, but the un-embodied *Voice* was contemporarily different; even in the land that he would give them and within their own community – the *Voice* indeed sound (from the Bible) as merciful as he purports. Of course, according to the Bible, he commanded the Jews to destroy the other nations and kill everyone in those lands but the Jews were not to destroy whoever was serving *Yahweh*. Death and destruction for the other nations were counted as punishments for going after *"false gods"*. However, if religion did not matter to the Jews as much as land and politics did, then the Jews would simply have been content to dispossess the other nations of their heritages, without respect to religious inclinations. In fact, they would have taken women as spoils, like the other nations, and they would not allow strangers to be circumcised and therefore joined to the Israel nation. The fact that they did not do as the other nations did implies that land and kingdom mattered less than religion; the purification and consecration and setting oneself apart unto the Almighty LORD God.

To be Jewish was to be devoted to the God of the patriarchs Abraham, Isaac and Jacob. The ancient Israel did not see themselves as the only descendants of the patriarch Abraham, to whom the land they sought to possess was originally promised. Neither did they believe that Abraham was the first person with whom God had an encounter. They believed and preached a God that has always pursued humans since the beginning of human existence – a God that did not only make the human body but also *breathed out* the human spirit. They believed that all the nations of the world are made *"from one man"*. Therefore, they were to be kind to all but quick to execute judgment on the wayward nations. The eternal *Voice* that they served was believed upon as *God over all nations* and not just over Israel. The principle was that if Israel complied with God's terms, then they would be *an example* unto other nations and through them all other nations would be blessed by *Yahweh*: if Israel refused *Him*, *He* would bypass Israel to go after the nations directly and relegate Israel before those nations.

> **The Bible invariably implies that man is as much an animal as he is a spirit being – a spirit in "the image and likeness" (nature) of God.**

Therefore, we can reckon that if the Israel nation had an ulterior motive in preserving the biblical records, the highest motive was not for the land or kingdom, but for the worship of *"the creator of the universe and Father of all humanity"*. Thus, we find that the Jews' "creation myth" maintained that *"the 'Spirit God' breathed out man's spirit and* **therefore** *all humans are children of the Most High"*. Verifying this seemingly bogus idea, that humankind is the offspring of God is the ultimate focus of this chapter of *Does God Truly Exist?* We should consider that if it can be proved that humankind has a special place as "offspring" in God's heart, it would make sense that God should be interested in seeking us out amidst the entire vast universe; and *He* would be humble enough to reveal himself to us.

The spirit of God in man.

The Bible invariably implies that man is as much an animal as he is a spirit being – a spirit in *"the image and likeness"* (nature) of God. Running through the entire Bible, we find the philosophy that man has a *"breath"* which the other animals do not have: that *"breath"* (which is translated *"spirit"* in our modern English language) is considered as a thing that could exist independently on its own without an animal body while maintaining its own consciousness. The Bible claims in the second chapter of Genesis that this *"breath"* was nested into *"the animal called man"* by God, at the creation.

The God-nested *breath* (or *"spirit"*) is also biblically considered as the *"**real**"* or *"inner"* man and it is believed by the writers of the Bible to be immortal, because it came from within the eternal immortal God. This *"inner man"* – not the outer, animal, form – is what is referred to as *"the image and likeness of the eternal God"*.

The *"inner man"* concept is the point where the Bible religions differ from Islam that attempts to preach the same deity (the God of Abraham) that Christians preach. It is a fundamental Islamic belief that *"God was not born, and neither does he give birth"*. However, Judaism and Christianity believe in a God whose eternal vitality is further attested to by the fact that he is not only auto-active but also reproductive. God, indeed, could not have been born if he is the **eternal** being that he is supposed to be, but if he is a barren God and if humans are not his children then it might make no sense that among all animals, humankind should be the species that seeks to worship God.

Some religions (such as Hinduism) believe that not only man, but also all living things have the nature of God within them. But we see that plants and other animals do not practise religion, unlike humankind. They do not build worship centres. They do not make obeisance to any idol or deity; they do not build altars and make sacrifices, oblations or offerings. Even Hindus would agree that at no time has any chimpanzee or gorilla been so *"enlightened"* as to practise yogi the way humans do. But according to the Bible, there is relationship between the Eternal Spirit, God, and humankind among every other animal upon the basis of man being God's offspring – not as animal but as *"breath"* or *"spirit"*.

> *The "inner man" concept is the point where the Bible religions differ from Islam that attempts to preach the same deity (the God of Abraham) that Christians preach.*

If humans are simply animals and no more, if humans are not inwardly the replicas of the *Spirit* of God, then we have no particular business with God and God should not have any business with us.

And neither should there be a basis for us among all living matters (animals and plants) to seek to worship him, as far as the Bible is concerned. And the same should normally apply to the basic principles of other religions for indeed if humankind is only an animal just as much as chimpanzee and gorilla, and if religion applies to humans, then it must apply (at least in lesser ways) to chimpanzee and gorilla as well. Again, if there is spirit in every living thing, then it still follows that chimpanzee and gorilla and potatoes and carrots should be religious to some reasonable extents. But if chimpanzee and gorilla do not practise religion at all, and not even in limited ways, then there must be a quality that humans possess but which chimpanzee and gorilla, and all the other living things – plants and animals – do not have in any measure. And that quality cannot be just a larger brain.

However, science has continually denied the existence of God while claiming that humankind is just an ordinary animal which simply evolved, and was not created. On the other hand, we find that the Bible's creation story was primarily written to highlight the powers of the Creator and magnify the un-embodied *Voice* that spoke with Moses. The authors of the biblical stories wished to give the readers a religious, rather than detailed scientific or historical account of what happened *"in the beginning"*. And when they tell us that *"God made man in his own image and after his own likeness"* [Genesis 1: 26], they could NOT have meant to tell us that God is a huge ape-like beast dwelling beyond the skies. They did NOT mean to tell us that he has blood, flesh and bones and also *"came from the dust and shall return to the dust"*. God, as presented in the Bible, is not an animal, and does not need to mate before producing *"His* own kind that is after his likeness"*. Of course, reproduction is not always sexual, several organisms reproduce asexually. For instance, the microscopic amoeba reproduces by binary fission – and presents an example of the manner in which the Bible portrays God's procreation.

> *If humans are simply animals and no more, if humans are not inwardly the replicas of the Spirit of God, then we have no particular business with God and God should not have any business with us.*

God is depicted in the Bible as a spirit, that is, [*living* (conscious, self-existent) *breath*] that could give birth to spirits by simply *"breathing out*" the replica (image and likeness) of *His* own being. Thus, the ancient Jews saw him as the **Father of our spirits** rather than the Father of our flesh:

> *Moreover, we have all had human fathers who disciplined us and we respected them for it. How much more should we submit to* **the Father of our spirits and live!**
>
> (Hebrews 12: 9)

> *Flesh gives birth to flesh, but* **the Spirit gives birth to spirit.**
>
> (John 3: 6)

> *'You are "gods";* **you are all sons of the Most High . . .'**
>
> (Psalm 82: 6)

In the Bible, though the word "*spirit*" is more often the same word "*breath*", the "*breath of life*" which every living plant and animal has is not the same as the "*spirit of life*" that is attributed to humankind alone. The biologically-respired "*breath*" that every plant and animal (including man) breathes, is not what Jesus referred to when he said "*God is a Breath*". Therefore, it does not automatically follow that anything that breathes has the spark of "*the Spirit God*" in it. The air that we breathe is just a mixture of gases. Yet the Bible says that God is "*Breath*" and that we are his children, who are in the real sense "*breath*" as well. "Breath" in this case is not the same as the mixture of material gases that we breathe.

Oral traditions: God, Man, and the Bible's six-day creation account.

From one perspective, we might say that the six-day creation account that opens the Bible in Genesis is rooted in a *religious* rather than scientific (or historical) motive – whoever wrote this account was apparently more interested in establishing a ground for the weekly Sabbath worship and the other tenets of Judaism rather than setting out the details of what actually happened. In fact, the ancient Jews often acknowledged the fact that what God called "days" could NOT have been the normal twenty-four hours that we know.

But do not forget this one thing, dear friends: With the Lord a day is like a thousand years, and a thousand years are like a day.

(2 Peter 3: 8)

Thus, as sceptics we might assume that the *"factual details"* of the Bible's creation story may not be preserved, but even if the details were lost, the moral of the story is still preserved. It is the morality of it that mattered, and still matters, to the religious minds.

Several Bible critics and historians have established that the stories of the creation, and indeed several of the stories in the book of Genesis, had passed from mouth to mouth over the generations (as *"traditions, fables and myths"*) before they were eventually penned down in a seemingly arranged manner. There is not much use in contending these opinions because they do not overrule the overall submission of the Bible stories.

To several scholars, the book of Genesis is apparently an attempt to trace the root of the Jewish slaves of the Egyptians. One prominent authority says, *"The whole book of Genesis attempts to show how and why the Jews became residents of Egypt and not much more"*. Thus, some scholars look at the stories as more of fiction than facts. But if the stories were indeed factual, and not made up, they would necessarily have passed from mouth to mouth all the same. Therefore, the singular fact that the stories probably passed from mouth to mouth does not negate their possible factuality. For example: if tomorrow morning you tell a friend that you have read a book titled *"Does God Truly Exist?"*, and state one or two things that you could remember from the book, your friend may in turn tell another person that a particular book says so and so. The singular fact the information pass from mouth to mouth would not automatically rule out the possibility of its being factual.

In the same way, if the Bible's creation stories are facts rather than fiction, they *may* not have been *entirely* received by prophecy from God. For instance, God would not have needed to tell the Jews about their immediate ancestors just as much you do not need any prophecy (or inspiration from God) to know who your grandfather was. When in the book of Exodus God sent Moses to the Jews that were in Egyptian slavery, God told Moses to tell them *"I am the God of Abraham and Isaac and Jacob"*. But how did God expect the Jews in Egypt to know Abraham, Isaac and Jacob and the fact that these three patriarchs worshipped a certain God if the people knew absolutely **nothing** about their ancestors? Likewise, it may not be that Moses was the original promulgator of the creation and *"Garden of Eden"* stories, even if he was the first person to commit the stories into writing. The stories (whether facts or fiction) would have necessarily passed from mouth to mouth over the ages long before Moses was born. Moreover, the Jews traditionally memorized stories maintained in a song-like manner: *"Jacob, which was the son of Isaac, which was the son of Abraham . . . which was the son of Seth, which was the son of* **Adam, which was the son of God***"* – an example of which we find in Luke 3: 23 – 38.

Thus, we find that the ancient Jews had always treasured stories – *"legends"*, *"sagas"*, *"myths"*, *"fables"*, whatever we call them – about the patriarchs. They apparently knew one or more things than Moses needed to tell them about the patriarchs. And then, the exact details of the events could have been lost due to inaccuracies of oral repetitions, but the morals of the stories could have been preserved all the same – because stories (traditions, fables, and myths) were often told for *"**moral** instructions"*. The possible fact that the stories passed from mouth to mouth over generations tells us why stories similar to the Garden of Eden story are also found in non-Jewish literature. But rationality lends much credence to biblical monotheism over polytheisms for indeed monotheism maintains that *"the LORD is God because he is the maker of all things"* whereas polytheism places many things under other gods besides the *"Supreme Being"*. But we know that rainfall and sunshine are parts of the cycles of the creation; and fertility and emotions are also parts of the cycles of the creation; things burn when they are heated to a certain temperature and bush fires probably occurred long before man *"invented fire"*. And through all these, we see that rationality does not support believing in so-called gods of rainfall, gods of sunshine, gods of love and hate, nor gods of fire. It is only rational to believe that the courses and causes of things have been instituted into the nature of the earth from the beginning of the earth. And if there was indeed an originator of the world, *He* alone could rightly be *"the God of everything"* by virtue of being *"the originator of all things"*.

The Egypt-fleeing Jews who had seen polytheism practised all their lives, more than any other form of religion, had a tendency to have become polytheistic also but they did not. And their tendency to go polytheistic is repeatedly suggested by the fact that the un-embodied *Voice* consistently warned them against it. The scenario could be vividly painted as the *Voice* telling them *"don't be stupid, rainfall and agriculture are parts of the earth's cycles, there cannot be a god of agriculture or a god of rainfall apart from the Creator"*. And Moses who we are told grew up in Pharaoh's palace amidst gods and magic had greater tendency than any other Jewish person to be polytheistic; but he became addicted to the *"all-sufficient God"* – a most insane idea at his time. If Moses did not probably have some mystic encounters, he could not have become so adamantly monotheistic all too suddenly.

The picture that the Bible paints of Moses is that he was so confident that the same *Voice* that spoke to him desired to speak to everyone else. This is another unusual thing about Moses' "all-sufficient God" for at that time access to most gods were limited to only a small cult of priests. But Moses boasted that *Yahweh* would rather make the entire nation of more than **six hundred thousand people** to **all** become priests and prophets:

*But Moses replied, "Are you jealous for my sake? I wish that **all** the LORD's people were prophets, and that the LORD would put his Spirit on them!"*

(Numbers 11: 29)

*'You yourselves have seen what I did to Egypt, and how I carried you on eagles' wings and brought you to myself. Now if you obey me fully and keep my covenant, then out of all nations you will be my treasured possession. Although the whole earth is mine, you will be for me **a kingdom of priests** and a holy nation.' These are the words you are to speak to the Israelites."*

(Exodus 19: 4 – 6)

> *Evolutionists do not want God in the picture at all and yet they attempt to answer every question only to conclude that "there are several unanswered questions".*

If God so desired that they all should be priests and prophets, then they were all destined to individually share in the special privilege of personal, two-way, communion with the deity. *"God wants to speak with **every** one of you"*, was Moses' message to the entire nation. But the ancient Jewish nation and indeed all humankind was not well used to the idea of speaking directly with the *"Creator of the universe"* – *"He is too magnificent to speak with us – let Him just leave us alone and speak only with His prophets"* was the reply of the Jewish nation and is still the answer of many humans today.

Evolutionists do not want God in the picture at all and yet they attempt to answer every question only to conclude that *"there are several unanswered questions"*. Creationists on the other hand do not care to know the details of *how* God worked in the making of the creatures. Creationists understand that because God is not a physical being, he could not have left physical fingerprints on anything he made. And evolutionists failing to find the invisible fingerprints of an *"invisible God"* assume that there are no fingerprints at all. But creationists would have us know that the invisible spiritual fingerprints of God are so profound on the human spirit. Perhaps it is only by examining *the spirituality (or religiosity) of humans* that we can find the fingerprints of God.

The spirituality of humans.

One thing is certain, humankind is the only animal that is known to worship or involve in mysticism and spiritualism. The belief that humankind has a spirit nature cuts across many religions, although what each religion teaches about the nature of the human spirit, and what happens to the spirit after death, varies widely. However, we find that a man need not die before he can express his spirituality.

Scientifically, one may easily take expressions of spirituality to be mere mental activities. In April 2000, the *New Scientist* magazine carried a feature article that opined, from one perspective, that *religious feelings are mere neurological functions.* However, spirituality is more than *"feeling the presence of God"*. Of course, we can feel someone if we touch the person, but there are several ways to interact with a person without touching (or feeling) the person. Spirituality does not even have much to do with the **feeling** of God's presence. Spirituality is more frequently expressed in supernatural occurrences (magic and miracles), prophecies and divinations, interactions with the spirit world, and other extra-mental experiences.

Supernatural encounters.

Many people believe that the supernatural world does not exist. But if the supernatural world does not exist, how do we account for many inexplicable events that surround us, of which there are several examples in various forms? I have heard of so many miraculous encounters – instant healings that did not involve any medical, surgical or herbal application; just communication with *"some supernatural forces"* resulting in instant healing. I have heard of other cases involving barren women conceiving without any In-Vitro Fertilisation or any medication or whatever. But let us leave aside what is not firsthand experience and come closer.

In my own experience of spirituality, I have always disdained whatever lacks proof. I had rather think like Thomas Didymus (whom the Bible says refused to believe that Jesus had actually resurrected until he dipped his fingers into the holes in the hands and feet of Jesus [John 20: 25]). So, very early in my inquest into Christianity I had shunned the much-publicised *"speaking in tongues"*. For me, the so-called speaking in tongues was not major evidence that anything supernatural was in place. After all, any one can babble empty noises and claim to be speaking in an unknown tongue. To me speaking in tongues was no proof, except the tongues had meaning to some other people. If a person who has never heard a single Spanish word and has never learnt Spanish from anywhere suddenly begins to make a coherent speech in Spanish, then that is miraculous, and it might well be taken as a proof of the reality of the supernatural. Such, I think, was the biblical experience of speaking in tongues described in the Bible [Acts 2: 1 – 21]. But I could not settle for the commonplace *I-am-speaking-to-God-and-only-God-understands* type of *speaking in tongues*. And when I would put supernaturalism to a test, I prayed that God should give me sign that is much surer than the usual noisome "speaking in tongues".

While I prayed that night, I heard *"God"* speak to me in the depth of my mind. The *Voice* beneath my mind told me that at 3.00 pm the following day, I would meet a particular person at a school compound that was not too far from where I was residing. The *Voice* gave me the description of how the person would look like; how he would be dressed; and some other details.

The next day, I was so eager to prove God that I got there much earlier, when it was minutes to three 'o' clock, I lost patience, perhaps because it was my first notable experience with the *Voice*. At 2.58 pm, I started to leave the place, because I started to think *"there's no much difference between 2:58 pm and 3:00 pm – after all, I was meant to "meet" the person here. If he's not here at this time [2.58 pm], how am I supposed to meet him even if I come at 3:00 pm"*. I was disappointed; *"Perhaps, God has not spoken anyway. Perhaps, he does not even exist at all"*. A second thought came, it brightened me a bit – *"well, if I have now proved that God does not exist, I am free to live anyhow I wish – no more Bible study, no more prayer, no church going. . . "*. (I was relatively new in the Christian faith and that brief moment was beginning to undo all the little that I believed about God.) However, it was not to be – because as I moved towards the exit of that school compound, I looked at my watch and it was precisely 3.00 clock, and I then glanced back into the compound (just to make sure), and was there anyone? **Yes**, the young man I was supposed to meet came in from the other exit. I was shocked. I was thrilled. *"God spoke to me! **Me?** I can't believe this!"*. I ran in excitement to meet the fellow and spoke to him about God. That was my first notable **firsthand** experience of prophecy. That was for me a proof of the supernatural. But right now, as sceptics, can we say that brief experience truly proved the existence of the supernatural, or the existence of God? Could it not have been that my *"imagination"* just happened to **coincide** with a futile reality by chance? But then, if it was coincidence, what a very outstanding coincidence it was, and how very much I have enjoyed multiple returns of similar *"**prayer-induced coincidences**"* ever since.

Prayer and Prophecy

Of course, it is not that I have since been catching a foreknowledge of what would happen at 3:00 pm every day. But I have ever since heard that inner *Voice* speaking to me concerning widely different issues.

If I could just be a sceptic for now; I would ask *why did God have to whisper beneath my mind rather than shout into my ears. Why didn't He call out to me from within "a fire burning in the bush without consuming the bush", as it was with Moses?* I may not really know why, but I do know that I am not the first person to whom that the *Voice* has spoken in the manner that he spoke to me. It has been an enduring phenomenon since the Bible days. All the biblical prophets, except Moses, reported that God spoke to them in their minds, dreams or visions or by some other similar means. And we should consider that they were prophets indeed, because the seeming *"fulfilment"* of their dreams and visions were also witnessed. It cannot be by mere coincidence alone that the dreams and visions of the *"seers"* came true to life.

As far as Physiology is concerned, dreams are simply part of our mental functions– everyone dreams every night during the REM (Rapid-Eye-Movement) phase of our sleeps. The position of science (as maintained by physiologists and psychologists) is that dreams are simply auto-concocted by our minds from our experiences and imaginations. A man who had lewd thoughts or watched nude pictures during the day has a tendency to have wet dreams at night. A woman who went to bed hungry and wishing she had some food to eat could no sooner dream of herself devouring a nice dish. The Bible also agrees that this is true:

As a dream comes when there are many cares . . .

(Ecclesiastes 5: 3)

As when a hungry man dreams that he is eating, but he awakens, and his hunger remains; as when a thirsty man dreams that he is drinking, but he awakens faint, with his thirst unquenched . . .

(Isaiah 29: 8)

However, the Bible also affirms that through dreams and visions, God reveals *His* mind to our minds, and the Bible maintains that this is made possible by God's *Spirit* communicating through the spirits that he had breathed into us, to our minds.

*For **God does speak** – now one way, now another – though man may not perceive it. **In a dream, in a vision of the night**, when deep sleep falls on men as they slumber in their beds, he may speak in their ears and terrify them with warnings, to turn man from wrongdoing and keep him from pride*

(Job 33: 14 – 17)

*"And afterward, **I will pour out my Spirit on all people.** Your sons and daughters will **prophesy**, your old men will **dream dreams**, your young men will **see visions.** Even on my servants, both men and women, I will pour out my Spirit in those days.*

(Joel 2: 28 – 29)

In the first week of January 1999, I had a dream. In the dream, I saw a shallow rectangular pit being dug in reddish brown soil near a wall. It was beginning to take the shape of a grave. I panicked and wondered why a grave was being dug. I frantically asked, *"Who died, where is the corpse, why dig a grave?"* But no one answered me. I woke up and was so embarrassed. Four days later, I received the news of a friend's demise. She was only seventeen years old. I visited her parents and siblings to commiserate with them. I was taken to see her grave – she was buried in reddish brown soil near a wall. Was that a coincidence?

Before and after that scary dream, I had not been thinking about my late friend, I had not even known that she was sick and dying. So, how could it be that my mind simply auto-concocted the dream from my imaginations or fears? And, how about the un-plastered grave in reddish brown soil near a wall?

In August 1992, I had a dream in which I was visited in my sitting room by a strange man – strange not only because I was not familiar with his face, but also because he looked and dressed like an Arabian while this is Nigeria. What was stranger about him was what he told me. He claimed to be an angel of God, which was quite funny to me (*"aren't angels supposed to be winged? How come you are without wings and also dress like an Arabian?"*, I thought). He gave me his message, notwithstanding my doubts. We talked about the Second Coming of Christ. When I asked him for a proof of his genuineness; he simply said *"read Luke chapter seventeen, verse thirty-two"*.

In the dream, I fumbled for my Bible and never found it. I woke up and realised *"it's only a dream"*. But I was curious to find out *what Luke chapter seventeen, verse thirty-two has to say*. I picked up my Bible and read it but the short verse made no immediate meaning; it simply says *"Remember Lot's wife"*.

Failing to find any meaning in the verse, I decided to read through to the end of the chapter, and then it made more sense. Consequently, I decided to read the preceding verses as well. I found that the entire passage speaks about the Second Coming of Christ. Notwithstanding, the *"angel"* seemed more interested in delivering his message to me than in confirming whether he is genuine because *"Remember Lot's wife"* reiterated his message to me about Christ's Second Coming. The dream's message tallied with the message of the verse referred. Was that a mere coincidence?

Is it by mere coincidence that such trances are "fulfilled" afterwards? Or is it a simple confirmation of humankind's spirituality?

I should spare you so many *"coincidences"* and dreams that were not resultant from activities or inherent desires or fears. But the fact is – over the ages many people have experienced the seeming *"coincidences"* of their dreams with subsequent real life experiences. This does not mean that every dream that a man has is a message from God or by any means from the *"spirit realm"*. The dream of a hungry man about doughnuts is not likely to be a message from God or from any spirit – it is more likely a message from the man's belly. But much more striking than dreams are "trances" and visions in which the *"seer"* is not asleep but has what may be called *"double sight"*. Is it by mere coincidence that such trances are *"fulfilled"* afterwards? Or is it a simple confirmation of humankind's spirituality? And are dreams and visions not the principal ways by which God reportedly spoke to the biblical prophets?

God spoke to the prophets in various ways.

> *In the past* **God spoke to our forefathers through the prophets at many times and in various ways,**
>
> (Hebrews 1: 1)

The Bible's position is that within nature, there is a super-nature; and within every natural human, there is the supernatural man – the offspring God that seeks to be reconciled to its source. The urge of the super-nature towards its eternal source is reckoned as what draws humans into mysticisms, spiritualisms, and religions of every kind.

Of course, there are different kinds of so-called worships and religions, but **true** *worship cannot and should not be just a mental affair. God is spirit, and his worshippers must worship in spirit and in truth.* [John 4: 24]. Worship, if it is indeed "worship", must transcend normal human experiences. The ordinary human mind does not know precisely what happens at 3.00 pm next day. The ability to foretell what would happen at a **precise** point in the future without having considered anything at all about it, transcends normal mental attributes. And true communion with God must be interactive and two-way. If we speak to God, and *He* does not speak to us, then it might well be that we have either not spoken through to him or *He* is simply not there. But dreams and visions, prayers and prophecies have been proven repeatedly to "*coincide predictably and interactively*" with actuality just as much as the ringing of a phone "coincides predictably and interactively" with the dialling of the number of that particular phone line.

> *The Bible's position is that within nature, there is a super-nature; and within every natural human, there is the supernatural man*

God had planted a Garden in the east, in Eden.

> *Now the* LORD **God had planted a garden in the east, in Eden;** *and* **there he put the man** *he had formed.*
>
> (Genesis 2: 8)

Finally, we return to the Garden of Eden and the Bible's creation story for the key evidence about humankind's spirituality. Humankind among all animals is apparently the only earthly species that concerns itself with supernatural phenomena. If the super-nature of God is not within humans in accordance with the Garden of Eden story, then there is no greater explanation for humankind's spirituality. The Bible tells us that humankind was in the garden and walked about naked like chimpanzee and gorilla, unashamed of his nakedness, and then humankind suddenly became ashamed. Evolution also maintains that "*the 'early man' did not wear anything to cover his nakedness*". And until today, no other animal makes clothes for itself for **shame of its nakedness**. The society still much considers that a man that is stripped to stark nakedness in the public is "*disgraced*". Extreme nudists do not come to the streets in the nude to mix with non-nudists – even if they wish to do so; they know the society would frown at it. Why was it once acceptable to "human societies" to walk about as nakedly as apes and then it became unacceptable?

A chimpanzee would not even bother to wear bamboo "*in the public*". The chimpanzee probably knows no such thing as "*public*". Of course, if it needs warmth, and finds anything that could warm it up on covering its body, the chimpanzee would take it, but a man would not throw off his entire clothes in the street just because he feels hot, because for man, cloth is not only for warmth – it also heals a sense of shame. That *sense of shame* apparently dates as far as religion, not evolution, dates.

Evolutionists may have theories on how the psychology of humans evolved to give us "*a sense of the shame of being naked*" and how humankind developed the knowledge of "**private** parts" which other animals do not regard as "private" at all. But, to speak scientifically, such a theory on the evolution of humankind's psychology cannot in anyway avoid the fact that humankind (as an animal) must have had an exclusive experience or habitat, or at least, an exclusive diet, which affected the development of *its* psychology. And that habitat/diet must have been one to which the "cousin apes" did not have access; otherwise, the other apes too would have developed similar psychology *of **religion**, and knowledge of **private** parts and the **shame** of being **naked**.*

If we go by the way of science and evolution, we must question how man among his "cousin apes" could have developed the shame of being naked if he lived together with them, simply contending with them for food and other essentials to emerge as *"the fittest"*. But in evolution, we know that *"isolation"* is a very important stage in the emergence of a new species or subspecies. Before a sample of a particular species can morph into a new species, *"isolation"* must have occurred. By way of science, the *"emergence of the fittest"* (as man's psycho-evolution may be described), could not have taken place while man was yet an ape, ate the same things, and walked in the same company with the other apes that did not *"emerge into humankind"*. But the Bible is not a textbook of biology or evolution, yet it does tell us that the *"Eternal Intelligence"* that created the world deliberately **isolated** "the animal called man" from other beasts.

The Bible does not deny the fact that the Creator made humankind from the same material substances of which other animals are composed. It tells us that both man and beasts were made from the *"dust"*. The human body consists of a proportionate combination of earthly minerals – phosphorus, calcium, sodium, iron, et cetera. But so also do the bodies of gorillas and chimpanzees and other animals. Both humankind and other animals are made of the "dusts" of the earth.

The Bible does not say that there were no other beasts [perhaps, *"man-like apes"*] that God made before *He* made man. BUT one thing it does maintain invariably is that *"man is NOT just an animal, man is ALSO spiritual"*. That man is an animal, just as much as apes (and whatever else), is not news. [Ecclesiastes 3: 18]. But what is unbelievable news to the scientists is that beneath the animal form of man and as an integral component of the complete human is a replica of the (nonmaterial) nature of God. What is news to the scientists is the fact that the very wide gap between the mental abilities of man and other apes resulted from a planned *"**isolation**"* in nature, experience, location and diets. The Bible teaches that in the Garden of Eden, the Creator planted *"trees that were pleasing to the eye and good for food. In the middle of the garden were the tree of life and the tree of the knowledge of good and evil"*. (Genesis 2: 9).

If we reckon with the Bible's Garden of Eden story and then reason as mere scientists, we might well say that at the *"emergence of man"* on earth, the *"Eternal Intelligence"*, or *Creator*, or *God*, or *Nature*, or whatever we wish to call *Him*, had given the animal man an exclusive access to a habitat and diet, which the other apes and beasts lacked. In the exclusive habitat, what the Bible implies might have transformed the psychological development of the animal human was the *"tree of knowledge of good and evil"* – a special kind of diet, perhaps, which humans had taken in the Garden of Eden.

Between chimpanzee and gorilla, there is only a narrow gap in mental capacities. But between them and humans, there is a wide gap. And when we consider what the Bible says about the tree of the knowledge of good and evil in the Garden of Eden, we find a tendency towards a scientific principle, although science cannot prove that the Garden of Eden existed. Yet when evolutionists plot graphs charting humankind's mental development over the ages, there is a sharp upward turn in the graph within the most recent six thousand years or thereabout, and *"coincidentally"*, the sharp upward turn in the graph begins at about the time that the Bible's Adam and Eve probably lived. Although, I am also curious to know what a *"natural garden"* would have looked like: common artists' impressions of the Garden of Eden look so artificial in the layouts.

Evolution (by rejecting the Bible's creation story) prejudges that there could not have been a *"natural garden"* on earth yet it agrees with other branches of science that *"floras"* that did not double as *"faunas"* probably existed. And yet again, it agrees that such floras could have been discovered and subsequently colonized by migrating animal species. But evolutionists will not agree that *Nature* could have led humankind into a flora or even that *"Nature prepared a flora in the east, in Eden"*.

Evolution agrees with other branches of science that the food we eat everyday affects not only our skeleto-muscular developments but also our psychological developments as well. Evolution agrees that it is not impossible to find natural psychochemicals [substances that affect the brain and its functions – including balance, coordination and thought] yet it does not agree with the Bible that humankind could have ingested some psychochemical substances from certain plants found within an exclusive wild flora. Perhaps, anyway, evolutionists are simply put off by the apparently **saga**cious language of the Bible and its interpreters. Notwithstanding the evolutionists' apparent prejudice against Bible's creation stories, however, the principles of evolution invariably reiterates the probable factuality of the Bible's creation and Garden of Eden stories. The conflict between evolution and creation may therefore not be a conflict of concepts but one of attitudes and perceptions. But we are not primarily interested in harmonising evolution and creation – if they do not blend, they simply do not blend and there is nothing to gain in trying to blend them. Yet it is important to point out what tends towards error on both sides. Evolutionists' stance that there could not have been a natural wild flora, in which humankind ingested a particular mental-enhancing "psychochemical" some six thousand years ago or thereabout, appears incongruent with the very principles of evolution. What the Bible says had happened to humankind in the Garden of Eden is a scientific possibility, even if it cannot be ascertained by science.

You must not eat from it!

> *The* LORD *God took the man and put him in the Garden of Eden to work it and to take care of it. And the* LORD *God commanded the man, "You are free to eat from any tree in the garden; but you must not eat from* **the tree of the knowledge of good and evil***, for when you eat of it you will surely die.*
>
> (Genesis 2: 15 – 17)

According to the Bible, there was a flora in which the Creator Spirit placed man and instructed man [*Spirit speaking to spirit*] that the human animal should not eat from a particular plant species. Where the Bible becomes difficult is that it does not tell us why the tree had to be in the Garden of Eden while God did not want man to eat from it. But in the long and short of the story, the Bible tells us that man disobeyed the un-embodied *Voice* and ate from that tree:

> *When the woman saw that the fruit of the tree was good for food and pleasing to the eye, and also desirable for gaining wisdom, she took some and ate it. She also gave some to her husband, who was with her, and he ate it. Then the eyes of both of them were opened, and they realised they were naked; . . .*
>
> (Genesis 3: 6 – 7)

The statement *"the eyes of both of them were opened"* does not tell us they had been physically blind for the author had told us earlier that they had **seen** that *"the tree was pleasing to the* **eye***"* before eating from it. What was *"opened"* after they had eaten from that tree was their *"mental eyes"*, so to say.

I am not interested in proving that there was certainly a Garden of Eden or that there was Adam and Eve, my sole objective is to verify (and reiterate if found true) the fact that God exists and that *He* both knows and could be known. But while pursuing this primal objective, I cannot simply overlook what those who testify of having known God had said about him and about us: what they have said about *"the proto-*

type humankind", Adam and Eve, cannot be simply brushed aside without examination. Yet while examining the Garden of Eden story I have found that the Bible tells us that man at first lived nakedly without paying attention to "*privacy*" and that at a particular point, man started covering his "*private parts*" – a fact that evolution and science also affirms. Who told man that those things are "*private*"?

It is interesting that at once evolution agrees with the Bible, that man had not always carried the "*private part*" idea. Evolutionists study the "*probable natural history*" of humankind by examining fossils and "*missing links*" – but apron/pant-wearing fossils of humankind do not date too much earlier than the probable time that the Bible's Adam and Eve existed. And this again makes one consider that there is a possible scientific corroboration of the Garden of Eden story. Evolution and fossils in fact make it appear that the "*eyes of man were not opened*" to the world in which he lived earlier than the time that the biblical Adam and Eve probably lived.

Proving that the opening of humankind's mental eyes coincides with the probable time that Adam and Eve lived and ate from the tree of knowledge is not the issue, though. What is more difficult to prove is how there could have been only one Adam ["*Adam*" means "man"] and only one Eve, in the "*isolated habitat*". Notwithstanding, we have arrived at the universal fact that the human species is an animal as much as other apes. We have also recognised the fact that man alone among all animals seeks after supernatural phenomena, with the implication that the urge towards the supernatural world could not have been basically animalistic otherwise "*lesser animals*" would possess this urge in lesser ways.

Evidence of an urge towards spirituality is totally absent in chimpanzee and gorilla, and it is a pointer towards the probable fact that within the animal called man alone is *the image and likeness* [that is, "*nature*"] of God. And we again recognise the fact that apart from the mental powers of our brains, humankind is also able to gain the precise knowledge of future events through dreams and visions, which bring "*messages and inspirations*" to us in a manner that transcends our normal mental capabilities.

Nevertheless not every man encounters "*spiritual dreams*" or "*visions*". In fact, a very small proportion of humans do. But the Bible offers an answer to why most men do not have "*spiritual dreams*" and are out of touch with the *Creator Breath*, God.

The Bible tells us that it was by Adam's lusts and sin in the Garden of Eden that humankind lost touch with the *breath* of God that is within us. If we lost that *"breath"*, then we must be spiritually irresponsive to God. **"Sin entered the world through one man, and in this way death** *came to all men"*. (Romans 5: 12). Therefore, as much we should have loved to do away with the Bible, we simply cannot; because even by trying to avoid God, or contact with God's Spirit, we corroborate the Bible's claims that Adam tried to avoid God **after** disobeying God in the Garden, and then passing on his spiritual-irresponsiveness (of trying to avoid God) to us all.

We may not all believe the Bible's story of Adam and Eve, but the story simply shows a typical man and woman; and when we re-examine the story we see the nature of Adam and Eve in today's men and women. If we are not true descendants of Adam and Eve, then why are we apparently so much like them? Why do we have the same attitudes toward God and *"lusts"* towards the things of this world as Adam and Eve had after they ate from the forbidden tree? If Adam and Eve did not exist, from where did humans get the idea of a *"Spirit God"* or spirits, generally? If "Adam and Eve" were simply Jewish fictitious "legends", then why do some other nations have indigenous stories that are similar to the Jewish one?

> *I think the undeniable truth is that when we remove prejudice from our sciences and religions, we cannot arrive at a better idea than that "the Spirit God" made the world*

As scientists, we disregard the Bible's creation story and the Garden of Eden story, but if we consider the fact that the Big Bang could not have occurred by itself unless there was an *Eternal Nonmaterial Being* in space, would this fact change what we believe about evolution? If the *Eternal Being* truly pre-existed the universe, and decided that the universe should *"hold together"*, could *He* not have influenced (or *"catalysed"*) the processes of evolution?

I think the undeniable truth is that when we remove prejudice from our sciences and religions, we cannot arrive at a better idea than that *"the Spirit God"* made the world and that man **alone** among all biological life on earth has an affinity towards God. This is the **only** rational conclusion that we can always reach. But if you cannot join in this conclusion, perhaps you might wish to review the discourse all over again or perhaps you might wish to show the world a better idea.

The import of the conclusion about the probable credibility of the creation stories is the factor of "*spiritual irresponsiveness*" towards God, which God called "*death*" in the Garden of Eden. It is essential to consider it.

Chapter Three

SIN AND VANITY

"Death and the Dead".

You will surely die!

In the Garden of Eden, so the Bible tells us, God had warned man about *"death"*.

> *The LORD God formed the man from the dust of the ground and breathed into his nostrils the breath of life; and the man became a living being. Now the LORD God had planted a garden in the east, in Eden; and there he put the man he had formed. And the LORD God made all kinds of trees grow out of the ground — trees that were pleasing to the eye and good for food. In the middle of the garden were the tree of life and the tree of the knowledge of good and evil . . . The LORD God took the man and put him in the Garden of Eden to work it and to take care of it. And the LORD God commanded the man, "You are free to eat from any tree in the garden; but you must not eat from the tree of the knowledge of good and evil, for when you eat of it you will surely die.*
>
> (Genesis 2: 7 – 17)

The Garden of Eden story may be considered as a theological idea, but evolutionists are seemingly not cognisant of the **fact** that the material world could not have originated of its own accord. Although, creationists reach their conclusions by believing in *"inspired"* teachings (as often asserted), yet what they believe are not necessarily incongruent with observable facts. First, we must consider the fact that the entire universe, from the greatest stellar systems down to the tiniest atoms, consists of a single pattern of spinning spheres revolving round a central sphere. This uniqueness and uniformity of pattern in the tiniest constituents of **every** thing is a probable indication that **all** things were originated by a unique eternal mind. Every detail of the material universe seemingly fits into a grand master plan written in *"spheres and circles"*, which are both symbols of infinity and eternality. But scientifically we may refuse to believe the biblical idea, which teaches that *"the Originator of the universe placed man in a wild flora in Eden"*, yet we cannot deny the absolute fact that unless the *Creator Spiritus* existed eternally, the material universe could not have come into existence.

> *evolutionists are seemingly not cognisant of the fact that the material world could not have originated of its own accord*

And if the entire universe therefore has an *"Architect and Builder"* and, by implication of this, a probable *"master plan"*, it is only rational to understand that in every master plan, every specific detail (such as the emergence of intelligent species) counts.

Thus, even if we cannot trace our way back to *"the flora eastward in Eden"*, through mouth-to-mouth "sagas" that were probably first promulgated by the original human inhabitants of that flora, or otherwise by prophetic encounters with the supposed *flora-Maker*, we can at least accept that the *Eternal Intelligence* must have included *"the emergence of species"* in *His "blueprints"*. And if the emergence of species were planned, likewise would have been the means by which the species should emerge.

Several study techniques used in evolution sciences have credibility – much credibility. But the singular fact that evolution has not considered that there must have been an eternal person behind the remote origin of the material universe is one reason that evolution may not be outright. Evolutionists build up theories from a combination of *"evidences and speculations"* but what is baffling to Christians is why evolutionists opine that such a wonderful eternal *Originator* of the material world could not have concerned himself with and controlled the origin of species on earth.

Indeed, evolutionists through the Big Bang theory have unwittingly arrived at the same basic idea that creationists have about the primal origin of the world. Big Bang theorists tell us that the *"the entire material world* **came out** *of absolute nothing"* while creationists tell us that *"the entire material world* **was brought out** *of absolute nothing"*.

By faith we understand that the universe was formed at God's command, so that what is seen was not made out of what was visible.

(Hebrew 11: 3)

Indeed, science agrees with the Bible that the visible things are built from invisible things – concerning science, this is true at least in terms of atomic protons and electrons that are invisible under the most powerful microscopes. And yet science has not probed into what makes up each of protons and electrons. What does an electron consist of? Suppose electrons consists of *"microelectrons"*, what does micro-electrons consist of? The question of what makes up something else would continue to surge up as long as we continue to probe until we have reduced all things to absolute **noth-ing**. It cannot be over-reiterated that science and the Bible both agree that before the exis-tence of the material world, there could not have been any material thing in space. Thus, the only **major** difference between the ideas of the evolutionists and the creationists is whether there was an *"Eternal Living Nonmaterial Energy"* behind the origin of the material world or not.

> *Indeed, evolutionists through the Big Bang theory have unwittingly arrived at the same basic idea that creationists have about the primal origin of the world.*

But, as absolute nothing would **only** have produced absolute nothing unless some energy was present and actively applied, the creationists seem to have a better case than the evolutionists do in respect of the primal origin of the material world. Therefore, whether we go by the ideas of the evolutionists towards the primal origin of the material world, or whether we go by the ideas of the creationists, we can only reckon that the *"Creator"* must have been there. And factually so.

Genesis describes the presence of the Creator God on the earth as *"Spirit"* (Genesis 1: 2) which implies that if it was possible that we were physically watching the creation processes, we would see only the crea-tures but not the Creator; and then species would appear to *"emerge"* as though of their own accord. But with regard to the emergence of spe-cies, the author of Genesis surprises us in his second chapter where he says that the Creator first formed man and then formed a woman from the body of the man.

So the LORD God caused the man to fall into deep sleep; and while he was sleep-

ing, he took one of the man's ribs and closed up the place with flesh. Then the LORD God made a woman from the rib he had taken out of the man, and he brought her to the man.

(Genesis 2: 21 – 22)

At the time Genesis was written, anaesthetic surgery was not known, yet what the author of Genesis described in the passage cited above might be called *"natural surgery"*. Today, however, humans have acquired the wisdom to clone and genetically engineer new variants of organisms from previous natural ones and we might well *"mould"* another living individual from a very small material sample taken from one individual. If we can do it, why do we suppose that the eternal powerful Spirit could not have done something similar and in a better, more natural way? Of course, if according to Genesis, God had moulded the man's body from *"dusts of the earth"*, he could as well have done the same for the woman's body. But why did God decide to *"surgically remove"* a sample from the body of the man and mould that small sample into an entire human being rather than mould afresh from dust?

> ***If Charles Darwin reckoned with the Originator of species, there are overabundant odds that his "Origin of Species" might have presented an approach that is different***

It is most probable that if the evolution theories were re-written today with a cognisance of the undeniable facts of the existence of the *Originator*, evolution theories would take a course different from their present forms. If Charles Darwin reckoned with the *Originator of species*, there are overabundant odds that his *"Origin of Species"* might have presented an approach that is different from what it is, if not a different conclusion.

Evolutionists believe that humankind descended from some kinds of apes. And in the way the Bible talks of the creation, apes should have lived on earth before humankind began to live on earth. But the singular fact that apes existed before humans and are made of the same earthly elements [*"dusts"*, biblically] of which humankind is made, does not necessarily translate that apes became humans. And interestingly, evolutionists have found that while trying to construct a chain between humans and ancient apes there are several *"missing links"* that have remained unfound. Is it not possible (in cognisance of the existence of an *Originator*) that such links do not exist in the first place? If it were possible that the Creator was building things in the way that we mould sculptures, would there remain a place for such missing links?

Let us take for instance a human sculptor who takes a large supply of clay and settles in his mind to mould a variety of things. The sculptor could first mould a completely flat "rectangular plate", seeing that "*it is good*", he could then mould a "rectangular plate with curved edges". Seeing that "*it is good*", he could next do a "circular plate". And seeing again that "*it is good*", he could next do a "circular plate that is slightly raised at the edge". And yet seeing again that "*it is good*", he could do a "circular plate that is well raised at the edge". By and by, he would mould a pot, and then a pot with handles, and then a pot with stands but without handles, and a pot with both handles and stands. In the long run, the last mould and the first mould would look so much different, but when the moulds are arranged in the order of their simplicities and similarities, a "*tree of relationships*" could be drawn up. But it would not automatically follow that the pot with both handles and stands was sculpted out of the very one without handles and stands. Of course, moulding a pot that lacks handles and stands could have inspired the sculptor to mould a pot that has both handles and stands, but it does not automatically translate that the sculptor added handles and stands to the very pot that lacked these. And it could well be. Nevertheless, the decision as to what means by which a sculptor would make his moulds rests solely with the sculptor. While recognising the fundamental right of every sculptor to freely choose thus, the Bible presents the *Creator Spirit* as man's sculptor.

> *Yet, O LORD, you are our Father We are the clay, you our potter, we are all the work of your hand.*

(Isaiah 64: 8)

However, indeed chimpanzees and gorillas resemble humankind. The Bible affirms that animals as well as humankind are made by the same "*Potter*" and both from "dusts" of the earth. According to the Bible, the fact that God made apes and "*saw that it was good*" and then also made humankind does not automatically translate that God made humankind from apes or converted apes to humans. The Bible's position is that both humans and beasts are "*made from dusts*", by the same maker, which implies that apes and humans originated from the same earthly materials ("*dusts*") but does not imply that God had brought man out of apes in the manner that he "*brought the woman out of the man*". And even if he decided to bring humans out of apes as he brought the woman out of man, it does not change his status as humankind's sculptor. But the Bible does NOT say that God had brought humankind out of apes or brought one animal out of another. The Bible only says that God made one kind of things, saw that it was good, and then made another kind, saw again that it was good, and by and by until he made humankind and saw that it was "*very good*". Yet the Bible is apparently correct about the FACT that there is an eternal God; a fact that Big Bang theorists apparently prove and yet refuse to acknowledge.

Nevertheless, even if we go with evolution and science to say that apes became humans, and if we disregard the missing links in the history of humankind's evolution while remaining cognisant of the primal origin of the material world, we must question the wide mental gap between humankind and "*the other primates*".

On its own part, the Bible asserts that when the Creator would make humankind, he purposed that man would be "*the administrator*" of the earth, ruling over even the "*great beasts*" and "*sea monsters*" that are much larger than man is. Considering the fact that the world of Moses' time did not know that the continent of Southern America (for instance) existed, Moses could not have known **experientially** that humankind is the greatest being on **whole** surface of the earth; there was at least a possibility that a creature greater than humankind lived on such unknown continents. But it turned out that what was written in Genesis even without an experiential knowledge of the whole surface of the earth, turned out to be true after all. And likewise were the other points that Genesis asserted about the earth, such as the "*continental drift*" which Moses could not have known experientially yet science discovered it afterwards. Time has again proved Moses right about man's dominion on earth over all other earthly creatures.

An elephant has greater strength than a human does but it is not by physical strength that humans dominate the earth. The whale is a hundred times bigger than humankind is, but it is not by body volume that humankind dominates the earth. Humankind dominates the earth by knowledge and designedly so, apparently.

We check out the facts (whether by evolution or creation) and find that the other animals species existed before humankind began to exist, yet **none** of them *"dominated the earth and also ruled over other creatures"* until humankind came into the scene. Humankind did not overthrow any other creature in order to gain dominion over the earth because indeed no creature had such dominion. Every other animal species simply concerns itself with its own affairs rather than managing the earth and the things in it. Thus, the fact that humankind emerged upon the earth and began to rule over the earth and all earthly creatures does not appear (given the context of the origin of the entire universe) to be by mere chance. To think as scientists, we must reckon that if man descended from apes, unless he was isolated from his generic order, he could not have been so much different from them. As scientists, we reckon that the mental capabilities of *"modern man"* could probably have soared in his isolation from other primates — an isolation that the *"special flora planted eastward in Eden"*, represents (or, describes). Apparently, the Garden of Eden fits more scientifically into the evolution of man (if origination was evolution) than *"missing links"* do because the development of man's advanced mental capabilities appear to be more recent than *"millions of years ago"*.

Christians would continue to believe in the Garden of Eden story, not only for theological reasons but also for the common sense reason approached from the fact that the universe has an *Architect* who must have planned to minute details the means by which species would emerge and subsist on earth. Much more that evolution also probably needs to identify specifically the isolation factor that separated man from the *"other primates"* and gave modern man the privilege to increase so much more in knowledge than modern chimpanzee and modern gorilla.

Whether the Garden of Eden appears nearer to us than the evolutionary separation of man from the primates, or not, the fact remains that a physical and dietary separation in the form of "colony" could have greatly enhanced the mental development of man among the other primates, and that separation is represented in the Bible as the *"Garden of Eden"*.

Back to the Bible's flora of Eden therefore, though it is theology, one could believe that the story came to the Bible writers either by prophecy (for the writer of Genesis could not have been an eyewitness of Adam's creation) or by mouth-to-mouth descent from the Garden, through Adam's generations. The latter possibility is equally reckoned with the former, because similar stories about *"first man and woman in a garden"* are also found in certain non-Jewish and non-Bible literatures, although with incompatible variations.

For the purpose of our quest, we would dwell on what the Creator Spirit reportedly told man in the biblical garden – *"in the day that you eat from the tree of knowledge,* **you shall surely die!** *"* – a warning that implies that the Creator did not want man to die. *Why* the Creator did not want man to die and *how* knowledge would kill man, is not detailed in the story but it is implied that if the man "died" [physically], he would no longer be in position to have dominion over the earth and all the creatures. Therefore, it makes sense that the Creator should want man to keep living in order to continuously take his destined place as the administrator of the earth yet he is supposed to govern the earth not by physical strength or body volume, but by knowledge. If knowledge would kill man, how shall he maintain dominion (by knowledge) over the earth?

"You made him ruler over everything".

Man, among beasts, is the king of the earth; the Bible and science agree on this.

> O LORD, *our Lord, . . . what is man that you are mindful of him, the son of man that you care for him? You made him a little lower than the heavenly beings and crowned him with glory and honor.* **You made him ruler over the works of your hands;** *you put everything under his feet:*
>
> (Psalm 8: 1 – 6)

Man, according to the Bible, is "lower than the heavenly beings" in the sense that he is not entirely a spirit being, unlike angels who are supposedly entirely spirits. The fact that man *"is also flesh [animal]"* limits him from fully enjoying his non-animal nature, the spiritual. But man has **dominion** over other animals, and according to the Bible, God had designed it thus.

In the creation story that we find in the Bible, God made all the animals including the "great" sea-dwelling creatures. But until God made the *"special animal that is capable of worship"*, he did not give any one of those animals dominion [ultimate control and administration] over the earth and everything that is on earth. But God [whom you might call *"Nature"* if you wish] gave man dominion over **ALL** things that are on earth just as soon as man emerged, according to the Bible. By nature, that task (the continual judicious administration of the earth and its resources) requires skills and experience which could not have been inherent in a then "newly emerged species". Thus, it makes sense that the *Creator* (or *Nature*) should have put (or led) man into an isolated habitat where he would grow to acquire the skills and experience required to govern the earth.

And it equally makes sense that God should train one individual towards maintaining dominion over the earth rather than to train a group who would no sooner begin contending with one another on who should be the dominator of the dominators.

The manager-in-training concept gives us a reason why the flora of Eden, if it was planned by the Creator, would probably have had only one Adam rather than many Adams. After all, if God wanted a species to dominate the earth, it would be easier for him to train a single couple, who would in turn train their own children, and the children would train the third generation, until there are as many administrators as would cover the face of the whole earth. And that dominion system would have a greater stability by vertical hierarchy than by horizontal control. In fact, a horizontal authority is almost impossible to exert. So, while Christians may not have immediate proofs that there was only one Adam in the flora of Eden, God's possible motive of managerial tutorage gives a reason to believe there could not have been more than one Adam in Eden.

Humankind, among every other animal, qualified for managerial tutorage because within man was that supernature, "the *breath* of God", the image and likeness of God, according to the Bible. When it is active and healthy, this *breath* enables man to commune directly with the Creator of the universe, by prayer and prophecy, and by spiritual dreams and visions.

However, as the Bible claims, this *"breath"* is unfortunately inactive in most human beings today because of what the Bible called "death" in the second chapter of Genesis, the death of which God had warned man *"when you eat from the tree of knowledge, **you will surely die!**"*.

According to the Bible, it was because of that "death" that we are often into this whole kind of discussions. An atheist believes that he is not spiritual and has no nature of God within him, because his spirit is "inactive" within him. He does not listen to God, and neither does he speak to God. Why should he believe then that God exists? After all, the so-called replica of the nature of God, by which humankind is able to relate with God, is inactive in most of us. Every human being who does not relate with God on a person-to-person basis probably affirms that it is true that "death" of the *breath of God*" in us has passed from the flora of Eden upon all men, as the Bible says. A man who is spiritually "dead" is therefore not wrong to say that he is no more than a mere animal. Of course, if humankind consists of both spirit and animal as the Bible teaches, and the spirit component is "dead", then it remains only the animal, and an atheist therefore has a sound reason to believe that he is not more than an ordinary animal. However, atheism would thus only reiterate that Bible's claim that because man's spirit "died" in the Garden of Eden, every ordinary man is born spiritually dead.

> *A man who is spiritually "dead" is therefore not wrong to say that he is no more than a mere animal.*

A man in whom the "*breath* of God" is dead cannot relate with God, and therefore may not believe that God truly exists. But if by reckoning thus, we are beginning to sound outright theological, let us return as sceptics to question what the Bible calls "death" of the "spirit".

You will NOT surely die!

The Bible says that God warned man that in the day man eats of the "*tree of the knowledge of good and evil*", man "*will surely die!*". But the Bible also tells us that another intelligent being also told man "*you will not surely die!*".

> *Now the serpent was more crafty than any of the wild animals the LORD God had made. He said unto the woman, "Did God really say, 'You must not eat from any tree in the garden'?" The woman said to the serpent, "We may eat fruit from the trees in the garden, but God did say, 'You must not eat fruit from the tree that is in the middle of the garden, and you must not touch it, or you will die.'* " ***"You will not surely die,"*** *the serpent said to the woman. "For God knows that when you eat of it your eyes will be opened and you will be like God,*

knowing good and evil.”

(Genesis 3: 1 – 5)

Ordinarily, many people consider the Garden of Eden story as rather childish. In fact, it brings up several questions – *“what kind of serpent was it that could commune with man?”*, *“how could a serpent with its tiny brain have known what man [a higher species] did not know?”*

“That Ancient ‘Serpent’, Satan, the Devil.

The great dragon was hurled down – **that ancient serpent called the devil, or Satan,** *who leads the whole world astray. He was hurled to the earth . . .*

(Revelations 12: 9)

By studying the Bible, we observe that the meanings of several Bible passages could be fetched from some other Bible passages. Reading Genesis alone, it does not make sense to us that a serpent speaks. But from Revelations we learn that what the author of Genesis called serpent was in fact not *“the craftiest among wild animals”* but *“the Devil, Satan”*, *“the beguiling spirit being”*. Although the story in Genesis makes it rather unclear whether this *“Satan”* was actually indwelling a particular physical serpent just as much as the “the *breath* of God” indwells man, or whether he was figuratively called “the serpent” because of the natural slithering “cunningness” of physical serpents. But even in the Genesis story, it is clear that the name *“the serpent”* refer to a particular being that is capable of intelligent communication. Therefore, the story-teller in Genesis could not have been talking literarily about the common *“wild animal”*, snake, but about a more intelligent being, that has a nature that places him *“above animal nature”*.

> *By studying the Bible, we observe that the meanings of several Bible passages could be fetched from some other Bible passages.*

In any case, what may (or may not) be an error of transcription removes the word *“serpent”* from one of the ancient manuscripts of the Bible; instead of the word *“nachash”* which means “serpent”, the manuscript reads *“cachash”* which means “lair”. Whichever way the original writing must have been spelt, it is settled that the focus of reference in the Garden of Eden story is that man was beguiled. The character of the “serpent” in the story points more to *“the beguiler”*, Ca-

chash, Satan, the Devil – a spirit being, rather than towards the physical serpent, *nachash*, snake. Nevertheless, whether it is *cachash* or *nachash*, the Bible's doctrine is that the deceiver in Eden was Satan, the Devil (whom we shall discuss more fully in the next chapter).

A thousand years in God's sight.

There is a little problem, and perhaps more, with the Garden of Eden story – we wonder how God expected man to know what the word "dying" meant when he said *"you will surely die"*.

If the first chapter of Genesis is right about God creating the world and everything that is in it in only six days, then all life would have been young and then, it was unlikely that anything should be dead. If nothing had died, how was Adam supposed to visualise what "dying" meant? However, it appears that what the author of Genesis called "days" were in fact not the [twenty-four-hour] days that we know to-day; probably he meant "phases". Those who would insist that "six days is always six days", should also consider that a natural "day" is not always twenty-four hours, anyway. In the polar regions of the earth, a sunset ("night") could last for about six months, and a sunshine ("day") could last for another six months such that if God were work-ing on the earth from the Polar Regions his *"evening and morning"* would have been six months each!

But we may expect God's "evening and morning" for the creation period to have lasted for more than six months each. God is a spirit, and spirits are thought to operate at the speed of light. If that is it, then moments of God's thoughts would have been extremely larger than moments of humankind's thoughts; such that what God would have considered "an evening and a morning" would have been nearly "647 998 evenings and mornings" for humans – going by the speed of light! And no wonder several Bible writers say, *"a [man's] thousand years are to God as an evening"*!

> For **a thousand years in your sight** *are like a day that has just gone by, or* **like a watch in the night**.
>
> (Psalm 90: 4)

> *But do not forget this one thing, dear friends:* **With the Lord a day is like a thousand years,** *and a thousand years are like a day.*
>
> (2 Peter 3: 8)

And such it would have been that if God had told anyone, "*I made the world in only six days*", the person may take the "*six days*" to be "*twenty-four hours in six places*", and not knowing that it could in fact have been six thousand, or six million, or six billion years – whatever it was is immaterial. To God, it was just "an evening and morning", even if to us it is ten thousand generations – it is apparently a matter of measures. The bigger the hands, the bigger the spans – a Bible prophet reported that God "*measured the oceans in the hollow of His palms*, and the skies by *His* span"; [Isaiah 40: 12]. To us they are vast oceans, but to *Him*, they are "*some 'palmfuls' of water*". Who knows whether what *He* called "six days" were six trillion years! Our immediate quest, however, is not about how long were *His* "six days" but whether Adam understood what *God* could have meant by "*you will surely die*", which Adam could not have understood anyway, unless God's "evenings" were truly "*thousands of years*" [figuratively] rather than twenty four hours – thereby giving the earth enough duration for there to have been an example of dead things.

From the Genesis story, it is apparent that Adam and Eve had an idea what "death" stood for. [So, they might perhaps have seen some form of death or dying. And that might well mean that God's "six days" were not our own six days but *His* own six "***days***". But then, if those six days were not "days" of twenty-four hours but "***days***" of "thousand generations", it could not have been that the Adam in the Garden of Eden was made on the sixth "day". For then he would have also witnessed God's seventh day, God's Sabbath, and would have been more than "a thousand years" old after the Sabbath, if a day counted for a thousand years].

Although, when we speak as sceptics we cannot take the creation stories of Genesis at face value because they would appear to preserve only "the morals of the story", and not the actual details. But the first chapter of Genesis also tells us that man was made on the sixth day, male and female, whereas the second chapter implies that man was made after God's Sabbath, making the man first, and then forming [morphing/cloning/whatever] the woman out of the man. This second account, which might imply that man was made after God's Sabbath, fits into the picture more rationally than the first account, although we cannot theologically disregard the first chapter.

In the second account, which also is the one that tells us of the Garden of Eden, we find that man kept God's charge of staying away from the "tree of the knowledge of good and evil" until Satan [Liar, the serpent], beguiled man. Satan told the woman, *"you will not surely die; God was only scaring you off! He doesn't want you to be wise like him"*. And indeed Eve and Adam did not surely die, bodily. Which means that Satan was right? Yes, somehow. But NO, because what God called "death" was not the physical death of the animal, which terminates the auto-activity of the body. The death that God warned humankind about is the death of the *"breath* that God breathed into the nostrils of man"; death of the "inner man".

The LORD *God formed the man from the dust of the ground and breathed into his nostrils the breath of life, and the man became a living being.*

(Genesis 2: 7)

The animal called man became a "living consciousness" when God breathed into that animal *His* "living *spirit"*. In respect to God, to be *spirit*ually alive is to be "*spirit*ually conscious".

The mind of the sinful man is death, but the mind controlled by the Spirit is life and peace; the sinful mind is hostile to God. It does not submit to God's law, nor can it do so.

(Romans 8: 6 – 8)

For to be **carnally minded is death***; but to be* **spiritually minded is life** *and peace. Because* **the carnal mind is enmity against God***: for it is not subject to the law of God, neither indeed can be. So then they that are in the flesh cannot please God.*

(Romans 8: 6 – 8, King James Version)

Thus, "*death"* in the warning that God gave humankind, meant that humankind would become carnally [bodily] minded as against being spiritually minded. Humankind's ordinary animal consciousness without an inner spiritual consciousness was thus regarded as "*death"* by God, for if humankind lost spiritual consciousness, and is left with only animal consciousness, humankind's two-way communication with God would become more difficult and humankind would therefore be alienated to God, and would no longer be submissive to God. To become alienated to God was to "*surely die"*.

Accordingly, we may consider the question again, did Adam and Eve "*surely die"* after eating of the tree of the knowledge of good and evil? Of course, they did. For after eating from that tree, they wanted

God no more. In fact, when next they were aware of the presence of the un-embodied *Voice* in the Garden, they hid themselves among the trees of the Garden. *"We don't want to relate with 'the Voice' any more"*, Adam and Eve conspired between them, according to the Bible. And thus, humankind lost the natural relationship with God.

> *When the woman saw that the fruit of the tree was good for food and pleasing to the eye, and also desirable for gaining wisdom, she took some and ate it. She also gave some to her husband, who was with her, and he ate it. Then the eyes of both of them were opened, and they realised they were naked; so they sewed fig leaves together and made coverings for themselves.* **Then the man and his wife heard the sound of the LORD God as he was walking in the garden in the cool of the day, and they hid from the LORD God among the trees of the garden.** *But the LORD God called to the man, "Where are you?". He answered, "I heard you in the garden, and I was afraid because I was naked; so I hid". And he said, "Who told you that you were naked? Have you eaten from the tree that I commanded you not to eat from?"*
>
> (Genesis 3: 6 – 11)

Man, where are you?

Eve ate from the tree because Satan persuaded her that she would not die [physically]; Satan's intent was not as friendly as it appeared. Satan did not tell her that by discovering mental knowledge on their own - without the guidance of God by spiritual knowledge - she and her husband would become alienated to God. And afterwards, she realised that indeed Satan had deceived her, thus justifying the warning of God that they will *"surely die"*.

> *And he said, "Who told you that you were naked? Have you eaten from the tree that I commanded you not to eat from?" The man said, "The woman you put here with me — she gave me some fruit from the tree, and I ate it." Then the LORD God said to the woman, "What is this you have done?" The woman said,* **"The serpent deceived me**, *and I ate."*
>
> (Genesis 3: 11 – 13)

As far as evolution and science are concerned, all kinds of food influence our mental developments, only to various degrees. Consequently, it is not unscientific that a particular food should be *"a food desirable for gaining wisdom"*; psychochemical-rich foods could affect ones mind, and thus the Garden of Eden story is compatible with the principles of science and evolution. But then, if God did not want humankind to eat from the tree of the knowledge of good and evil, why did *He* plant it in the garden in the first place? Rather than warn humankind to keep off from the tree, why did not God avoid planting the tree in the Garden? And why did God not prevent Satan from entering the Garden to tempt humankind?

To begin with, it was apparently not God's plan that humankind should remain in ignorance forever. The moral of the Garden of Eden story is not that God did not want *"humankind's eyes to be opened"*. The story shows that God only wanted to be humans' instructor, providing knowledge to both the inner [spirit] human as well as the outer [animal] human. According to the story, God had in fact started man on the pathway of knowledge and wisdom by making man to name all animals. (Genesis 2: 19 – 20). Identifying and distinguishing the animals was a basic stage in God's curriculum for man's mental development. So, perhaps, God had some subsequent plans to use the tree of knowledge to teach humans the knowledge of good and evil, after humans might have graduated from all the necessary elementary stages. Just perhaps.

And as for why God did not keep Satan out of the Garden, it could be opined that it was also a necessary stage in God's plan for humans' growth in knowledge and wisdom. It was not a bad idea that humankind should be tempted by the devil; to be tempted is NOT sin. **Yielding** to temptation (against a stated instruction) is sin. It was possible that Eve and Adam should have overcome Satan's temptation. Eve could have said, *"thank you, Mr. Serpent, I would consult Adam and we would both challenge God to his face about what you have just said"*. But it was not so because she *became enticed and drawn away by **her** desires*. It is the enticement and drawing away that was sin.

> *When tempted, no one should say, "God is tempting me." For God cannot be tempted by evil, nor does he tempt anyone; but each is tempted when, by his own evil desire, he is dragged away and enticed. Then, after desire has conceived, it gives birth to sin, and sin, when it is full-grown, gives birth to death.*
>
> (James 1: 13 – 15)

Eve went through this cycle, she saw the tree as *"good for food"* [lust of the flesh]; *"pleasant to the eyes"* [lust of the eyes]; and *"a tree to be desired to make one wise"* [the pride of life – for *"knowledge puffs up"* (1 Corinthians 8: 1). She must have been concentrating on the seeming benefits of the tree without considering the danger that God warned. She observed the tree long enough for all the seeming benefits of the tree to turn into "lusts" [strong, hardly resistible desires]. And then, she got enticed [became overwhelmed by the urge to eat the fruit], and ultimately she ate from the tree, thus breaking God's commandment. To break God's commandment was to take a step without being guided by God through the inner [spirit] man. And to thus gain knowledge in the animal [outer] form without gaining knowledge in the spirit [inner] form was to "kill" the inner form, for the "*breath* of God" in humankind was thus suppressed and alienated to its eternal source, God. By making their own spirits far more "inert" than their animal components, Adam and Eve in the Garden of Eden became alienated to God and spread the "*inertness of the inner man*" upon all humankind – so the Bible teaches. And while we may not be willing to believe the Garden of Eden story for the simple fact that it is theology, we know at least that humankind has the "spiritual inertness" of which the story informs us.

Nevertheless, when we lay aside theology and disregard the Garden of Eden, to look at humankind in the society and in all histories, we find that the more humankind becomes "intelligent", the less the human society becomes religious; which seem to reiterate the moral of the Garden of Eden story. If there was no Garden of Eden, why does humankind continue to reiterate the moral of the Garden of Eden story?

If today we have so grown in the knowledge of good and evil to the extent that we do not only run away from the un-embodied *Voice*, but also deny his existence, then we only confirm the reality of God's existence and the reality of the "death" of which *He* warned humankind in the Garden of Eden.

Without question therefore, the Bible's teachings about the creation of the world, the spirituality of man, and the Garden of Eden, have greater tendency to be true than otherwise. The story may (if possible) have lost its original form, sequences and details, but it certainly has not lost its principles and essence. Science may not be able to prove precisely the reality of the Garden of Eden, but neither can science disprove it; because *why* the Garden was probably planted, *what* probably happened in the Garden, and *the implications* of human actions in the Garden as reported by the Bible, are all in accordance with scientific principles.

The author of Genesis tells us that humankind was driven out of the Garden of Eden after eating from the forbidden tree. He also tells us that God determined that humans should not find entrance into the Garden anymore.

> *After he drove the man out, he placed on the east of the Garden of Eden cherubim, and a flaming sword flashing back and forth to guard the way to the tree of life.*
>
> (Genesis 3: 24)

Today, many people claim that they have experienced the rebirth of the "*breath* of God in man", and have experienced prophecies and "spiritual dreams" and visions, and these testify to the probable fact that the replica of the nature of God is in humankind. The fact that most humans run away from relating with God, prefer to be in their own world, discovering things they never knew and advancing in mental knowledge without spiritual experience, also concurs with the Bible's claim that humankind "*surely died*" in the Garden of Eden. However, if these hold true, human life without a healthy relationship with God would be vain. Without spirituality, human life is no more than animal life – it is pointless, and there is no proper place for morality in the life of humans.

Dogs eat dogs, and for dog's morals, it is morally acceptable. If humans are no more than animals, there is no point frowning at cannibalism – if life is no more than "survival of the fittest", then the question of fairness and societal laws should not even arise. If humans are no more than animals, then a human has no moral responsibility at all.

Vanity of vanities – everything is meaningless!

> *The words of the Teacher, son of David, king in Jerusalem. "Meaningless! Meaningless!" says the Teacher, "Utterly meaningless! Everything is meaningless". What does man gain from all his labor at which he toils under the sun?*
>
> (Ecclesiastes 1: 1 – 3)

There is no specific purpose to life on earth if humankind is simply an animal that originated from earthly elements (dusts) and no more than that. In the story of the Garden of Eden, God reportedly told man – "*you are soil, and unto soil shall you return*". (Genesis 3: 19). And truly when a human corpse is buried in the soil, the dead flesh decomposes into soil elements. But in the creation story, an element in humankind was not taken from the soil, and therefore cannot return unto soil – and that element the *breath* of God in humankind, must "*return to the one that gave it*".

> *Then the* LORD *said, "My Spirit will not contend with man forever, for he is mortal, his days will be a hundred and twenty years.*
>
> (Genesis 6: 3)

> *And the* LORD *said, My spirit shall not always strive with man, for that he* **also** *is flesh: yet his days shall be an hundred and twenty years.*
>
> (Genesis 6: 3, King James Version)

> *. . . Then man goes to his eternal home and mourners go about the streets. Remember him – before the silver cord is severed, or the golden bowl is broken; before the pitcher is shattered at the spring, or the wheel broken at the well, and the dust returns to the ground it came from, and the spirit returns to God who gave it.*
>
> (Ecclesiastes 12: 5 – 7)

When a human's life [the silver cord] is severed, the dust [flesh that is composed of soil elements] normally turns again into ordinary earthly elements, but the inner [spiritual] being returns to God, the Father of spirits. If there were no spirit of God in humankind, chimpanzees too would normally pray and prophesy and see spiritual visions. But it is only humans that pray and prophesy, and see spiritual visions, and gain understanding of things by means other than mental activities;

> *But* **it is the spirit in a man**, *the* **breath of the Almighty, that gives him understanding.**
>
> (Job 32: 8)

> *But* **there is a spirit in man**: *and* **the inspiration of the Almighty giveth them understanding.**
>
> (Job 32: 8, King James Version)

Human life therefore has meaning and purpose only when we consider humankind's spirituality, by which humans could appropriately lean on God, spiritually, for direction. As long as the modern humankind tries to evade the presence of God, trying to hide from God's continual effort to reconcile with humans and restore humans back to that healthy spiritual state, modern humankind continues to reiterate that there was probably a Garden eastward in Eden, for such was the behaviour of Adam and Eve after their spirits "died".

To this end, whether we are creationists or evolutionists, we cannot but reckon that the universe could not have come into existence without a *Maker*, God. The God who made the universe must have largely planned it to the details. He must have planned the emergence of humankind as the earth's dominant species. According to the Bible, the *Originator* has put his "image and likeness" [nature] within humankind, so that humankind is capable, among all kinds of animals, to relate with God. And we cannot but agree that only an eternal Creator of the universe can rightly be the *"true and living God"* whilst all other [so-called] gods are false. This is the submission of creationists and the Bible, and it is a position that science cannot rationally rule out, as long as the Big Bang theory and human behaviours reiterate the biblical concept of an eternal God and human spirituality. These we have proved thus far.

However, the Bible traces humankind's present perpetual and inherent enmity with God to Satan, the Liar. But there are several conflicting concepts people have about Satan. To some, Satan is just a personification of the forces of evil; to others he is just an unreal, imaginary being; and yet to many others he is a real person, as real as you and I. Knowing whom Satan really is further sheds light on the Garden of Eden story and humans' spirituality. For this reason, we should examine the probable facts of Satan's existence and nature.

> *whether we are creationists or evolutionists, we can-not but reckon that the universe could not have come into existence without a Maker, God.*

Chapter Four

SATAN

"*Your Enemy The Devil*".

An ugly, black man with a tail and horns.

In paintings, Satan is often a black ogre-like man with horns, hoofs, wings and a tail – a product of idle imaginations. But the Bible's description of Satan differs from this.

In the Bible, the name "Satan" stands for two entities – first, it stands for a particular living being, a person, and second it is a "non-being" personification of the forces of evil.

Both as a living being and as personification of the forces of evil, Satan is invariably identified in the Bible as an instigator of evil deeds. Hence, the responsibilities for many evils are placed upon him. And hence, pronouncements on the human perpetrators of such evils are as well attributed to Satan who is believed to be the underlying performer of such evils. For instance, therefore, Satan is believed to be equally identified with the Babylonian King referred to as "*Lucifer*" by prophet Isaiah as well as the King of Tyre referred to by prophet Ezekiel as "*the guardian Cherub*". [Isaiah 14 and Ezekiel 28].

Indeed, Satan was a **perennial** figure constantly referred to across all generations of the Bible days. But it was not possible that this ultimate evil being whose perpetual existence spanned across all the generations of the Bible days should have been the physical (flesh, blood and bones) occupiers of the thrones of Babylon and Tyre, but neither could the king of Tyre, for instance, have been a "*guardian cherub*" or "*defending angel*". Thus, only a careful analyses and juxtaposition of the biblical poetry and prophecies in which the person of Satan is discussed or represented can give his full biblical picture.

You Will Crawl On Your Belly!

When, as critics, we carefully look into the Genesis story (of Adam and Eve in the Garden of Eden), it appears that the literal integrity of the story is distorted. But what is certainly NOT distorted is the fact that Satan was *"the person referred to as the Serpent or the Liar"*. In what physical form he could have presented himself, if at all he presented himself physically, is not clear as the word "serpent" as used in the story in fact appears allusive.

What further obscures the literal details of the story is the curse that God placed on the serpent in the garden. If it was Satan the spirit being ["Liar, the Devil"], that beguiled Eve, why does it appear that a physical serpent was cursed? However, the curse neither perfectly fits a physical serpent as we see in the passage:

Then the LORD God said to the woman, "What is this you have done?" The woman said, "The serpent deceived me, and I ate." So the LORD God said to the serpent, "Because you have done this, Cursed are you above all the livestock and all the wild animals! You will crawl upon your belly and you will eat dust all the days of your life. And I will put enmity between you and the woman, and between your offspring and hers; he will crush your head, and you will strike his heel.

(Genesis 3: 13 – 15)

The wordings of the curse implies, that the serpent did not *"crawl on its belly"* until the curse, which looks improbable for a physical serpent that in the first instance could not even have had the intelligence to commune with Eve. Therefore, it is only possible that the allusion refers to the *"Liar spirit"* (Satan the Devil) rather than to a physical serpent just as much as the Prophet Ezekiel made the allusion of *"the guardian cherub"* to the King of Tyre. (Ezekiel 28: 14). For the purpose our discussion therefore, we would uphold that "the serpent" (Hebrew: *nachash*) or "the liar" (Hebrew: *cachash*) was figurative in the Garden of Eden story. Whether as "serpent" or "liar", whichever is the true word used by the original author of Genesis, the author only intends to tell us of the same *"Old Serpent called Satan the Devil"* of which the writers of the other books Bible also tell us. And it should be very sad indeed (if the author of Genesis is right) that Adam and Eve, the first true humans, fell from spiritual consciousness (or, aliveness) to

108

ordinary mental consciousness by the guile of "the Liar".

As far as all rational evidences can prove, it is more probable than otherwise (if not entirely certain) that there was a Garden in Eden. And to consider that man's emergence on earth must have been taken into account by the architect and builder of the universe (as certainly the universe could not have come into existence without one), the author of Genesis seemingly tells us the very right thing about man's spirituality among all animals. Having been right about creation, and about the spirituality of man, we can safely take for granted that he should be right that "the Liar", "the serpent" beguiled man. What he did not tell us, however, cannot be taken for granted. He did not tell us whence came the Liar, (if it was liar) or whence the serpent got "his" intelligence and power of speech, if it was simply a *"wild animal"* and no more. But since the reference to *"serpent"* in other Bible usages were allusive, and because the perpetual *"beguiler"* could not have been an ordinary physical serpent which of course would have had a limited life span, we can only examine the origin of Satan as known, or implied, by the authors of the other books in the Bible, and identify him as the same *"serpent"* that beguiled Eve in the Garden of Eden.

> *As far as all rational evidences can prove, it is more probable than otherwise (if not entirely certain) that there was a Garden in Eden.*

Satan's origin and nature should not have been a topic worth discussing at all if all that he ever accomplished was the beguiling of Eve and Adam. But other writers of the Bible would have us believe that Satan is a perennial figure, a completely spirit being who did not and does not have an outer animal form unlike Eve and Adam that were outwardly animals but inwardly *"image and likeness of God"*. Other writers of the Bible would have us believe that, being a spirit, Satan exists perpetually and continues to be a deceiver of human beings and a continual disrupter of humans' relationship with God. In fact, the rest of Bible implies that Satan continues to work on earth waging a war against humans in fulfilment of his enmity towards God and in accordance with the curse that the author of Genesis reports:

So the LORD God said to the serpent, "Because you have done this, Cursed are you above all the livestock and all the wild animals! You will crawl on your belly and you will eat dust all the days of your life. And **I will put enmity between you and the woman, and between your offspring and hers; he will crush your head, and you will strike his heel.***"*

(Genesis 3: 14 – 15)

> **But we cannot rationally deny the existence of God, for all indications (scientific and non-scientific) point with clear certainty to the fact that the universe has an "eternal intelligence" behind its origin.**

It is taught biblically, that the serpent, the liar, was by this curse destined to fight with the woman and her child. Of course, the woman was not yet with child, so the curse spoke futilely. But the curse insinuates that the serpent, the liar, would stay on beyond that first generation – having fought the woman, and while the serpents' offspring would also fight woman's offspring, the serpent himself would yet fight the woman's offspring, thus staying beyond the first generation of both the woman and himself. We could care less, whatever all these means. But if certainly the liar, the serpent, was destined to fight the offspring of Eve, while we are also told that Eve is the *"prototype mother"* ("mother of all the living [humanity]" Genesis 3: 20), then we must be careful to observe that the curse meant to the writer of Genesis that Satan would fight perpetually against *"all the living"* [humankind], and that means until now.

Many people who do not believe in spirituality, or that God exists also do not believe also that Satan exists. But we cannot rationally deny the existence of God, for all indications (scientific and non-scientific) point with clear certainty to the fact that the universe has an *"eternal intelligence"* behind its origin. If then, God exists, and lives from eternity to eternity, and Satan is also identified in the Bible as a spirit of perennial existence, we have a strong reason to give thought to Satan's existence and nature.

The goal of this book does not include proving that Satan exists. Our question is *"does God truly exist?"* and *"could his existence be proved beyond reasonable doubt?"* – and our answers to this question we had settled with the conclusion that *"it is certain that the material world was created by an eternal ethereal being, God"*. What now remains is to grasp a fuller understanding of the spiritual nature of man and his relationship with God. Pursuant to this, therefore, we have explored the "flora of Eden" and there met not only God and humankind, but the Liar, Serpent, as well – and thus we have an imperative to look at him within the context in which we find him in the Bible.

"You were in Eden"

Earlier in this chapter, we overviewed the fact that Bible scholars attribute statements made in respect of a particular King of Tyre to Satan. In the particular Bible passage, the "King of Tyre" was alleged to have been *"in Eden, the garden of God"*. If indeed, the passage refers to the same "Garden of Eden" in which Adam and Eve lived, then it is not possible that the human "King of Tyre" to which the message was directed could have been with Adam and Eve who had died many centuries earlier.   Further still, the same passage refers to the "King of Tyre" as a "cherub" – [spirit being]:

> *The word of the* LORD *came to me: "Son of man, take up a lament concerning the king of Tyre and say to him: 'This is what the Sovereign* LORD *say: " 'You were the model of perfection, full of wisdom and perfect in beauty.* **You were in Eden, the garden of God***; every precious stone adorned you: ruby, topaz and emerald, chrysolite, onyx and jasper, sapphire, turquoise and beryl. Your settings and mountings were made of gold; on the day you were created they were prepared.* **You were anointed as a guardian cherub***, for so I ordained you. You were on the holy mount of God; you walked among the fiery stones.   You were blameless in your ways from the day you were created till wickedness was found in you. Through your widespread trade you were filled with violence, and you sinned. So I drove you in disgrace from the mount of God, and I expelled you, O Guardian cherub, from among the fiery stones. Your heart became proud on account of your beauty, and you corrupted your wisdom because of your splendor.*
>
> (Ezekiel 28: 11 – 17)

But we know that the author of Genesis identified only four persons that were **in** the Garden of Eden – these are God, Adam, Eve and the Serpent. If the "King of Tyre" *"were in"* the Garden and is not God, Adam, or Eve, he could only be the Serpent, the Liar. This is not because the physical King of Tyre is considered a cherub [completely ethereal being] but because it is believed that the king was working by the instigation and power of the Serpent.

Prophet Ezekiel wrote that the "King of Tyre", as a cherub, was at first perfect until he *"became proud"*. Prophet Isaiah also maintained that the "King of Babylon" also *"fell from heaven"* because of pride. The book of Revelations also maintains that a leader of angels was "cast out from heaven", and was cast to the earth:

And **there was war in heaven**. *Michael and his angels fought against the dragon, and* **the dragon and his angels fought back**. *But he was not strong enough, and they lost their place in heaven.* **The great dragon was hurled down – that ancient serpent called the devil**, *or Satan, who leads the whole world astray. He was hurled to the earth, and his angels with him. Then I heard a loud voice say: "Now have come the salvation and the power and the kingdom of our God, and the authority of his Christ. For the accuser of our brothers, who accuses them before our God day and night, has been hurled down. They overcame him by the blood of the Lamb and by the word of their testimony; and they did not love their lives so much as to shrink from death. Therefore rejoice, you heavens and you who dwell in them! But* **woe to the earth and the sea, because the devil has gone down to you! He is filled with fury, because he knows that his time is short."**

(Revelations 12: 7 – 12)

How have you fallen from Heaven?

So, here is the full picture – from the passages we read in Isaiah, Ezekiel and Revelations – Satan was created as an archangel – *"the anointed guardian cherub"*, a "spirit being" created to lead other "spirit beings" of his type. But he fell from this position by sinful pride.

How have you fallen from heaven, O morning star, son of the dawn! You have been cast down to the earth, you who once laid down the nations! You said in your heart, "I will ascend to heaven; I will raise my throne above the stars of God; I will sit enthroned on the mount of the assembly, on the utmost heights of the scared mountain. I will ascend above the tops of the clouds; I will make myself like the Most High." But you are brought down to the grave, to the depths of the pit. Those who see you stare at you, they ponder your fate: "Is this the man who shook the earth and made kingdoms tremble, the man who made the world a desert, who overthrew its cities and would not let his captives go home?

(Isaiah 14: 12 – 17)

There was war in heaven.

By juxtaposing the fallen, ambitious *"dragon and his angels"* that we see in Revelations with the ambitious *"guardian cherub"* of Ezekiel, and the proud Lucifer [*"Morning star"*] of Isaiah, Christian traditions have upheld that the perpetual ethereal evil being, Satan, was an archangel who fell from God's grace because of his pride and evil ambitions. It is believed that angels are spirit creatures of God, who like the *Creator Spiritus* also have the attribute of perpetual existence – not dying like animals. Satan is believed to have fought God's loyal angels in Heaven (God's abode) resulting in his expulsion from heaven together with his angels.

Woe to the earth.

Thus, the Bible wants us to believe that Satan and his co-rebels were expunged from God's spiritual abode, Heaven, and for a "temporal" punishment "*hurled down*" to the physical world, while an eternal spiritual torment awaits them.

From grace to grass, the Serpent with his angels was hurled into this material world. Coming here is not a pleasurable adventure for him – he came down "*filled with fury*". (Revelations 12: 12)

According to the Bible, Satan hates all – he hates himself much less everyone else. Out of hatred for God and man, he tempted man to sin against God in the Garden of Eden so that he might taunt God and disrupt God's purpose for making man. And from that day that Eve fell for his ploy, Satan continues to wage war against God's purpose for humankind.

The author of Genesis says that the offspring of the serpent (that is, by allusion, fallen angels and their cohorts) would wage war against the offspring of the woman. By and by, the Bible unfolds the allegory in affirming that "the offspring of the woman" refers to a righteous generation of humankind – righteous because they have been restored back to the full vitality of the *breath* of God in humankind. Thus, Satan, and his angels are continually at war with humankind, and especially anyone who identifies with God.

There is a war!

If the Bible is right about Satan, then unknown to many, there is a perpetual spiritual war on earth. Human life is caught in-between God's forces and Satan's forces. Humanity is divided into two between these two forces – God's army and Satan's army and there is no neutral ground as far as the two spiritual armies are concerned – everyone belongs to either God's army or Satan's army. Even a person who believes that neither God nor Satan exists also belongs to Satan's army because the belief that God does not exist is falsehood [facts about the origin of the universe proves that God exists]. So long as Satan is the "prototype Liar", "the father of falsehood" [John 8: 44] those who believe in the lie that God does not exist also aid Satan's falsehood.

> *You belong to your father, the devil, and you want to carry out your father's desire. He was a murderer from the beginning, not holding to the truth, for there is no truth in him. When he lies, he speaks his native language, for he is a liar and the father of lies.*
>
> (John 8: 44)

It is evident that Atheism is strongly against belief in God's existence. If it is not for God, then it is against God, and certainly, it is not neutral in respect to God. Atheism strives against belief in God, and in turn, belief in God strives against atheism. Satan, according to the Bible, is fully aware that God exists – but in his tradition of falsehood and guile, he would rather tell a man that *"God does not exist"* just as much as he told Eve *"you will not surely die"* knowing fully well that the dying refers to "spiritual death" and not physical death. And knowing fully well that Eve would *"surely die"* spiritually. In essence, the Serpent actually murdered the truth and murdered the spirituality of humankind.

The Liar

Who has never told a lie? Perhaps we may find one exception among a billion. But the excellence of lying is not in saying things that are completely false but in burying a pinch of lie leaven in a whole loaf of truth; knowing well that the pinch of lie is enough to mislead.

According to the Bible, Satan is an excellent liar – he would hardly tell you a thing that is absolutely false; just enough falsehood buried deep into an otherwise all-true claim, is all he needs to deceive you. Check out what he told Eve in the Garden, everything seems true:

> *"You will not surely die," the serpent said to the woman. "For God knows that when you eat of it your eyes will be opened, and you will be like God, knowing good and evil."*
>
> (Genesis 3: 4 – 5)

Of course, that much was considerably true. Their [mental] eyes were opened and they knew good and evil. Moreover, they did not surely die physically. But Satan had deceived them because they surely died spiritually.

Likewise, if Satan would beguile a man today – he would do so perfectly; he would give every good reason why God does not seem to exist but will not tell of the indisputable evidences that prove God's existence. All what he would say would be considerably true but he would thus have succeeded in leading one into a false conclusion.

In the light of the Bible, one way Satan and his cohorts can ruin a human member of God's army is by propaganda. If Satan had tried to deceive such a person without success, he simply retorts to spreading false news about that person.

We cannot deny the fact that scandals have been done by many people who identify with the name of God. But false news of scandals widely spread about a "man of God" might do so much damage that a latter open rebuttal may never rectify.

The Destroyer

The Bible warns people who identify with God to beware of Satan's threats:

Be self-controlled and alert. **Your enemy the devil** *prowls around like a roaring lion looking for someone to devour. Resist him, standing firm in the faith, because you know that your brothers throughout the world are undergoing the same kind of sufferings.*

(1 Peter 5: 8 – 9)

Many people consider a lion's roars to be a simple "*free expression of itself*". But the roar does threaten other species and helps the lion to break down the courage of the "prey".

The Bible teaches that like a lion, Satan and his cohorts use threats to discourage many people who identify with God. But as sceptics, we may wonder how he does this? The Bible-writers, who apparently believed or even know more about Satan than we do, answer that Satan uses human beings to fulfil his wicked plans on earth. Since they were "experts in their own field", we need not argue with them unless we have contrary evidences. They be-

> *We cannot deny the fact that scandals have been done by many people who identify with the name of God. But false news of scandals . . . do so much damage*

lieve that Satan can "possess" a man by entering into the man like breath enters ones nostrils, like the *breath* of God entered "the nostrils" of man in the Garden of Eden and the earthly "man" who would otherwise had remained an ordinary animal then began to commune with God.

The Bible does not say that God was seen physically by Adam in the Garden of Eden. It only says that Adam *heard* and *spoke* with God – and who knows whether that was often not more than an inner "still small voice", which subsequent prophets also got used to? In fact, the God that the author of the Genesis creation story knows was at first pictured as "*a mighty moving breath/wind*". (Genesis 1: 2).

> *Some people gather together to worship Satan. They do so simply because they opine that Satan is the equal-opposite of God.*

Like that "*breath*", Satan "enters" people who have an inclination towards his purpose and instigates them all the more to do wickedly and spread guile.

However, Satan *himself* does not possess just anybody. Satan possesses the person with the *best* advantage to deliver a strategic blow on God's plans and God's army. In the Bible, he used mostly kings (not pheasants), people with far-reaching effects. He seeks the best advantage, though; not just royalty: whoever is in the *best* position to deliver the deadliest blow on God's army at any particular moment serves Satan's purpose.

The equal-opposite of God.

Some people gather together to worship Satan. They do so simply because they opine that Satan is the equal-opposite of God. They reason that if God is deemed the "*ultimate good one*" and Satan is deemed the "*ultimate evil one*", then he is everything that God is, only in the opposite direction. Unfortunately, these people do not know Satan as he had always been known. Much more that they do not really know who God is.

God is "the eternal source" and Creator, the eternal and first person. Satan was not eternal, and could not have been, for he and God could not have been both first. If Satan were eternal, then he would have only been the same person with God, as the only one eternal person. But God cannot be "the opposer" of *His own self* and purposes, the *Eternal Spirit* cannot double as both God and Satan. If God is the "eternal source", then Satan cannot be. Satan can only be God's creature and would more appropriately be identified with the "fallen archangel" that God's loyal angels expelled from God's abode (as we read in Revelations). Consequently, Satan should not be worshipped in the place of God – for he is not the Creator of the universe and has no right to being worshipped.

Many other people do not worship Satan but they reverence him. These people think that Satan automatically knows the thoughts of men just as much as God knows everyone's mind, according to the Bible. But God being the eternal source, and "the only *Master Mind*" in the universe has the power and wisdom to know man's thoughts, BUT Satan does not have this privilege. He does not know everything but God does know everything. He cannot do everything but God can do all things. The supremacy of God is demonstrated by the fact that God can work while holding Satan bound, but Satan cannot hold God bound. This is the picture that the Bible paints, and it appears very rational.

> *Many other people do not worship Satan but they reverence him. These people think that Satan automatically knows the thoughts of men.*

By some means, the tempter has tempted you.

Many people do things that they do not originally intend to do. In most cases, they are "tempted" to do it. Satan is known to be "the tempter". But Satan does not personally execute every temptation. It is biblically wrong to say, *"If Satan does not exist, people would never be tempted"*. *What* tempts is not Satan, but "the thing desired", Satan is only chief among *who* tempts. The Bible's apostles said:

> *When tempted, no one should say, "God is tempting me." For God cannot be tempted by evil, nor does he tempt anyone; but* **each is tempted when, by his own evil desire**, *he is dragged away and enticed. Then,* **after desire has conceived, it gives birth to sin;** *and sin, when it is full-grown, gives birth to death. Don't be deceived my dear brothers.*

(James 1: 13 – 16)

Now, the apostles did not say that *"each is tempted by* **Satan**" but that *"each is tempted by* **his own evil desires**". The distinction between what and who tempts is important.

If a man likes soup, and has decided not to take soup on a particular day, he should not sit down by a soup bowl and start to observe the appearance and aroma of the soup. Merely looking at the soup, or smelling the aroma of it, would increase the man's desire to take the soup. When the man's desire has increased considerably, it becomes an urge, an enticement, which he would find more difficult to resist than if he had avoided sitting by the soup in the first place. To develop an *urge* towards the soup, or indeed anything else, is to be *tempted*. If by yourself, you sit by the bowl of soup and feed your nose with the aroma, you are simply the *tempter* of your own self. What tempts you is the soup, but who tempts you is yourself, in this case.

But if someone else had come around, and had encouraged you by any means – guile, pretext, threat, or otherwise – to sit by that bowl of soup, then that person is the *tempter*. It is important to know that if within you, you had been tempted to do a thing or another, unless Satan had possessed you, then Satan is not at that point the *tempter*, you were. But if you were possessed by Satan or by any of his fallen angels, and the possessing spirit had held your mind captive or urged you to do what your own mind would not have done, then the possessing spirit is the *tempter*.

Whilst everyone is tempted from to time, not everyone is "possessed" and Satan himself cannot possess more than one person at a particular moment – he cannot be in Jane, tempting Jane, and at the same time be in John, tempting John. At best, he would be in Jane, tempting Jane, and Jane in turn may tempt John.

In the Garden of Eden, the Bible tells us, Satan did *not* deceive Adam; he deceived only Eve. Satan did not even tempt Adam; Eve was the one who "tempted" Adam. Eve (not the Serpent, the Liar) persuaded Adam to disobey God and yet the Serpent did not possess Eve:

> *And he said, "Who told you that you were naked? Have you eaten from the tree that I commanded you not to eat from?" The man said, "**The woman** you put here with me – she gave me some fruit from the tree, and I ate it." Then the* LORD *God said to the woman, "What is this you have done?" The woman said, "The serpent deceived me, and I ate."*
>
> (Genesis 3: 11 – 13)

> *For Adam was formed first, then Eve. And **Adam was not the one deceived**; it was **the woman who was deceived and became a sinner.***
>
> (1 Timothy 2: 13 – 14)

The Devil tempted me!

Well, some people do not believe whatever is said about Adam and Eve, although the same people would ever act like Adam and Eve by never accepting responsibility for their own faults. God asked Adam, *"have you eaten from that tree that I forbade?"*; the simple answer should have been *"Yes, I ate. I am very sorry that I broke your commandment"*. But no, he answered as though God had said *"who made you eat from that tree?"* and we are just like him whether we believe or not that he lived as our first father. We say, *"that fault was not really mine, so-and-so made me do it"* – we sound pretty much like Adam.

Again, some people think that the Bible upholds that Satan is the one responsible for every temptation. But in the Bible, he is pictured as the Commander-in-chief of the anti-God forces. In most cases, Satan has more administrative work to do than to zoom about from Janets to Johns tempting them to buy porn videos. He has a duty to himself as a "prince" to organise and strategise his army towards fighting God's army; he would rather spend a moment planning (and executing the plan) towards ensuring a steady flow of porn videos than spend that moment trying to persuade a non-influential individual to watch a film. And in any case, he is not omni-present. He is not once tempting Jean in France and Kim in Korea. He does move about *"like a blowing wind"* but he is not omni-present. You and I have a responsibility for the various ways in which every man tempts his own self and Satan on his own part has a responsibility for the specific temptations he does. And when as a cherub, the archangel that would later become Satan fell; he was not tempted by any other tempter. He tempted himself just as much as a man may tempt himself to eat soup by simply feeding his nostrils on the aroma of some soup. Just as much as a man may tempt himself to sleep with a harlot by strolling idly up and down amidst the one-night-standers. The man would be tempted to "help" anyone of the prostitutes that *poises* to need some help; and that idle stroll (not Satan) and the seeming "compassion" towards the prostitute is all that is needed to start a man towards adultery. However, if the man had been taken there by a friend and marshalled idly up and down that street, then the man that took him down is the *tempter*. Anyone who is in sin is a tempter whether or not possessed by an evil spirit. [1 Timothy 2: 13 – 14]

The sum of all the biblical references on Satan therefore is that he is a perpetual spirit being that wages a spiritual war against God; and against humankind through deceits, threats and temptations. Knowing these about the biblical Satan, the fallen archangel is enough for the purpose of our quest in this book. Now let us talk about the angels that fell with him – the spirits that we now know as demons or "evil spirits". Do demons really exist and influence people?

Chapter Five

DEMONS AND BONDAGES

"Spiritual Wickedness".

Spirits are unreal !!!

Ghosts, **genies**, **kobolds**, **elves**, **fairies** – whatever we call them – *"are no more than products of our imaginations and phobias. They are not real"*. Of course, how could they be real when *"real"* means *"tangible"*? Ethereality is not *"real"* – because (so-called) *"incorporeal beings"* are not sensually perceptible; and if a thing cannot be seen [with the naked eye], cannot be tasted, cannot be felt, cannot be heard, and cannot be smelled, then it is not *"real"*.

Several tabloids carry stories of "haunted houses" from time to time. People sell those stories to the papers and many people simply read for the "horror-novel" experience it gives them, even when they do not believe an iota of the stories. While many of the stories could be deliberately made up for pecuniary reasons, quite many others are told with the interviewee's strong conviction that he or she has been truly haunted. Nevertheless, it is typical of people who are sure that they have been "truly haunted" to show signs of phobias. Perhaps they "saw and heard" ghosts just because that is what their phobias looked out for. A woman who had spent most of her time half-believing tabloid ghost stories, and now lives alone in a large eighteenth century beach house would likely "see and hear" ghosts on dark cold windy nights. Apparitions would haunt her dreams at night and the ones that have haunted her dreams would eventually begin to take shape in the unlit corners of the house. When a strong wind slams a door upstairs, it would be taken for a ghost closing the door. Then, ethereality would become reality.

However, the final judgement on the reality of a thing is not made by our five senses, but the sixth sense, which is often fed by the five. Every real thing is "real" only when the mind recognises the perceptions of the other senses that the thing is real. The hallucinated mind, however, has conflict with the five senses. The lunatic eyes see things that other people do not see, and the body of the lunatic accommodates situations that are unbearable for other people.

Psychologists and psychiatrists probe into the nature and functions of minds and conclude that some form of therapy could help restore "the sufferer" to normality. To talk of "normality" with regard to ethereality, one might well opine that the human race had long been a "sufferer" species because over the ages, humans have blended ethereality with reality.

In former times, people were brought to public squares and stoned to death on accusation of witchcrafts. Yet people consulted mediums for necromancy. They bought charms for protection or otherwise. They visited the sorcerers for divinations. And might we well say that human society in those days was generally afflicted with neurosis – for believing in the reality of the ethereal? Probably not: because those divinations and charms seemingly worked for many people. Why would people not have believed in the soothsayers and sorcerers when several things that the diviners predicted were apparently *"fulfilled"* before their very eyes? What obtained for the *"prophets of [the invisible] God"*, also obtained for the soothsayers and sorcerers – they all knew what ethereality had in common with reality and that common ground was the mind.

Ordinarily, men looked to prophets, diviners and sorcerers as people with *"special mental talents"* but these so-called *"gifted people"* themselves affirmed that their *"special talents"* were not implanted in their brains and that anyone who followed some form of *"initiations"* could as well acquire the same *"special talents"*. That was why there were "schools of prophets" and "schools of magicians" and the sorcerers too had apprentices under them. Some pupil soothsayers never approached the expertise of their masters, while others simply transcended their masters. But soothsaying, unlike music or arts, required more than skills alone. Often, soothsayers and prophets said things that were considered ordinarily impossible. For instance, at the peak of a famine, the biblical prophet Elisha affirmed that on the morrow, food would be ridiculously cheap. By all indications, it looked like an idle talk, much more because the prophet did not tell *how* his prediction would be fulfilled; he only said *what* he felt would certainly be. Now, let us pick some lessons about ethereality from the full length of the Elisha episode:

Some time later, Ben-Hadad king of Aram mobilized his entire army and marched up and laid siege to Samaria. There was a great famine in the city; the siege lasted so long that a donkey's head sold for eighty shekels of silver, and a quarter of a cab of seed pods for five shekels. As the king of Israel was passing by on the wall, a woman cried to him, "Help me, my lord the king!" The king replied, "If the LORD does not help you, where can I get help for you? From the threshing floor? From the winepress?" Then he asked her, "What's the matter?" She answered, "This woman said to me, 'Give up your son so we may eat him today, and tomorrow we'll eat my son.' So we cooked my son and ate him. The next day I said to her, 'Give up your son so we may eat him,' but she had hidden him." When the king heard the woman's words, he tore his robes. As he went along the wall, the people looked, and there, underneath, he had sackcloth on his body. He said, "May God deal with me, be it ever so severely, if the head of Elisha son of Shaphat remains on his shoulders today!" Now Elisha was sitting in his house, and the elders were sitting with him. The king sent a messenger ahead, but before he arrived, Elisha said to the elders, "Don't you see how this murderer is sending someone to cut off my head? Look, when the messenger comes, shut the door and hold it shut against him. Is not the sound of his master's footsteps behind him?" While he was still talking to them, the messenger came down to him. And the king said, "This disaster is from the LORD. Why should I wait for the LORD any longer?" Elisha said, "Hear the word of the LORD. This is what the LORD says: About this time tomorrow, a seah of flour will sell for a shekel and two seahs of barley for a shekel at the gate of Samaria." The officer on whose arm the king was leaning said to the man of God, "Look, even if the LORD should open the floodgates of the heavens, could this happen?" "You will see it with your own eyes," answered Elisha, "but you will not eat any of it!" Now there were four men with leprosy at the entrance of the city gate. They said to each other, "Why stay here until we die? If we say, 'We'll go into the city'-the famine is there, and we will die. And if we stay here, we will die. So let's go over to the camp of the Arameans and surrender. If they spare us, we live; if they kill us, then we die." At dusk they got up and went to the camp of the Arameans. When they reached the edge of the camp, not a man was there, for the Lord had caused the Arameans to hear the sound of chariots and horses and a great army, so that they said to one another, "Look, the king of Israel has hired the Hittite and Egyptian kings to attack us!" So they got up and fled in the dusk and abandoned their tents and their horses and donkeys. They left the camp as it was and ran for their lives. The men who had leprosy reached the edge of the camp and entered one of the tents. They ate and drank, and carried away silver, gold and clothes, and went off and hid them. They returned and entered another tent and took some things from it and hid them also. Then they said to each other, "We're not doing right. This is a day of good news and we are keeping it to ourselves. If we wait until daylight, punishment will overtake us. Let's go at once and report this to the royal palace." So they went and called out to the city gatekeepers and told them, "We went into the Aramean camp and not a man was there-not a sound of anyone-only tethered horses and donkeys, and the tents left just as they were." The gatekeepers shouted the news, and it was reported within the palace. The king got up in the night and said to his officers, "I will tell you what the Arameans have done to us. They know we are starving; so they have left the camp to hide in the countryside, thinking, 'They will surely come out, and then we will take them alive and get into the city.' "One of his officers answered, "Have some men take five of the horses that are left in the city. Their plight will be like that of all the Israelites left here-yes, they will only be like all these Israelites who are doomed. So let us send them to find out what hap-pened." So they selected two chariots with their horses, and the king sent them after the Aramean army. He commanded the drivers, "Go and find out what has hap-pened." They followed them as far as the Jordan, and they found the whole road strewn with the clothing and equipment the Arameans had thrown away in their headlong flight. So the messengers returned and reported to the king. Then the peo-ple went out and plundered the camp of the Arameans. So a seah of flour sold for a shekel, and two seahs of barley sold for a shekel, as the LORD had said. Now the king had put the officer on whose arm he leaned in charge of the gate, and the people trampled him in the gateway, and he died, just as the man of God had fore-told when the king came down to his house. It happened as the man of God had said to the king: "About this time tomorrow, a seah of flour will sell for a shekel and two seahs of barley for a shekel at the gate of Samaria." The officer had said to the man of God, "Look, even if the LORD should open the floodgates of the heavens, could this happen?" The man of God had replied, "You will see it with your own eyes, but you will not eat any of it!" And that is exactly what happened to him, for the people trampled him in the gateway, and he died.

(2 Kings 6:24 – 7:20)

Reading this long passage, one must sympathise with that king of Israel but one must also wonder why his royal wrath was turned to-wards Elisha rather the Arameans or, perhaps, God. After all, it was not Elisha that besieged Samaria. But the king must have been won-dering why Elisha could not talk to God about the situation and bring out a solution, so long as Elisha was deemed the major prophet of God in Israel, who might well be called "Heaven's ambassador", at that time.

The king was ready to severe every *"diplomatic relationship"* between *"the eternal God"* and the nation of Israel by first killing God's ambassador. He sent an executioner but before the killer got to Elisha, the prophet knew (somehow) that the killer was coming and directed that the door be shut; and indeed the executioner arrived so soon. How did Elisha know within him what the king had done while indeed no person had come from the king to tell him?

What is more baffling is that when the king himself who had simply followed the executioner came to Elisha's residence, the prophet told him *"This is what the LORD says . . ."* and went on to affirm that food would be surplus the following day. The royal private secretary made the very statement that every reasonable person would have made — *"even if the eternal God rains down from heaven, can food be surplus tomorrow?"*. Well, we have been told the rest of it. But one thing to consider is this – how did Elisha hear the word of the LORD and the elders sitting with him did not hear? If God had at least spoken audibly, then not only Elisha but also the elders sitting by his side should have heard. But they did not hear. And the fact that Elisha's predictions were fulfilled on the next day proves that he was not speaking out of hallucinations – he really must have heard what he claimed to hear God speak. Nevertheless, the hearing of God's voice was not in Elisha's external [fleshy] ears, but in his mind.

> *The mind is the point where ethereality meets reality, where the spiritual meets the physical. In humankind, the mind is the highest at-tribute of the animal, but the lowest attribute of the spirit.*

The mind is the meeting point.

The mind is the point where ethereality meets reality, where the spiritual meets the physical. In humankind, the mind is the highest attribute of the animal, but the lowest attribute of the spirit.

It is in the mind that humans connect with ethereality. When prophets and sorcerers speak, we look at them as though they are lunatic. But when what they predict happens, we say they have "special talents". It is not talents, because everyone can do what prophets and sorcerers do.

The things a man sees are "seen" in the mind; if the eyeballs receive light and images but the optic nerve, which connects the eyes to the brain, does not function properly, the man's vision is impaired.

If you enter a large hall and face the crowd, your eyes automatically take a photograph of the entire audience within their scopes. But later on, you meet a friend who tells you he was sitting on the second row and liked the way you spoke, and then you just say *"Aaaah, but I didn't see you!"*. Of course, your eyes took his photograph, but because his face was not focused, your mind did not register seeing him. Thus, it is in the mind, not the eyes, that the true "seeing" takes place.

If a prophet or sorcerer dies, arranging with a surgeon to exchange the eyeballs of the prophet with yours by transplant would not make you see what the prophet was seeing. The visions of the prophet or sorcerer are not in his eyeballs but in his mind. The diviner's mind hears things clearly, as though the sounds were in the ears but you sit by his side and hear nothing, so his ears could not have been hearing, the hearing was in his mind.

Swerving brains with the prophet would also not work, because the divining consciousness is not dependent on physical senses, unlike the brain. The divining mind is incorporeal because that mind speaks of things that are not corporeally perceived. However, the fact that what it does perceive materialise afterwards proves that it indeed perceives. Consequently, one might opine that beneath the embodied mind of the diviner, lies an "incorporeal mind" by which the diviner perceives things independent of his senses. What we call spirits can be simply described as "incorporeal minds". And divinations and predictions, made outside bodily perceptions, are proofs that such "minds" exist.

Predictions made incorporeally.

One day, a boy walked up to me and said *"Senior, please tell me if I would repeat my class again this year"*. I looked at him baffled; *"what do you mean?"*. We were both in secondary school and the previous session I was a class ahead of him. It was typical in Nigerian boarding secondary schools to call anyone *"Senior"* who enters a school at least a session ahead of one.

The fellow reminded me that he had offended me the previous term and out of annoyance, I had cursed him that he would repeat his class. I recollected that he had so insulted me in the dining hall, and being not physically bigger than him, I could not bully him as other stronger "seniors" would have done. But I took succour for my physical helplessness in cursing him. I only voiced out of provocation what

I wished should happen to him. Alas, it turned out that at the end of the term he passed his subjects well enough for the school authorities to promote him to the next class. So, was the curse I pronounced on him fulfilled? Yes, it was. The boy told me that when he got home for the end-of-session vacation, his father was not satisfied with his performance and insisted that he could have done better and therefore must repeat the class. The father came to the school to ask the class teacher and the principal to let the child *"repeat the class and be more serious"*!

I felt so sorry for the boy – my anger had waned with time. Presently, I would wish he should not repeat the class. He looked at me with curious fear evident in his eyes as though I had made it happen or could make anything happen. *"Look here, ol' boy"*, I tried to assure him, *"I am as harmless as yourself. I didn't cause it. I only cursed you the normal way that everyone else would have cursed if they cared!"*. But he did not appear persuaded.

Perhaps that occurrence was simply coincidental – perhaps not. Just thinking about it today, I wonder why human beings *"curse"* and *"bless,"* and when the practise really started. [Can any social psychologist or anthropologist unravel that?]

We shall return to the curses and blessings issue, but let me tell you another experience. There is a game played with dice called Ludo. In my final year at secondary school, I played Ludo with a friend named Kola. The Ludo board has four groups of four seeds each. You throw a pair of dice and try to get all your seeds home first. One way to get home quickly is to "peck" any of your opponent's seed by throwing a figure on either or both of your dice to land your seed exactly where his own rests. The other way is to keep counting the number shown on your dice until you have gone round the board all the way home.

So we played, my friend and I, until we were left with a seed each. I still had my seed in the dock; either or both of my dice must have a "six" side facing up before my seed could get out of the dock. If both dice showed "six", then I would replay and count everything cumulatively, beginning from the first "double six".

As it turned out, my friend's last seed was about to hit home. Just then, I paused and decided to count how many figures I would need to take my seed home; I found I would need ten "six" and a "two". I looked straight at my friend, who was beginning to urge me to *"stop wasting time and throw the dice"*; and I said *"I would have ten 'six' and 'two"*. He answered, *"Just play!"*.

And so I played. I threw the dice first time; I had "double six". I was pleased. I diced the second time; I had "double six". I was thrilled. I diced the third time; I had "double six". We looked at each other. Then I diced the fourth time, I had "double six". As I picked the dice cup again, I prayed inwardly, "*Lord, just let it be*". Then, I diced again, "double six". And the last time, I had "double one". We were both too surprised to count; of course, there was no need to do so anymore; I had won the game despite the fact that Kola had a far better likelihood of winning. I should have lost but for a "stupid" idea, which I should normally not have believed. Kola looked at me and said "*please do it again*"; his eyes widened in amazement as he continued to stare at me. I shook my head and said "*No. It won't happen again*". I just could not believe it would happen again. Kola persuaded me to try it again, and I tried, but it did not happen again.

Perhaps that occurrence was also coincidental – perhaps not. But one thing I have found over the years, repeatedly, is that when the human mind (or at least mine) is deeply stirred, one confidently makes some statements – positive [blessings] or negative [curses] – and one feels a strong conviction that these statements would happen as one wishes. Oftentimes, all the five senses would present evidences that go against the "predictions", but the predictions just become eventually fulfilled, somehow.

Humankind, from the beginning, has always practised "*cursing*" and "*blessing*". However, many times neither the blessings nor the curses one pronounce are apparently fulfilled. You do not just go out there and say, "*By this time tomorrow, a bag of rice would be sold for a cent*", and turn to whoever doubts you to say "*you would see it but won't eat of it*". No, it does not always happen that way. There must first be a "*stir*", deeper, beneath your ordinary mind, feeding your mind with a conviction that it will happen even when every circumstantial evidence oppose the statement. That divining "*stir*", or "*inspiration*", or "*moving*", comes not from the corporeal mind that is fed by the five corporeal senses, but from ethereality.

You shall not divinise!

I have **skimmed** quite some volumes (and have **read** several pieces) on evolution. None of them talk about **why** humankind curses and blesses, or why curses and blessings, and "*religious predictions*", generally are apparently fulfilled, mysteriously. The evolutionists obviously do not concern themselves with such. But theologians tell us, and the

Bible most of all.

The Bible's answer is that within humankind, and as inherent part of the complete human is an "inert" ethereality, *"the image and likeness of God"*. According to the Bible, if humankind had not fallen in the Garden of Eden, the inner ethereal nature would have helped humankind to keep charge over the earth simply by spiritual authority, naturally. By simple inspired pronouncements, humankind would have controlled the entire environment. And, probably Adam and Eve did control the earth and its creatures by this means before they fell. But because they "killed" the ethereality in them by eating from that forbidden tree and thereby submitting control of humankind to the corporeal mind rather than to the incorporeal under God's authority, humankind lost spiritual authority over the earth.

But unwitting that the spiritual authority that came with that inner ethereality has been lost to *"carnal mindedness"*, *"death"*, humans still want to continue the use of making pronouncements, only to wish futilely that the pronouncements be fulfilled. By and by, some humans learned that ethereal powers are required to make pronouncements and predictions effective and gave themselves over to witchcraft, necromancy, sorcery and other forms of divination. However, according to the Bible, the etherealities beneath these practises are not the same with what God gave humankind originally; it makes sense therefore that God should warn man against these practices:

Let no one be found among you who sacrifices his son or daughter in fire, who practices divination or sorcery, interprets omens, engages in witchcraft, or casts spells, or who is a medium or spiritist or who consults the dead. Anyone who does these things is detestable to the LORD, and because of these detestable practices the LORD your God will drive out those nations before you. You must be blameless before the LORD your God. The nations you will dispossess listen to those who practices sorcery or divination. But as for you, the LORD your God has not permitted you to do so.

(Deuteronomy 18: 10 – 14)

Notwithstanding this counsel of God to humankind, as exemplified by the words of Moses (the prophet who led the ancient Jewish nation out of Egypt), many men continue to practise divinations of different forms until today. But the etherealities by which they do these are ["allegedly", if so preferred] those angels that fell with Satan, the Liar, that ancient Serpent, who deceived man in the Garden of Eden.

The difference between the diviners and God's prophets.

The ordinary carnal [animal] mind in humankind does not understand the difference between God's prophets and other diviners. Neither does it understands why the Bible approves of prophecies but forbids necromancy, soothsaying, astrology, other horoscopes, and the likes. To the carnal mind, there is no difference between these and those, although the reason is not far-fetched. The principle, according to the Bible is that God wants humankind restored back to that original state in which man related with his *"Maker and Father"* appropriately. But in their sworn enmity towards God, the fallen angels (or, "evil spirits") are determined to ensure that every human is kept off from the true and living God as much as possible. The prime goal of the fallen angels is to confuse humankind by providing several seemingly equal alternatives to God. According to the Bible, there is a continual war between God's army and Satan's army for the control of every human mind on earth. God is working towards restoring humans into that original ethereal aliveness that humankind had and enjoyed with God, while Satan and his cohorts are bent on making sure that God's plan for humankind is not realised.

Anyone in Satan's shoes would strategise in the same way. Once you know there is only one original, the best way you can prevent people from choosing the original is to produce as many similar counterfeits as possible and the more counterfeits you produce, the greater the chance that people would choose one of them.

The Bible tells us that fallen angels are spiritually wicked towards humankind. By lending their own ethereality to the corporeal minds of the humans that are not in terms with the true and living God, they give such humans spiritual power – to predict, to divinise and seemingly do what the prophets of God do, except that such humans are not brought into appropriate relationship with the true and living God. That is why astrologers and necromancers would rarely tell the truth to a person about Adam and Eve or being reconciled to the true and living God, who is the *"Maker and Father"* of humankind.

The ordinary carnal mind considers the idea of "relationship with God" as just "religion" and in doing so also thinks, *"there are all sorts of religions"*. Satan and his cohorts have successfully achieved this. The ordinary person thinks, *"if you want to be religious, just choose the religion that you enjoy most, they are all towards the same objective – morality"*. However, even if we must so reduce the objective of religion to only morality, we should wonder why religion marks humankind out from among all animals. How many religions bother to tell us the reason why human-kind must be moral while chimpanzee and gorilla are not? How many religions tell us why and how humankind is spiritual?

The doctrines of demons.

Apostle Paul warned about the doctrines of demons:

The Spirit clearly says that in later times some will abandon the faith and follow deceiving spirits and things taught by demons. Such teachings come through hypo-critical liars, whose consciences have been seared as with a hot iron. They forbid people to marry and order them to abstain from certain foods, which God created to be received with thanksgiving by those who believe and who know the truth.

(1 Timothy 4: 1 – 3)

This passage states certain possible facts that common sense already tells us – first, ethereal beings are ordinarily separated from corporeal beings. For spirits to relate with bodies, they usually must work through minds. Demons [evil spirits] would not sit down at a computer, type a misleading article, and send it to a publisher. No, they would not, because they do not have bodies – they have no [animal] fingers with which they can type and envelope papers. But if there is any human being who lives in disobedience to God [as Adam and Eve lived after eating from the forbidden tree], not having the holy spirit of God, the mind of such a person is prone to being "inspired" by demons. And the person would type out what was in the mind of the evil ethereal being. Traditionally, Christians describe such persons as "possessed". Such a person, whose mind "heeds" the doctrines of demons, would in turn "speak (Satanic) lies".

To make real effects in this world, ethereal beings often need to possess [take control of] corporeal minds. Persons inspired by spirits other than the God-given one, often might recognise that they are "inspired" but they may not often understand that such inspirations are not from the *"true and living God"*, or they simply do not care about the source of their "inspirations". It is not the fact that they are inspired that counts, what matters more is what [*who*] inspires them.

The angels that sinned.

In the last chapter of this book, we examined the person of Satan and noted from the Bible that Satan is a fallen archangel. The Bible teaches also that some other angels fell with Satan. The angels that fell together with Satan are what Christians call "demons" or "evil spirits".

Earlier in this chapter, we have considered the fact that the human corporeal mind could be "inspired" by ethereal minds such that a man could know things precisely without the use of his corporeal senses. Traditionally, it is believed by Christians that the *prophecies* of the Bible are inspired. However, many other religions also lay claim to the inspiration factor – some without understanding the import of the written records that has been inspired in the Bible. One such religion is Hinduism. Just as the Bible is often regarded by Christians as "inspired", the Vedic literatures of the Hindus are taken by Hindus as "inspired".

While there may not be many reasons to doubt that the Vedic literatures are inspired, one must look well into the source of inspiration because of the very claims of the so-called inspired literatures. While also we may decline to comment critically and extensively on the Vedic literatures in this book, as it is not our focus, we must observe at least a few important things because among the world's widest accepted religions, it is the Vedic beliefs that present the closest look-alike of the Christian idea of spirituality [that within the animal man is the spirit man], although with several unchristian conclusions.

First, Hinduism purports that a *"spark of God"* is in everything that is in the world, while it also maintains that the *"anti-material [spark of God]"* or *"spirit"* is greater than minds and intelligence. But one question Hinduism seemingly evades is this – if the *"anti-material"* is in cattle, donkey, dog, and all animals, and the *"anti-material"* is greater than intelligence, why does the anti-material not enlighten the animal minds or intelligence of these species as it does for man? Of course, we have earlier examined situations in which information that are acquired without the body's material perceptions *"inspires"* the otherwise ordinary animal mind of humans. But we see that humankind rules on earth over all other animals; if Hinduism is right that every animal and plant has in it a *"spark of supremacy"* (while we know that if a thing is supreme it cannot be inferior to any other thing), why then are other animals not "inspired" or "enlightened" by the *"spark of supremacy"* in them? Why are they inferior to us?

However, Hindus by yogi explore the universe with "their consciousness" and meet non-terrestrial consciousnesses who poise as "spiritual guides" or "enlighteners" towards the Hindus. Yet Hindus believe that *"all the consciousnesses that are within the material universe are in 'material contamination' because they are counted 'unworthy' to live in God's Heaven"*. Why are they unworthy? And if what Hindu teaches about the eternality of the *"anti-material"* is true, it means then that the non-terrestrial consciousnesses within the "material world" must have earlier been in the "anti-material world". If true to Hinduism these consciousnesses are now *"banished to the material world"*, then certainly they must have offended the *"Supreme Godhead"* before *"His Supremacy"* banish them to the material world.

On their own part, Christians do not practise yogi but by knowledge that are believed to be *"inspired"* [gained without the use of the bodily sense], Christians believe that some angels [ethereal beings] were banished from God's Heaven into *"the material world"*. Christians believe that these angels *"were hurled down from [the spiritual] Heaven"* along with Satan and though they are so many, are less in number than the ones that remained loyal to the Supreme Being, God. It is interesting that the Hindus also believe that the *"consciousnesses"* in the *"anti-material world"* are more than the one within the *"material world"*.

> *Then another sign appeared in heaven: an enormous red dragon with seven heads and ten horns and seven crowns on his heads. His tail swept* **a third of the stars** *out of the sky and flung them to the earth. . . . And there was war in heaven. Michael and his angels fought against the dragon, and* **the dragon and his angels fought back.** *But he was not strong enough,* **and they lost their place in heaven. The great dragon was hurled down – that ancient serpent called the devil, or Satan, who leads the whole world astray. He was hurled to the earth, and his angels with him.** *Then I heard a loud voice say: . . . woe to the earth and the sea, because the devil has gone down to you! He is filled with fury, because he knows that his time is short."*
>
> (Revelations 12: 3 – 12)

What the prophet who wrote Revelations called *"stars of heaven"* is what he afterwards called *"angels"*, even as other Bible prophets also call angels *"stars"* [Job 38: 7]. According to the Bible, the population of the stars that fell appeared to the prophet to be about one-third the population of the holy angels. The Vedic literatures of the Hindus also teach that the population of the *"consciousnesses"* that are in the *"material world"* is *"**one-third**"* the population of the *"consciousnesses"* in the *"anti-material world"*. According to the Vedas, ethereal *"consciousnesses"* are in the material world because they are *"counted unworthy"* of God's Heaven. And according to the Bible, there are angels [ethereal beings], that "**sinned**" [became "unworthy"] and were cast out of God's heaven. When one compares the biblical knowledge and the Vedic knowledge, one is likely to conclude that the *"consciousnesses"* that Hindus say are *"banished to the material world"* are possibly the same with the ones that Christians refer to as the *"angels that sinned"*.

How did you fall from Heaven, O Lucifer?

Many Christians refer to Satan as "Lucifer" but not many people know that the name *"Lucifer"* means *"Morning Star"* or *"Light-bringer"* or *"Enlightener"*. Yet Prophet Isaiah was *"inspired"* to know that the *"Enlightener"* had fallen from God's Heaven.

How have you fallen from heaven, O morning star, son of the dawn! You have been cast down to the earth, you who once laid down the nations! You said in your heart, "I will ascend to heaven; I will raise my throne above the stars of God; I will sit enthroned on the mount of the assembly, on the utmost heights of the scared mountain. I will ascend above the tops of the clouds; I will make myself like the Most High". But you are brought down to the grave, to the depths of the pit.

(Isaiah 14: 12 – 15)

It is a basic Christian belief that Satan still goes about poising as the *"Enlightener"* or *"one who inspires"* or *"(teaching) master"*, and the angels that fell together with him are believed to so poise with him. In the typical manner that *"the ancient Serpent"* performed in the Garden of Eden, Satan and his angels still mislead people by revealing partial truths. And indeed many people are misled accordingly.

While some people advocate for inter-religious unity, on the assumption that *"the monotheistic religions are the same in principle"*, what matters to Christians is not just the confession of the fact that there is only one Supreme Being in existence; Christians believe that the fallen angels also acknowledge the fact that only God is Supreme. Every *"ethereal consciousness"* knows the fact that there is only one Supreme Being, God:

You believe that **there is one God**. *Good! Even* **the demons believe that** *– and shudder.*

(James 2: 19)

Moslems are used to saying *"There is no God, but Allah"* and *"Allah, Most Gracious, Most Merciful"*. But as fundamental as these recitations are to Islam, it must be noted that even the Hindus who attend many "gods" or "*expressions of God*" [so-called] also believe that "*there is the only one Supreme God, Krsna, Most Gracious and Most Merciful*". And this the Hindus maintain while also fellowshipping (in their yogi travels into the space) with the "*angels that sinned*", who also acknowledge the fact that "*There is only one Supreme God, Most Gracious and Most Merciful*". Therefore, simply believing that there is only one Supreme God does not make one better than "*the angels that sinned*" which Christians call "*evil spirits*" or "*demons*", which the Hindus also believe have "*become unworthy*" of God's Heaven.

If true to the teachings of Hinduism (and many other religions) the etherealities that are now in "*material contamination*" were once "*worthy*" to live with the *Supreme Ethereality*, then those contaminated etherealities cannot but *know* without doubt that *there is only one God*. But just as Satan did to Eve, they would acknowledge this fact to anyone as long as by so doing they succeed in preventing the person from truly following God.

> *Gorillas and Homo sapiens may be of the same primate family, but it does not translate that a man is therefore a gorilla or that a gorilla is therefore a man.*

Woe to the earth for the devil is come down unto you!

According to the Bible, the etherealities that were banished from God's Heaven into the material world ("*earth*", so-called) came down with "*great wrath*"; they wish they could have an opportunity to return into God's Heaven. But there is a difference between them and human beings. This is one fact that the Bible acknowledges but the Vedas does not. The fact that there is naturally in humankind an "inert" ethereal nature does not mean that man is automatically one of those "*angels that sinned*".

Gorillas and *Homo sapiens* may be of the same primate family, but it does not translate that a man is therefore a gorilla or that a gorilla is therefore a man. Of course, both may be "apes" [so-called], but they are yet different. Likewise man (as a spirit "*image and likeness of [the Spirit] God*") differs from the other spirits that the Hindus by yogi meet when they journey into the astral and planetary constellations.

Rationality and common sense re-affirms that we are not the same with them even if like them we have an inner ethereal nature, which is naturally "inert" in our own case, anyway. The simple fact that those non-human etherealities out there are not by nature attached to animal human consciousness implies that they are different from us.

But Satan, the Liar, leads the fallen angels, as *"deceivers of the world"* to ensure that humankind does not find the path to the true and living God. By corrupting humankind's ethereality, Satan and his angels seek to destroy *"the image and likeness of God"* in humankind. Rationality dictates that a man who has spent his lifetime associating his mind with *"fallen angels"*, who are *"unworthy"* in God's view, cannot be thus made acceptable to God. Rationally, *"travelling to other planets"* to meet with *"contaminated spirits"* that are *"unworthy"* of God's abode cannot make one *"worthy"* of God's abode. This is one of the reasons why Christians do not practise yogi. Much more because one never meets *"the Supreme Godhead"* during yogi travels, and all the spirits that one meets out there are the same ones that were *"once worthy of God's Heaven"* but are now *"unworthy"*, because they are *"the angels that sinned"*, the *"evil spirits"*, the *"demons"*.

Christians believe that it is very important to understand the plots of Satan and his cohorts so that one would not be caught in their guile – because they have overabundant guiles. First, it must be recognised that humans are not *"fallen angels"*. We were originated by the Creator Spirit here on earth, according to the Bible. Though having inherited an *"inert"* spirituality from Adam, we too are in transgression – but our case is different from *"fallen angels"* who are also in transgression; they fell from Heaven, we were born here. They do not have an *"outer"* animal form, we do. And therefore, we should not believe them when they try to beguile us into thinking that we are the same with them. Of course, they would beguile by making statements that are apparent *"truth"*. But as much as Satan beguiled Eve by simply telling her the *"truth"* (so-called), although incompletely and perversely, those who fellowship with *"fallen angels"* are prone to being beguiled through the very *"truths"* (so-called) that those evil spirits out there would reveal to them.

Secondly, Christians believe that we must neither fear nor love the *"unworthy spirits"* and by any means have no relationship with them. But what is surprising is the fact that in spite of the abundant teachings of the Bible on the nature of evil spirits, many "Christians" nurture several unbiblical ideas about "evil spirits". Many Christians [wrongly] blame every evil thing on *"evil spirits"*. For instance, I once told a Christian friend that I was feeling cold, he turned to me, lifted up one hand, and placed the other on my shoulder, and said *"Father, I rebuke the spirit of cold in this brother"*. I had to rebuke this Christian friend as well. I corrected him that *"I didn't tell you I have 'the spirit of cold', I said I feel cold. It is the weather. After all it just rained and I have been wearing only a singlet. What good cause do you have to believe I have the spirit of cold?"*.

But that is the way it is with many people, they see spirits behind everything – if they were cooking rice and it gets burnt, they would say there is a *"spirit of rice-burning"*, if they have pain in their broken ankle, they would pray against a *"spirit of pain"*!!!!!. Nothing could be farther away from rationality and actuality than this.

Normally, if one pours hot oil on one's skin, one will have blisters, not the *"spirit of blisters"*. Spirits may indeed be associated with sicknesses and misfortunes but certainly not in such simplistic ways that are popularly believed.

The contact point between flesh and spirit is the mind, often more than not. If an evil spirit needs to set a house ablaze, for instance, it must usually find some human cohorts to work with, or at least anything with *both* mind and body. The cycle flows from the ethereality to the mind and from the mind to the body. Even a network of several persons may be employed.

A spirit decides to set a house ablaze. A smoker walks by, gets to the house that the ethereality has determined to burn down and thoughtlessly throws off his unfinished cigarette into the lawn that has dry leaves. A moment later, he wonders why he had just thrown away his unfinished cigarette and lights another one, but he forgets the fact that the unfinished cigarette could start a fire in the lawn. He had been used.

It is much easier for a farmer to move a plough by making an animal to move its body, on which the instrument had been girded, rather than the farmer moving the plough by himself. Likewise, it is much easier for spirits to destroy a skyscraper by instigating men to bomb the skyscraper than for the spirits to pull down the building without using men. Evil spirits, therefore, work more often by making suggestion to human minds.

Suggestions (or, might we say "inspirations") from evil spirits are projected towards the minds of people who live without the aliveness of the *breath* [spirit] of God in them. Pornography and prostitution, for instance, persuade people to attach their minds to the desires of the human animal rather than the desires of the human spirit, which is the image and likeness of God. Evil spirits would rather have humans to be always animally conscious and thus remain "dead" to God; therefore, evil spirits would encourage pornography and prostitutions. But evil spirits have no human bodies of their own which they could display nude in gloss magazines; but they would rather suggest to the minds of some idle folks to start a pornography business and to some other minds to legalise it. And like a single spark from a matchstick, one demon-inspired person does it, and tempts other "un-inspired" people to follow suit.

As far as Bible principles are concerned, a *"spirit of pornography"* does not necessarily possess everyone who is in the pornographic chain (from producers to consumers) just as much as a *"spirit of fruit-eating"* did not possess Adam and Eve. There is a difference between temptations and demonic suggestions and that difference can only be appropriately discerned by a man whose inner natural ethereality is "alive" towards God.

Evil spirits and sicknesses of the human body.

We know that a man who imbibes contaminated food and drink is prone to bacterial diseases. When a person has been bitten by mosquitoes and the plasmodium passed into his blood weakens him to a feverish point, such a man has malaria and not *"the spirit of malaria"*. No matter how great an exorcist one is, one cannot *"cast out"* malaria from such a fellow because malaria is plasmodia-induced, and plasmodia are not ethereal, they are material. But indeed, we sometimes see one or two (so-called) exorcists trying futilely to *"cast out the spirit of malaria"* rather than try to treat or heal the malaria patient. This is unbiblical and irrational as well.

However, more debated than "physical ailments" are "mental ailments" – far too many people believe that *"mental illnesses are caused by demons, no more, no less"*. What makes it even more interesting is that several mentally ill people are called *"demoniacs"* in some versions of the Bible and several other *"holy books"*. But in modern psychiatry, we employ chemotherapy on the so-called demoniacs and it helps restore them to normalcy. The rational question to ask those who believe that *"everyone who has a 'mental sickness' is possessed"* is this: can drugs and chemicals cast out demons? After all, anti-depressants help to heal many mental patients just as much as chloroquine and other anti-malarial drugs help in treatments of malaria. If malaria is truly caused by a "spirit of malaria", then chloroquine should not be able to drive out the spirit, and likewise in the mental illnesses, drugs should have no effect on spirits.

Nevertheless, not all mental patients respond positively to chemotherapy or indeed any form of therapy [not even extensive psychotherapy] because of a persistent "suggestive force" beneath their minds. In certain cases of this nature, patients have tried "alternative medical practices" or "medical arts" (including extortions) with "*surprisingly positive results*". But there is a difference between a mental illness resultant from physical and emotional injury to the brain or mind and one resultant from so-called "non-determinable causes".

Evil spirits and occults.

It must be observed that Satan and his "fallen angels" have certain unashamedly dedicated human cohorts. We call them "occultists" because they maintain a sworn bond with the evil etherealities. They entice one to join them, one joins (in many cases under an if-I-quit-I-must-die treaty), but one soon finds that the group is committed to making the world a "sad and frightful" place just in bid to get more members. One becomes Satan's "bondman" – one maintains a bond that one is under threat not to break.

People join occult groups by either of two principal means – enticement and threats. In their guile, the angels that sinned would divide their human partners into seemingly opposing occult groups but all the groups simply fish into the same basket. It makes their "fishing" easier.

One occult group threatens a man while another occult group (which poises to be more powerful) offers to protect the threatened man; and the man falls for it. He ends up being an occultist too. Soon he finds that his own group threatens some other persons and drive them into membership of another group. [Satan's ambidextrous trapping]. "*Woe to the inhabiters of the earth . . . for **the devil is come down unto you having great wrath!**". (Revelations 12: 12, King James Version).

Spiritual wickedness in the skies.

Finally, one must take a bird-eye view of the world as regards the nature and works of evil etherealities. A myopic view may simply tell you that occults do not exist just as much a man who lives in a remote African village may never know that there are "white-skinned humans".

While the "inert" natural ethereality in humankinds wants to be attuned again to God, humankind is constantly fought against by the "fallen angels" and their deceived "companions" and sworn "bondmen". But the major fight that humans must win is not against the human cohorts of the evil spirits but against the evil spirits themselves.

For our struggle is not against flesh and blood, but against the rulers, against the authorities, against the powers of this dark world and against the spiritual forces of evil in the heavenly realms.

(Ephesians 6: 12)

In Africa, we see how much people dread the charm-wearing occult grandmasters. A witchdoctor goes into the forest and plucks some leaves. [There is a difference between an ordinary herbalist and a witchdoctor. The herbalist believes in the chemical powers of the leaves, whereas the witchdoctor believes in the spiritual powers]. The witchdoctor claims that the leaves have some special spiritual powers. But he does not pluck them in the way that I prune the hibiscus behind my bedroom window. He must make incantations *"to invoke the powers of the leaves"*. If an *"uninitiated"* (as the occultists regard non-occultists) plucks the same leaves, the leaves would seemingly not work for him because the uninitiated does not know the required incantations. Thus, when the leaves work for the witchdoctor, they work not because of the chemo-physical properties of the leaves but because of the *incantations*, which only *"the initiated"* knows. And the incantations would not work unless one has thus successfully *"invoked"* the associated etherealities.

The successful witchdoctor brings home his "leaves", and concocts a charm out of them, again chanting incantations. The next day he uses the charm, often with incantations, by which he must invoke the *"powers of the earth, the ancestors and the globins"*. He *"pays homage to the bond of the initiated"* and pleads that *"the 'initiated' should join hands"* with him. Then he gains an ethereal conviction springing up within him that he is *"being escorted"* by the *"powers"* he had invoked. Nevertheless, when he is face-to-face with the person on whom he hopes to use his charms, he chants again his incantations until that person is frightened or mesmerised. Most charms usually fail to have a bodily effect on the "victim" until the victim's mind is subdued, because it is easier for spirits to attack the mind rather than the body; because they have minds but not bodies.

It is interesting to note that the witchdoctors were at the highest echelons of the typical West African society before the Europeans colonised this region and even before the slave trades. But the witch-doctors could not bewitch the Europeans because they could not successfully mesmerise them. The Europeans did not care whatever the witchdoctors were chanting. In the first place, the fact that they did not understand the witchdoctors' languages made the deliberately frightening words of no effect. Nonetheless, it is not only by mesmerising a person that occultists can gain advantage over the person.

Evil spirits can disturb the consciousness of animals and use them to wreck great havoc against a person and in some cases can "energise" inanimate objects. Energies are convertible. Chemical energies can be converted into electrical energies, electrical energies can be converted into kinetic energies, and kinetic energies can produce heat energies, and so on. Likewise, ethereal energies can have effect on our material world. Nevertheless, ethereal beings most often affect the material world through the manipulation of human minds, or at least animal minds and ethereal energies are considered superior to all forms of energies [chemical, nuclear, et cetera] associated with the material world.

It is believed that evil spirits are not particularly limited to the planet Earth. Christians believe that many *"evil spirits dwell in the skies"* [Ephesians 12: 12], that is, the many stellar galaxies that lies beyond the earth's immediate atmosphere. It is also believed that evil spirits organise themselves into "territorial" and "occupational" hierarchies working together to influence (directly and indirectly) all ramifications of human life on earth. Whatever they are, anyway, and however they live or operate in the world, we are primarily concerned about God, and not about them. But the very importance of knowing who they are is just so we would not be deceived by them.

We must know that the ethereal consciousnesses that are bound into the material world are principally the angels that sinned and were driven out of God's Heaven. Drawing inspirations or enlightenment of any sort, or fellowshipping with these "unworthy" spirits only exposes a person's mind more to the deception of the devil and one cannot through any of these, escape from the spiritual "death" that Adam and Eve died in the Garden of Eden and passed by birth into us all.

And as per whether evil spirits truly exist, the reality of inspirations – knowledge gained independent of the perceptions of our corporeal senses – probably indicate that there are incorporeal minds in existence that can interact with human minds.

Chapter Six

NICOLAITANES

"The Leaven of the Pharisees and of Herod".

Much ado about leavened bread.

Traditionally, the Jews regard the unleavened bread as a symbol of spiritual purity. Certain Jewish religious festivals are celebrated with the unleavened bread and no one dares "profane" the "holy" festivals by doing so much as handle a leavened loaf of bread while the unleavened bread is being used for religious purposes. Any leavening substance was considered in this wise as a thing that adulterates or pollutes.

So it was one day, the Bible says, after eating bread with the small group that he led, Jesus met some Pharisees who questioned him on some issues. When he left the Pharisees, he entered the ship in which were his disciples and told them *"take heed, beware of the leaven of the Pharisees, and of the leaven of Herod".* (Mark 8: 15, King James Version).

Jesus' disciples began to murmur to one another that their master spoke sharply to them because they had not taken any food along with them into the ship. But Jesus corrected their mistaken notion by pointing out to them that he was not particular about edible leavened loaves.

*The disciples had forgotten to bring bread, except for one loaf they had with them in the boat. **"Be careful,"** Jesus warned them. **"Watch out for the yeasts of the Pharisees and that of Herod."** They discussed this with one another and said, "it is because we have no bread." Aware of their discussion, Jesus* *asked them:* **"Why are you talking about having no bread?** *Do you still not see or understand? Are your hearts hardened? Do you have eyes but fail to see, and ears but fail to hear? And don't you remember? When I broke the five loaves for the five thousand, how many basketfuls of pieces did you pick up?"* *"Twelve," they replied. And when I broke the seven loaves for the four thousand, how many basketfuls of pieces did you pick up?" They answered, "Seven." He said to them,* **"Do you still not understand?"**

(Mark 8: 14 – 21)

There have been several sceptic approaches to the possible realities of the Bible's miracles and some people without paying close attention to the multiple proofs of ethereality that surround us, have opined that Jesus' miracles of multiplying loaves were nothing more than pre-arranged frauds. Some have even advanced the theory that Jesus probably pre-arranged to hide loaves around the premises of the places in which he reportedly multiplied the loaves. While presently declining to pursue for or against the cynical arguments about Jesus' miracles of the loaves, we should dwell on the fact that in the passage that we have just read, Jesus eventually persuaded his disciples that he had his own way of getting them loaves if ever there arise a dire need for loaves. Whether by "miracles", according to believers, or by "pre-arrangements", according to cynics, the most important fact remains that Jesus provided more than enough loaves to feed the gathered thousands on the recorded two occasions and how much less would be the task of providing for only twelve people. And the import of this fact for our present discussion is that while warning his disciples about *"the yeasts of the Pharisees and that of Herod"*, Jesus could not have been bothered by the fact that they had not taken baked edible loaves with them; but rather, he warned them about figurative loaves – *"do you still not understand?"*.

What Jesus referred to as *"yeast"* of the Pharisees and of Herod were *"doctrines"* or *"ideologies"* and not the oven-baked loaves. But while this symbolism perfectly fits the Pharisees who were promulgators of doctrines, one might think that Herod (who tried to play "secular") had nothing to do with doctrines. However, it is clearer from Herod's approach to religious affairs that his "secular" stance was as much im-portant as the zealously committed stance of the Pharisees.

The Yeast of the Pharisees, which is hypocrisy.

Jesus and his disciples associated more closely with the Pharisees than the other equally popular Judaist sect of their days, the Sadducees. This is understandable considering the fact that the Pharisees, like Jesus and his disciples, believed in existence after death, which the Sadducees did not believe. But the Pharisees with whom Jesus associated more closely were often the same people that he criticised most frequently. And although the Pharisees were the most respected Judaist sect at that time (among whom were chief priests and the very pillars of Judaism), their doctrines were frequently attacked by Jesus.

Meanwhile, when a crowd of many thousands had gathered, so that they were trampling on one another, Jesus began to speak first to his disciples, saying: **"Be on your guard against the yeast of the Pharisees, which is hypocrisy."**

(Luke 12: 1)

To Jesus, the Jews [who practised Judaism] knew *"the true and living God"* [John 4: 22] and the Pharisees were the best Judaists at that time. Therefore, when he warned his disciples to *"beware of the yeast of the Pharisees"*, he did not mean *"beware of Judaism"*; rather he meant *"beware of* **hypocrisy***"*. Of course, in the Bible, Jesus even says he was not particularly against Judaism.

"Do not think that I have come to abolish the Law or the Prophets; I have not come to abolish but to fulfill them."

(Matthew 5: 17)

Fulfilling the Jewish scriptures, *"the Torah and the Prophets"*, according to Jesus, is the declared reason for the "founding" of Christianity. This is why the lengthier part of the Christian Bible consists of the Jewish scriptures and the remaining part consists of books that seek to prove that the prophecies and purpose of the Jewish scriptures were being fulfilled in the days of Jesus and his disciples.

Outward versus inward righteousness.

With particular emphasis on the pharisaic doctrines, Jesus once admonished that his followers should practise what the Pharisees *taught* but not what they *practised.*

Then Jesus said to the crowds and to his disciples: "The teachers of the law and the

Pharisees sit in Moses' seat. **So you must obey them and do every-thing they tell you.** *But do not practice what they do, for they do not practice what they preach.*

(Matthew 23: 1 – 3)

Considering the fact that Jesus approved of what the Pharisees taught, one might well opine that he was contradicting himself by warning his disciples to keep off from the proverbial *"leaven"* of the Pharisees. Nevertheless, it must be equally considered that while approving what the Pharisees *taught* (being *"the Torah and the Prophets"*), Jesus disapproved their practices. Definitely, the Bible-day Pharisees had specific *"practices"* that were not acceptable to Jesus – so long as they do not teach people to do those *"practices"*, Jesus told his disciples to follow them, but no more than that because those *"practices"* contradicted the underlying principles of the Judaism religion which the Pharisees advocated. The problem was, the Pharisees *"practised"* according to what they considered as the proper interpretation of the Torah and the Prophets.

From the same Bible passage in which Jesus identified the *"yeast"* of the Pharisees as *"hypocrisy"*, we find a more vivid description of what he regarded as hypocrisy, or, *"yeast"*:

> *"Woe to you, teachers of the law and Pharisees, you hypocrites! You are like whitewashed tombs, which look beautiful on the outside but on the inside are full of dead mean's bones and everything unclean. In the same way, on the* **outside** *you appear to people as righteous but on the* **inside** *are full of hypocrisy and wickedness.*

(Matthew 23: 27 – 28)

The central theme of Jesus' public ministry emphasised that Judaism was at that point in time unfulfilled and that the sole purpose of his life on earth was to fulfil the very doctrines of Judaism, "the Law and the Prophets". The fulfilment was to make the *"inward"* human righteous, considering that Judaism already made the *"outward"* human *"righteous"*.

Judaism, as practised by the Pharisees, was primarily concerned about the righteousness of the animal [outward] human, it was about morals and it is still about morals. But Christianity as Jesus taught is not about *"the moral animal"*; rather, it is about that *"**breath** of God in man"*, which the Torah says had *"surely died"* in the Garden of Eden.

Today, many people think of religion only in the moral and social import of it. People say *"all religions are established towards the goal of instilling morals into society"*. According to Jesus, in the Bible, if religion is all about morals, then Judaism was enough for the Jews and Christianity would be unnecessary. Therefore, the reason that Jesus considered the Pharisees as *"religious fraudsters"* was simply because they believed in human existence after death while at once practising religion as though it concerns only social morality of the animal human and no more.

The *"Torah and the Prophets"* indeed say things that emphasise that the difference between man and other animals is not simply *"the biggest brain"* issue but the *"inward ethereality"*. Therefore, if the Pharisees were being true to the principles of Judaism, they should have emphasised the *"resurrection"* of *"the inner man"* as much as they looked forward to the eventual resurrection of the human body. Pharisees taught that *"if a man obeys scriptural commandments faithfully, then his body would be resurrected from death at the end of the world"*, whereas Jesus was particular about the resurrection of the *"breath"* [spirit] which *"surely died"* in the Garden of Eden, according to the Torah. To Jesus, the more important resurrection was that of the *"inner man"* which brings the human spirit nature back into vitality towards God.

Jesus believed and taught that the perpetual existence of *"the animal man"* is NOT of primary importance to God; he maintained that God is a Spirit and wants *"the spirit that God breathed into man"* to resurrect within every man and relate with *Him*, rather than the animal human trying futilely to relate with *"the Spirit God"*. This Jesus' stance was in accordance with the fundamental principles of *"the Torah and the Prophets"* and hence he charged his disciples to beware of the teachings of the Pharisees, which emphasised the righteousness of the animal human – *"do you still not understand?"*.

However, one wonders why Jesus had to warn his disciples against *"the yeast of Pharisees"* as it was generally obvious that Jesus was already separating his disciples from Judaism into *"a new sect"* and they might after all no longer be under the Pharisees. When we study Jesus and Christianity more critically, though, we find that it was justifiably important to Jesus to have warned his disciples about the religious hypocrisy, which purports that God wants to be worshipped by *"the ani-*

> *The "Torah and the Prophets" indeed say things that emphasise that the difference between man and other animals is not simply "the biggest brain" issue but the "inward ethereality".*

mal called man". Alas, "Christianity" as popularly known today has fallen from what Jesus intended, and has come into the same *"yeast"* for which Jesus condemned the Pharisees. This means that, if we examine things according to the Bible's principles, popular Christianity is not in any way more acceptable to God than any other religion that stipulates the submission of the animal human to the laws of God.

God wants worshippers who are spiritually alive.

The basic principle of Christianity is that God does not want to be worshipped by animals – of which *Homo sapiens* is the chief species. To Jesus, according to the Bible, it is hypocrisy while believing that every human has an inner spirit nature that had *"surely died"* through Adam in the Garden Eden, and at once to teach that the human, without first coming back to life spiritually, can truly worship God [a Spirit]. *"God is spirit, and his worshippers must be spirits"* *"Do you still not understand?"* [John 4: 24 and Mark 8: 21]

Also in the Bible, Jesus met a woman who argued with him about acceptability of religious beliefs and forms of worship. Jesus was Jewish, and the woman was Samaritan, both tribes trace their genealogies to the same patriarch, Jacob. Jesus and the woman met at *"the well of Jacob"* and the woman was beginning to make a big issue of Jesus being a Jew, so much that she could not spare him a single cup of water. Then, he told her some facts about herself, which she opined Jesus could not have known by ordinary mental reckoning. She immediately believed Jesus was a prophet, who had known those facts by incorporeal perceptions.

> *"Sir," the woman said, "I can see that you are a prophet. Our fathers worshipped on this mountain, but you Jews claim that the place where we must worship is in Jerusalem." Jesus declared, "Believe me, woman, a time is coming when you will worship the Father neither on this mountain nor in Jerusalem. You Samaritans worship what you do not know, we worship what we do know, for salvation is from the Jews. Yet a time is coming and has now come when the true worshippers will worship the Father* **in spirit** *and truth, for they are* **the kind of worshippers the Father seeks.** *God is Spirit, and his worshippers must worship* **in spirit** *and in truth."*

> (John 4: 19 – 24)

If God is truly Spirit [incorporeal], the true worshippers must primarily worship *Him* "inwardly" – not in the mental "mind" of the animal human, but in an incorporeal consciousness.

The mental mind being an animal consciousness is yet regarded as part of the "outward" (animal) human. For religious purpose, in the principles of Jesus, deep religiousness – so deep it goes beyond behavioural devotion into "mental addiction" is "*hypocrisy*" as far as "*the Torah and the Prophets*" is concerned. To Jesus, a man who spends his entire lifetime in a secluded home, keeping his body and surroundings so clean, who does not get angry or wish anybody evil, who spends twenty four hours everyday praying and studying the scriptures, who commits no "sin", and obeys all scriptural commandments, is NOT holy. To Jesus, even if the man goes further to be so kind as to give up every material possession he

> *However, most religions, including the popular form of Christianity deviate from Jesus' stance on God's nature and man's spirituality while also purporting that God is a Spirit.*

has for the benefits of others, and has no "sinful" friends, lives a life of total abstinence from all defilements, the man still remains "inwardly" unholy. To Jesus, if a man spends his entire life mediating on God and chanting God's holy name and holy commandments, and the man's mind is absolutely focused on God even from birth till death, the man is still "inwardly" unholy. This is simply because a man's mental consciousness is a function of his animal body – no one can have mental consciousness without a brain, which is still an integral part of the animal body of the man. But if God is completely a Spirit, then animal life is not part of God's life. Therefore, animal life, no matter how morally excellent, is NOT reckoned with by God. This is the basic principle upon which Bible-day Christianity was founded and it is a principle without which any form of Christianity is false and "hypocritical".

However, most religions, including the popular form of Christianity deviate from Jesus' stance on God's nature and man's spirituality while also purporting that God is a Spirit. But Jesus was simply emphasising the import of "*the Torah and the Prophets*" which maintain that man in the image and likeness of God has an "*inner*" [*spirit*] component.

The brain is the seat of our mental consciousness. Our ordinary thoughts, speech and actions are originated and governed in the brain. Structural or chemical alterations made to the brain can alter the way in which a person thinks, speaks and acts. For those among us who have been privileged to study the anatomy and physiology of the human brain, we appreciate the fact that the brain is indeed *"the mind organ"*, or put another way, *"our organic mind"*. That is why psychosurgeries and psychochemicals affect the "mind" while in fact their direct touch is on the material brain and it is also why physical *"brain damage"* can lead to a *"loss of information from the mind"*. Along these lines, if religious purity simply consists of *"purity of the mind, and purity of thoughts, speech and actions"*, it remains as *"purity of the animal called man"* and is therefore of no import to God who has no animal parts. Thus, original Christianity teaches in accordance with *the Torah and the Prophets* that there is an "inward" incorporeal nature within man, with which God reckons, and an "outward" animal nature, which is not of primary import to God; anything less than this is the *"yeast"* of the Pharisees, which Jesus considered as "hypocrisy" and "iniquity".

> *Structural or chemical alterations made to the brain can alter the way in which a person thinks, speaks and acts.*

There shall be false teachers among you.

The Christianity that most of us know today is at variance with what was reckoned as being "Christian" in the very Bible that Christians read, teach and poise to believe. In the Bible, Peter, one of those that Jesus warned about the yeast of the Pharisees, also warned about false teachers:

> *But there were also false prophets among the people, just as there will be false teachers among you. They will secretly introduce destructive heresies, even denying the sovereign Lord who bought them — bringing swift destruction on themselves. Many will follow their shameful ways and will bring the way of truth into disrepute.* **In their greed these teachers will exploit you with stories they have made up.** *Their condemnation has long been hanging over them, and their destruction has not been sleeping.*
>
> (2 Peter 2: 1 – 3)

Everywhere on earth today where the words "Christian" and "church" are familiar, *"big church means big business"*. Christians and churches [both so-called] have widely embraced *"the yeast of the Pharisees"* which preaches the "outward" righteousness of maintaining *"pure minds, thoughts, speech and actions"*. And if there is any religion at all on earth that obscures the original teachings of Jesus the most, it is none other than popular Christianity. Unfortunately!

The greatest, most effective "enemy" of original Christianity is the popular but false Christianity that is preached and practised in many churches worldwide – it is as much "hypocrisy" as the pharisaic Judaism, which taught and practised things that were contrary to the basic principles of its scriptures. And just as much as Jesus openly berated the Pharisees as *"fools and blind"* [Matthew 23], so might we as well berate popular Christianity as *"blind and foolish"* considering that its teachings and practices are as much at variance with its scriptures as was the case of the Pharisees of Jesus' days.

How is it that you do not understand?

While biblical Christianity teaches that only spirituality (not animality) can rightly relate with God's spiritual nature, popular Christianity advances a religion that is based on purported relationship between the animal man and the Spirit God. Popular Christianity fails to discern that our ordinary minds and our mental thoughts are animalistic and hence "outward" while only ethereality is spiritualistic and "inward". It may be decisively stated therefore that there are two forms of Christianity – the false and the true.

While Jesus warned that his disciples should beware of the yeast of the Pharisees, he admonished them to keep to the scriptures of the Pharisees. This implies what Jesus condemned was not the Judaist scriptures but the wrong interpretations and practises that the Pharisees purported to derive from the scriptures. The same applies to popular Christianity. Even Jesus himself and his apostles insinuated that there are two opposing forms of Christianity. On one occasion, he warned his disciples about what he called *"the broad road"*:

> *"Enter through the narrow gate. For wide is the gate and broad is the road that leads to destruction, and many enter through it. But small is the gate and narrow the road that leads to life, and only a few find it. Watch out for false prophets. They come to you in sheep's clothing, but inwardly they are ferocious wolves."*
>
> (Matthew 7: 13 – 15)

This passage of the Bible is one of the widest read and most frequently quoted among Christians. But it is equally one of the most misinterpreted. Contrary to what most Christians and the churches want us to believe, Jesus was not teaching about life generally when he mentioned *"the broad road"* and *"the narrow road"*; he was teaching about what he called *"the kingdom of heaven"*. But most churches and most Christians tell us *"there are two roads in life, the broad road and the narrow"*, thinking they are "expounding" this passage. They fail to see that Jesus also talked about "gates". If Jesus was talking about life generally when he spoke about *"the two roads"*, he would not have mentioned anything about gates; or at least about the wide gate in particular, because we should have already "entered" it by natural birth into human existence and we would be left with only the narrow gate to choose, then there would not be any need to *"make every effort to enter"* [Luke 13: 24]. We can no longer be left with two options if true to popular Christian opinion we have already entered by birth into the wide gate and are walking in the broad road.

Indeed many Christians and churches simply "read" the portions of the Bible at random without considering the context and primary audience that the passages addressed. But when we consider Jesus' audience in this passage, we see that he was speaking to an audience that consist primarily of those who believed in him and were *"seeking to enter the kingdom of God"*. And he implied that his followers shall by so seeking discover two gates that both purport to be the same thing – entrance into the kingdom of heaven. The entire *"Sermon on The Mount"*, from which this passage is culled, addresses people that already believed and followed Jesus, and it is to them [seekers of the kingdom of heaven] that the *"broad road"* and *"narrow road"* parable specifically applies; not to entire humanity. And today it might well apply to all who seek to enter the Kingdom of heaven as preached by Jesus.

The "broad road" Christianity.

Jesus who had warned the disciples to beware of the leaven of the Pharisees also warned them against "false prophets". But the false prophets were not supposed to be non-Christians and non-churchgoers; they were to be *"false prophets among Christians"* as the apostles further testified. (2 Peter 2: 1 – 3). And this is again reaffirmed in the very sermon by which Jesus warned his followers about *"the broad road"*:

"Watch out for false prophets. They come to you in sheep's clothing, but inwardly they are ferocious wolves. By their fruit you will recognize them. Do people pick grapes from thornbushes, or figs from thistles? Likewise every good tree bears good fruit, but a bad tree bears bad fruit. A good tree cannot bear bad fruit, and a bad tree cannot bear good fruit. Every tree that does not bear good fruit is cut down and thrown into the fire. Thus, by their fruit you will recognize them."

(Matthew 7: 15 – 20)

It is very easy to say *"by their fruits you shall know them"* which is unfortunately the only expression that many Christians remember the most from this passage. Christians often overlook the fact that Jesus had earlier said the false Christian prophets would *"come in sheep's clothing but inwardly they are ferocious wolves"*. For non-Christians, *"wolves in sheep's clothing"* is the most memorable expression taken from this passage. But the import of Jesus' warning is often overlooked. Nevertheless, in the subsequent verses from the same passage, the import of Jesus' widely adapted expressions is made clearer:

"Not every one who says to me, 'Lord, Lord,' will enter the kingdom of heaven, but only he who does the will of my Father who is in heaven. Many will say to me on that day, 'Lord, Lord, did we not prophesy in your name, and in your name drive out demons and perform many miracles?' Then I will tell them plainly, 'I never knew you. Away from me, you evildoers!' "

(Matthew 7: 21 – 23)

For a flock, nothing could be more dangerous than wolves that have grown much pure wool and have learnt to bleat and chew grass as well. While it is very easy to recite *"by their fruits you shall now them"*, it is virtually impossible to distinguish, by mere mental reckoning, a wolf that is perfectly disguised as a sheep. One just looks for the "fruits" [attributes] and conclude that *"if it has the face of a sheep, if it has much pure wool, if it bleats, if it chews grass and treads gently among the flock, if it does not pounce on any sheep, and it does no one any harm, then it is a sheep"*. But Jesus taught that these are all "outward".

We take a man who believes the entire Christian scriptures; who mediates on several Bible passages every day; who never misses church attendance; who never hurts anyone, who devotes his entire life to the services of the name of God and benevolence towards humanity; we look at him and say *"that is a true Christian"*. Moreover, if his prayers seem to get quick results; if he professes to be "born again"; if he keeps his words faithfully, if he breaks no religious or societal laws; with all these, if he also freely forgives and "speaks no evil of anyone"; we say *"if every Christian is like that man, I too would like to be a Christian"*. But that same man is one of those that Jesus say would not enter into the kingdom of heaven because all his righteousness are simply achievable by a serious discipline of *"the animal called man"*. Yet such men are the best that popular Christianity can afford.

What makes it more unfortunate for those who follow popular Christianity is that the Bible talks of their best men (exemplified in the immediate previous paragraph) as ones that would be *"cast away"* at last from the kingdom of heaven. Just as Jesus and Peter warned about false prophets among Christians, Paul (also an Apostle) warned about false apostles:

For such are false apostles, deceitful workers, transforming themselves into the apostles of Christ. And no marvel; for Satan himself is transformed into an angel of light. Therefore it is no great thing if his ministers also be transformed as the ministers of righteousness; whose end shall be according to their works.
(2 Corinthians 11: 13 – 15, King James Version).

We say *"if they are transformed, then it is acceptable"*. But Jesus and his apostles say the transformation of the animal called man to as great an extent as one might say *"that man is an angel"* is unacceptable to God; for God being a Spirit, reckons with spirit and not with animals. It does not matter whether the animal is moral or immoral, God would only be worshipped in **spirit**, not in the mind of the animal humans. The transformation of the outer man seemingly into Christian excellence is mere **masquerading**.

For such men are false apostles, deceitful workmen, masquerading as apostles of Christ. And no wonder, for Satan himself masquerades as an angel of light. It is not surprising, then, if his servants masquerade as servants of righteousness. Their end will be what their actions deserve.
(2 Corinthians 11: 13 – 15)

Popular Christianity teaches that men whose "minds, thoughts, speech and actions" have been transformed into "angelic" [perfect] standards are acceptable to God – but this contradicts the principles of the Christian scriptures, and hence popular Christianity is false and hypocritical, according to the Bible.

Keeping to one's lanes.

Finally, in respect of *"the broad road Christianity"*, we must observe that Jesus implied there is a disguised similarity between it and the true ["*narrow road*"] Christianity. It is unusual for an expressway to consist of only one lane. The *"broad road"* Christianity, cannot be an exception to the rule. Like every other highway, it must be made up of *"narrow"* lanes, which in this case the *"denominations"*, *"sects"* and *"movements"* of false Christianity apparently represents.

As no one travelling on the highway covers the entire way but simply takes to a lane on it, irrespective of whatever probable causes might have given birth to denominations and movements within popular Christianity, the fact remains that the Christian scriptures disapprove of denominational Christianity.

For followers of Jesus' teachings, the implication of denominational Christianity is that one narrowly follows a particular sect and its teachings thinking he is walking on the *"narrow road"* that Jesus talked about – whereas that *"narrow road Christianity"* that Jesus advocated could not in any wise be sectarian, for Jesus invariably reiterated that his followers *"must be one"*. [John 14 – John 17].

Contrary to the form of worship that Jesus approves in the Bible, sectarianism was an attribute of the Pharisees, who for the noble reason of wanting to please God as perfectly as possible formed a sect within Judaism. If in spite of their moral and religious excellence as far as the Jewish scriptures, they were unacceptable to Jesus, then also the widespread sectarian Christianity practised today cannot be acceptable to Jesus unless it satisfies the fundamental requirement of *"worshipping in the inner [spirit] man"*. Of course, the Pharisees were *"blameless"* as far as the *"righteousness of mind and body"* as stipulated in their holy scriptures was concerned. [Philippians 3: 5 – 6].

But it is noteworthy that like the Pharisees of Jesus' days, those who practise *"the broad road Christianity"* today, even with a sincere purpose of wanting to please God as perfectly as possible, are simply *"blind"* to the facts of the very Bible that they read and believe. Jesus, without any compunction, called the pharisaic chief priests *"blind leaders of the blind"* and so might we rightly call the *"chief priests"* of popular Christianity today. True Christianity advocates the righteousness and aliveness of the *spirit* man, which the godliness of the *mind* in the outward animal man complements but does not substitute. True Christianity is NOT about being *"morally upright"* and *"being good and useful to the human society"*, it is about being *"**spiritually** upright and being determined to* *join the heavenly society of God and the holy angels"*. And it is in this capacity that religion makes sense, if God truly exists and humans have the nature of God within them. According to the Bible, anything less than this is blind and foolish both to the things prophetically written in respect to God and in fact to common sense as well.

> *Then the disciples came to him and asked, "Do you know that the Pharisees were offended when they heard this?" He replied, "Every plant that my heavenly Father has not planted will be pulled up by the roots. Leave them; they are blind guides. If a blind man leads a blind man, both will fall into a pit."*
>
> (Matthew 15: 12 – 14)

Beware of the yeast . . . of Herod.

Jesus had warned his disciples against **both** the yeast of the Pharisees and that of Herod. But while he did identify the yeast of the Pharisees as *"hypocrisy"*, he did not plainly tell them what "the *yeast* of Herod" meant. Yet we know that Herod was a *"secular"* king and stood firmly for secularism as much as he could. The *yeast* of Herod may therefore be regarded as "the practices and teachings of secularists" as much the *yeast* of the Pharisees stood for the practices and teachings of sectarian worshippers who preach *"blamelessness in minds, thoughts, speech and deeds"* rather than in the spirit. And it should be interesting to dig deeper into why Jesus was against the *"yeast"* of the secularists, after all secularists are seemingly neutral and harmless persons.

The only thing for which most Bible readers remember the biblical Herod the First [Herod the Great] is that he murdered infants when his royal heritage appeared threatened by the birth of a *"destined King"* as reported to him by the Magi. Only a few people realise that Herod was simply typical of our modern politicians. Herod's principle was to serve himself first, his family next and then his society to the best of his abilities. Herod rebuilt the Judaist Temple even though he had a flagrant disregard for the *"Judaists' God"* and prophets, and could well have believed that *"there is [really] no God"*.

If Herod believed in the God of the Jews and in the importance of the Jewish Temple that he had built, he would not have also built worship places for the other religions at the same time because the Jewish God and laws forbade such. Thus, in the view of Herod, religion (of whatever form) only served *"to help moralise the society"* and the state laws were superior to any religious laws that might exist, in his view.

Herod maintained that the religious freedom of everyone must be guaranteed so long as no religion poised a threat to the state or the stability of the society, or offended the state authorities. That was why Herod gave state support to *"every peaceful form of religion"* – giving the greatest succour to the widest accepted and the least succour to the least accepted. Herod rated the religions according to the popularity of each religion among his subject because his basic belief might simply have been that *"there is really no God and religions have only invented 'the so-called God' or Gods"*. He was a typical secularist who welcomed all priests so far they do not try to force their respective religious convictions on him. Of course, he had a dedicated "Royal Portico" within the Jewish Temple premises but the portico simply served for him to "grace" the Temple with his personal presence and thus fulfil a state role. He hardly worshipped there. He fulfilled the same "state role" while attending the worship places of other "less important" religions.

There is no God.

There is something rather *"funny"* about secularism – it "recognises" God but ensures that allegiance to the State is greater than allegiance to God. It says *"you cannot teach about God in State schools unless the students themselves have opted to learn about God"* yet it gives out currency notes that are labelled *"in **God** we trust"* or *"**God** save the King"* to be spent on the same students.

Secularism says, *"The State has approved designated worship centres and any form of worship outside the designated centres, except in private homes, has no defined legal backing"*. But when the question arises on what to teach children about the origin of the world, and the origin of humanity, secularism says, *"evolution is okay, since it proves scientifically that man is an animal, which no rational person can deny"*. Secularism aims for peaceful neutrality focused on maintaining the stability of the State and opines that "evolution" and "science" are religiously neutral. The *yeast* of Herod forgets that evolution and science tend towards the belief that *"there is no God"*.

In 1997, a Danish couple reportedly moved into a zoo for a while in order to remind the zoo's visitors that humans are closely related to the apes. But the religious person who has observed evidences of incorporeal perceptions (*"inspirations"*) in humankind considers it **foolish** to believe that *"man is no more than an animal and there is no God"*.

The fool says in his heart, "There is no God." They are corrupt, and their ways are vile; there is no one who does good. God looks down from heaven on the sons of men to see if there are any who understand, any who seek God. Everyone has turned away, they have together become corrupt; there is none who does good, not even one.

(Psalms 53: 1 – 3)

The prophetic king, David, who wrote this passage, opined that it is due to lack of understanding that some humans think that there is no God. But evolutionists and other atheist scientists have invariably sought for evidences of God's existence well enough before concluding, *"there is no Creator"*. We say that *"they have their evidences against the existence of God"*, yet we know that it is one thing to have evidences but another thing to make correct inferences from the evidences, and yet another thing for the evidences to be complete and conclusive.

Evolutionists have until now made inferences from only material evidences without completing even the material evidences much less including incorporeal evidences. We look upon evolution as "mentally sound", but when we consider that the evidences are incomplete and inconclusive, can we really uphold the "soundness" of evolution? Did evolutionists consider the impossibility of the Big Bang theory in view of the factors of source of energy and decision required for the first *Matter* to come into existence at the precise moment it did? Most probably, they did NOT – and no wonder that Jesus warned against the *yeast* of the secularists.

It must have been this way or that.

What the spiritually conscious people, such as King David, regard as not thoughtful in secularism and atheism is the manner in which **speculations** are transformed into authoritative theories. Evolutionists pick up fossils here and there and after doing some work on the dating of the fossil rocks, they turn their speculations into **conclusions**. While it appears *"mentally sound"* to do so, there is the danger of arriving at an incorrect conclusion.

For a typical example of being misled by evidences, we might consider again a biblical example in the story of Joseph. It is a popular Bible story and again we are not after proving whether the story was fact or fiction; we are chiefly after *the demonstration* (whether by fact or fiction) that evidences could mislead.

The story is told of twelve brothers among whom one, Joseph, had been strongly resented against, because he had told his parents and brothers his dreams of becoming the greatest among them all. At an opportune time for them, his brothers caught him and thought of killing him. But the eldest suggested that Joseph should rather be kept in a dungeon, hoping to rescue him afterwards. But while this eldest brother, Reuben, was not there, the rest conspired again and sold Joseph away as slave to some foreign merchants in order that his dreams might not be fulfilled.

*Judah said to his brothers, "What will we gain if we kill our brother and cover up his blood? Come, let's sell him to the Ishmaelites and not lay our hands on him; after all, he is our brother, our own flesh and blood." His brothers agreed. So when the Midianite merchants came by, his brothers pulled Joseph up out of the cistern and sold him for twenty shekels of silver to the Ishmaelites, who took him to Egypt. When Reuben returned to the cistern and saw that Joseph was not there, he tore his clothes. He went back to his brothers and said, "The boy isn't there! Where can I turn now?" Then they got Joseph's robe, slaughtered a goat and dipped the robe in the blood. They took the ornamented robe back to their father and said, "**We found this.** Examine it to see whether it is your son's robe." He recognized it and said, "It is my son's robe! Some ferocious animal has devoured him. Joseph has **surely** been torn to pieces." Then Jacob tore his clothes, put on sackcloth and mourned for his son many days.*

(Genesis 37: 26 – 34)

As we see in the story, their father arrived at a "mentally sound" conclusion *based upon the evidences at his disposal* that a wild animal had killed his son. There is no "mentally sound" person in Jacob's situation that would not have arrived at the same conclusion. After all, his favourite son was not back at home and his brothers had brought home his torn clothes soaked in blood. Their voices were probably laden with mournful concern as they enquired from their father, *"is Joseph home and well? We found clothes that look so much like Joseph's and we brought them to verify. Where is he, please?"*. And the father had no other rational option than to conclude that a wild animal must have killed Joseph. *"Joseph"*, he said, *"is **without doubt** torn in pieces"*. The conclusion was "mentally sound" based upon

> *The Bible teaches that by mere mental reckoning of material evidences, it is impossible to fully know the nature and attributes of God*

evidences, but the conclusion was simply NOT the **TRUTH**. The truth was that Joseph had been sold to the Ishmaelite merchants, but the evidences in support of that were not within the reach of Jacob.

For evolutionists themselves, who find fossils, and study them carefully, and for the secularists who seemingly weigh the evidences that the evolutionists present, it is pathetic that as long as they base their judgments on the incomplete evidences, saying *"we have found these"*, they are prone to arrive at a *"without-doubt"* [nevertheless wrong] conclusion – just like Joseph's father.

Conclusively, the *yeast* of Herod, of which Jesus warned his disciples, could therefore be reckoned as the worldly mental wisdom similar to the kind that is secularly celebrated today. If God is indeed nonmaterial, it could be nothing but "foolish" to look for the primary evidences of God's existence among material evidences. The Bible teaches that by mere mental reckoning of material evidences, it is impossible to fully know the nature and attributes of God because God being Spirit can only be spiritually understood:

Where is the wise man? Where is the scholar? Where is the philosopher of this age? Has not God made foolish the wisdom of the world? For since in the wisdom of God the world through its wisdom did not know him . . .

(1 Corinthians 1: 20 – 21)

We do, however, speak a message of wisdom among the mature, but not the wisdom of this age or of the rulers of this age, who are coming to nothing. No, we speak of God's secret wisdom, a wisdom that has been hidden and that God destined for our glory before time began. None of the rulers of this age understood it, for if they had, they would not have crucified the Lord of glory. However, as it is written: "No eye has seen, no ear has heard, no mind has conceived what God has prepared for those who love him" **but God has revealed it to us by his Spirit.** *The Spirit searches all things, even the deep things of God. For who among men knows the thoughts of a man except the man's spirit within him? In the same way* **no one knows the thoughts of God except the Spirit of God.** *We have not received the spirit of the world but the Spirit who is from God, that we may understand what God has freely given us. This is what we speak, not in words taught us by human wisdom but in words taught by the Spirit, expressing spiritual truths in spiritual words. The man without the Spirit does not accept the things that come from the Spirit of God, for they are foolishness to him, and he cannot understand them, because* **they are spiritually discerned.** *The spiritual man makes judgments about all things, but he himself is not subject to any man's judgment.*

(1 Corinthians 2: 6 – 15)

This is the basic principle of the "narrow road Christianity" – that God is known by incorporeal perceptions; by *"inspiration"*; by comparing ethereal things with ethereal; by comparing prophecies and "things precisely known without bodily perception or mental adductions". Popular, "broad road Christianity" differs from this and so does the now widely state-sanctioned "evolution theory and science". But for those who sought to enter the kingdom of God, Jesus' primary warning was to beware of false [popular] Christianity; beware of those who preach blamelessness of mind, thought, speech and deeds; and beware of secular science-based atheism, which appears neutral and harmless but was originally against *"the birth of the Christ"*.

Here is the bottom-line: commonplace Christianity as well as secularism is outright anti-Christian, no more, no less.

Chapter Seven

BACKSLIDERS

"Some Are Already Turned Aside".

No one is lost, except the son of perdition.

Judas Iscariot is a name that is almost as widely known as Jesus. Though he was one of the closest people to Jesus, on one occasion Jesus referred to Judas as *"the son of perdition"*:

While I was with them in the world, I kept them in thy name: those that thou gavest me I have kept, and none of them is lost, but the son of perdition; that the scripture might be fulfilled.

(John 17: 12, King James Version)

What Judas did is typical of what many other people have since done – he had learnt about the "narrow road" religion that Jesus preached and had tasted it, but decided to "decamp".

Between religions, people decamp endlessly. In any given year, many Muslims become Christians, while many Christians also become Muslims. Christians become Buddhists and Hindus, and *vice versa*. There is probably no religion on earth to which Christians have not "decamped". Likewise, Christianity has gained converts from probably all religions, including so-called "New Age" religions. When a person quits Christianity and joins any other religion or even Atheism, the remaining Christians label such a person "backslider". According to the Bible, Judas was the first major "backslider", in that among the many followers of Jesus that deserted Jesus' teachings, he was the closest to

Jesus and a key officer [the treasurer] among Jesus' closest twelve disciples. Perhaps that is why Jesus called him *"the son of perdition"*.

However, as sceptics, when we consider whatever a religion has to offer, we must also consider why it failed to satisfy those who decamped from it. If Judas had been with Jesus all through Jesus' public ministry; had imbibed all his public and private lessons about God and eternity; and had been sent out as an evangelist together with the other eleven, what good reasons did he have to turn back from Jesus?

The writers of the Christian scriptures did not offer us in Judas' own words his reason for turning away from Jesus. We are only told that he sold Jesus to the priestly prosecutors for *"thirty coins of silver"*. [Matthew 26: 15]. Whether the recorded price at which Jesus was "sold" is the **literal** price or the **proverbial** price, it was far less than Jesus' normal worth; because *"thirty silver coins"* used to be a compensatory price, recommended in the Torah, in regard of wounded slaves. [Exodus 21: 32]. If he were really after making money, Judas should have taken far much more money than he reportedly took. Therefore, Judas, though possibly enticed by the "compensatory price" paid to him for betraying Jesus, must have had some other motivation besides the money. Moreover, he *"kept the purse"* for the thirteen [Jesus and the twelve] and probably had been pilfering from it (as the other apostles alleged) under the pretext of spending on the poor.

> *But one of his disciples, Judas Iscariot, who was later to betray him, objected, 'Why wasn't this perfume sold and the money given to the poor? It was worth a year's wages." He did not say this because he cared about the poor but because he was a thief; as keeper of the money bag, he used to help himself to what was put into it.*
>
> (John 12: 4 – 6)

A worthless sum of money.

Thirty pieces of silver was just about a hundred and twenty pence, while (according to this passage) Judas suggested that the perfumed ointment that Mary had "wasted" on Jesus could rather have been sold for three hundred pence and perhaps put into his care in trust for the poor. It could be reasoned that if the amount quoted as the price for which Judas betrayed Jesus is the literal value; it might have been quite small compared to what he had managed while in charge of the common purse. [He did not consider three hundred pounds an amount too big for him to give out to the poor]. And if the recorded price at which Jesus was sold were proverbial, it was after all still counted for a worthless sum by the other apostles. Moreover, they were not a poverty-stricken group. They probably did not live in luxury, but neither were they so impoverished. Although, they had given up their daily businesses, yet their daily needs were invariably met and they probably had some change in the purse, which Judas managed for buying occasional necessities and giving to the poor as well.

At "the last supper", Jesus had told Judas *"what you have to do, do quickly"* and the rest of the disciples had thought he was sending Judas to buy things or give out to the poor. If these were unusual practices, they should not have thought so.

Since Judas had charge of the money, some thought Jesus was telling him to buy what was needed for the Feast, or to give something to the poor.

(John 13: 29)

Jesus and the twelve were not eating miracle loaves everyday. Whenever they went on evangelistic missions, it was probably typical for them to receive "freewill gifts and helps" from those to whom they had rendered "spiritual services", and enough of such that they literarily "lacked nothing":

Then Jesus asked them, "When I sent you without purse, bag or sandals, did you lack anything?" "Nothing," they answered.

(Luke 22: 35)

Moreover, Jesus himself went through the cities and villages, together with the twelve, and "received gifts" from the people to whom he rendered "spiritual service" (Luke 8: 1 – 3). In fact, he taught the apostles (by example) to make their living from preaching the gospel [1 Corinthians 9: 14]. Therefore, Judas' primary motivation for betraying Jesus might not have been the "worthless money" paid to him in return. He perhaps could have had the opportunity to pilfer twice that much over the coming year if he did not betray Jesus. Something fundamental must have changed in Judas' value system for him to exchange Jesus for "a worthless sum".

When Judas gave away Jesus, he was not giving off only Jesus but everything that Jesus meant including the "new doctrine" about the "kingdom of heaven" and "worshipping in the spirit". After all, Judas was among the twelve when they had earlier declared (in view of the eternal-life factor) an unflinching support for Jesus at a time that most of the other disciples had departed.

From this time many of his disciples turned back and no longer followed him. "You do not want to leave too, do you?" Jesus asked the twelve. Simon Peter answered him, "Lord, to whom shall we go? You have the words of eternal life. We believe and know that you are the Holy One of God."

(John 6: 66 – 69)

Why did Judas stop believing in Jesus?

"Eternal life is worth more than all the riches of the whole world", Jesus had taught them, [Mark 8: 36]. Therefore, for Judas to sell off Jesus for any sum at all, he must have stopped believing in Jesus, or perhaps he really never believed him. While Peter spoke on behalf of the twelve that they *"believe and are* **sure***"* that Jesus was the Christ and Son of God, Judas did not object; which implies that he was either consenting to Peter's declaration or just hanging on in order to keep his job of managing the purse. Even Thomas Didymus, who often sought for proofs before believing most things, did not object to Peter's statement. But it appears unlikely that Judas never believed in Jesus because he probably did not become Jesus' disciple simply because of the treasurer job. "The twelve" were chosen from among a larger number of disciples:

When morning came, he called his disciples to him and **chose twelve of them**, *whom he also designated apostles:*

(Luke 6: 13)

It may therefore be reasoned that Judas must have been an ordinary "follower of Jesus", numbered among those who believed in Jesus' teachings and claims, **before** he was chosen together with the twelve and among them again chosen to be the treasurer. It is unlikely for him to have become a Jesus' follower simply with a view to becoming the treasurer – a position that was probably not available at the time that Judas became Jesus' disciple. Judas could therefore not have always disbelieved Jesus. He only must have changed. But why, what good reasons made Judas change his mind about Jesus and about the worth of eternal life, and about the Jesus' claim to Christhood? More importantly, if a person who saw Jesus face to face, lived with him for several years, was an eyewitness to his teachings and miracles, and believed in his Christhood, turned away from all these and gave him up at *"the price of a redundant slave"*, why should we who live two thousand years away believe in Jesus?

We shall chew these questions again, but let us first consider another important "backslider" who decamped from the form of worship that Jesus advocated.

Demas has forsaken me.

Demas was a dedicated associate of Paul the apostle [Philemon 1: 24], although not much is written in the Bible about him. But Paul reported that Demas *"abandoned"* him because of the *"love of this temporal world"*.

> *For Demas, because he loved this world, has deserted me and has gone to Thessalonica . . .*
>
> (2 Timothy 4: 10)

Paul himself was committed to the doctrines of Jesus, and Demas too should have been while he remained Paul's associate. But Paul lived a more strenuous life than most of the other apostles; in fact (according to the Bible), at several instances, he personally declined several apostolic benefits including the right to make a living from preaching the gospel.

> *If we have sown spiritual seed among you, is it too much if we reap a material harvest from you? If others have this right of support from you, shouldn't we have it all the more? But we did not use this right. On the contrary, we put up with anything rather than hinder the gospel of Christ.*
>
> (1 Corinthians 9: 11 – 12)

Paul confidently boasted of being often poor and suffering [2 Corinthians 12: 22 – 33]. However, the typical apostolic life was not so much rosier than Paul's was. Jesus had taught them to be content once their basic needs (food for subsistence and clothing *to cover nakedness*) were met, [Matthew 5 – Matthew 7], and they probably lived up to his charge and example. Indeed, what they "earned" in gifts and offerings were probably over and above what they could have earned by practising their former pre-apostolic occupations, yet the apostles lived below the comfort they would normally have enjoyed without the "huge apostolic incomes" because they were compelled by the doctrines of Jesus to "*lay up treasures in heaven*" rather than on earth.

> *Sell your possessions and give to the poor. Provide purses for yourself that will not wear out, a treasure in heaven that will not be exhausted, where no thief comes near and no moth destroys. For where your treasure is, there your heart will be also.*

> (Luke 12: 33 – 34)

The higher apostolic income, which should have otherwise been an advantage, apparently became a disadvantage in effect, because of "*laying up treasures in heaven*". Paul most probably braced up to the multiple disadvantages of apostolic missionary life and Demas too might have endured together with Paul until he broke off from Paul to pursue the "*love of this temporal world*". But we consider the fact that the authorship of almost half the entire Christian part of the Bible is attributed to Paul, who is also reputed to have performed "*special miracles*" in the name of Jesus [Acts 19: 11]. And we wonder that if Demas, who lived with Paul, and as a probable eyewitness of his miracles, could "decamp" from the original Christianity that Paul preached, why must we embrace it? What were Demas' good reasons for preferring the "*love of this temporal world*"?

If any man loves the world, he does not love God.

Judas and Demas were the first generation of "true Christians" who decamped. For both of them, the reason that the Bible submits is that they returned their preferences towards material profits as against the spiritual profits that Jesus preached. It would have been nice, though, if we have their versions of the story – especially that of Judas who is alleged to have pilfered money from the common purse. Nevertheless, if Judas' method of stealing money from the purse (as alleged) is by guise of gifts to the poor [John 12: 6], then it is probable that the thirteen lived as considerably a self-denying life as Paul lived. If they had spent their increased incomes towards their personal gratifications as freely as they received it, then Judas would not have needed to "pilfer" under guise, he would have had more than enough. As a group, they probably earned a high income from preaching the gospel, but they must have lived far below the standard that they would normally have enjoyed without this income. In fact, the apostles lamented that they *"left all"* in order to live the Jesus-kind-of-life (in pursuit of spiritual profits) and they **"lost"** what otherwise would have been gain to them. The apostles said to Jesus *"****we have left all we had****, to follow you."* (Luke 18: 28).

*But whatever was to my profit I now consider loss for the sake of Christ. What is more, I consider everything a loss compared to the surpassing greatness of knowing Christ Jesus my Lord, **for whose sake I have lost all things**. I consider them rubbish, that I may gain Christ.*

(Philippians 3: 7 – 8)

Judas too probably left all that he had in order to live the Jesus-kind-of-life. However, he afterwards returned to the love of those things. But the Jesus-kind-of-life was in accordance with the fundamental principle of Jesus' teaching as well as that of the *"Torah and the Prophets"*. And the principle was that in man, there is a nonmaterial *"breath of God"*, which like God shall exist forever, even after the death of the animal human. Consequently, if God truly exists, and as a nonmaterial being, to whom our inner nonmaterial natures shall return at death (as *the Torah and the Prophets* taught), then the Jesus-kind-of-life (of placing more value on spiritual profits rather than material profits) has great merit and rationality. If the philosophy underlying the Jesus-kind-of-life is therefore perfectly justifiable in accordance with the principles already given in *the Torah and the Prophets*, then his warning to the disciples to desist from the love of money could not be less justifiable. He had taught them that they could not love spiritual profits and material profits at once.

"No servant can serve two masters. Either he will hate the one and love the other, or he will be devoted to the one and despise the other. You cannot serve both God and Money.

(Luke 16: 13)

The charge to love spiritual profits against material profits was also passed on by the other apostles who did not decamp.

Do not love the world or anything in the world. If anyone loves the world, the love of the Father is not in him.

(1 John 2: 15)

But in the end, Judas, Demas and the likes, decided that in spite of all these injunctions, they had good enough reasons to quit. As no one but a person who had travelled on a particular road is better able to dissuade another from following the same road, we can only reckon that the backsliders send us a strong signal that they were not perfectly satisfied by following Jesus. However, in all fairness, we can only consider the philosophy underlying the Jesus-kind-of-life to be perfectly agreeable with belief in infinity, eternality and God's existence. To have turned back, for whatever reason, from the Jesus-kind-of-life consequently implies denial of God's existence, denial of the reality of infinity and denial of the reality of incorporeal consciousnesses. But as we have earlier observed that infinity is real; that unless God exists, the universe could not have originated; and that in many instances humans have demonstrated knowledge acquired by incorporeal perceptions, we might better decide that the backsliders are at fault in this matter. They probably erred.

Let him that stands take heed lest he falls.

Whenever a major Christian, especially a leader, boldly decamps [or, "backslides", if you prefer], people pay some keen attention. In fact, such persons may be invited to give press briefings, which undermine the faith of several other people.

> *Their teachings will spread like gangrene . . . who have wandered away from the truth . . .*
>
> (2 Timothy 2: 17 – 18)

As a precaution against falling into the errors of the backsliders, the simple advice that Paul the apostle gave in the Bible is *"being careful"*, keeping watch against the possibility of drifting into error.

> *So, if you think you are standing firm, be careful that you don't fall!.*
>
> (1 Corinthians 10: 12)

Inasmuch as Eve probably fell to Satan's ploy in the Garden of Eden (as earlier discussed) just by not retracting her focus early enough from the fruits of the tree from which she had been commanded not to eat, it is not impossible that the reason Judas and Demas, and their bedfellows, quit Christianity is because they failed to retract their tempted focuses early enough from material profits. From typical examples, we observe that however strongly a person determines to despise anything, as long as one keeps focusing on that thing, one is prone to yield it.

> *But godliness with contentment is great gain. For we brought nothing into the world, and we can take nothing out of it. But if we have food and clothing, we will be content with that. People who want to get rich fall into foolish temptation and a trap and into many foolish and harmful desires that plunge men into ruin and destruction. For the love of money is a* **root of all kinds of evil***. Some people,* **eager for money, have wandered from the faith** *and pierced themselves with many griefs.*

(1 Timothy 6: 6 – 10)

The deceitfulness of riches.

For Judas and Demas, this was probably the case; they might indeed have originally desired to keep the doctrines of Jesus as demonstrated by the sacrifices they had made at the onset of their commitments to Christianity. But once they underrated the deceitfulness of material profits [Mark 4: 19], and thereby failed to control their focus from wandering away from spiritual profits, an eventual decamp from the "narrow road" Christianity was inevitable. It is an unequivocal Christian principle that focusing on material gain leads away from spiritual gain, and focusing begins with nurturing a single thought. According to the Bible, it is difficult and uncommon for a person to be at once wealthy and also remain faithful to the Christian doctrines. But where possessing wealth becomes deceitful is that it appears at first sight to be compatible with the Christian faith, whereas Christians that receive high incomes from their own labours and trade or from bequests are by Christian principles charged to reckon themselves as holding such incomes in trust for the entire Christendom and humanity at large.

It is in practise hard to have toiled, studied much, laboured strenuously and by dints of one's hard work and genius amassed a small fortune only to be compelled thereafter by religious reasons to reckon oneself as not the real owner of one's properties and incomes. The fact is, when you get your salary at the end of the week/month; when you get your shares' dividends; when your business flourishes and you make a huge profit; or when as a church leader someone walks up to you and says – *"Pastor, here is a cheque for you as a person, I have already drawn another cheque for the church account"*, you have the feeling that these are your rightful incomes. Moreover, the "broad way" Christianity teaches that *"ten percent of all your incomes are God's and the rest is yours, feel free and enjoy it as you wish"*. However, the "narrow road" Christianity that Jesus taught would say, *"thank you for all your hard work, commitment and faithfulness, but ten percent of all your incomes are God's as well as the ninety percent besides. Take care of your necessities (not wants, but needs) and use the rest as God further directs, because all your incomes are entirely God's, not yours!"* Then, you would certainly wonder why you have to strenuously belabour yourself only to gain a high income that you cannot use as you please, and must render for the benefit of even those that have not laboured as strenuously as you have. How shall it go down well with you? How did it go down well with Paul, but not Demas? They preached and got gifts – probably more incomes from gifts than they would have gained from the practising their own trades – but Paul reckoned that in view of spiritual and eternal profits, he had to *"share with people who are in need, practise hospitality, mind not high things and condescend to a man of low estate"*. (Roman 12: 13 – 16).

Perhaps all that sacrifice was too much for Demas who may have began to wonder why he should go to that extent – to reckon, *"Well, because God is the one who gives me the strength and intellect with which I get my incomes, God is consequently the rightful owner of all my money and properties, and I am only holding them in trust for Him and for His people. I have only gathered all these together just so I can disburse it to meet the needs of humankind – God's offspring."* Whereas it looks so easy at first sight, and almost everyone would pray, *"God make me a millionaire and see what I would do for you"*, in all likelihood most persons would spend more than a quarter or a half of the million on his or her own affairs. But suppose one considers it in the light of the "narrow road' Christianity that he or she has only been employed by God to gather the million together in trust for the rest of humanity – (not for one's immediate neighbours, but for the entire human race – all the six and half billion individuals on earth), shall one be able to spend up to a quarter of the million on one's own personal delights? And if one is thus limited from freely spending one's income as one wishes, but as God directs, shall one still find delight in strenuously working to earn more only to spend more on alleviating the sufferings of other people?

You may say to yourself, "My power and the strength of my hands have produced this wealth for me." But remember the LORD your God, for it is he who gives you the ability to produce wealth . . .

(Deuteronomy 8: 17 – 18)

The earth is the LORD's, and everything in it, the world, and all who live in it.

(Psalm 24: 1)

At times we wonder how Judas Iscariot was expected to contain himself if after abandoning all his personal belongings to become a disciple of Jesus he is entrusted with greater wealth than he abandoned and yet enjoined to "condescend to low estate" even to the extent of spending his own rightful incomes on the poor rather than freely spend them. In fact, not only Judas and Demas but so many other disciples of Jesus at that time, and from then till now, have found it too hard to reckon their rightful incomes as belonging hundred percent to God, and if to God, then to the entire human race being God's offspring.

They go away sad and disappointed.

In the Bible, the story is told about a man who came to Jesus and wished to follow the "narrow road" religion that Jesus preached:

A certain ruler asked him, "Good teacher, what must I do to inherit eternal life?" "Why do you call me good?" Jesus answered. "No one is good — except God alone. You know the commandments: 'Do not commit adultery, do not murder, do not steal, do not give false testimony, honor your father and mother.'" "All these I have kept since I was a boy," he said. When Jesus heard this, he said to him, "You still lack one thing. Sell everything you have and give to the poor, and you will have treasure in heaven. Then come, follow me." When he heard this, he became very sad, because he was a man of great wealth. Jesus looked at him and said, "How hard it is for the rich to enter the kingdom of God!" Indeed, it is easier for a camel to go through the eye of a needle than for a rich man to enter the kingdom of God."

(Luke 18: 18 – 25)

Probably, if on that day Jesus had told the man to sell ten percent of all his possessions and give to the poor, the man might well have jumped at it. Probably, if Jesus had said, "*sell **half** of all your possessions, give that to the poor and keep the rest*", the man might well have considered it. Perhaps, if Jesus had said, "*give away three-quarter and retain one-quarter*", the man could have taken his time over the calculations and returned a positive answer eventually. But Jesus asked him to give away **everything** – one hundred percent. And there is where the "narrow road" Christianity is often deserted by many people. When they reach this level of understanding in the faith, most Christians have just two options to choose from – either quit Christianity entirely or go for the "broad way" Christianity, which endorses *"ten percent for God, the rest is yours"*.

Indeed, not many people can maintain the "hundred-percent-for-God" kind of faith that Jesus taught. Many people go into Christianity not knowing about the hundred-percent requirement, often because the louder, and more popular, but false form of Christianity teaches that *"it is only ten percent of your incomes that God requires"*. Consequently, many people embrace Christianity with an under-estimate of the requirements of the faith. That is why Jesus had also warned that anyone who would follow his teachings should first *"sit down and count the cost"*. (Luke 14: 25 – 30). Of course, most so-called Christians jump into Christianity without first counting the cost. Possibly Judas and Demas did not. And possibly most "backsliders" since then prepare for the "ten-percentile Christianity", not knowing that the full extent of what is required.

The argument remains open for whoever wants to pursue it further in defence of the "backsliders" in order to conclude whether or not they are at fault. But one fact is certain and most important, backslidden Christians are anti-Christian, just as much as secularists and those who practise the popular denominational ten-percentile Christianity that advocates *"righteousness of mind, thought, speech and actions"* rather than righteousness of the inner [spirit] person.

> *Dear children, this is the last hour; and as you have heard that the antichrist is coming, even now many antichrists have come. This is how we know it is the last hour. They went out from us, but they did not really belong to us. For if they had belonged to us, they would have remained with us; but their going showed that none of them belonged to us.*
>
> (1 John 2: 18 – 19)

The backslidden Christians can only lead one away from the Jesus kind of life, which advocates that God being Spirit must be worshipped in spirit, not just in the mind, speech and actions. Backslidden Christians wage war (on Satan's side) against true Christianity.

Chapter Eight

THE WAGES OF SIN

"You shall surely die".

What is man?

Homo sapiens **perennially ponder at** questions regarding the nature of the entire universe while in fact we have not all reached a common idea of what humankind is, in the absolute sense.

However, one thing a man could always do without remorse is to throw his arms around the necks of *"Cousins Chimpanzee and Gorilla"* and acknowledge that humankind also is an animal. But why humankind unlike its primate cousins must be mindful of God, or rather why God must be mindful of humankind, among all terrestrial life is quite baffling for the ordinary animal human mind.

The Bible tells us how God gave laws to the Jews at Mount Horeb but it does not tell us when God gave laws to chimpanzees and gorillas.

As animals, our animal minds crave for the apish things that monkeys do. We want to eat the most palatable foods, watch the most pleasant scenes, and sleep with the most attractive mates we find. And when we look at *"our wild cousins"*, many of us wish we are as wild as they are – bullying off every competitor and mapping out "territories" for ourselves that our "rivals" must not step into without paying due homage to us. Interestingly, when we look at the anatomy and physiology of chimpanzees and gorillas, their life cycles, and their "societies", we simply muse over the fact that *"man too is monkey"*. [Ecclesiastes 3: 18]. But the other fact that we cannot just muse over is our sense morals and religiousness, which the wild apes do not have.

When male mountain gorillas are about fourteens years old, they are delighted to discover that they have reached *"the mating age"*. Nature teaches them so by changing the colour of their furry back. The fourteen-year-old *"silver back"* (as "he" might now be called) must now be the head of the family, the one that "boastfully" defends the group, and leads them in search of daily food, in other words, *"the bread winner"*. But then, he does something that his *"tame cousin"* would not normally do – he kills the older, weaker males and their young offspring, and then sleeps with all the matured females in the "family", siring new young ones of his own to replace the ones he killed!

Many of us have not been in the wild forests to study gorillas and chimpanzees but we at least believe the report of the researchers among us who have been to the forests to study gorillas. While believing that we are "apes" as much as our wild cousins are, some humans have argued that it is proper for one to have as many sex partners as one wish. But there is an issue about the gorillas' sex life, which even those who advocate for the apish "sexual liberty" would find repulsive. How would the human society take it, if a young man kills his immediate elder brother with the all the children, and then marries his brothers' wife – the mother of the slain children? How would the woman herself take it? Just imagine that you are a man who travelled abroad for two years and come back to discover that all your children have been killed by your own immediate younger brother, who has claimed all your possessions and your wife and even fathered a child by her, then on sighting you, the only thing he could think of is killing you. How much do you wish that happens? But it is just the **normal** life of the mountain gorilla – one kills his brothers and their children, takes their wives, and **does not feel bad** about it, so long as one is a gorilla. However, humankind feels bad about it. What is humankind? Is humankind just a moral gorilla or a tame chimpanzee?

Just as toddlers say to the "twinkle, twinkle stars", we might well say to one another *"how I wonder what you are!"*. This is not just because humankind has the sense of morals, but also because humankind lives longer than **most** other animals and yet a hundred-and-twenty-year-old man still wants to stick around. But one other thing we can say to one another is *"you will surely die!"*. This very statement, with its particular emphasis on the certainty of death reminds us of the biblical story of the Garden of Eden. Whether we believe the Garden of Eden story or not, we have at least a "quotable quote" to pick from it – *"you will surely die, for dust you are, and to dust you will return"*. [Genesis 2: 17, Genesis 3: 19].

No one dies twice – everyone dies just once. The life of a human being ceases at death. The lungs stop breathing. The heart stops beating. The limbs no longer move. The body warmth is gone. There is no more auto-activity. The body is flogged but the dead man feels no pain, in fact, he is not aware that he is being flogged. He is not aware of anything; not even of the fact that he is dead.

For the living know that they will die, but the dead know nothing; they have no further reward, and even the memory of them is forgotten. Their love, their hate and their jealousy have long since vanished; never again will they have a part in anything that happens under the sun. Go, eat your food with gladness, and drink your wine with a joyful heart, for it is now that God favors what you do. Always be clothed in white, and always anoint your head with oil. Enjoy life with your wife, whom you love, all the days of this meaningless life that God has given you under the sun – all your meaningless days. For this is your lot in life and your toilsome labor under the sun. Whatever your hands finds to do, do it with all your might, for in the grave, where you are going, there is neither working nor planning, nor knowledge nor wisdom.

(Ecclesiastes 9: 5 – 10)

Everyone will surely die – death will come by any means; a gunshot, a bomb blast, an auto crash, a heart attack, a domestic accident, suffocation in the subway, drowning, earthquake – no one really knows precisely when and what his or her own would be. Do you know yours? When, where and how? No one really knows. But we are all certain it will be. And then, when it happens, your relatives and friends (if they are aware of your death) would mourn for you who cannot mourn for yourself. They would miss you, but you would not miss them, because while they remain conscious you no longer are. And then if there is a commendation service, the parish priest comes around and tries as professionally as he could to make people reflect, feel some pain, some sympathy, some guilt, and some comfort. However, he (perhaps unwittingly) would have given the Joneses a point to debate for the rest of the evening – existence after death.

What happens to a man's mind after death?

The religions have all sorts of ideas (rational and otherwise) among

177

them about what happens to a human soul [so-called] after death. Some tell us that when a human being dies, the "consciousness" would be reincarnated in another body, which may or may not be a human body. Some others tell us that the "consciousness" would go into a place where it would be temporarily tormented and then accepted into God's heaven. And yet some others tell us *"nothing happens to the consciousness; it is gone and gone forever"*.

Indeed, when we look at humankind and consider the fact that the **mental** consciousness of a human being is seated in the brain, we reason that when the human dies physically, and the brain dies too, and so should the mental consciousness that is rooted in the brain. Certainly, a man's thoughts and his awareness of things around him cannot exist outside of his brain and therefore, a man's mental consciousness should go nowhere at death. In fact, we should consider that once a human dies, the **mental** consciousness **ceases to exist**; the mind (being a function of the brain), and all the information and experience treasured in it, is consequently lost. So, when we speak in terms of the animal called man who is in fact just an ordinary [living] body, death is the terminal end of existence; the **animal** called humankind does not exist as a conscious being after death. A human dies as an animal dies and there is **no difference** between the ordinary **mental** consciousnesses of humankind and that of all other animals.

Man's fate is like that of the animals; the same fate awaits them both: As one dies, so dies the other. All have the same breath; man has no advantage over the animal. Everything is meaningless. All go to the same place; and all come from the dust, and to dust all return.

(Ecclesiastes 3: 19 – 20)

As the heartbeat is a physiological characteristic of the heart, so are awareness, memory and thought physiological characteristics of the brain. When a woman dies, one does not ask where her heartbeat has gone because the heartbeat goes nowhere, it simply ceases. Likewise is the mental consciousness, the ideas, the knowledge, the experience, the awareness, the attitude, and every vital function and attribute of the brain; they do not go anywhere, they just cease. Unless humankind has a latent nonmaterial nature, there is nothing at all to consider about human existence after death. And since no one has died for, say, some ten months to come back and tell us what obtains beyond here, not *ALL* of us can be **sure** that there is a latent nature in humankind that survives death. But what we can all be **sure** of is that the material world does have a nonmaterial Creator; for even atheistic evolutionists believe that the material world had an origin and an origin implies an *Originator*, as a matter of course and causes.

Evolutionists believe that the material world originated from "absolute nothing" and yet they know that absolute nothing could not have produced anything at a particular point within *"an infinity of time"*, unless there was an energy that was capable of decisions, with the power and wisdom to spool matter out of absolute nothing. That *"nonmaterial energy"* (that decided to build such a vast material world from empty and void spheres and circles) whether the eternal energy is a *Thing* [if it is right to call *Him* "thing"] or a *Person*, is the *Originator*, whose eternal existence and immortality we cannot rationally deny. What we can also be **sure** of is that humankind takes interest in discovering and perhaps also relating with that nonmaterial *Originator*, and many of us testify that the *Originator/ Creator* himself takes interest in humankind, among the many millions of animal and plant species that live on earth.

When I consider your heavens, the work of your fingers, the moon and the stars, which you have set in place, what is man that you are mindful of him, the son of man that you care for him?

(Psalms 8: 3 – 4)

Why does God care about humankind?

When the gorilla kills all its brothers, nephews and nieces and marries its sisters-in-law, religion does not tell us that God cares. But when man does the same, the human conscience does not agree, the society feels strongly irritated, and most of all, the *Creator* of the world is displeased, (as religions tell us). Nevertheless, a single human is just too insignificant in size compared to the entire universe. So much smaller than a two-millimetre ant in comparison with the Pacific Ocean, is a man in comparison with the entire universe. Consequently, it does not make sense at all to the ordinary human mind that the *Creator* of such a magnificent universe should care about humans – very insignificant humans.

However, humankind seeks the *Creator* and the *Creator* seemingly seeks humankind, at least by "transmitting" prophecies, trances, dreams and visions, into human minds such that a man could know several future events without the using his animal senses to work at knowing such events; and these happens often more than not to those who seek after the *Creator*. The mutual interest in one another between humankind and the *Creator* most probably corroborates the biblical belief that the *Creator* (himself being "*Breath*") **nested** his "*breath*" into the animal human in the beginning.

A nest is very important to the bird. The tree upon which the nest rests is most special among a billion others to the bird. Not unless the animal human is indeed the "nest" of "*that which is born of the Spirit (Creator)*", the *Creator* should not take any particular interest in the animal human among humankind's "wild cousins", [so-called]. But if the author of Genesis is right about humankind being the "*image and likeness of God (the Creator)*", and if the author is right about the rest of the Garden of Eden episode, then humankind must indeed have an inward "*irresponsive spirit*", a "*spirit corpse*" that has lost its "*aliveness*". The question is, "*can we be* **sure** *that the author of Genesis is right about the statement that man is the image and likeness of God?*"

Let the dead bury their dead.

Coma is a taste of death. The comatose person does not know that he is comatose. But if he is fortunate to be recovered from that state and comes alive again, he learns that he had been in coma and recognises other people that are yet in coma who themselves cannot know that they are in coma. In this wise, we should consider that we could prove whether the author of Genesis is right or wrong about the "*death*" of the "inner" man, if by any means we can experience "*spiritual aliveness*".

If we are in spiritual coma, our best bet at proving whether there is indeed anything like "*spiritual coma*" is to gain spiritual aliveness. This is another basic principle of Christianity. Jesus upheld that those who can be **sure** that one had been spiritually dead are those who "*have passed from [spiritual] death to [spiritual] life*". This principle appears rational considering the fact that it is not the dead but the living that knows what death is. The bodily dead know nothing because the organ [brain] by which they know things is dead.

On one occasion, Jesus invited a man to be his disciple. But the man asked for permission to first go and bury his father. Jesus' answer was typical of his principle about spiritual aliveness; he told the man to leave the burial for "*the dead*" to perform.

He said to another man, "Follow me." But the man replied, "Lord, first let me to go and bury my father." Jesus said to him, "Let the dead bury their own dead: but you go and proclaim the kingdom of God."

(Luke 9: 59 – 60).

Of course, we know that a physically dead man cannot bury another physically dead man. If *"the dead"* that Jesus said should *"bury their own dead"* were still capable of performing the burial ceremonies, then they were not physically dead. And indeed it is only those who are physically alive that could bury the physically dead. But Jesus called those men *"dead"* that should perform the burial of that man's father probably because they were reckoned spiritually dead.

For our mental [animal] consciousness, there is little that we can comprehend about the spiritual world. Usually, our animal minds regard etherealities as though there are no such things, because we are naturally ***"dead"*** to the ethereal world. Even when by thorough examination of the rudiments of life we come to recognise that incorporeal consciousnesses exists, our animal minds still do not **understand** the specific attributes of spirit beings. However, those who testify of having passed from the natural spiritual stupor into spiritual vigour would have us believe that consciousness is **not** the **only** attribute of spirits. We are told that spirits have distinct forms in their own *"realities"*. But such *"spirit forms"* remain incomprehensible and meaningless to the ordinary animal mind of humankind because we reckon that if a thing is spiritual, then it cannot have a distinct body or form. Yet we also know that without a distinct corporeal form (however tiny), nothing in the material world can have a consciousness. But in an interactive manner, some of us acquire precise knowledge in our corporeal minds of future or concurrent events without the use of our corporeal senses; and this proves that there probably are *"incorporeal consciousnesses"* in existence that we can relate with and that are capable of *"inspiring"* our corporeal minds. We find, however, that one *"inspiration"* [of the prophets, for instance] conflicts with another *"inspiration"* [of the sorcerers, also for instance]. And therefore we reckon that if *spirit beings* are the ones that feed our mental minds with these inspirations, then the ethereal beings must be distinct persons, each with his own distinct form or *"nonmaterial body"*, because it is usual that minds must be functions of "bodies" just as our animal minds are functions of our brains. But the term *"nonmaterial body"* is unintelligible to our brains.

*All flesh is not the same: Men have one kind of flesh, animals have another, birds another and fish another. **There are also heavenly bodies** and there are earthly bodies; but the splendor of the heavenly bodies is one kind, and the splendor of the earthly bodies is another. The sun has one kind of splendor, the moon another and the stars another; and star differs from star in splendor. So will it be with the resurrection of the dead. The body that is sown is perishable, it is raised imperishable. It is sown in dishonor, it is raised in glory; it is sown in weakness, it is raised in power; it is sown a **natural body**, it is raised a **spiritual body**.*

(1 Corinthians 15: 39 – 44)

The spiritual body.

While indeed our brains might not comprehend the idea of a *"spiritual [nonmaterial] body"*, it does approach the fact that the evolutionists' Big Bang theory tells us that at first, there was absolutely no material particle at all in the entire material universe, and yet the entire material world came into existence. And by the Big Bang theory, we further know that some [*"nonmaterial"*] energy must have been used to originate the material world. As every sort of energy must have "a source" in which it is inherent or from which it originates, we reckon that the *"nonmaterial energy"* that produced the first iota of material substance in the universe must have been inherent in a *"nonmaterial substance"*. The borrowed word is "substance" because it is associated with materiality whereas we wish to describe a nonmaterial **phenomenon.**

Summarily, therefore, we can say that as much as the scientists among us can only **reckon** (rationally) that protons and electrons of atoms of material substances exist, without being able to give an accurate description of the structures and components of these *"invisible"* sub-particles of material elements, *"nonmaterial substances"* can also be **reckoned** but not described. We know (rationally) that they exist, and can prove (from their actions) that they exist, but they are simply *"indescribable"* relative to our material world. We compare them to breath, wind, light – whatever is distinctly recognisable but intangible yet all these comparisons are material and CANNOT perfectly describe a spirit.

However, existence after death is reckoned upon the basis of the "spiritual [nonmaterial] body" and not the animal body. Christians believe in existence after death upon the basis that the replica of the *Creator's "nonmaterial form"* was *"breathed"* into the animal called man. This distinct *"nonmaterial entity"* (regarded as *"the inner man"*) is believed to remain of a human even when the material entity of the person is dead and decayed. Debates about existence after death are all about whether this *"inner [spirit] man"* really exists and what happens to it after the death of the *"outer [animal] man"*. And when religionists talk about where a man's consciousness [or, soul] goes after death, they seek to talk in regard of the *"inner man"* rather than the *"outer man"*.

How are the dead raised?

*But someone may ask, "**How are the dead raised? With what kind of body will they come?**" How foolish! What you sow now does not come to life unless it dies. When you sow, you do not plant the body that will be, but just a seed, perhaps of wheat or of something else. But God gives it a body as he has determined, and to each kind of seed he gives its own body. All flesh is not the same: Men have one kind of flesh, animals have another, birds another and fish another. **There are also heavenly bodies** and there are earthly bodies; but the splendor of the heavenly bodies is one kind, and the splendor of the earthly bodies is another.*

(1 Corinthians 15: 35 – 40)

Usually, the material body of a human corpse is buried, cremated, or by any other means prevented from decomposing openly such that the corpse does not detrimentally affect the health and comfort of the society. Although religious beliefs play large roles in deciding the manner by which corpses are done away with, yet the health and comfort of the living is also an important consideration. However, some people are neither buried nor cremated, their entire bodies simply become "irrevocable" as for instance those that are killed and eaten by wild animals, whose remains are not found.

In 2001, some geologists working the mangrove forests of the Nigerian petroleum-rich Niger Delta captured a large snake whose belly was swollen towards its head parts. When they had taken the snake out of the forest and electrocuted it, they found that what it had swallowed was a grown-up man. For the little I know about snakes, I would not know how the snake could have managed (had it not been killed) to digest its six-foot-tall several-pounds prey together with the singlet and boxer shorts. But what I know is that if the snake had not been found, that man's corpse would not have been extracted from its belly for burial.

If it had happened fifty years ago, that a lioness had pounced on a man and had torn him apart to feed her cubs and the rest of the pride. The flesh, blood and brains of the slain man would have been absorbed to nourish the body of the lions. It is in fact possible that the lions were subsequently captured and taken into zoological gardens in separate countries. The lions themselves would die not too long after, and their decayed carcasses would have been absorbed by the roots of some plants, say a mahogany tree. It is possible that through a long "food chain", some phosphorous and nitrogen samples from the body of the man that a lioness killed fifty years ago have somehow found their way into the wooden desk of your office table. However, when we consider the Bible doctrine on existence after death, we find that it implies a resurrection [returning to life] of humans for eternal existence, and we are curious to find out how such a man that was killed by the lioness (and have become part of desks in many different locations) would be raised. If the Christian idea of resurrection holds true, how would such people whose bodies have been eaten, digested and defecated by wild animals be raised back to life?

"Do not be amazed at this, for a time is coming when all who are in their graves will hear his voice and come out — those who have done good will rise to live, and those who have done evil will rise to be condemned."

(John 5: 28 – 29)

The resurrection of the dead and existence after death as far as the Bible is concerned is not limited to only those who are properly interred in graves. In fact, the Bible teaches that **every** dead human shall be raised back to life whether buried in the grave or not. But while wondering at the question *"how are the dead raised?"*, we find in the Bible specific prophecies that has greatly influence what most Christians believe about existence after death:

Then I saw the beast and the kings of the earth and their armies gathered together to make war against the rider on the horse and his army. But the beast was captured, and with him the false prophet who had performed the miraculous signs on his behalf. With these signs he had deluded those who had received the mark of the beast and worshipped his image. ***The two of them were thrown alive into the fiery lake of burning sulfur.*** *The rest of them were killed with the sword that came out of the mouth of the rider on the horse, and all the birds gorged themselves on their flesh. And I saw an angel coming down out of heaven, having the key of the Abyss and holding in his hand a great chain.* ***He seized the dragon, that ancient serpent, who is the devil, or Satan, and*** *__bound him for a thousand years.__ He threw him into the Abyss, and locked and sealed it over him, to keep him from deceiving the nations anymore until the thousand years were ended. After that, he must be set free for a short time. I saw thrones on which were seated those who had been given authority to judge. And I saw the __souls of those who had been beheaded__ because of the word of God. They had not worshipped the beast or his image and had not received his mark on their foreheads or their hands. __They came to life__ and reigned with Christ a thousand years. (The __rest of the dead did not come to life__ until the thousand years were ended). __This is the first resurrection.__ Blessed and holy are those have part in the first resurrection. The second death has no power over them, but they will be priests of God and of Christ and will reign with him for a thousand years. When the thousand years are over, Satan will be released from his prison and will go out to deceive the nations in the four corners of the earth – Gog and Magog – to gather them for battle. In number they are like the sand on the seashore. They marched across the breadth of the earth and surrounded the camp of God's people, the city he loves. But fire came down from heaven and devoured them. And __the devil, who deceived them, was thrown into the lake of burning sulfur__, where the beast and the false prophet had been thrown. __They will be tormented day and night for ever and ever.__ Then I saw a great white throne and him who was seated on it. Earth and sky fled from his presence, and there was no place for them. And I saw the dead, great and small, __standing__ before the throne, and books were opened. Another book was opened, which is the book of life. The dead were judged according to what they had done as recorded in the books. The __sea__ gave up the dead that were in it, and death and Hades gave up the dead that were in them, and each person was judged according to what he had done. Then death and Hades were thrown into the lake of fire. The lake of fire is the second death. If anyone's name was not found written in the book of life, he was thrown into the lake of fire.*

(Revelations 19: 19 –20: 15)

The "*lake of fire burning with fire and brimstone*", reminds us of what historians say about the ancient Jerusalem, in which at the outskirt of the city, the deep narrow valley ("*valley of Hinnon*") by Mount Zion, was used as "*the dumping place*" for the dead bodies of animals and "*disgusting evildoers*". This valley, which was previously the former worship place of the "pagan gods", Molech and Baal, to whom human sacrifices were made, was converted into the latter use as "*dumping place*" or "*hell*", and a fire aided with sulphur and brimstone was kept burning in it. Thus, traditionally, when the Jews say that a person "*would end up being cast into hell*", the attached idea was that such a person would die the death of a "*disgusting evildoer*" and rather than being buried in a decent tomb within the city in hope of resurrection, would be thrown into the Valley of

Hinnon, "*hell*".

However, from the book of Revelations, one might as well relate that the apostle John, being Jew, was merely hoping that the earthly Jerusalem would be rebuilt with much grace and splendour for "*the saints*" to inherit, while evildoers would be rejected and thrown into a "*hell*" similar to the earthly one as known to Jews. But Jesus himself had also expressed that "*the kingdom of heaven*" "*is likened to*" welcoming just people into the city while casting the evildoers into a "*furnace of fire*", [perhaps deliberately avoiding the word "*hell*" and its literal attachment to the earthly "*dumping place*" just outside the then Jerusalem].

> *Then he left the crowd and went into the house. His disciples came to him and said, "Explain to us the parable of the weeds in the field." He answered, "The one who sowed the good seed is the Son of Man. The field is the world, and the good seed stands for the sons of the kingdom. The weeds are the sons of the evil one, and the enemy who sows them is the devil. The harvest is the end of the age, and the harvesters are angels. As the weeds are pulled up and burned in fire, so it will be at the end of the age. The Son of Man will send out his angels, and they will weed out of his kingdom everything that causes sin and all who do evil. They will throw them into the fiery furnace, where there will be weeping and gnashing of teeth. Then the righteous will shine like the sun in the kingdom of their Father. He who has ears, let him hear."*
>
> (Matthew 13: 36 – 43)

Consequently, we might consider that John's prophetic concept of a "*lake of fire burning with sulphur and brimstone*" was **less** about the annihilation of the material **bodies** of evildoers in the "*hell*" located outside Jerusalem, but **more** about the "*furnace of fire*" of which Jesus spoke. And along this line of thought, we might well consider that John the apostle wrote that Satan was also cast into the "*lake of fire*" to be "*tormented for ever and ever*", after being "*bound for a thousand years*". And yet we know that the person whom John referred to as "*Satan*" could not have been human being even for the simple fact that humans do not normally live for "*a thousand years*". The Satan that John wrote about must therefore have been an ethereal being, but one with a distinct form that may also be called "*body*", otherwise it would have been impossible for an "*angel*" to "*lay hold*" of Satan and bound him for a thousand years. We may therefore consider Paul's idea of "*spiritual bodies*" to be such "*bodies*" as spirits may have, which unlike our material bodies could abide in fiery torment "*for ever and ever*" without being burnt into ashes: spirits in the Bible are not considered to be without a form that one could "*lay hold*" upon.

Nevertheless, as sceptics we have no immediate means of verifying whether there is indeed a "*lake of fire*", and anyway, if there are indeed spirits, and spirits (such as Satan) are destined to be cast into a "*lake of fire*", many of us are less bothered because "*that is a problem for spirits, not animals*". Certainly, the flesh of humans and other animals cannot stay in fire "*for ever and ever*"; in only a matter of hours (at most), a human being (dead or alive) thrown into a furnace in which the fire is aided with sulphur and brimstone would be reduced into ashes and cannot by any means feel "*tormented forever*". Therefore, unless humans indeed have an inward spirit form that is distinct from our animal bodies, eternal torment in a lake of fire constitutes no threat. And if the *Creator* by any means raises the dead and brings "*evildoers*" into judgment only to cast them again into a lake of fire, it obviously would be a sheer waste of time, if the resurrected bodies would be such as we presently have.

However, John says that in his vision, the "*beast and the false prophet*" were already cast into the lake of fire a thousand years before Satan was cast into the lake of fire. From John's earlier description of the "*beast and the false prophet*", he had insinuated that they were humans, leaving us to wonder how a thousand years in the fire did not reduce them into ashes.

In the light of the foregoing, when we pursue the Christian idea of eternal existence, we reckon that the idea of eternal human existence as animals makes no sense at all, unless within our animal nature we also have a spiritual nature [which is, of course, what Christians believe and teach]. The doctrines of other religions that believe in human existence after death are also built upon the spirituality factor – maintaining that humankind has an inner (spiritual, nonmaterial) "supernature" that subsists even after the complete annihilation of the material human body. The various ideas about existence after death are consequently altogether built upon the concept of "*spiritual consciousness*" rather than of the "*animal consciousness*" such that a man whose body parts have found their ways into various mahogany desks (through the long food chain earlier outlined) remains as "*a whole person*" that one could lay hold upon. What we must prove, therefore, is whether humans indeed possess an inward (spiritual) nature that would subsists even after the human body has been completely cremated or, "*turned into dust [soil elements]*", if it were buried instead.

As earlier stated, the best means by which we can prove whether humankind has an inward spiritual nature is by moving from spiritual irresponsiveness into spiritual vitality, and the Christian idea of *"passing from (spiritual) death to life"* is what we shall consider in the subsequent chapters of this book. But now, in consideration of the claims of those who assert that they have passed from spiritual irresponsiveness into spiritual vitality, we would **presume** (for the purpose of our discussion on existence after death) that humankind indeed have an inward spiritual nature that, in the image and likeness of God, is immortal and non-annihilable. But the animal body of man is annihilable and is considered incapable of eternal existence, and rationally so.

I declare to you, brothers, that flesh and blood cannot inherit the kingdom of God, nor does the perishable inherit the imperishable.

(1 Corinthians 15: 50)

Moreover, the Christian apostles tried to explain the resurrection of the dead by giving example of the springing up of new plants from a buried seed [1 Corinthians 15: 37], but we know that in a buried seed, what springs forth into a new living plant is not the very portion of seed that had decayed. If a seed were **completely** decayed, it cannot spring forth into a new plant anymore. In the buried seed, there yet remains a very tiny living speck of the seed, from which life springs again. And likewise, it is reckoned by Christians that when the entire human body (flesh and bones) decays, there remains yet one "thing" that does not decay – the *breath* of God in humankind, which is considered nonmaterial and non-annihilable, and yet with a definite form such that ethereal beings could *"lay hold upon"*. But the idea of a non-material and non-annihilable component of humankind is not limited to the Christian religion.

In both Christian and non-Christian beliefs, the [supposed] nonmaterial and non-annihilable component of human nature is often referred to as *"spirit"*, but more often as *"soul"*. The word *"soul"* itself in the ordinary literal meaning stands for *"psyche"* or *"mind"* [as the *"seat of thought"*], but as a synecdoche, the word is often used to represent anything that is conscious – be it humans, animals or spirits. Sometimes also, the word *"soul"* is figuratively used to represent *"life"* as it is often reckoned that unconscious things are dead, and *"consciousness"* (which *"mind"* represents) is in this respect counted as *"life"*. The Bible is not an exception to contemporary literary styles and it incorporates all uses of the word *"soul"*, to the confusion [perhaps] of some people who have not paid attention to the different figurative and literary uses of the language. Nevertheless, when the Bible speaks of the *"psyche"* as subsisting after the decaying or cremation of the dead human body, it speaks in respect of *"psyche of the spirit"* rather than *"psyche of the body"*. But our quest as far as the discussion has progressed is not to prove whether *"spirit, soul and body"* are *three distinct and separable* things, yet it is important that we do not just gullibly recite that *"humankind is composed of spirit, soul and body"* without seeking to understand what the three consist of and imply.

Spirit, soul and body

As we have earlier observed, the mental consciousness of humankind is dependent upon the brain, which is an integral part of the body. We know that an unconscious body cannot do anything of its own accord. For instance, if there were food by the side of a sleeping hungry man, normally the man's mouth would not automatically begin to eat the food until the man is **aware** of the food. But it is the mind, not the mouth, which becomes aware of the food and desires it. And in the same way, no part of the human body has a *"desire"* by itself; desire is an issue of the mind.

Among and within the belief systems, there are often differences of opinions in respect of whether humankind consists of *"body, alone"*, *"separable soul and body, alone"*, *"separable spirit and body, alone"*, or *"separable spirit, soul and body"*. These differences of opinions also extend into within the Christendom in which all parties assert that they derive their opinions from the Bible. Nevertheless, we might consider that the differences are simply routed in misrepresentations of ideas and language uses. For a way out, we should consider that in the non-religious fields, among people who do not believe in spirituality there are also differences of ideas and language uses when it comes to what should be classed as "mental" or "physical". In particular, we talk of *"mental assaults"* as against *"physical assaults"* and *"mental retardation"* as against *"physical retardation"*. But the brain is in fact a physical component of the body, as much as the liver and kidney *et cetera* yet we cannot physically separate the brain and mentality. Yet still brain surgery is not necessarily mind surgery but certain brain surgeries can alter the state of a human mind, for instance. And we therefore think of the relationship between the brain and mind in the way we think of a piece of paper and the information printed on it. The brain is the paper; the mind is the *"information"* (the knowledge or idea conveyed). If the piece of paper is burnt into ashes, without the information having been read or by any other means retrieved from the paper, then the information has been burnt as much as the paper. Similarly, the physical death or destruction of the brain implies a death/destruction of the mind as well.

However, while talking about spirit, soul and body, the factor of intricate figurative expressions in source materials must be reckoned with. Outside religion, in the everyday conversations, we could say *"White House spoke this morning…"* when in fact we mean that *"the chief officials resident in the White House spoke this morning"*, but the meaning is immediately clear because we have a preset idea value that *"houses do not speak"*. Nevertheless, a conflict of ideas could arise if a headline says *"White House collapsed this morning"* [God forbid] and offers us no details. Someone might believe that *"the **building** in which the president resides fell apart"*, while another person might believe *"the **president's aides** fell apart"*, and yet another person might believe *"the **president [himself]** had a major breakdown [of ideas – or whatever]"*. The trouble is that all the three interpretations are genuine, but which of them a person would choose, will come with the preset values and idiosyncrasies that the person already attaches to the name *"White House"*, be it as a building or an institution.

Similarly, the expression *"may God preserve your head, brain and mind"* could generate a conflict of ideas, just as well as the expression *"may God preserve your spirit, soul and body"* [1 Thessalonians 5: 23]. However, while the brain could be physically removed from the head, the mind cannot be physically removed from the brain, yet brain and mind are different things as much as the paper and the information printed on the paper are different things. And yet we can talk of *"weak head"* or *"weak brain"* while in fact we mean *"weak mind"*, while though neither "head" nor "brain" is the "mind". But the import of our present discussion is not about heads, brains and minds; we are particular about spirit, soul and body.

In deciding whether the Bible projects the idea that humankind indeed consists of a separable *"spirit, soul and body"*, we might regard the implication of the statement *"a person's uppermost part consists of the head, brain and mind"* and run similar parallels of arguments through the meanings of the words *"spirit, soul and body"* as used throughout the Bible. By this, our most rational conclusion of the biblical idea of *"spirit, soul and body"* would show that in the literal [non-figurative] meaning of the word "*soul*" as "*psyche*" ["*consciousness*"], it is not represented that the "*soul*" (as "*consciousness of the body*") is structurally separable from the body, or that the "*soul*" (as "*consciousness of the spirit*") is structurally separable from the spirit. Indeed, brain and mind are **not structurally separable** yet they remain **distinct** things, reckoned as distinguished from each other. But head and brain are structurally separable, and the Bible presents the human spirit and the human body as structurally separable, while presenting the body as definite material and the spirit as definite nonmaterial. But a Bible passage that states "*the soul would be separated from the spirit, the body would be separated from the soul*" could be multiply misrepresented if in the passage the word "*soul*" synecdochically refers first to "*body*" and then to "*spirit*", and indeed such figurative uses of the word "*soul*" run through the Bible.

God will not leave the soul in hell.

King David who wrote the question "*what is man that God should care about?*" also wrote another famous line expressing his hope in the resurrection from the dead, by which he asserted that he would not be abandoned in "*the world of the dead*".

> *For thou wilt not leave my soul in hell; neither wilt thou suffer thine Holy One to see corruption. Thou wilt shew me the path of life: in thy presence is fulness of joy; at thy right hand there are pleasures for evermore.*
>
> (Psalm 16: 10 – 11, King James Version)

Again, dictions play an important role in this passage. The word interpreted as "*hell*" here is not the "*valley of Hinnon*", in which the bodies of "*disgusting evildoers*" were burned with sulphur and brimstone. The dug pit, grave, in which corpses were interred, was contemporarily called "*hell*" and so was the (imagined) place in which the nonmaterial essences of humans (were believed to) congregate after death. David lived in hope of the resurrection, for which everyone at that time generally wished. However, the apostles would later argue that David's grave lied still in Jerusalem at their own time (many hundred years after David) and that the body of David had "*seen corruption*", that is "*decayed*":

> *"For when David had served God's purpose in his own generation, he fell asleep; he was buried with his fathers and his body decayed."*

(Acts 13: 36)

Practically, if David had meant that his own material body would not decay, that hope certainly failed. And as long as his body and brain had completely decayed, so would have been all the information, thought, memories, and desires of his mental mind because mental consciousness cannot subsist without the brain. But in Revelations, Apostle John says he *"saw the dead, great and small, stand before God"* for eventual judgment [Revelations 20: 12]. And we reason that if they could *"stand"* then they are not *"dead"*, for dead men do not stand. But equally, if they had not *"died"*, they would not have been in *"death and hell"*. Nevertheless, John had made himself clear by stating that what he saw *"standing"* before God were the *"souls"*, which he projects to us as capable of being *"tormented in fire and brimstone for ever and ever"* without being reduced into ashes. He in fact implies the immateriality of both *"the lake of fire, burning with sulphur and brimstone"* as well as the *"souls"* that were cast into it. Certainly, if material *"souls"* were cast into the kind of *"fire"* that burned in the *"valley of Hinnon"*; then the "souls" would in a moment turn to ashes, and the idea of being tormented for ever and ever would perish.

Again, John says he saw *"the sea gave up the dead that are in it"*, but we know that graves are not normally dug in the sea. Yet many human corpses have been permanently lost into sea through the capsizing of ships, sea wars, *et cetera*. The human corpses in the sea do not remain intact forever. Most often, they are eaten by fishes and other sea animals, or simply decomposed into basic organic matter and diluted away into the water or absorbed by sea plants and planktons. But if true to John's vision, the dead are raised, what would be raised cannot be the material essence of flesh, bones and blood that have been consumed by sharks and fishes because neither John nor any other biblical character hoped that sharks and fishes would resurrect. The biblical idea of existence after death therefore does not imply that our biological bodies would live forever and ever. Yet while defending the idea of resurrection, the apostles refer to the resurrection of Jesus as evidence that people would be raised.

> *But if it is preached that Christ has been raised from the dead, how can some of you say that there is no resurrection of the dead? If there is no resurrection of the dead, then not even Christ has been raised. And if Christ has not been raised, our preaching is useless and so is your faith. More than that, we are then found to be*

false witnesses about God for we have testified about God that he raised Christ from the dead. But he did not raise him if in fact the dead are not raised. For if the dead are not raised, then Christ has not been raised either. And if Christ has not been raised, your faith is futile; you are still in your sins. Then those also who have fallen asleep in Christ are lost. If only for this life we have hope in Christ, we are to be pitied more than all men.

(1 Corinthians 15: 12 – 19)

There are multiple arguments about the resurrection of Jesus that we shall also review in subsequent chapters. [Some argue that he was not killed, some argue that he was killed but was not buried, some argue that he was buried but did not resurrect]. For now, however, let us consider the importance of Paul's argument in respect of the resurrection of Jesus. From the passage, Paul had argued that religion makes meaning if **only** there is resurrection from the dead, and he further stressed that the resurrection of Jesus from the dead was a proof of God's ability to bring the dead back to life. The complex issue is that the body of Jesus did not decompose, according to the apostles while the bodies of most of the persons that have died from the beginning until now would certainly have decomposed.

If Jesus' body indeed returned to life, it should rightly prove God's ability to raise the dead, and prove that resurrection is real. But there is in the instance of Jesus a relation between the body that was interred and the risen one. However, if the corpse of a person had totally decomposed and had been absorbed by a tree as *"soil nutrients"* and the tree had subsequently been made into desks, we are curious to know the manner in which the resurrected body of such a person would bear a relationship with the former body. If such a person would be raised in a manner similar to that of Jesus, then every material element from his body that had been absorbed into leaves and desks must also be drawn back together otherwise the resurrected body would bear no direct relation with the former body. But the apostles and Jesus himself implied that the dead persons that would be raised for *"the Great White Throne Judgment"* would bear a relation with their former selves.

If Jesus' body indeed returned to life, it should rightly prove God's ability to raise the dead, and prove that resurrection is real.

Furthermore, Paul had further stated that the resurrected bodies of those that would be raised *"at the last trump"* would be *"spiritual bodies"* instead of the natural bodies that died, whilst the natural bodies of those Christians *"who remain alive"* would also be *"changed"*. Besides, Paul (as well all the other apostles, and Jesus himself) believed that humankind consists of an outer annihilable being and an inner non-annihilable being.

> *For which cause we faint not; but though* **our outward man** *perish, yet* **the inward man** *is renewed day by day.*
> (2 Corinthians 4: 16, King James version)

> Therefore we do not lose heart. Though outwardly we are wasting away, yet inwardly we are being renewed day by day.
> (2 Corinthians 4: 16)

In the pre-Christian era, worshippers of Yahweh also expressed views similar to Paul's views. The three Hebrew captives that served King Nebuchadnezzar are examples of such. These three men, Hananiah, Mishael, and Azariah, (also called Shadrach, Meshach, and Abednego) reportedly dared the Babylonian King at the risk of being burnt alive.

> *Shadrach, Meshach and Abednego replied to the king, "O Nebuchadnezzar, we do not need to defend ourselves before you in this matter. If we are thrown into the blazing furnace, the God we serve is able to save us from it, and he will rescue us from your hand, O King. But even if he does not, we want you to know, O King, that we will not serve your gods or worship the image of gold you have set up."*
> (Daniel 3: 16 – 18)

If these three men did not have an assurance of existence after death, they would not have dared the king and taken the risk of being reduced to ash in the furnace. We consider that adherence to Yahweh at the risk of being cremated alive would have been most stupid of them unless they considered that there is benefit in it for them. But if the hope of rising back to life were built upon being decently buried and having an intact body, then being burnt in the furnace would have terminated their hopes. Nevertheless, they were willing to be cremated alive for the sake of God, and in firm belief that being cremated is no loss to them. But if they were absolutely cremated, then what would rise after death cannot be their animal form, but the breath form, which the furnace could not destroy. In the Bible, the "breath" or "inner form" is called "spirit", in the complete sense of it, and also called "*soul*", synecdochically.

Summarily, from all biblical views, we can only deduce that the concept of existence after death in all religions is based upon the belief in an inner nonmaterial nature, which is believed to subsist even if the entire animal being of a person were cremated or by any other means annihilated. In the next few chapters, we shall examine what the Bible prescribes for humans who want to experience spiritual aliveness and could then be **sure** that humankind indeed has an inner (spirit) nature that in the likeness of the Creator, God, subsists eternally. But before we go ahead to examine "*spiritual aliveness*", in the Christian concept, we must first sum up what Christians regard as "*spiritual death*" because it is these two concept of death and aliveness of the "*inner form*" that separate Christianity from all other religions.

The Wages of Sin is Death.

"*You will surely die*" was the reiterated warning given to man in the Garden of Eden, according to the Bible. We earlier considered that if there were nothing dead, the word "*death*" would have been vague to Adam and Eve. But "*death*" for Adam and Eve was considered a consequence of sin.

For the wages of sin is death . . .

(Romans 6: 23)

Several people have interpreted the Bible to imply that if Adam and Eve had not sinned by breaking the commandment of God about eating from the forbidden tree, they would probably be bodily alive today. But in Genesis, God had not given any commandment to the animals, which also die, and yet did not sin. So, why should animals too die? Or why were things dead before man sinned? Or else, why did the word "*death*" make meaning to Adam and Eve if there was nothing dead before they sinned?

Every Christmas, millions of turkeys and chickens die. Millions of rams also die for Moslem celebrations yearly. But we do not read from the Bible that the first turkeys, chickens, and rams committed sin. And interestingly, when God reportedly cursed Adam that he would "*return to dust*", he did not curse animals, though he cursed the ground for man's sake. So, why then do animals die, if biological death is the wages of sin?

Moreover, when we consider the anatomy and physiology of the animal body we discover that the animal nature seems to grow naturally from pre-birth towards death. For animals, birth and death, are terminals of the same line. Of course, growth in animals (including humankind) takes them through from small embryos into some maximal adult sizes and then the increase in size stops. The animal subsists at the *"adult size"* for a while, produces offspring and then gradually degenerates towards death. Death of the animal is also often quickened by environmental factors and the food chain structures.

Lions normally eat flesh and not grass. And their dentition is well adapted to carnivorous feeding. If God had indeed created the animals in forms similar to their present ones, then he had probably designed that the lions should feed on flesh and not grass. And it does not appear from the Bible or any other source that true lions ever ate grass instead of flesh. And by such designs, we know that *"the Architect and Builder of the universe"* must have thus designed that the lion should kill and eat other animals. And therefore, death must have prevailed over those preys of the lions ever before man sinned. And thus, man's sin (if it were the cause of biological death for humankind) could not have been what brought biological death upon animals as well. Plants also are living things and they grow from tender age towards death. In fact, in the creation story of Genesis, plants were destined to be food for animals but the grasses eaten by cattle were not supposed to remain alive in the belly of the cattle. So, death reigned upon plants, which did not sin.

However, when we consider the normal life spans of plants and animals, we find that plants (such as trees) generally live longer than animals. Nevertheless, plants also *"die of old age"* as animals do. The summary is that biological death is a terminal point of the life of living things, whether they are plants or animals. And if then, it leaves us wondering what the Bible means by saying *"death is the reward of sin"*. Yet, we know that in the book of Romans, Apostle Paul went further to declare the outright meaning of what *"death"* he called the *"wages of sin"*.

For they that are after the flesh do mind the things of the flesh; but they that are after the Spirit the things of the Spirit. For to be carnally minded is death; but to be spiritually minded is life and peace.

(Romans 8: 5 – 6, King James Version)

In the long and short of it, therefore, we consider that **living only in our animal nature** is what Paul considered *"death"* when he called it *"the wages of sin"*. By the same token, we consider the same thing to be what God called *"death"* when he said to Adam and Eve, *"you will surely die, in the day that you eat from that tree"*. According to Genesis, Adam from the very day he ate from the forbidden tree lived solely as an animal; he remained biologically alive for a long while after eating from the tree that was supposed to kill him **in the day** he eats from it, but he was spiritually irresponsive towards God. So, rather than biological death, *"death"* as *"carnal mindedness"* seems more to be *"the wages of Adam's sin"*.

However, many Christians have always opined that if Adam had not sinned, he could have lived since then without tasting biological death, while indeed we know that the animal nature of humankind seems "programmed" to grow to old age and then die. And considering the fact, as we have examined earlier, that the hope of eternal existence in the Bible is not based on living with a material animal body forever but living with a nonmaterial spiritual body, we reckon that the idea of Adam living biologically forever is somewhat unbiblical. Indeed, the Bible insinuates that God did not want Adam to die; yet living forever with an animal nature does not seem to be the perfect Bible idea either. The Bible idea is that if God does not want humankind, as animal, to taste death, he would simply *"translate"* humankind into the *"spiritual world"*. In fact, the Bible gives us at least two examples of people that were thus *"translated"*, one of which is Enoch.

> *By faith Enoch was translated that he should not see death; and was not found, because God had translated him: for before his translation he had this testimony, that he pleased God.*
>
> (Hebrews 11: 5, King James Version)

> *By faith Enoch was taken from this life, so that he did not experience death; he could not be found, because God had taken him away. For before he was taken, he was commended as one who pleased God.*
>
> (Hebrews 11: 5)

By this example, we might as well reckon that if Adam also had pleased God, he too could have been *"translated that he should not see (biological) death"*. And if Adam had continued to *"walk with God"*, humankind might have continued to please God and be continually translated into the spiritual *"kingdom of heaven"*. For further examples of this biblical idea, Elijah the prophet was also *"translated"* and did not see death; and as well, Paul expressed the hope that those who please God and remain physically alive *"at the last trump"* would be similarly *"translated"*.

> *Listen, I tell you a mystery: We will not all sleep, but we will all be changed — in a flash, in the twinkling of an eye, at the last trumpet. For the trumpet will sound, the dead will be raised imperishable, and we will be changed. For the perishable must clothe itself with the imperishable, and the mortal with immortality.*
>
> (1 Corinthians 15: 51 – 53)

> *According to the Lord's own word, we tell you that we who are still alive, who are left till the coming of the Lord, will certainly not precede those who have fallen asleep. For the Lord himself will come down from heaven, with a loud command, with the voice of the archangel and with the trumpet call of God, and the dead in Christ will rise first. After that, we who are still alive and are left will be caught up together with them in the clouds to meet the Lord in the air. And so we will be with the Lord forever.*
>
> (1 Thessalonians 4: 15 – 17)

In the Bible, Jesus himself also taught that those who please God could be *"translated"* [that is, *"transferred"* or *"changed"*] from this material form into nonmaterial form without tasting death while he also stressed that those who pleased God, even if they have died physically could be raised and also *"translated"*.

> *Jesus said to her, "I am the resurrection and the life. He who believes in me will live, even though he dies; and whoever lives and believes in me will never die. Do you believe this?"*
>
> (John 11: 25 – 26)

Jesus had earlier said that believing in him and in his message about *"spiritual aliveness"* automatically leads to pleasing God. And here again he reaffirms that if anyone truly pleases God, such persons could be translated, without tasting death, into eternity. The biblical idea that Adam would not have died biologically is therefore built upon the *"translation"* factor for those who please God rather than living in the flesh as animals forever, because indeed the animal body is not designed to subsists forever; for *"flesh and blood cannot inherit the kingdom of God"*, according to the Bible.

Notwithstanding, we know that biological death comes from *"natural and unnatural causes"* and we might consider that even if God had arranged that humankind would not die of natural causes, humankind might have died of unnatural causes. But again, the *"spiritual aliveness"* factor could have prevented humankind from unnatural causes because *"spiritual aliveness"* would have enabled every person to continually hear the voice of God, as Adam did at first. The superior spiritual knowledge would have continually guided every person (in the manner by which *He* knows the precise timing of future events) and humankind would have continually avoided natural and unnatural causes, if **every** person were prophetic, and if it so pleases God.

Thus, in the Bible, it is reckoned that the first *"death"* (of *"carnal mindedness"*) that Adam died paved way for death (in every form) to reign over man. According to the Bible, death (in every form) is therefore *"wages of sin"* for humankind BUT NOT for other earthly living things, because humankind is the one deemed to be *"translatable"* among all earthly creatures, not because humankind is the greatest animal but because in humankind is the ethereal *"image and likeness of God"*, the *"spirit"*, the *"breath"*.

Furthermore, we find that the word *"death"* in the Bible has three meanings. In the first occurrence, it implies *"carnal mindedness"* or *"spiritual irresponsiveness towards God"*. In the second occurrence, it implies *"losing biological life"*. And in the third occurrence, it implies *"being tormented eternally"*. But the apostles did not count the loss of biological life as real death but as *"sleep"* because they reckoned that the spiritual essence of a human is not destroyed even when the entire body is cremated. What they regard as the *"essential man"* without which man would not count as *"man"* but as other animals, was the *"inner man"*, the *"spirit man"*. But there is indeed a shortfall of this *"spirit nature"* in us, so much that we argue among ourselves that there is or there is not such a nature.

The first death.

From biblical perspectives, the first *"death"* of man as *"wages of sin"* was not punitive but consequential. The *"death"* [*"spiritual irresponsiveness"*] that Adam died on the day he ate the fruit of the forbidden tree was NOT a punishment imposed by God upon Adam for breaking *His* law, it was simply the *"next stage"* of eating the fruits. Genesis implies that God wanted man to grow and increase knowledge in the inner [spirit] man **as well as** the outer [animal] man. But by stepping up the outer animal nature ahead of the spirit nature, man had made the inner spirit nature become irresponsive towards God.

For all have sinned and fall short of the glory of God,

(Romans 3: 23)

In Christian doctrines, to "sin" simply meant and still means to live by the will of animal (outward) man rather than the dynamic will of God's Spirit. This Adam did and *"fell short of the appearance [likeness – similarity of nature] of God"*: by descent, we too have inherited the shortfall of the nature of God. And by this, we all have inherited a nature of sin [gratification of animal nature at the expense of that of *"the image and appearance"* (*"glory"*) of God]. Indeed, we can only **reckon** that Adam lived, without being able to lay outright indisputable claims to his existence, but what is outright and indisputable is that in us there is a shortfall of the **likeness/nature** of God. However, Christians believe that Adam truly lived not only because the Bible says so, but also because our present nature (with the shortfall of the likeness of God and yet a capacity to become *"spiritually alive"*) does **corroborate** the biblical information on Adam.

In biblical Christianity, to be a sinner does **not** mean to be a person who **commits** offences against stated laws or to one who **omits** obligations. To be a sinner means to have a shortfall of God's spiritual nature, that is to be *"spiritually irresponsive"* towards God. Therefore, as far as biblical Christianity is concerned, every natural person who is not *"spiritually alive"* is counted a sinner even if he is a dedicated Christian priest who does not commit any offence against stated commandments and does not fail to perform all obligations. In Christian doctrines, the *"spiritual aliveness"* factor is what determines whether God (a Spirit) takes pleasure in a human or not. In Christian doctrines, those who are not *"spiritually alive"* are *"dead"* as far as God is concerned, and however good or religious they are in the outer (animal) man – which comprises of the animal body and bodily consciousness [mind] – the *"spiritually irresponsive"* are a heart sore to God.

When we consider Christian doctrines, we wonder why the natural humankind must be made to answer for the sins he has not committed. We wonder why a person should be counted a *"sinner"* when he maintains **blamelessness** in mind, thought, speech, and actions. But the Bible teaches that humans are sinners **not** just because of what they think, say or do, but because *"spiritual irresponsiveness"* is disgusting to God, just as much as decomposing fleshy corpses are disgusting to our animal perceptions. Rationally, therefore, it does not count

200

whether we are guilty or blameless in mind, thought, speech and actions, so long as our inner (spirit) nature, which is the image and glory [likeness] of God, is *"irresponsive"* towards God, we are simply *"spiritual corpses"*. In any case, *"spiritual irresponsiveness"* which we inherit by birth is NOT our individual faults but in the rational perspective, that singular fact is not reason enough for God to cherish our *"spiritual corpses"*, the irresponsive *"inner man"*.

However, there is an apparent rationality in the Christian doctrine of sinfulness as expressed by this example: supposing that a stray bullet kills someone close to you [God forbid], it would certainly not be that person's fault to have died by the stray bullet. Yet the singular fact that it was not his or her fault does not make the corpse responsive to you; the corpse cannot dance with you, cannot eat with you, cannot drink with you, and in fact, cannot respond to you in anyway. So, you would be left to decide doing away with the corpse by burial, by cremation, or by any other means, yet the death was not the corpse's fault. Christians believe that in like manner, God must do away with the **spirits** of everyone whom he finds to be spiritually irresponsive, even though *"spiritual irresponsiveness"* is not our original fault; we inherit from our parents, naturally. This is *"the first death"*, the death that Adam died when he ate the fruit that advanced his mental prowess at the expense of spiritual prowess, and we inherit it, naturally.

Therefore, just as sin entered the world through one man, and death through sin, and in this way death came to all men, because all sinned — for before the law was given, sin was in the world. But sin is not taken into account when there is no law. Nevertheless, death reigned from the time of Adam to the time of Moses, even over those who did not sin by breaking a command, as did Adam, who was a pattern of the one to come.

(Romans 5: 12 – 14)

In Christian doctrines, therefore, "sin" is not only the breaking of God's commandments, because ever before the popular *"Ten Commandments"* were given through Prophet Moses, there were gratifications of the animal desires. Before the commandments were given through Moses, people were doing all the things that the Ten Commandments forbade but the fact that there were no commandments against such actions did not imply that the actions were consequently pleasant to *Yahweh*. For example, if you returned from office one evening and found that your child had smashed the television set; you belch at him *"John, why have you done this!*!*!*"*; but the child simply says,

"I'm sorry, Dad, but you didn't tell me not to do so". You shout *"what!*"'!'*, but the child replies unruffled, *"Common, Dad, after all you hadn't told me not to do it. I did it simply because smashing things have recently become my pastime; it gives me pleasure. And after all, you didn't tell me you won't like it!"*. And that is it. You would not like what the child had done, but (as a matter of logics) you cannot justifiably tell him *"that was wrong"* because he had not broken any rule. In Christian doctrines, similarly, the failure to please God, with or without rules, is sin – displeasure to God. Yet by birth, we have an inherent irresponsiveness towards God. It **was** not our fault; but whether or not a person has caused his or her own death, the corpse must be *"taken care of"*.

The Second Death.

Finally, as far as the wages of failing to please God is concerned, the Bible talks of *"the second death"*; having reckoned that biological death is no death at all since it annihilates only the outward (animal) person but not the inward (spirit) person, whereas the *"first death"* (*"spiritual irresponsiveness"*) affects the inner person as well as does the *"second death"*.

> *But the cowardly, the unbelieving, the vile, the murderers, the sexually immoral, those who practice magic arts, the idolaters and all liars – their place will be in the fiery lake of burning sulfur. This is the second death.*
>
> (Revelations 21: 8)

Earlier, we had reckoned with John's use of language in respect of *"the lake that burns with fire and brimstone"* and observed that he probably borrows the idea of *"hell"* [*"Valley of Hinnon"*] to express what he saw. Describing it as *"hell"* or *"lake of fire"*, being figurative, therefore, may or may not perfectly capture the view that John saw in the revelations. But whatever we call the place that is designated as *"the place of eternal torments"*, anyway, the summation of the idea from Christian perspectives is that it is a place that God originally planned for Satan and *"the angels that sinned"*, because they were the first sinners: it was planned for spirits who have no material animal bodies such as we have. Ordinarily, we cannot argue whether there is such a place or not, but what we know is that if indeed there are spirits (who being in the nature of God cannot be annihilated), one rational way that God could dispose of them is to put them into **eternal** torments. The other thing that we know, from what the Bible teaches, is that if the *"inner man"* of any human would also be put in this place of eternal torments, it would not be because of whatever the animal man has done or failed to do, but because the *"inner man"* has failed to respond to God. Such might as well be counted as corpses for cremation, except that unlike the cremation of fleshy corpses, the *"spirit corpses"* cannot turn to ash and yet would have the feelings of being tormented.

No sane parent would cremate his/her child alive for the mere fact that the child had disobeyed him/her. Neither would you keep the corpse of a very good and useful child and let it decay in your bed just because the child was good and useful. That is just the way it is with the Christian idea of God and eternal torments – not for the good or bad done, thought or said, and not for anything our animal nature does or fails to do, would God punish any human eternally: God would simply inter into the eternal lake of torments everyone that to *Him* is dead, whose name is not found among those of the *"spiritually alive"*.

According to the Bible, those who have been revived in the inner man and have become *"spiritually responsive"* towards God are the same that he keeps their names in his *"list of the living"*, the *"book of life"*. Excluded from this list would be all those who, even though they have so dedicatedly given themselves up for the benefits of humankind and have lived very penitent lives, with stringent abstaining from all sorts of so-called *"defilements"*, but who are nevertheless *"irresponsive"* in the *"inner man"* towards God. So, it matters less whether we are morally decayed or morally excellent in the outward animal human. So long as God is spirit and **only** those who are alive in the spirit could please him and walk with him, all our religious virtues in the animal (outward) man, earns us no credit towards God. Being hurled into the eternal *"lake of fire"* would not be upon weighing the goods and evils we have done to determine which is greater; it would simply be based upon the issue of life and death.

According to the Bible, many good persons would be in hell, as well as many *"selfless philanthropists"*. Moral excellence would not be a guarantee against being hurled into the *"lake of fire"*, because God is not a moral animal, he is Spirit and only spirits that are responsive to *Him* are counted by him as being alive. The rest may just as well remain *"dying forever"*.

Of course, there are those who are spiritually active, but their spiritual activities (in their astral projections – or whatever) is not counted as *"spiritual aliveness"* in the sight of God, because they do not fellowship with God but with the *"angels that sinned"*. Here rests the big difference between just hooking on to any form of *"spiritual activity"*. It is not enough to be active spiritually; what really counts is the person towards whom we are found spiritually responsive. If *"the spirits that have been found unworthy to live in the immaterial world of God"* are the one towards whom we are spiritually responsive, we should not expect to be welcome by God who has ever tried to make every one of us, humans, spiritually responsive towards him. Since the angels that sinned are already excommunicated by God, communicating with them cannot earn us the eventual privilege of communicating with God.

Finally, on the issue of eternal death [that is, dying continuously without coming to the end of dying and yet without diminishing] – that the *"lake of fire"* represents in the Bible – Christians believe that once a human is physically dead, the opportunity to become spiritually responsive towards God is irrevocably lost. But certain other religions preach that the inner man is always reincarnated at death, and therefore giving people a reason not to be seriously bothered about spiritual irresponsiveness towards God. Yet these religions unwittingly concur with the Bible that a person is destined to die just once and thereafter to face judgment.

Just as man is destined to die once, and after that to face judgment,
(Hebrews 9: 27)

By preaching that what a person does in his or her earthly lifetime, good or bad, would determine the form in which he or she would be further reincarnated, these other religions do agree with the Bible at least up to the point that what a person does in the earthly lifetime does determine the person's state in the existence thereafter.

Thus they presuppose also that there is a judgment after death – a judgment of how every human has lived his or her lifetime on earth. However, what these religions fail to acknowledge is the fact that if there would be a **judgment**, there must as a matter of course be a **Judge**. And who then could rightly be the judge of humankind besides the *Maker* and *Lawgiver* of humankind? The Creator himself, not just some (so-called) superior *Brahmas* living in some *"higher universes"*, must of course be the judge. As long as those *Brahmas* are the same spirits that were once worthy of living with the Sovereign God, and they had somewhere along the line, displeased God so much as to be *"counted unworthy"* to live any more with him, they cannot rightly judge humankind.

Let us look at it in this example: a prisoner who is awaiting execution and who spoke his cell mate, *"Hey, buddy, on your final judgment day, the Judge of the court would count himself too dignified to judge you, because you are so much a worse criminal than I am, so I would be your judge!"* By the Bible doctrines, that is just the picture that could be painted from what the *"angels that sinned"* are doing to those who among humankind go against the word of God to fellowship with evil spirits, who *"transform themselves into angels of light"*.

Whether we all like it or not, and whether we all believe it or not, as long as the God is the *Originator* of the world, our *Potter* and *Father*, the *Architect* and *Master Builder* of the entire worlds, material and immaterial, known and unknown, he alone shall continue to remain our *Lawgiver* and our *Judge*.

> **For the LORD is our judge**, *the* **LORD is our lawgiver**, *the* LORD *is our king; it is he who will save us.*
>
> (Isaiah 33: 22)

> *The* LORD *reigns forever; he has established his throne for judgement. He will judge the world in righteousness; he will govern the peoples with justice.*
>
> (Psalm 9: 7 – 8)

It is possible for any of the angels that sinned to possess a human and after the death of that human may possess yet another human, and hence give the impression of reincarnation. But according to the Bible, the human spirit is different from the angel spirits that sinned. Unlike the angels that sinned, the natural human spirit cannot possess another human and neither can it reincarnate.

According to the Bible, there is a judgment after biological death for every human, and this much is acknowledged even by the angels that sinned – for they also know God's truth and shudder [James 2: 19].

So, here we are, the best we can do is just to note that while a human still maintains his complete nature, while a spirit-reviving message could still be passed through by any means to the *"image and likeness"* of God within, the person should avail himself or herself of the chance to be listed among those whose are spiritually alive in God's reckoning, and whose names are in God's book of life.

> *The* **sea** *gave up the dead that were in it, and death and Hades gave up the dead that were in them,* **and each person was judged according to what**

he had done. *Then death and Hades were thrown into the lake of fire. The lake of fire is the second death.* **If anyone's name was not found written in the book of life, he was thrown into the lake of fire.**

(Revelations 20: 13 – 15)

PART II

THE KINGDOM OF GOD

This section of *Does God Truly Exist?* has six chapters. Chapter Nine, the first in this section, goes a considerable length to examine the most fundamental distinctive claims of the Christian faith – especially as it relates to the restoration of man's spiritual aliveness. Perhaps the most popular Christian quotation is found in John 3: 16 – *"For God so loved the world that he gave his one and only Son that whoever believes in him shall not perish but have eternal life"*. But how exactly is Jesus the Son of God? And why do Christians believe that he is the ONLY one in whom and through whom one could find eternal life in God to escape *"the lake of fire"*?

Chapter Ten discusses the other widely known Christian concept – being *"born again"*. Also in John Chapter 3, we read that *"Unless a man is born again, he cannot enter the kingdom of God"*. But what exactly does it mean to be born again, and how is this achieved? Why must one be born again before he could rightly relate with God?

In Chapter Eleven, there is a re-examination of the doctrine of grace. Christians believe and preach that the "grace of God" [God's gifts freely given to humankind] is more than abundant to take us through everything and is all we need in life. But in this chapter, we would question whether *grace is* **enough** indeed and what in fact does grace consists of or excludes?

Chapter Twelve examines why Christians put up with so many troubles and disadvantages in a seemingly gullible manner. Is there any good sense at all in denying oneself of the pleasures and benefits of this life? Is there any good sense at all in surrendering oneself to torture and even execution just for the sake of religion?

Chapter Thirteen deals with the two greatest strengths of the Christian faith – prayer and evangelism – by which the Christian religion has been able to sustain itself and grow over the centuries from one small persecuted sect into the widest embraced religion in the world today. But does prayer really work? Does God, a Spirit, really hear and pay attention when humans (as animals) pray to him? How does God manage to hear when five hundred million people are praying simultaneously? And as for evangelism, how right is it for Christians to work tirelessly at converting people from other religions while they do not want any of their own members to be converted into other religions?

The last chapter in this part re-examines the hope of all Christians to live forever together and with God in *"a paradise far above the skies"*. How real and rational is this hope? Is there really a heaven where Christians would go after existence on earth? If there is indeed such a place as heaven and if God is as kind and merciful as Christians claim that he is, why must it be Christians alone that would be admitted into God's heaven? Is Jesus really coming back to take Christians to this heaven?

Chapter Nine

GRACE AND FAITH

"So Great A Salvation".

The Kingdom of God is like a Garden.

In the previous chapters, we reviewed issues that concern the existence of God and the spirituality of man. Beginning with considerations that lead us to reckon that God's existence cannot be denied, we looked at what "sin" has done to humankind by pitching man against God, in the Garden of Eden. Then we considered also the person of Satan, the importance of evil spirits, false Christianity, secularity, and *"backsliders"*.

In the war that life is, according to the Bible, there is an army that is waging a perpetual war against God's kingdom. This army consists of Satan as the generalissimo, evil spirits as his chief cohorts, as well as false Christians, secularists, backsliders and the ordinary natural man. Together, these all form the "root of sin" (*"sin"* being *"failure to please/respond to God"*) and it is by them that the reality of **God's existence and his kingdom** is being obscured in the world today.

Talking about the reality of God's kingdom, every curious mind would eagerly seek to know what the kingdom of God truly consist of and how one could be sure that he or she is part of it. In this chapter, and throughout the next five, we shall examine what the Christian perception of the kingdom of God is. Along this line, we shall deal more properly with issues that form the basic (rather difficult) doctrines peculiar to Christianity as distinct from all other religions. Of course, the other issues that we have previously considered in this book are also linked to Christianity to a large extent – for instance, Christians believe in God's existence; but it is not only Christians who believe that God exists. However, now we shall consider the themes that are peculiar to Christianity, such as belief in the deity of Jesus, and belief in his crucifixion and resurrection. These are more specific to Christianity, and the correct understanding of them would help us to fully understand why Christianity maintains an either-for-us-or-against-us standpoint.

Christians believe that the world consist of basically two categories of people – Christians (perceived as *"God's people"*) and non-Christians (perceived as the *"Satan's people"*), and whoever is not a Christian is deemed by Christians as *"heading towards eternal doom"*. But in fact, not all *"Christians"* [so-called] are really Christians, if we reckon with biblical principles as highlighted in the sixth chapter of this book", and as such we need a clear definition of what is considered in Bible terms as authentic Christianity, or *"the kingdom of God"*.

When the Bible does talk of God as "The King" over the entire world and over all that exists, it as well sums up everything under the dominion of God and within his territory. And when it talks of God as "The Judge and Lawgiver", the Bible also sums up everything and everyone under the jurisdiction of God. As such therefore the Bible reckons everyone to be **God's subject**, while he remains *"The Eternal King"*. However, even among men, not all of a king's subjects are in perpetuity automatically subject to the king. That is why we have such words as "rebellion", "treason", "insubordination" and the likes.

As far as he is eternally sovereign, the eternal Creator Spirit holds all rights to authority and dominion for being the first and eternal person by whom all things came to be and the one at whose word all things hold together. Nevertheless, a king's true subject is not just one who simply subsists within the royal territory but one who while thus subsisting remains subject and loyal to the sovereign. It is in accordance with this rationale that Christians consider as "members of God's kingdom" only the subjects of God who are subject to God. For others, (be they such spirits as *"the angels that sinned"* or humans – who also have spirits within their animal natures) Christians reckon them as God's subjects, because they all subsist within the infinite space which entirely is God's domain and jurisdiction: but they are counted as *"not belonging to the kingdom"* because they are perceived as living in rebellion to the will of God.

We can borrow the explanation of the Christian idea of the Kingdom of God from a biblical parable:

Jesus told them another parable: "The kingdom of heaven is like a man who sowed good seed in his field. But while everyone was sleeping, his enemy came and sowed weeds among the wheat, and went away. When the wheat sprouted and formed heads, then the weeds also appeared. The owner's servants came to him and said, 'Sir, didn't you sow good seed in your field? Where then did the weeds come from?' " 'An enemy did this,' he replied. "The servants asked him, 'Do you want us to go and pull them up?' 'No,' he answered, 'because while you are pulling the weeds, you may root up the wheat with them. Let both grow together until the harvest. At that time I will tell the harvesters: First collect the weeds and tie them in bundles to be burned: then gather the wheat and bring it into my barn.' "

(Matthew 13: 24 – 30)

Such is the "kingdom of God". The entire garden is the farmer's garden, but not every thing that grows within that garden is the farmer's delight. It is arguable that since the weeds subsist on his farm they are also his weeds, but as long as they are weeds, they cannot make it home to the farmer's barn. Of course, they may yet subsist on the farm but long before the time at which they would be pulled up, they have been disowned by the farmer. *"These weeds do not belong to me"*, the farmer says, *"but let's leave them within the garden until an appropriate time so we do not hurt the tender wheat while trying to get rid of the weeds"*. By the same token, any being that subsists within the whole infinite space but does not please *The Originator* are deemed by Christians as already disowned by *Him*. They yet subsist within his domain and jurisdiction, but they are already marked as not belonging to the Kingdom, because he has found no pleasure in them. It is those in whom God is pleased that are counted as members of the Kingdom of God. If then, why is it that Christians think they are the ones in whom God is *"well pleased"* and count every other people as *"displeasure"* to God? What is the basis for this belief and is it at all justifiable?

The Kingdom of God is Within You!

Once, having been asked by the Pharisees when the kingdom of God would come, Jesus replied, "The kingdom of God does not come with your careful observation, nor will people say, 'Here it is,' or 'There it is,' because the kingdom of God is within you."

(Luke 17: 20 – 21)

For the kingdom of God is not a matter of eating and drinking, but of righteousness, peace and joy in the Holy Spirit,

(Romans 14: 17)

The Christian scriptures have been widely interpreted over time. Many people simply read their own meanings into the scriptures rather than read out what the scriptures originally stood for. Of particular import at this moment is the apparent misinterpretation of what Jesus had said about the Kingdom of God being *"within you"*. Not a few people have taken it to mean that *"the kingdom of God is within the mind of every person"*. But unlike our English language in which both the singular and plural forms of the word "you" are spelt the same way, there is a difference in the original Bible language between *"you"* as a singular pronoun, and *"you"* as a plural pronoun. The manuscripts of the Bible used the plural form of the pronoun *"you"* in the line *"the kingdom of God is within you"*. So, when Jesus said, *"the kingdom of God is within you"*, he had not meant that the kingdom of God is *"within every one of you [as individuals]"*; rather, he had said the kingdom of God is *"present among you [as a people]"*. Apart from the fact that he had used the plural form of the word *"you"*, there would have been no relevance to all his messages about repentance and *"spiritual aliveness"* or *"eternal life"*, if he had meant that the kingdom of God is within the mind of every human.

Paul subsequently made it clear that the kingdom of God that Jesus preached is a matter of *"righteousness, peace and joy in the Holy Spirit"* and, of course, if every human is already having the kingdom of God within him or her, then it means everyone already has *"righteousness, peace and joy in the Holy Spirit"* within. And then there would be no further need to preach the message of the kingdom of God to anyone anymore. All of Paul's messages and epistles, and indeed everything about Christianity would be null and void.

Besides, the kingdom of God is specifically an issue of *"spirits"*; *"God is Spirit"*, Jesus had said; and to think of God's kingdom as the *"righteousness, peace and joy of mind"* (as some interpret Jesus' statement to mean) is far from what Jesus had said – if "mind" as used here refers to the ordinary animal mind of humankind. The Christian scriptures, and indeed the entire principles of Christianity, distinguish between the embodied *"mind"* and the *"spirit"*. In Christian principles, a person may be pure and upright in mind, but he or she is not counted as part of the kingdom of God unless he or she is righteous in the *spirit* and made thus righteous by *the Spirit*, God, himself.

In fact, all that Jesus had taught was that (in accordance with the Torah and the Prophets) all humans were already condemned and counted out of God's kingdom, not because of what they individually **do or fail to do daily** but because of what Adam and Eve **did** and passed on to all humans by birth. How could anyone think then that it is consistent for Jesus to say that *"the kingdom of God is within the mind of everybody"*? Of course, the author of Genesis wrote that *"God was* **grieved***"* because *"every thought and intents of mind"* of the natural human was continuously against God's own. How then could such minds be the kingdom of God, where God reigns and rules? Moreover, our animal minds are simply functions of our brains which are made of "dusts" [earthly elements, that is] and shall return at biological death to dust. According to the Bible, it is not primarily our animal mind that God reckons with, but our spirit minds. And as long as we inherit by birth a natural irresponsiveness of our spirit minds towards God, the natural humankind cannot be reckoned with by God as belonging to his kingdom.

Jesus told the Pharisees that the kingdom of God is not such as one would have to look out for; the Pharisees had been looking forward to a time that God would send them a political ruler, who would reign over Israel in all godliness and peace and prosperity after the order of David, their most beloved king. They were expecting a Christ that would live as though he was an angel incarnate – surpassing all humans in virtue. They were expecting such a kingdom on earth here, with its capital in Jerusalem, governing an entire world from which all evildoers have perished and into which "all the dead who have done well" would have resurrected. But Jesus told them that the kingdom of God was not to come in such a manner. He told them *"the kingdom of God is already present among humans; you only have to become a part of it"*. His doctrine is that God being Spirit, reigns from the spirit realm and relates with those who have righteousness and joy and peace in the Spirit, which all humankind had lost through the sin of Adam and Eve.

One night, a most respected Pharisee visited Jesus privately. This noble man was a righteous man as far as the righteousness of the human animal was concerned. It was typical of the Pharisees to aim at moral and religious excellence – they paid attention to the even least matters of the Torah. And here was a man who belonged to the highest council (Sanhedrin) of the Judaist religion – a man who had righteousness and peace and joy in his (corporeal) mind! But Jesus had to tell him that the kingdom of God is not about (corporeal) minds, but about (incorporeal) spirits. And from his discussions with Jesus that night came the popular *"born again"* term that we shall review in greater details in the next chapter.

> *Now there was a man of the Pharisees named Nicodemus, a member of the Jewish ruling council. He came to Jesus at night and said, "Rabbi, we know you are a teacher who has come from God. For no one could perform the miraculous signs you are doing if God were not with him". In reply Jesus declared, "I tell you the truth, no one can see the kingdom of God unless he is born again". "How can a man be born when he is old?" Nicodemus asked. "Surely he cannot enter a second time into his mother's womb to be born!". Jesus answered, "I tell you the truth, no one can enter the kingdom of God unless he is born of water and the Spirit. Flesh gives birth to flesh, but the Spirit gives birth to spirit. You should not be surprised at my saying, 'You must be born again.' . . . For God so loved the world that he gave his one and only Son, that whoever believes in him shall not perish but have eternal life. For God did not send his Son into the world to condemn the world, but to save the world through him. Whoever believes in him is not condemned, but whoever does not believe stands condemned already because he has not believed in the name of God's one and only Son".*

(John 3: 1 – 7, 16 – 18)

In the Bible, when Jesus told Nicodemus *"you must be born again"*, he again used the plural *"you"*, probably signifying that it was not a condition limited to Nicodemus in person alone, but one that applies to everyone who wishes to be part of God's kingdom. Jesus emphasised the fact that there is an actual **birth** involved in becoming part of God's kingdom, and that had made Nicodemus wondered. Jesus had told him *"you people would have to be given birth to all over again before you could become part of God's kingdom"*, and that sounded quite incomprehensible – an adult man would be normally bigger than his mother, much less his mother's womb. How then could a man be born again? But Jesus explained further that he was not talking about the (outer) animal form of humans, of which the brain mind is a constituent; rather he talked about the (inner) spirit form of humans.

The Pharisees, unlike the Sadducees, believed that spirits exist and that God is Spirit but all their righteousness and observation of the Law and the Prophets dealt with the actions, attitudes and minds of the (outer) animal human. The whole *"born again"* and *"righteousness of the inner man"* teachings that Jesus introduced to Nicodemus were therefore totally new to him.

214

However, Jesus further told Nicodemus, *"That exactly is why I am on earth here. I have come to admit people into God's kingdom. And no one can come in into the kingdom of God unless he believes all these things that I am telling you about the righteousness of the inner man. Anyone who would be part of God's kingdom must believe in me, and whoever does not believe in me remains in condemnation before God".*

What manner of man is this!

According to the Bible, that night with Nicodemus, Jesus had referred to himself as *"the Son of God"*. Until Jesus, there had been so many public preachers and teachers, and even nationally-respected prophets, in Israel, but none of them ever referred to himself as *"Son of God"*. Of course, it was bearable to know that Jesus was the first to preach being *"born again"*, but to claim an exclusive authority for admitting people into God's kingdom and eternal life was outrageous. In fact, another day he had said *"I am the way and the truth and the life. No one comes to the Father except through me"*. (John 14: 6).

Really, not many people could be comfortable reading or hearing all the statements attributed to Jesus in the Bible. Many people actually prefer to believe that Jesus never really said such things. Of particular note are our Moslems, who insist that the Bible has been multiply doctored and does not contain most of Jesus' original words. But then, if the Bible of which several manuscripts have been found that are dated as early as within a century of Jesus' estimated lifetime on earth, is reckoned to contain not much of Jesus' original words, the Koran that came after about six hundred years of Jesus' time cannot be taken as the one that faithfully reports Jesus' original words. The Moslem prophet who penned down the Koran does not even claim to be an eyewitness of what Jesus did and said; but several of the Bible's books have been passed on from one generation to another by people who believe that the original message of the New Testament books came from several eyewitnesses of Jesus' teachings and actions. It is also important that different copies and versions of New Testament manuscripts collected from different locations compare favourably with one another (even though there are many transcript discrepancies that albeit come in a manner that strongly suggests against the possibility of deliberate manipulations). And for the Koran, it cannot precisely pinpoint the particular individuals or group of persons that could have doctored the manuscripts of the Bible, or precisely where, when and why such changes to the manuscripts were made, yet it refers to the seemingly inadvertent errors of transcriptions as though they were planned, notwithstanding errors of manuscript transcriptions are not limited to the Bible's manuscripts alone; many other books fall into the same category.

Let us not drag that too far, and come to really think of the man Jesus and what he said about himself in the surviving Bible manuscripts. Whatever is so important about this man Jesus that many millions of people argue every day, and many hundred thousands have died contending on his reported words and actions?

Some time ago, I happened to sit by an elderly preacher who talked to a younger man about Jesus. The young man retorted, "*Who is this Jesus?*" Before that instance, I had frequently taken for granted that every human has at least a basic common idea about Jesus. But this young man's four-word question reminded me that even in Jesus' own days, according to the Bible, people had asked similar questions:

> *When Jesus entered Jerusalem, the whole city was stirred and asked,* **"Who is this?"**.
>
> (Matthew 21: 10)

> *. . . In fear and amazement they asked one another,* **"Who is this?** *. . .*
>
> (Luke 8: 25)

> *. . . And they being afraid wondered, saying to one another,* **What manner of man is this!** *. . .*
>
> (Luke 8: 25, King James Version)

Yeah, what manner of man is this for whom many people have died while disputing between themselves about his words and actions? Is this not the greatest puzzle on earth that a single man was born to this world about two thousand years ago and has since remained the most-discussed person in the world, and yet there is no universal answer? Some say he was "*just a good and brilliant religious leader*". Others say he was "*just a cunning opportunist*". Many others say he was "*a prophet of God*", and while some others even doubt whether he really existed at all, or is "*just the invented subject of a widespread fable*". However, according to the Bible, Jesus himself had also inquired in his own days to know what men say of him.

> *When Jesus came to Caeserea Philippi, he asked his disciples, "Who do people say the Son of Man is?" They replied, "Some say John the Baptist; others say Elijah;*

and still others, Jeremiah or one of the prophets."

(Matthew 16: 13 – 14)

Jesus could not have been at once "John the Baptist", and "Elijah", and "Jeremiah", and "one of the prophets". If at all he were any of these, he would have been only one of them and not all. But who really is this Jesus, whose singular life ended one social era for humankind and began another? Who really is this Jesus whose name has forever changed the way the world is?

When his disciples had told him what other men thought of him, Jesus further asked the disciples what they themselves thought of him.

"But what about you?" he asked. "Who do you say I am?" Simon Peter answered, "You are the Christ, the Son of the living God."

(Matthew 16: 15 – 16)

The Son of the Living God?

Of all that Jesus said and did, as reported in the Bible and contemporary literature, probably what gave the greatest public offence, and still generates the greatest controversies about him till today is the claim that he is *"the Son of the Living God"*. It was one claim way too much for the Jews of his time and for many persons ever since. How could a man, with flesh, blood, and bones, like us, be *"the Son of God"*? How could he be, when he was actually carried in the womb and born of a human mother as much as every other human?

Again, we cannot but consider it as it were from the biblical records, because what is written in the Bible books about him were spread around by word of mouth as early as the very century of his lifetime. Although contemporary literatures did not attribute as much personal statements to him as the Bible books do, the fact that he had claimed to be the Son of God was not contended in any of the literatures. Perhaps the only book of wide circulation and influence that denies the fact that Jesus claimed to be the Son of God is the Koran which in fact came after six centuries of Jesus' lifetime. But even the Koran says that the Jews had plotted to kill Jesus, and that brings up questions on why the Jews would have wanted to kill Jesus. We should reckon that if Jesus was not practising or teaching things that were fundamentally contrary to the Jewish laws

How could a man, with flesh, blood, and bones, like us, be "the Son of God"?

and customs, or by any other means giving offence, then the Jews would not have seriously considered killing him.

In the Bible, the Jews themselves testified that they had nothing else against Jesus except the fact that he claimed to be the Son of God.

> *Again the Jews picked up stones to stone him, but Jesus said to them, "I have shown you many great miracles from the Father. For which of these do you stone me?" "We are not stoning you for any of these," replied the Jews, "but for blasphemy, because you, a mere man, claim to be God."*
>
> (John 10: 31 – 33)

From contemporary literatures, we gather that many Jewish authorities of Jesus time regarded him as a "magician" and "blasphemer", but at once his disciples regarded him as a "miracle worker" and "the Christ". We know that when personal interests come into play, human choice of descriptive words vary according to our interests. For instance, when a man girdles himself with explosives and walks into a bus only to kill himself and the other people in that bus, certain people refer to him as "terrorist", others refer to him as "suicide bomber", and yet some others speak of him as "martyr". Whatever the name by which people choose to describe such a person according to their respective interests in him, the fact would remain that he had basically used some explosives to kill himself along with other people. And such might we also say of Jesus that whether his works were described as "magic" (according to those who did not accept him as the Christ) or as "miracles" (according to those who believe in him), the fact remains that he had a reputation, within and without his circle of followers, to have performed "acts of extraordinary nature". To describe those "extraordinary acts" as "magic" or "miracles" then depends on the personal interests of the people making the description. The singular fact that his contemporaries who did not believe in his Christhood recognised the extraordinariness of his acts leaves little room for those who argue that his reported "miracles" were simply make-believes.

Back to the person of Jesus, it is indeed possible that, as some say, the reason he was killed was because the contemporary Jewish authorities were jealous of his reputation for performing extraordinary acts. But then they would not have been able to successfully prosecute him unto death under the State if the only charge against him was that he was using (so-called) "magic" or "miracles" to excite the masses. Apart from his probably wide reputation for extraordinary acts, two other reasons could have made the Jews want to kill Jesus. According to the Bible and contemporary literatures, one reason is that he had a habit of breaking some Sabbath rules, and another reason is that he threatened to destroy the temple, which had taken more than forty-six years for the Jews to build. The issue is that these reasons were not terminal in themselves. There was more to breaking the Sabbath rules than really concerns Sabbath-keeping and there was more to destroying the Temple than concerns bricks and mortar. The question is, *"what was Jesus trying to prove by breaking the Sabbath and what would he have proven if he destroyed the Temple?"*.

As for the Temple, he had said *"if this Temple were destroyed, I will raise it up in only three days"*. But what he intended to prove by that was that he is the "Son of God" – according to the Bible. For unless he had such power as could have created the world, it would have been impossible for him alone to finish a nation's work of forty-six years in only three days.

Likewise was the issue of breaking the Sabbath. Jesus was close to several top Jewish rabbis and was himself also probably considered a rabbi. According to the Bible, there were times he had taught publicly in the synagogues and within the Temple premises. As a Jewish religious leader, he would normally have been bound by every bit of the Judaist laws as much as the priests and the Pharisees considered themselves bound. But Jesus did not only personally break some Sabbath traditions by working on the Sabbaths, he also taught people to do away with some of the traditions and elements of the Torah, as for instance the *"an-eye-for-an-eye"* rule and some laws on divorce, among others. The issue with breaking and changing the Torah rules was not just the rules in themselves, but the fact that he laid claim to having the authority to do so and yet be guiltless, and he also claimed an authority to single-handedly forgive the sins that are committed against God, which the Jews deemed only God alone could forgive.

When Jesus saw their faith, he said to the paralytic, "Son, your sins are forgiven." Now some teachers of the law were sitting there, thinking to themselves, "Why does this fellow talk like that? He's blaspheming! Who can forgive sins but God alone? . . . and he said to them, ". . . But that you may know that the Son of Man has authority on earth to forgive sins . . ."

(Mark 2: 5 – 12)

At that time Jesus went through the grainfields on the Sabbath. His disciples were

219

hungry and began to pick some heads of grain and eat them. When the Pharisees saw this, they said to him "Look! Your disciples are doing what is unlawful on the Sabbath." He answered, "Haven't you read what David did when he and his companions were hungry? He entered the house of God, and he and his companions ate the consecrated bread — which was not lawful for them to do, but only for the priests. Or haven't you read in the Law that on the Sabbath the priests in the temple desecrate the day and yet are innocent? I tell you that one greater than the temple is here. If you had known what these words mean, 'I deliver mercy, not sacrifice,' you would not have condemned the innocent. For the Son of Man is Lord of the Sabbath.". . . But the Pharisees went out and plotted how they might kill Jesus.

(Matthew 12: 1 – 14)

The Koran wants us to believe that Jesus never said these things that the Bible says he did. Yet it wants to believe that the Jews plotted to kill Jesus. When we consider the fame that surrounded Jesus, and his popularity among so many ordinary folks, we reckon that it would have been impossible for the Jewish leaders to win national condemnation against him to the point of death unless they could lay such a charge as would affect the interest of the ordinary folks against him. It may be possible that their basic motive was jealousy of his popularity and the fact that they *"could not bear the truth that he was teaching"*, as the Koran says. But then, they would not have been able to successfully prosecute him before a cross-section of the entire nation if their only excuses were his popularity and that he *"taught truths"*. If the "truths" that he was teaching did not in any way contradict what was written in the Torah and the Prophets, there could not have been a way for the Jewish leaders to publicly condemn him to death, because there would have been portions of the Torah and the Prophets that would stand in his defence as for instance the ones he cited about David and the priests.

The Pharisees were experts at "the Torah and the Prophets", and they aspired towards keeping it to the details. If Jesus was entirely like the Pharisees in this respect, keeping the Sabbaths rules as much as they did, and observing all the minor specifics of the Jewish scriptures that the Pharisees paid attention to, he could not have given a public offence enough for the nation to endorse his execution. If he was entirely like the Pharisees, he could not have said, *"I am the Son of God"*. We therefore cannot but reckon with the biblical report that Jesus was

> ### The Koran wants us to believe that . . .the Jews plotted to kill Jesus

counted a blasphemer on account of claiming to be the Son of God. Nothing less than this would have made the Jewish nation support the plan of the Pharisees to execute him publicly.

Is this not the Son of the Carpenter?

In spite of Jesus' more excellent fame, the Pharisees, who basically controlled the Sanhedrin, could have somehow managed to put up with Jesus, but his unbelievable claim about being Son of God, sent from the Father [God] above made it impossible. It is indeed understandable that the Jews should have every human reason to wonder at this claim, considering the fact that Jesus had flesh, blood, and bones, and a family, like everyone else.

"For I have come down from heaven not to do my will but to do the will of him who sent me. And this is the will of him who sent me, that I shall lose none of all that he has given me, but raise them up at the last day. For my Father's will is that everyone who looks to the Son and believes in him shall have eternal life, and I will raise him up at the last day." At this the Jews began to grumble about him because he said, "I am the bread that came down from heaven. They said, "Is this not Jesus, the son of Joseph, whose father and mother we know? How can he now say, 'I came down from heaven'?"

(John 6: 38 – 42)

When Jesus had finished these parables, he moved on from there. Coming to his hometown, he began teaching the people in their synagogue, and they were amazed. "Where did this man get this wisdom and these miraculous powers?" they asked. "Isn't this the carpenter's son? Isn't his mother's name Mary, and aren't his brother's James, Joseph, Simon and Judas? Aren't his sisters with us? Where then did this man get all these things?" And they took offense at him. . .

(Matthew 13: 53 – 58)

We must consider the fact that Jesus had a childhood and a family. He had neighbours and contemporaries who knew Joseph and Mary and the other children of the family. In that village, in which he probably grew up and also visited as an adult, no one could have been comfortable to hear from him *"I am the Son of God, I came down from heaven, I am eternal and I only can give eternal life"*. Whether he was sired by Joseph or not, the fact remains that he was raised to public knowledge as *"son of Joseph, the carpenter"*. The public idea of his paternity was that Joseph was his father.

The Son of Mary.

When we read the Christian part of the Bible, we are already told about the miracle conception before we meet the public Jesus and the idea that he was not sired by Joseph remains fixed in our minds when we eventually read about the publicly-known Jesus. But for the Jews of his days, and especially the people of Nazareth, many of them were not conscious of the miracle birth, that is if at all they were originally aware of it. The issue was that Jesus' birth was not in Nazareth: he was born in Bethlehem, according to the Bible. More importantly, Joseph had married Mary before Jesus was born and the messages of the angels to Mary and Joseph as reported in the Bible were probably not public knowledge. So, the people of Nazareth and the rest of the nation did not share the same knowledge with us about the miracle conception, or of the appearance of the angels to the shepherds, or of the star that appeared to the three wise men. The public may have been able to re-member that Herod had killed infants at about the time that Jesus was born, even as non-biblical contemporary sources reveal, but to them that could not have been significantly about Jesus. The Bible tells us that it was because of Jesus that Herod had killed all the infants; but it was Herod and not the entire nation that the three wise men had vis-ited, and the public may therefore not have known the real reason why Herod killed infants. Of course, they knew Herod as someone who could do that for no sound reason at all – Herod had killed even his own grown-up son, so why should he count it anything special to kill the infant children of other people? Nevertheless, Jesus as far as the public knew was born as every other child. If the people knew what Mary and Joseph had known between them, would Jesus have been born in the manger? Of course, many people would rather have slept in the streets than let the child be born in a manger, if they knew what Joseph and Mary kept between them. Moreover, the Bible expressly says that what the angels had told Mary about her conception, she "*kept in her mind*" – she did not go about to tell everyone.

> *But Mary treasured up all these things and pondered them in her heart.*
>
> (Luke 2: 19)

Mary had not made the secrets of her pregnancy a public knowl-edge and further still, she had referred to Joseph as Jesus' "father" out-side the home.

When his parents saw him, they were astonished. His mother said to him, "Son, why have you treated us like this? Your father and I have been anxiously searching for you.

(Luke 2: 48).

In all fairness to the Jews of Jesus' days and village, when we put ourselves in their shoes, we find they could not have so readily imbibed his claim as *"the Son of God"* because to them he had always been known, referred to, and regarded as, *"the Son of Mary and Joseph, the carpenter"*.

Given that, why would the public not have endorsed his execution when he stood firm by his claim as *"the Son of God"*? The Jews were a nation very jealous for the name of God as we have considered earlier in this book. It was to them a blasphemy of the highest order that a man, whose mother, brothers, sisters, and [publicly supposed] father they have always known, should come to openly say *"I came down from heaven, I am the Son of God, God does nothing without me, and I do nothing without him"*! According to the Bible, the Jews at first could not believe that Jesus was in fact serious about his claim. Some of them even told him *"You are mad!"*. But to them, and as much as we read from writings about him, he appeared to be sane in every other respect, therefore he carried responsibility for claiming to be the *"Son of God"*. On that charge, no judge or jury could pronounce a verdict of "not guilty for reason of insanity", because Jesus showed no sign of insanity at all. He carried full responsibility for the claim to the Christhood.

Many of them said, "He is demon-possessed and raving mad. Why listen to him?" But others said, "These are not the sayings of a man possessed by a demon. Can a demon open the eyes of the blind?"

(John 10: 20 – 21).

Whether we like it or not, we must sympathise with the feelings of the Jews of Jesus days. Here is man who taught them from the scriptures in more powerful and soul-stirring ways than they ever had before. Here is a man who taught them to be kind; forgiving, forbearing, giving, holy, dedicated, and virtuous in every way; a man who did many more acts of wonder before their very eyes than they ever heard about; a man who taught them that the greatest of all commandments is to *"love the LORD God with all your might, soul and heart"*. And yet here is a man claiming the eternality and authority that only God could rightly claim. They had no problem accepting him as "prophet" or "Rabbi" or "teacher" or "master". But to say, *"You are Christ, the Son of the Living God, you are the Lord from heaven"* conflicted with their settled knowledge that *"this is the Son of Mary and Joseph the carpenter, and his brothers and sisters are here with us"*.

Crucify Him!

So it came to pass that the Pharisee-controlled Sanhedrin eventually contrived to arrest and put Jesus to trial. They did not even take laws into their own hands. The way it is with many Christians when the name "Pharisees" is mentioned is as though the Pharisees were the vilest of men. But the reverse could have very well been true. If it was a matter of simply killing him to get rid of him, the Pharisees could easily have sent an assassin, or once they laid their hands on him, could have by themselves stoned him to death without putting him through the State trial. But rather than use jungle justice, they took him to Governor Pontius Pilate to be tried.

That night at both the Palace of the High Priest and the Governor's mansion, they had laid against Jesus the accusation of blasphemy. Before then, many of the Jewish leaders and the nation had received his fame and reports of his acts of wonders. Many of them were eye-witnesses of these things, but most people simply heard about him. However, in the week of his arrest, the most important Jewish celebration of the year was being held: the Passover was being commemorated. Jews came to Jerusalem not only from all over the nation but from various foreign lands. The Sanhedrin in council and the High Priest were there to perform their most important functions of the year. There and then Jesus was asked to confirm the claim that he is the Christ; the long-awaited King of Israel; the Son of God. He simply told them *"I am"* and they replied *"that's a blasphemy"*. According to the Bible, they blindfolded him, and slapped him in turns, asking him *"can you tell who among us had slapped you?"* Now, suppose Jesus had just spoken up then, suppose he mentioned the name of just one of them correctly, would that have changed the situation? Suppose he took a stone and turned it into a loaf of bread, suppose he took a rod, cast it to the ground and it became a snake, would that have changed the situation? But at the trial he did nothing of that sort. He only re-affirmed his statement that he is the Christ.

With the Governor, he had one more opportunity to escape death. Governor Pilate was not a Jew and did not count it anything much that Jesus claimed to be the Christ. Left to him alone, he could as well have let Jesus go. To him it was not a serious offence – it probably went like "So, *he is claiming that he is the King of Israel? Uh? But is he reigning over you? Has he threatened to overthrow the present Government? Does he have any military force or militia group? Is he planning a revolt?*". Jesus himself had answered Pilate, "*my kingship is not political*". [John 18: 36]. And as long as Pontius did not consider Jesus to be a political threat, he was ready to release him. But the Jews insisted that "*this blasphemer must be crucified – he is a man but he is claiming to be our God. If you do not kill him, he would destabilise the whole nation and that would not be in the interest of the Emperor*".

Again the Governor saw another opportunity to free Jesus, since he considered him harmless and thought the Jews were simply moved by the envy of Jesus' fame: he asked to release him under the festive amnesty. But the Jews preferred to free a prisoner that was known for murder and robbery, Barabbas.

*Now it was the governor's custom at the Feast to release a prisoner chosen by the crowd. At that time they had a notorious prisoner, called Barabbas. So when the crowd had gathered, Pilate asked them, "Which one do you want me to release to you: Barabbas, or Jesus who is called Christ?" For he knew it was out of envy that they had handed Jesus over to him. . . . But the chief priests and the elders persuaded the crowd to ask for Barabbas and to have Jesus executed. "Which of the two do you want me to release to you", asked the governor. "Barabbas," they answered. "What shall I do, then, with Jesus who is called Christ?" Pilate asked. They all answered, "**Crucify him!**". . .*

(Matthew 27: 15 – 26).

And so he was crucified. The Bible and contemporary literatures tell us that Jesus was actually crucified. But the Koran says he was not the one that was crucified. The Koran tells us that an angel had rescued Jesus from the midst of the Jews and had replaced him with an exact look-alike who was crucified instead of Jesus. But by the same token, the Koran in fact is implying that "*a man publicly believed to be Jesus was actually crucified*". By the charge of blasphemy laid against him, according to the Bible and other sources much older than the Koran, we know that the Jews would not have exchanged Jesus for another person. Not for any reason. At the Governor's mansion, they had rather freed a notorious robber and murderer than free "*a blasphemer*", as they called Jesus. The issue is that what happened after that crucifixion generated too much controversy and the Koran seemingly tries to avoid the arguments about the resurrection of Jesus by saying he was not really crucified in the first place. But the escape from death that the

Koran paints is as much difficult to believe as the resurrection that the Bible depicts. If God was powerful enough to have miraculously rescued Jesus from the cross and replaced him with an exact look-alike, so much that the Jews could not know that the man crucified was not the same Jesus that they had arrested and tried, and guardedly led from the Governor's mansion, God would have been equally powerful to raise Jesus back from death. But if the biblical account [resurrection] were considered implausible, so would be the Koran account [substitution with an exact look-alike]. The power capable of either of this would have been equally capable of the other. So, we cannot realistically substitute the Koran account of Jesus' crucifixion for the biblical and contemporary ones, until we have well examined all possibilities. Besides, we have to consider why God would have even freed Jesus from death in the manner that the Koran describes. What advantage would that have been to God? What would God have thus achieved in the minds of the Jews when in fact the person crucified does not appear to them to have changed from the same person that they had arrested and tried? The way the Koran puts it, the people who handled Jesus have no reason at all to doubt that he was the same person that they had crucified. The substitution, if it was real, would have been a secret known to God and God alone.

Whether we like to take it or not – the fact remains that it was widely believed that Jesus was actually charged and crucified for blasphemy, and what was counted as "blasphemy" in his case was that he claimed to be *"the Christ, the Son of God"*.

He was crucified with the wicked and buried with the rich.

This man, Jesus, had so much controversy surrounding him – and so many contradictions too. For being in the views of the Jews a sinner of the highest order, he was executed in the manner that was considered fit only for the worst criminals. But by a sudden twist, he ended up being buried among the crème-de-la-crème of the Jewish nation. For sceptics, we would rather believe that it is all a legend that Jesus was thus buried. However, given the offence for which he was charged, the many controversial statements attributed to him, and the circumstances in which he died, it was not possible for his burial to have been otherwise.

The issue is that Jesus' closest disciples had fled for their own lives when he was arrested and taken to trial. None of them that were known with him wanted to identify with him at that point lest they should be charged with being an accomplice of a man who dared claim he is *"as eternal as the Creator of the universe, without whom the Creator does nothing"*. The greatest hopes of the last remaining eleven disciples were destroyed when they saw him executed without any miraculous intervention. They expected more from him than they got at that hour – when he was captured, their confidence in him was captured, and when he died, so died every hope left in them.

His prosecutors however recollected that he had spoken of being the *"resurrection and the life"*, and had ever emphasised having the power of *"eternal life"*. They could not under any circumstance afford to release the corpse to just anybody. Even if his disciples could somehow find the courage to come forward for his body, the Sanhedrin could not afford the risk of releasing him to those who were capable of taking the body to some obscure places and then claim that he had resurrected. The only people to whom such a controversial corpse could have been entrusted were men in the leagues of those identified in the Gospels – Joseph of Arimathea and Nicodemus. Since these men were members of the Sanhedrin, the council that prosecuted Jesus, it was only to men like them that such a corpse could have been entrusted. It was a corpse of national importance; the Sanhedrin could not afford to lose sight of the corpse until it would have decayed. Normally, they would not even have allowed it to be buried in the first instance, at least not until the first three days would have passed – giving them enough time to prove wrong Jesus' boasting of rising up on the third day. But the day after his crucifixion was the Sabbath of the Passover, it was the high point of the celebrations; for the Jews, it was the most important day of any year. Leaving a corpse hanging or decaying in the open would defile the whole festival for them, it would defile the whole year. So, it had to be buried. Yet the corpse was such that must not be released to his family or friends or disciples lest they should hide it and claim he had risen. That was probably why it ended up being given to a member of the Sanhedrin for burial.

Although the Bible writers tell us that the man who went to Governor Pilate to request for the body was also a disciple of Jesus, they also remind us that he was a ***"secret disciple"***: the rest of the Sanhedrin probably did not know him as a disciple of Jesus at all. When he went to Governor Pontius Pilate, he could not have gone in the capacity of a disciple but as *"an honourable member of the Sanhedrin and an influential rich man in the society"*. Moreover, the Bible records show that the Sanhedrin was fully aware of the burial processes. Joseph did not go to the governor in secret. And if he thus had gone openly to the knowledge of the other members of the Sanhedrin and the public, he could not have gone as a disciple or friend of Jesus, lest he would have won the disfavour and wrath of the Sanhedrin. He may probably have gone with the excuse of not wanting the Passover Sabbath to be defiled.

For Joseph, we might question why he had to spare the grave he had prepared for his own self. One possible reason is that since it was a ready grave, it was immediately usable. Another possibility is that since it was very close to the city, it would be easier to keep an eye on it as the Sanhedrin wished. Yet another possibility is that he did not want to lose the favour of either parties – the Sanhedrin, on the one hand, and Jesus (if haply he should resurrect), on the other hand. These are just possibilities. We may never know why really he spared his own grave for Jesus. But we know that the eleven people who were closest to Jesus among the disciples did not probably take part in the burial arrangements; they had gone into hiding for their own lives, and had also been devastated as their master died the most shameful death helplessly. They were the only ones among the disciples who when other disciples had deserted Jesus for claiming to be the Son of God, stood by him and testified that they *"believe and are sure"* that Jesus is *"the Christ, the Son of the Living God"*. [John 6: 66 – 69].

Joseph certainly did not share the same strength of confidence in Jesus' Christhood as the eleven men had. If he was as "sure" as Peter, or James, or John, that Jesus was the Christ, then he would have abandoned all he had – his wealth and his position in the Sanhedrin both of which Jesus frequently spoke against. Like Nicodemus, Joseph probably believed too that Jesus was God-sent and had no problem taking him as *"Rabbi"*. But to take Jesus as *"Son of God"*, when in fact Jesus had the reputation of *"Son of the carpenter"* hanging about him, was probably too much for Joseph. But as Jesus had been crucified and had earlier said that the sign he would give for his Christhood would include being dead for three days, Joseph probably saw the opportunity to finally prove whether Jesus was truly the Christ. He could well have thought that burying Jesus in such a decent tomb would win him the favour of the resurrected Christ, if by any means he should resurrect. And of course he had nothing much to lose if Jesus did not resurrect after three days; he had not left the Sanhedrin or his wealth and therefore would have more favour with the Sanhedrin if he reports back to them that the corpse had been watched for three days and had not resurrected. In fact, Joseph appears to be someone who ever wanted to gain on both sides – otherwise why would he have been a (secret) disciple of Jesus and at once a member of the Sanhedrin?

He is not here, he is risen!

So it happened that Jesus was killed with the wicked and buried with the rich. It was such a rare combination for someone who had died the most shameful of deaths to also get a very decent burial in the cemetery of the elite.

The climax of the whole issue came on the day after the Sabbath when it was found that the grave had become empty. The very thing that the Sanhedrin feared had happened. The Sanhedrin had thought well ahead by providing guards for the tomb to ensure that the body would not be removed by Jesus' disciples or family. They could not have used Jewish guards because every Jew present in Jerusalem must be part of the Passover Sabbath. Guarding the tomb that Saturday would have meant "working", which would break the Sabbath rules – and the Sanhedrin being Pharisees would be the last to endorse such. Therefore, they had to request for Roman guards from Governor Pilate. But in spite of the Roman guards, who had the reputation of never toying with duty, it was found on Sunday that the body was missing from the tomb.

Many arguments surround the empty tomb and volumes upon whole volumes have been written about it. This book would not become one of those volumes. But we have to wonder how the body managed to be missing from the grave. Some people have suggested that perhaps the Roman guards abandoned duty and therefore created opportunity for the disciples of Jesus or his family to steal the corpse. Others have suggested that the guards were bribed by Jesus' disciples. Yet others have suggested that the body was in fact not buried there – some of these people believe that it was the larger-than-required volume of spices that Nicodemus provided that were enshrouded and buried under pretence. The propositions are listless. But it would have been most difficult, if not impossible, for the Sanhedrin to take anything for granted and allow spices to be buried instead of such a controversial corpse. Even if the only two people that represented the Sanhedrin at the burial were Joseph and Nicodemus, it would have been impossible to bury spices instead of the corpse. Joseph and Nicodemus probably had as much doubts about the Christhood of Jesus as many of us do, and to have swindled the Sanhedrin council by burying spices and giving the body away to Jesus' relatives or disciples would equally mean swindling their own selves. They had personal interest in keeping an eye on the corpse for the sake of their own faith, as much as it was in the interest of the Sanhedrin and the entire nation. It would have been a miracle for them to bury spices instead of the body. In all probability, that corpse had a 99.99% chance of making it into that tomb – it was a corpse of national importance, which also meant so much to Joseph of Arimathea who undertook to bury it; spices could only have been substituted for it if only Joseph was absent, which is most unlikely.

In all probabilities, that all-important corpse was interred in that tomb. The real question is how it managed to be missing from it. That brings us back to the Roman guards. If at all they abandoned duty, who could have cared or dared to go there and remove the corpse? Hardly would any Jew have done that on the most sacred Sabbath of the year, much more that the man killed the previous day is one who himself had broken some Sabbath rules. It would have taken so much gut for any Jew to steal the corpse on that Sabbath. Neither his family nor the eleven remaining disciples who probably did not know where he was buried could have gone to steal the corpse; if at all the Roman guards that are renowned for not abandoning duty somehow happened to toy with duty that day. And the issue about bribing the soldiers too could have taken some guts – the eleven disciples who had gone into hiding could not have found money enough to bribe the guards for the corpse. Besides the fact that they were not rich men, whatever amount they had would have been with Judas Iscariot who was the treasurer until the night of the arrest and who had not handed over his office or the chest, nor returned to join the eleven.

If anybody probably had motive enough to steal the corpse or bribe the guards for it, and probably had money enough to do so; if any Jew could have cared less about Jewish laws concerning handling corpses at that most sacred festival, perhaps Judas Iscariot would have been the best suspect. Overwhelmed by the grief of having betrayed his beloved master and friend, he may perhaps have decided to make up by making Jesus seemingly resurrect; and could have done anything to achieve that. But the most important thing about the resurrection was not that the tomb became empty, rather it was the word subsequently spread about that Jesus was seen alive thereafter. Even if Judas or anyone else had managed to get the corpse out of that guarded tomb by any means, he could not have been able to make Jesus seen alive thereafter. The question is how many people actually saw Jesus alive after the crucifixion and burial and how many people believe he truly resurrected?

Who has believed our report?

Though, the eleven disciples did not originally know where Jesus was buried, some women who were close to them knew the place, according to the Bible. When on that Sunday morning the women told the eleven that Jesus had resurrected, they invited the men to visit the tomb for evidence. But merely sighting an empty tomb did not persuade the eleven that Jesus had truly resurrected. They wanted Jesus himself – not his empty tomb. Later on, according to the Bible, Jesus appeared to them. Thomas Didymus – the Bible tells us – was not with them and refused to believe the report that Jesus had actually resurrected and had been seen alive by the rest. He it was who after Jesus appeared again to them asked to touch the holes in Jesus' hands and side.

> *The question is how many people actually saw Jesus alive after the crucifixion and burial and how many people believe he truly resurrected?*

*Now Thomas (called Didymus), one of the Twelve, was not with the disciples when Jesus came. So the other disciples told him, "We have seen the Lord!" But he said to them, "Unless I see the nail marks in his hands and put my finger where the nails were, and put my hand into his side, I will not believe it." A week later his disciples were in the house again, and Thomas was with them. Though the doors were locked, Jesus came and stood among them and said "Peace be with you!". Then he said to Thomas, "Put your finger here; see my hands. Reach out your hand and put it into my side. Stop doubting and believe." Thomas said to him, "My Lord and my God!". Then Jesus told him, "**Because you have seen me, you have believed**; blessed are those who have not seen and yet believed."*

(John 20: 24 – 29)

This is the point where it becomes most difficult: the eleven remaining disciples were NOT fully persuaded that Jesus had resurrected until they saw him, even though they had seen his empty tomb. Thomas stepped ahead to touch him. We are told that Jesus then ate bread and fish with them. But how are we to believe that he truly resurrected, when we have not seen him, nor touched him nor yet eaten with him as the disciples did – according to the Bible? If they had not seen and touched him would they have believed that he resurrected in spite of his empty tomb? Since they were not part of the burial activities, would they even have believed that he was truly buried in the same tomb that women showed them?

Questions tumble upon questions as we review the resurrection issue. Jesus in fact want men to believe that he resurrected – going by what he told the disciples that *"blessed are those who have not seen but yet believe"*, according to the Bible. But why did he not make personal efforts to make sure that ALL men do believe? Why did he not appear, for instance, to Governor Pilate, or High Priest Caiaphas, or the Sanhedrin, or at least Nicodemus and Joseph of Arimathea? The Bible does not tell us that he appeared to any of these persons. That leaves us to wonder why Jesus did not appear to as many people as saw him crucified so that he would have enough witnesses of his resurrection. Why did he choose that people should believe just **the report** of his resurrection rather than see him personally, touch him, and eat with him, as did the disciples? In fact, how many people believed the report of his resurrection, and how many can really do?

The Koran spares us most of these questions about the resurrection by telling us that Jesus was actually **not** crucified. The author of the Koran tells us that God had sent an angel to rescue Jesus by replacing him with an exact look-alike who was then killed instead of Jesus. The Koran in fact implies that Jesus had been seen alive by many people after that weekend so much that the Jews widely contended with themselves on the identity of the "Jesus" that was killed. As it were from the Koran, there was no reason to doubt that the man seen after that crucifixion weekend is Jesus; but whereas those who witnessed his crucifixion were certain that he was the one they had killed, those who did not witness his death and who had found him alive thereafter believed that another man must have been killed in his stead. Whereas at once the author of the Koran tells us that the man that was arrested and tried and sentenced to death was **unmistakably** the same Jesus, "Son of Mary and Joseph". The Koran implies that *"**except** a miracle had happened, the Jesus that was crucified was certainly the same Jesus that was arrested"*. But the Koran also goes further to imply that the man that was seen after that Passover weekend of the crucifixion was also undoubtedly the same Jesus that was arrested.

However, the Koran knowledge is extra-biblical information; which the author of the Koran got probably because he received some versions of the story that have not survived through other sources. Nevertheless, the information he gives us is very sensitive and the sum of it is that Jesus, *"the Son of Mary and Joseph"*, was seen alive after that weekend by as much a number of people as was enough to cause public arguments about his crucifixion.

Was there really a miracle that weekend?

When we gather together all the available information [be they (so-called) "reports", or "legends" or whatever else we might call them] about the crucifixion of Jesus and the aftermath, the sum of it all is that the general public as well as his eleven remaining disciples, at that time, had every reason to believe that Jesus was undoubtedly crucified. Sources outside both the Bible and the Koran inform us that Jesus was undoubtedly crucified. The Bible informs us that Jesus was undoubtedly crucified. The Koran informs us that, barring a miracle, Jesus was undoubtedly crucified. The sources outside the Bible and the Koran inform us that there were "rumours" of his empty tomb and appearances shortly after the weekend of the crucifixion. The Bible informs us there were "reports" of his empty tomb and appearances beginning from the first day of the week that followed his crucifixion. The Koran implies that he was certainly seen alive after that weekend so much that it became a public argument that he may not have been the one crucified.

We must carefully observe that the Koran does not want to present Jesus to us as "the Christ, the Son of the living God". But it informs us that a miracle happened that weekend. The miracle it puts to us is that an angel had delivered Jesus from the hands of the executioners without the knowledge of the executioners, who did not for a moment stop handling Jesus. It directly implies that if miracles do not happen, then Jesus was certainly the person crucified. The Bible also says a miracle had happened that weekend but the miracle it puts to us is that Jesus was raised back to life after his crucifixion. In its own case it implies that if miracles do not happen, then Jesus certainly did not resurrect, and still remains dead till today. The non-Bible-non-Koran sources that inform us of his crucifixion do not claim that a miracle had happened, their own account is that his body was fraudulently withdrawn from the grave (either by not being placed there in the first place or by bribing the soldiers that guarded the tomb to release the body to his disciples). Nevertheless, given the offence for which he was charged, the unflinching interests of the Sanhedrin and the public in his corpse, and reputation and interests of the Joseph who led the burial, the claim of non-Bible-non-Koran sources implies that it would have taken a (near) miracle for the body not to have been buried in that tomb or for it to have been stolen from it or yet for the body to have been sold by the guards to the disciples. By wide implication, whether they seek to buttress Jesus' claim to the Christhood or not, all the primary sources that discuss what happened to Jesus that weekend seek refuge in "miracles" – that is, *"phenomena beyond human comprehension"*.

When we think of Jesus and the circumstances that surrounded his death and how within a few days thereafter it began to be spread about that he has resurrected, and the natures of the "reports" and "rumours", all the explanations put forward on how the "reports" or "rumours" managed to gain ground rise beyond human comprehension. Can we indeed believe the "reports" (or "rumours")?

Unless we believe in miracles, we cannot rationally explain the aftermath of the arrest of Jesus. If we go with the non-Bible-non-Koran sources, we find that it would have been a miracle if the Sanhedrin had allowed the corpse to go to anyone apart from someone they could trust (such as Joseph of Arimathea). It would have been a miracle if Joseph had buried Nicodemus's spices instead of the corpse in which he personally had interest in verifying whether it would resurrect or not. It would have been a miracle if the Sanhedrin had allowed the corpse to be left in an unguarded tomb. It would have been a miracle if the guards at the tomb had abandoned the duty assigned them by Governor Pilate, when they in fact had been well briefed and paid by the Sanhedrin, and in spite of being renown for not abandoning duties even in the face of dangers. It would have been a miracle if the corpse were stolen from amidst the guards, when none of them had been killed. It would have been a miracle if the guards had sold the corpse to anyone when in fact the Sanhedrin was more than jealously prepared to overpay for the head of anyone who dared offer to buy the corpse. Something special must have happened for the all-important corpse to be missing from that grave and unless we believe in miracles, we cannot rationally uphold the non-Bible-non-Koran explanations of the empty tomb.

If we go with the Koran, we may find it plausible to believe that Jesus was not the person killed. But unless we believe in miracles, the explanation of the substitution cannot be imbibed. And even then, if Jesus had been thus miraculously rescued from crucifixion, how about the corpse of the person that was killed in his stead; the corpse that would have been supposed (according to the Koran) as the corpse of Jesus? Whatever happened to that corpse? Did the angel that rescued Jesus further steal the corpse of his substitute from the tomb? Was it a double miracle? The Koran has in fact implied that it could not be conclusively proven that the Jesus was not the person killed – that is probably because the corpse of the (so-called) substitute was missing from the guarded tomb while at once Jesus was being seen alive after the crucifixion. It would have been a miracle if the corpse of Jesus' (so-called) substitute were missing from the guarded tomb while the real Jesus was subsequently seen about.

For the Bible's explanations, unless we believe in miracles, we cannot believe that Jesus actually resurrected. It was the same eleven disciples who had ran into hiding for their own lives during the trial and the crucifixion that came out again and dared death to publicly testify that they had seen Jesus alive, had touched him, spoken with him and eaten with him. If Jesus had not resurrected, it would have been a miracle if Simon Peter (who on the night of the arrest denied ever knowing Jesus) return again to testify before the Sanhedrin that he is a witness and disciple of Jesus. If Jesus remained dead while Peter openly undertook punishments on account of testifying that Jesus had resurrected, Peter must have gone insane. But Peter's insanity would have been immediately provable if the corpse remained in the grave, or if there was a rational explanation of the missing corpse. There was no such incontrovertible explanation from the Sanhedrin. Yet at the moment that he denied Jesus, Peter could no longer have been sure that Jesus was truly the Christ. But after that weekend, he gladly submitted himself to stripes and lashes and imprisonments and ultimately death. What happened to Peter, if miracles do not take place?

Only a miracle could have persuaded the siblings of Jesus to join the rank and file of those who believe that their own blood brother is the "*Son of God*" – as we found from the Bible that they did not believe this until after that weekend. A mere empty tomb would not have persuaded the brothers of Jesus to join the company of Peter and the sons of Zebedee. If they had not seen their brother alive again after that weekend, the simple fact that Peter or John or Thomas reports to them that they had seen him could not have persuaded them that the son of their mother is also the Son of God. Neither would his empty tomb or the report of the women that visited the tomb have persuaded them [Jesus' siblings].

The whole issue about that weekend is so entangled. But Jesus was in all probability crucified and buried in a guarded tomb before the Sabbath. After the Sabbath, he was no longer found in the tomb while at once "reports" or "rumours" began to spread about that people are seeing him alive after the Sabbath. And then also the unlikeliest people began to believe in his Christhood, not least among these were the very people who came out of the same womb from which he came and sucked the breasts that he had sucked. It is they, more any of us today, who had enough reasons to never believe in his Christhood. Yet that weekend changed them and made them believe in him, leaving us to wonder whether a miracle had actually taken place and what exactly the miracle could have been. But before we can decide what the miracle could have been, we must first resolve whether miracles happen at all.

Do miracles truly take place?

Oftentimes when the word "miracle" is used, many of us immediately retort that "miracles are 'make-believes' and 'hear-says'". For the "make-believes" part I may not be qualified to comment extensively, but for hearsays, I know that I have never been an eyewitness of blind persons regaining sights, nor deaf persons regaining their senses of hearing, nor yet lame persons jumping up and walking, nor even yet corpses regaining lives. I have also met only a few people who claim they were eyewitness of such miracles, but most people simply report the testimonies of others. Yet I have not found such reports implausible because I reckon that the universe itself is a miracle, and also because the prayer and prophecy cycle of which I have ample personal experiences are "miracles" in their own rights.

When we talk of miracles, the greatest miracle that ever took place is the origination of the universe. Even if no further miracles take place, we cannot but reckon with the power and wisdom that originated the universe because the origination of the universe surpasses human comprehension in every way.

Science informs us that the Universe as we know it has not always been as it is. The universe is constantly expanding with new stars and planets being formed while others have disintegrated. At a particular time, everything was compacted together in one singular mass. That mass of matter itself had not eternally existed. It has an origin. But how it managed to come into existence without a material source remains the greatest miracle ever.

Without having to repeat the whole discourse on what the world and everything in it consist of, we should borrow the wisdom in the fact that the world consists entirely of absolute nothing when we reduce everything to its smallest constituents. Our human wisdom knows how to "create" a thing using specific source materials, but the *Originator* of the universe brought out the entire world from no source material at all, and that alone is the greatest miracle ever. And there is no way we can say there is no *Originator* considering the fact that cosmology agrees that the entire universe came out of absolute nothing. The eternal power and wisdom by which that was accomplished is reposed in the sole *Originator* of the universe, and that same *Originator* is capable of any thing such that nothing is in fact impossible for him to do.

As humans, we are always quick to conclude that whatever we cannot do, cannot be done. Many years ago, some people imagined humans flying in the sky – moving from one geographic location to another without touching the ground. People told them *"it is impossible"*. But today, not only have humans been able to fly from on place on the earth to another, humankind has visited even the moon. It was impossible. But suppose people knew the wisdom and power that is required to actualise these, they would not have concluded that such was "impossible".

In the Bible, God is reported to have told a ninety-year-old woman that she would conceive a child sired by her hundred-year-old husband. It was impossible; the woman was far beyond menopause. In fact, many of her age mates' daughters must have passed menopause at that time. But God assured her that there is *"**nothing** too difficult"* for him to do.

Then the LORD said, "I will surely return to you about this time next year, and Sarah your wife will have a son." Now Sarah herself was listening at the entrance to the tent, which was behind him. Abraham and Sarah were already old and well advanced in years, and Sarah was past the age of childbearing. So Sarah laughed to herself as she thought "After I am worn out and my master is old, will I now have this pleasure?" Then the LORD said to Abraham, "Why did Sarah laugh and say 'Will I really have a child, now that I am old?' Is anything too hard for the LORD? I will return to you at the appointed time next year and Sarah will have a son." Sarah was afraid, so she lied and said "I did not laugh". But he said, "yes, you did laugh".

(Genesis 18: 10 – 15)

Who would not laugh at God's ridiculous boast? A ninety-year-old woman becoming pregnant was totally unheard of. But because God had by his own wisdom and power brought out the sub-proton-sized particle, *Matter*, from no source material at all, and had from that sub-proton-sized *Matter* created the entire Universe that is many billion of trillion times larger in volume and mass than *Matter*, it was a small issue to him to rejuvenate a womb that was doubly dry. Many of us still laugh at the story today because it sounds so unrealistic to us [far more than the Wright brothers' airplanes sounded impossible to their contemporaries], but the *Eternal Noumenon* did fulfil his promise and gave Sarah a son, however ridiculous it originally sounded – according to the Bible.

Now the LORD *was gracious to Sarah as he had said, and the* LORD *did for Sarah what he had promised. Sarah became pregnant and bore a son to Abraham in his old age, at the very time God had promised to him. Abraham gave the name Isaac to the son Sarah bore him. When his son Isaac was eight days old, Abraham circumcised him, as God commanded him. Abraham was a hundred years old when his son Isaac was born to him. Sarah said, "God has brought me laughter, and everyone who hears about this will laugh with me." And she added, "Who would have said to Abraham that Sarah would nurse children? Yet I have borne him a son in his old age."*

(Genesis 21: 1 – 7)

I do not know of you, but I am laughing here with Sarah. Not only to share with her the joy of going to her grave with her ninety years of barrenness removed, but also to share with her the preposterousness with which she had received God's promise initially. Unfortunately, the latter reason for laughter is the only one that many of us share with her – we find it hard to believe that she eventually had the longer latter laughter of satisfaction and joy.

Many other things are laughable today – cloning was **impossible**, decoding the human genome was **impossible**, tissue culture was **impossible**, laser surgery was **impossible**, email was **impossible**, ecommerce was **impossible** – we could keep listing impossibilities forever. Perhaps the word "impossible" itself is the impossible – our perennial enemy. Perhaps, it should be replaced by the phrase "yet to be discovered".

Now we return to the crucifixion weekend and consider Jesus, his arrest, his burial, his empty tomb, and view the fact that unless something beyond normal human comprehension or capabilities had taken place during that weekend, the corpse would have remained in the guarded tomb, at least until after the first three days or until after it had decayed. We also consider the fact that the siblings of Jesus accepted him as "the Christ" after that weekend while yet we know that a mere empty tomb could not have persuaded them. For this last reason, if not for any other, we reckon that the non-Bible-non-Koran propositions about the empty tomb cannot rationally hold. The incomprehensible event that took place that weekend and forever changed the way the world lives could not have been that spices were buried in place of Jesus, or that by any means he was not buried in that tomb, or that the corpse was stolen or bought from the soldiers. The actuality of the incomprehensible event that took place should lie between the Bible's account and the Koran's.

Without prejudice, I would personally have wished to completely believe the Koran version – but the Koran version does not realistically account for how the corpse of the (so-called) "substitute Jesus" was buried or how it managed to escape from the guarded tomb, since he was taken for the real Jesus, according to the Koran. The Koran implies that not only did God replace the real Jesus with an exact look-alike before the crucifixion; God must also have taken care of the corpse of the substitute. If the incomprehensible event of that weekend went the way of the Koran, what impression would it have created on the minds of Jews? In the Koran way, the Jews would have killed the substitute Jesus that looked exactly like the real Jesus, after capturing the real Jesus and never letting go of him, and because of the controversial claim for which the real Jesus was charged, the tomb of the substitute Jesus would have remained guarded. But when subsequently the real Jesus was seen alive and about so much that it became public arguments whether he was really the one killed or not, if no miracle had taken place, the corpse of substitute Jesus would have been found in the tomb and that would have immediately put to rest the arguments about the identity of the person crucified. But the arguments persisted, probably because no corpse was in the tomb – and no shrouded spices either. For those who may have been privileged to follow the whole events, the impression on their minds (even if indeed there was a substitute Jesus) would have been that the real Jesus that was captured is the same that was killed and buried and still the same that was seen alive thereafter. The sum of the impression would be that Jesus had resurrected. The issue is that, from all the miracles recorded in the Koran and the Bible, God is never known to perform "look-alike miracles". All the miracles attributed to God in both of these books present

God as one who would do his miracles straight through – God would not do a thing that would look like a miracle when in fact it is not. God would not normally do two minor miracles [of replacing the real Jesus with an exact look-alike and then removing the substitute Jesus from the tomb] in order to create the impression of having done a greater one [of letting the real Jesus be crucified and resurrected]. Although, indeed no miracle is greater (in the absolute sense) than another – but because they make varied intensities of impressions on our animal minds we can call some, *"great"* and others, *"minor"*. Nevertheless, we reckon that if the Koran is right in what it says about the crucifixion of Jesus, the series of events would have only created the impression that the real Jesus had resurrected. But God, as depicted throughout the Koran and the Bible, does not normally create mere impressions – he simply does the real things.

Without any prejudice, and in consideration of the information gathered from religious and non-religious sources about the person of Jesus, his death and burial, his empty tomb and subsequent appearances, those among humans who have given thought enough to all these things more often than not conclude that it was the real Jesus (and not a substitute) that was crucified, certified dead, and buried in the jealously guarded tomb that became empty during the same weekend. The Bible explicitly tells us that by a miracle of God – the *Originator* of the universe – Jesus actually resurrected. The Koran does not want us to believe this, but at once it fails to give us a satisfactory alternative explanation – its explanation in fact suggests what the Bible explicitly states. Non-Bible-non-Koran sources also fail to give us satisfactory alternative explanations. Yet the Bible's own submission is as laughable as the birth of Isaac by a ninety-year-old woman, or indeed the origination of the entire vast universe from the difficult-to-imagine sub-proton-sized *Matter*, which itself came out of absolute nothing. But as a matter of logic, whatever power was capable of rejuvenating a doubly dry womb or originating the universe from absolute nothing should as a matter of course be also capable of making Jesus resurrect in that guarded tomb. The resurrection of the dead indeed sounds preposterous – but so also sounds every miracle recorded in religious literature, and so sounded even the human accomplishments that were once in actual fact **"impossible"**. Cloning, for instance, was a laughable idea. Today, it is a reality.

Now know we no man after the flesh.

Within two months of the crucifixion, the emptiness of the tomb, and the widely reported appearances, more than three thousand people at a go joined the eleven disciples that had abandoned Jesus on his night of arrest – according to the Bible. And from then on many people have continued to join the rank and file of those who believe that Jesus is the Christ. Nevertheless, the Bible itself says that the Sanhedrin intimidated the disciples of Jesus and charged them to stop testifying of his resurrection and Christhood. But by a twist, these helpless men who had lost all hope and respect when their master was shamefully crucified, dared the council and were willing to die rather than yield to the warnings of the Sanhedrin. In that again is a reason to believe that they were not merely resting their conviction on the fact of an empty tomb alone. If all they had found was that the tomb became empty (as implied by non-Bible sources), there would have been no gain for them in the sufferings they turned about to willingly embrace.

Among those who joined the eleven was Stephen. Stephen testified before the Sanhedrin that the same Jesus that they had prosecuted and used the State authority to execute publicly had resurrected. He argued that the human history and person of Jesus matched the scriptural prophecies about the expected Christ. For us, we do not all know how he managed to link the prophecies of the Torah and the Prophets with the person of Jesus, but at least we find that he quotes the psalmist king, David, who had said that *"God will not leave my soul in the grave nor allow His Christ to decay"*. [Psalm 16: 10]

Stephen argued that David remained in the grave and had decayed, whilst Jesus did not decay and could no longer be found in the grave. The submission of Stephen was that David could therefore not have referred to himself as the Christ. He argued that what David said about the Christ was apparently fulfilled by the obvious resurrection of Jesus. Nevertheless, Stephen was eventually stoned not only because what he was saying about Jesus did not go down well with the Sanhedrin, but also because he called the chief priests, and even the high priest *"obstinate people and murderers"* to their face, and went ahead to declare that he could see Jesus in a vision standing in the skies by the throne of God.

At Stephen's stoning, the Bible says, was a most zealous Pharisee, Saul (who also had the name Paul). Paul, we are told, endorsed the killing of Stephen and was making spirited efforts to exterminate Christianity and all Christians. Paul himself became a Christian in the very process of trying to exterminate Christianity – the Bible says. Authorship of about half the Christian part of the Bible is attributed to Paul, and the forcefulness of the writings shows how aggressively he must have pursued his goal of seeing Christianity exterminated, if he had applied his typical enthusiasm in pursuit of exterminating Christianity.

We must of course bear in mind that the most fundamental reason why the Pharisees and the Sanhedrin executed Jesus and determined to abort Christianity in its infancy was the fact that Jesus had always been publicly acknowledged as *"Son of Mary and Joseph, the carpenter"* but was claiming later in life to be *"the Son of God, as eternal as God himself, without whom God does nothing"*! But from all indications, Paul never met Jesus as *"Son of Mary and Joseph"*, he seems to have embraced all that the Jewish leaders said about Jesus, and accordingly furiously sought to quench Christianity before it would spread far too wide. For the noted legality of the Pharisees, Paul did not wish to take laws into his hands and decided to first obtain the support of higher authorities before laying his hands on any Christian. Armed with authority, he suppressed the Christians in Jerusalem to a large extent and while seeking to exterminate Christianity from other locations, he ran into a miracle – according to the Bible: Jesus interacted with him.

Paul's encounter with the resurrected Jesus is registered three times in the Acts of Apostles. In the first entry, [Acts 9: 1 – 9], we are told that Paul and his companions saw a light that was brighter than the sun, and heard a voice, the "sounds" of which his companions also heard. In the second entry, [Acts 22: 1 – 11], Paul testified that he saw a light brighter than the sun and heard a voice; he said his companions saw the light but did not "understand" the voice. In the third entry, [Acts 26: 4 –18], Paul testified that he and his companions saw a light brighter than the sun; and that a voice spoke to him in his tribal language. Some people have argued that there are discrepancies in the descriptions of Paul's encounter with the light and sound – and indeed the details do not exactly tally but that is not by any means a suggestion that they contradicted one another. Particular attention has been drawn to the difference between first and second entries, laying emphasis on the fact that in one Paul said that his companions **did not see** "anyone" but heard the **"sounds"**, and in the other he said that his companions **saw** the "light" but did not "understand" the **voice**. But when we look at it logically, we see that Paul did not mean that the *"light"* is the same as the *"anyone"* that was not seen, and neither did he mean that *"hearing the sounds of the voice"* is the same as *"understanding the speech of the voice"*. Probably, what he meant by mentioning in the third entry that the voice spoke in his ancestral language is that his companions did not understand that language, even though they heard the sounds of the speech.

Without pursuing further the minor details about the entries, we should also consider those who argue that Paul was drawn to Christianity for pecuniary or similar reasons and in order to gain an esteemed reputation. But we should at once cautiously acknowledge the fact that there was no good enough reason other than such a miracle as he described that would have made Paul abandon a bird in his hand to futilely pursue two in the bush. Here is a man who had it all going for him in the Judaist religion. Even if the then nascent Christianity promised Paul any material or social benefit better than Judaism had to offer him, the mere fact that it was a start-up, and had no track records, and had all hands against it, should have dissuaded Paul from it. The mere fact that Christians had many chances of being stoned to death by the Pharisees should have dissuaded him from becoming a Christian. Besides, Judaism was by far more formidable and widespread, was patronised by a larger number of wealthy individuals, and Paul had the favour of the very pillars of Judaism. He could not have changed his mind suddenly to embrace a poorer and weaker, start-up religion, and abandoned the one for which he could be guaranteed a firm success, unless something special had happened to him. Unless he had encountered a miracle, he could not suddenly embrace a religion that he was continuously succeeding at exterminating. Moreover, he later encouraged himself so much and prided in the **sufferings** that came with the new religion; only a miracle could have been able to change him from Judaism unless he had run insane (as Governor Festus supposed – Acts 26: 24).

However, Paul's speeches and writings as reported in the Bible show no sign of mental illness. They show a deep and firm conviction. But if by any means he had run insane at the very point of almost completely wiping out Christianity from the face of the earth, what a time to have run insane! The timeliness of the insanity would have in itself been a miracle. Notwithstanding whatever is said against Paul's conversion, something wondrous must have affected Paul's mind so much that he became irrevocably persuaded that Jesus is the Christ to the extent that he was willing to die for the conviction and also encouraged all men to **"endure all things"** just in order to please the Christ. If what so affected him was not the miracle that he had described, it could not have been anything of lesser wonder. Paul wrote later:

Who will bring any charge against those whom God has chosen? It is God who justifies. Who is he that condemns? Christ Jesus, who died – more than that, who was raised to life – is at the right hand of God and is also interceding for us. Who shall separate us from the love of Christ? Shall trouble or hardship or persecutions or famine or nakedness or danger or sword? As it is written: "For your sake we face death all day long: we are considered as sheep to be slaughtered." No, in all these things we are more than conquerors through him who loved us. **For I am convinced** *that neither death nor life, neither angels or demons, neither the present nor the future, nor any powers, neither height nor depth, nor anything else in all creation, will be able to separate us from the love of God that is in* **Christ Jesus our Lord.**

(Romans 8: 33 – 39)

What! Paul? The same Paul who had endorsed the killing of Stephen for saying that *"Jesus is the Christ standing at the right hand of God"*? This is laughable – as laughable as Sarah's pregnancy and the birth of Isaac. Yet Paul stood by this conviction through so many things, encouraging himself and others to embrace untold sufferings on account of testifying that Jesus had risen from the dead and is the Christ. He gave a summary of some of his sufferings afterwards:

Are they Hebrews? So am I. Are they Israelites? So am I. Are they servants of Christ? (I am out of my mind to talk like this.) I am more. I have worked much harder, been in prison more frequently, been flogged more severely, and been exposed to death again and again. Five times I received from the Jews the forty lashes minus one. Three times I was beaten with rods, once I was stoned, three times I was shipwrecked, I spent a night and a day in the open sea, I have been constantly on the move. I have been in danger from rivers, . . . for Christ's sake

(2 Corinthians 11: 22 – 12:10)

To Paul himself it sounded insane that he who had sought to destroy Christianity should now boast of his untold sufferings in order to testify that Jesus is the Christ. If Paul did not experience the miracle he had described, would a mere empty tomb have changed his belief about Jesus? I do not think so. Moreover, Paul eventually could resolve between what he had learned about Jesus from the Jews and from his own personal encounter with the *Voice*. He acknowledged the fact that Jesus had always been known as a man – *"Son of Mary and Joseph, the carpenter"* – but could not be known any more as such:

So from now on we regard no one from a worldly point of view. Though we once re-

garded Christ in this way, we do so no longer.

(2 Corinthians 5: 16)

Wherefore henceforth know we no man after the flesh: yea, though we have known Christ after the flesh, yet now henceforth know we him no more.

(2 Corinthians 5: 16, King James Version)

While he pursued the extermination of Christianity, Paul reckoned with Jesus as a mere man – since Jesus was reputed as Son of Mary and Joseph. But after a mysterious encounter, according to the Bible, he turned to believe that Jesus is the Son of God and that the Christhood is not a political office, in contrast with what he would have always believed as a Pharisee. From then on, he related with Jesus as Christ rather than as the Son of Mary and Joseph. As it were, when Paul first heard the Christians preach Jesus as Christ, he reckoned with the outer man [flesh, blood and bones – human animal] of Jesus. However, his encounter with the *Voice* on the road to Damascus made him reckon no more with the outer man, but with the inner (spirit) being. But he therefore leaves us to wonder whether it is wrong to regard Jesus as the Son of Mary and Joseph, when in fact that is what people had always known Jesus to be.

The Son of David?

While he lived as the Son of Mary and Joseph, the Bible says Jesus had himself asked Jewish leaders about the paternity of the Christ:

While the Pharisees were gathered together, Jesus asked them, "What do you think about the Christ? Whose son is he?" "The son of David," they replied. He said to them, "How is it then that David, speaking by the Spirit, calls him 'Lord'? For he says, " 'The Lord said to my Lord: "Sit at my right hand until I put your enemies under your feet." ' If then David calls him 'Lord,' how can he be his son?" No one could say a word in reply, and from that day on no one dared to ask him any more questions.

(Matthew 22: 41 – 45)

One issue is that David did not specifically state that he was writing about the Christ when he wrote the Psalm that Jesus referenced. [Psalm 110]. Yet as it is in the Gospel of Matthew, the Pharisees who were experts at the Torah and the Prophets did not retort that the psalm was not about the expected Christ. Possibly, then, it was generally accepted that David was speaking about the expected Christ. Nevertheless, the expectation of the Jews was that the Christ would be a prophet as well as political king just as much as David was – in fact better than David – but from the lineage of David. But since he is expected to be David's son, we too should wonder why David should call him "Lord". Moreover, David had said in that same psalm that God has sworn to this his "Lord" to be *"a priest forever, in the order of Melchizedek"*. [Psalms 110: 4]. Yet David knew that priesthood for the Jews had been covenanted under Moses to be perpetually in the order of Aaron. But under the Torah and the Prophets it was not done that a king should also be a priest; of all the priests of the God of the Jews, only Melchizedek was at once a king as well as a priest. And the priesthood of Melchizedek was many years before Moses gave the Law to the Jews, and as such he was not made a priest under the Levitical codes.

In his psalm, David addressed a new priest that would be made in the order of Melchizedek. Apart from David's psalm, Melchizedek was only mentioned once in the whole Torah and Prophets and that was when he met Abraham and blessed Abraham in God's name. [Genesis 14: 18 – 20]. Apart from the three short verses that reports that instance, the Torah and Prophets have no other documentation of Melchizedek's genealogy. But the Jews reckoned with his priesthood, even though they could not tell his predecessor or successor. Yet he was counted a greater high priest than Aaron not only because he was a priest much long before Aaron was born, but also because Aaron's great ancestor, Abraham, had been blessed by Melchizedek. In the Jewish way, it was reckoned that it is the greater that blesses the lesser [Hebrews 7: 7] – and yet Abraham was counted greater than Aaron; how much far greater than Aaron, therefore, would Melchizedek have been counted?

While the Jews of his days questioned him about his claim to Christhood, Jesus said to them, *"Abraham had so longed for my presence, and when he found it, he was glad"*.

Jesus replied, ". . . You father Abraham rejoiced at the thought of seeing my day; he saw it and was glad." "You are not yet fifty years old," the Jews said to him, "and you have seen Abraham!" "I tell you the truth," Jesus answered, "before Abraham was born, I am!" At this, they picked up stones to stone him, but Jesus hid himself, slipping away from the temple grounds.

(John 8: 54 – 58)

Jesus could not certainly have meant that Mary had given birth to him before Abraham was born, so how could he have said that Abraham was glad at his presence if he perceived himself as mere flesh, blood, and bones? And how could David have called him "Lord" who would be the Christ, if the Christ were to be no more than mere flesh, blood and bones? Yet even Paul agrees that Jesus is from the tribe of Judah [Hebrews 6: 14], whilst the Jews do not reckon a man's nativity by his maternity but by his paternity. For Jesus to have been counted as *"descending from Judah"* and as *"son of David"*, his paternity – routed through the progenitors of Joseph the carpenter – must have been reckoned with. [Matthew 1: 1 – 16 and Luke 3: 23 – 38].

The Jews apparently had conflicting ideas on how the expected Christ should be. They had expected he would be the *"Son of David"* – that is, a descendant from David's lineage. Yet at once they believed that *"the Christ would come from nowhere"*:

At that point some of the people of Jerusalem began to ask, "Isn't this the man they are trying to kill? Here he is, speaking publicly, and they are not saying a word to him. Have the authorities really concluded that he is the Christ? But we know where this man is from; when the Christ comes, no one will know where he is from."

(John 7: 25 – 27)

The Jews probably counted that the Christ would be *"in order of Melchizedek"* [whose genealogy was not known], as they believed David had foretold. So, the Christ was expected to be at once without genealogy and yet be of Davidic ancestry. As a man, and as long as he was counted the son of Joseph the carpenter, Jesus matched the Davidic ancestry part. But the Jews could not by any means link Jesus with the Melchizedek part of *"unknown genealogy"*. It is in fact amazing how they could have realistically expected to blend the two "thumb prints" – David's and Melchizedek's – in one man: whoever would be known as the *"Son of David"* could consequently not be of *"unknown genealogy"* and vice versa. Yet the Jews were not to accept as Christ whoever could not fulfil both qualities. Could anyone indeed ever fulfil both qualities at once?

The Lord is that Spirit.

Paul, when he made his case to the Corinthians on the difference between the "Old Testament and the New", referred to Jesus [whom he often called "Lord"] as *"the Spirit"*.

Now the Lord is the Spirit, and where the Spirit of the Lord is, there is freedom. And we, who with unveiled faces all reflect the Lord's glory, are being transformed into his likeness with ever-increasing glory, which comes from the Lord, who is the Spirit.

(2 Corinthians 3: 17 – 18)

Until Paul had become a Christian, he was used to regarding a man as just the (outward) animal man. As a Pharisee, he believed in the existence of spirits but he made no distinction between the "outward [animal] man" and the "inner [spirit] man". But on the road to Damascus, he encountered Jesus not as an "outward" man, but as an "inner" man. What changed his mind about the reported resurrection of Jesus was not that he dipped his fingers into holes of Jesus hands, feet and side, or that he ate bread and fish with Jesus. He was changed by a *Voice* which spoke with him from the midst of the brightness that was greater than the sun's, and yet he and his companions did not see anyone in that brightness – just in the way Moses too had encountered a *Voice* in the fire that was present in the bush without burning up the bush, and yet did not see anyone in that fire. From then on, Paul who had endorsed the killing of those who believed that Jesus doubled as both the Son of David and Lord to David also reverted to the same belief. He then began to reckon that Jesus was counted as Son of David only in honour to David, but in real terms Lord to David, in the order of Melchizedek.

To Paul, and indeed to all the apostles, what makes Jesus qualify as "Christ" and "Lord" was not the issue of the (controversial) virgin birth. In fact, they did not originally attach so much significance to the virgin birth factor. Like every other person around them, they too must have originally believed that Jesus was sired by Joseph the carpenter. By emphasising the virgin birth in the Gospels, the disciples were not trying to present God as a "sperm donor"; Jesus was not taken by them as "Son of God" on account of being *"born by a virgin, who conceived by the semen of God"*. God was not depicted as having slept with Mary, or by any such means, fathered the flesh and blood that was born by Mary. Jesus himself had said, *"Spirit gives birth to spirit and flesh gives birth to flesh"*, so he claimed to be the Son of God not on account of the virgin birth. What was counted as *"Son of God"* is essentially not the flesh and blood that came out of Mary's womb, what was counted as Son of God is in essence the Spirit of Jesus. Yet, the apostles did not do away with the virgin birth doctrine, because for them to reckon Jesus as having being sired by Joseph the carpenter meant that his complete nature [outer plus inner man] might as well have descended from Joseph. But because they believed that his *"inner man"* is the Son of God, rather than the Son of Man, they reckoned that Jesus could indeed not have been sired by Joseph. However, if it is just the *"inner man"* of Jesus that is the *"Son of God"*, whose son was the *"outer man"*, God's, Joseph's or just Mary's?

You all are gods and offspring of the Most High.

According to the Bible, while Jesus argued with the Jews about his being the God's Son, he asked them to consider what had been written about being offspring of God.

> *Again the Jews picked up stones to stone him, but Jesus said to them, "I have shown you many great miracles from the Father. For which of these do you stone me?" "We are not stoning you for any of these," replied the Jews, "but for blasphemy, because you, a mere man, claim to be God." Jesus answered them, "Is it not written in your Law, 'I have said you are gods'? If he called them 'gods,' to whom the word of God came — and the Scripture cannot be broken — what about the one whom the Father set apart as his very own and sent into the world? Why then do you accuse me of blasphemy because I said, 'I am God's Son'?"*

(John 10: 31 – 36)

David in the psalm that Jesus referenced here had said to men *"you are gods and sons of the Most High"* [Psalm 82: 6] and it ever went down well with the Jews that men were called *"sons of the Most High"*. Yet it did not go down well with them that Jesus should call himself *"God's Son"*, whereas he that would be Christ, as David foretold, was such that David himself addressed as "Lord". If among David's descendants, David's Lord should be born to be *"a priest forever in order of Melchizedek"*, could it be preposterous that David's Lord would be *"the Son of God"* in a greater way than other men are *"God's sons"*? David himself had after all insinuated that his foretold Son and Lord would be far greater than him in that he spoke of the Christ's priesthood as belonging to an order much greater than the order of Aaron, in the pattern of

249

a priest that was greater than even Abraham.

One other question is that when men are called the *"offspring of God"*, is it just in honour to God or are we in reality children of God by descent? Paul while correcting the Athenians against superstitions reminded them that even one of their own poets acknowledged men as God's offspring.

> *"The God who made the whole world and everything in it is the Lord of heaven and earth and does not live in temples built by hands . . . 'For in him we live and move and have our being.' As some of your own poets have said, 'We are his offspring.' Therefore since we are God's offspring, we should not think that the divine being is like gold or silver or stone – an image made by man's design and skill."*
>
> (Acts 17: 24 – 29)

From Paul's argument here about the way the eternal being should be regarded, he does not take it as just a point of honour to call God our Father, he in fact implies that by **descent** we are the offspring of God. However, the Torah and the Prophets from which Paul received his elementary ideas about the nature of God says that God had formed man from the dust of the earth. And since the entire Bible further presents God to us as Spirit rather than animal, and one who does not give birth to animals, it submits that there is more to us than our animal nature. Nevertheless, when it speaks of our spirit nature as offspring of God, the Bible does not suggest that our individual inner beings born by God when our animal forms are being born by our natural parents. Rather, the Bible suggests that having once for all breathed his nature into the animal man, Adam, the human spirit supernature is replicated together with the animal nature at birth, such that by a long chain of births, our inner spirit natures have descended from God through Adam, whose inner spirit nature came from God. [Luke 3: 38]. When it says that Adam *"was the son of God"*, the Bible does not refer to the complete nature of Adam (comprising the outer animal nature as well as the inner spirit nature, because the outer animal nature was taken from the physical earthly elements, according to the Torah), the Bible's reference to Adam as Son of God more exactly refers to the inner (spirit) nature.

Paul wrote to the Corinthians and made a comparison between Adam and Jesus:

> *So it is written, "The first man Adam became a living being"; the last Adam, a life-giving spirit. The spiritual did not come first, but the natural, and after that*

the spiritual. The first man is of the dust of the earth, the second man from heaven.

(1 Corinthians 15: 45 – 47)

In Genesis, God took the first Adam from the dust of the earth. But the "breath" that God breathed into man was not taken from the dusts of the earth and hence the man was not completely dust. For Jesus, even though Paul argues that he is a "life-giving *breath*", Jesus was not completely "breath"/"spirit" because Jesus had flesh, blood and bones, which like that of "the first Adam" must of course have been composed of "dusts". The body of Jesus was no semblance, his flesh, body and bones were as those of every other human. But as it is preached that God formed man from the dust of the earth and put his spirit within that living dust, it is also preached that God formed the body of Jesus in the womb of Mary and put in it the eternal spirit of the Christ.

Jesus himself confessed that he has true flesh and bones [Luke 24: 39], and I have a good cause to suppose that when the disciples touched his body and felt his flesh and bones, the body was not any different from that of any other human. Therefore, the body of Jesus must have been as much terrestrial and earthly as the body of *"the first Adam"*. Nevertheless, Paul preached that the Christ is a *"life-giving breath that came from heaven"*; and as such what came from heaven as Paul meant could not have been the body of Jesus.

Even though it refers to "the first Adam" as "son of God", the Bible yet recognises that the animal form of that Adam was not born by God. By the same token, when it calls Jesus the "Son of God", the Bible does not submit that the body of Jesus was born by God. It simply puts it to us that as God took the body of Adam from the dusts of the earth, so God also took the body of Jesus from the womb of Mary, but what is essentially *"Son of God"* is the inner spirit being. But for humans, we reckon a man in entirety and by that we often do not make distinction between Jesus as Son of God and Son of Mary, he is often to us the one and same person.

The Roman Catholic Church teaches that Mary was immaculate – that is, free from the *"Original Sin"* of Adam and Eve in the Garden of Eden. But when and how Mary managed to be immaculate is neither clearly defined nor precisely defendable from the books of the Bible. Going by the Bible, unless Mary had descended from a lineage of immaculate humans that did not descend from Adam and Eve, she could not indeed inherited immaculacy. To reckon Mary as immaculate by birth would necessitate reckoning her entire line of ancestors as immaculate. In the Bible, the apostles did not ascribe the quality of being immaculate to Mary or her ancestors; rather they ascribed it to Jesus.

The apostles preached that Jesus was immaculate on the account of being the Christ. They counted that the Christ had to be immaculate because he, unlike other humans, was deemed to have been in existence before he was born. For other humans, the Bible does not regard anyone has having been in existence in any form before being naturally born. Consequently, the Bible teaches that every human sired by a human father takes his or her entire being (spiritual and animal) from both of his or her biological parents. For Jesus, however, the Bible teaches that because he already existed as Spirit, his spirit could not any more be formed by a union of human parents, and on that basis it is believed that Jesus did not have the natural human spirit that is born together with the outward animal form.

The apostles preached that Jesus was immaculate. And the rationale for that rested upon the fact that they identified him as the one concerning whom the Torah and the Prophets had foretold would be the Christ. The Christ as foretold was such that would have been in existence (spiritually) long before he would be born naturally, which implies that the foretold Christ would not derive his entire nature from his human parents. Having matched the person of Jesus with the various prophecies already made concerning the foretold Christ, the apostles reckoned that Jesus was immaculate and indeed born without being sired by a human father. Nevertheless, we are burdened with the task of verifying that Jesus the Son of Mary is the one of whom the Torah and the Prophets had foretold as the Christ.

Meanwhile, calling Jesus the Son of Mary also brings up one more question: if Jesus was not indeed sired by Joseph, how exact is it to call him the Son of Mary? This question leads us through the surrogate conception methods that are fast becoming popular today. By In-Vitro-Fertilisation some women are made to carry the children conceived using other women's ova. The question then arises, who is the real mother of a child — the woman whose ovum is used to form the foetus, or the one who carries the foetus in her womb and gives birth to it as a baby? The indisputable answer to this last question may be difficult to contrive. But as for Jesus, while the Bible does not tell us whether God had used Mary's ovum to form him or not, it does at least tell us that Jesus was carried in the womb of Mary from conception unto birth. Nevertheless, how exactly the foetus was formed in Mary's womb and how exactly it avoided having a human spirit remains as incomprehensible to us as how Adam was formed from the earthly dusts and how the spirit that God breathed into Adam is replicated together with the animal form of humans that are born thereafter. For both of these "miracles", the Bible in its typical manner does not tell us "how" but "what".

While we leave aside what is incomprehensible, we should examine issues that are comprehensible to specific extents, such as how the apostles managed to match the person of Jesus with the person of the foretold Christ.

The Priests of Bread and Wine.

Eddie Murphy's film, *Coming To America*, did not only become a bestseller, it also kept selling for many years. In the film, the King and Prince Akeem usually walked with "Rose Bearers" going ahead of them, making a carpet of rose petals for the King or the Prince to step upon. Once, when the Prince had gone to America to find love as a common man, he got to the doorsteps of his apartment one day and found rose petals strewn along the corridor. He instantly knew that the King must have been there. The carpet of rose petals was a signature.

Signatures vary in forms and uses. But wherever a signature is found, it represents a particular identity. A signature is usually unique. Many media stations have peculiar signature tunes each of which forms a peculiar identity for the particular media station that uses it. Whenever I hear a particular tune, even without going near the television screen I could tell it is the BBC World Service, because I have found that the BBC plays that particular tune very often in-between its scheduled programmes and the tune is unique (as far as I know) to the BBC World Service.

Concerning he that would be the Christ, David said the Most High had sworn to establish an eternal priesthood.

The LORD has sworn and will not change his mind: "You are a priest forever, in the order of Melchizedek"

(Psalm 110: 4)

The priesthood of Melchizedek was different from that of Aaron. Melchizedek was a priest that ministered with bread and wine. When he met Abraham, he did not make a sacrifice of flesh or blood as a priest in the Levitical order would have done. As Abraham was returning from a battle, it was incumbent upon any priest that would meet him to make a sacrifice of atonement for him. In most battles, there are no guarantees that all innocent people would be spared. Abraham could have shed some innocent blood while fighting against the five kings or by any other means would have delivered some injustice. Whether it was so or not, however, any priest that happened to have met Abraham would have considered it necessary to make an offering for atonement and purification for a man returning from shedding blood. But rather than kill an animal or make any such sacrifice, Melchizedek administered bread and wine to Abraham. No other priest in the entire Bible administered bread and wine as an atonement for sin to any person. For Melchizedek, bread and wine was a peculiar sanctification offering.

However, Jesus, who by (supposed) descent was not qualified to be a traditional priest, administered bread and wine to his twelve disciples for the *"atonement of sins"*. Of course, Jesus had been familiar with the psalm that spoke of the Christ as having a perpetual priesthood in the order of Melchizedek, and one might think that he was merely imitating Melchizedek in order to claim the Christhood but then Jesus performed his own bread and wine rite in an original way. When he did administer bread and wine to his disciples, neither did Jesus speak to the disciples about Melchizedek, nor did the disciples link his actions with that of Melchizedek or regard what Melchizedek did to Abraham in the light of what Jesus was presently doing to them. In both the instance of the Melchizedek that Abraham met, and in that of Jesus to his disciples, the rite of bread and wine were performed as original rites. Yet the rites were the same signature – an offering for sanctification from sins. No other person in the entire Bible repeated the rite that Melchizedek had made until Jesus came, and no other person repeated the rite after Jesus except the people who believed that Jesus is the Christ and to whom Jesus had committed the rite as a perpetual ordinance. By the bread and wine rite, Jesus signed the Melchizedek signature.

The significant thing about the bread and wine rite was that it laid foundations for a righteousness that comes by faith rather than by the keeping of specific rules and commandments, although *"righteousness by faith*" does not imply that rules and laws should be disregarded. According to the Bible, Abraham was "*declared righteous*" because he simply "*believed God*" rather than because he kept a certain set of laws and rules. Melchizedek sanctified Abraham with bread and wine in preparation for a coming promise. After he had received the sacraments of bread and wine from Melchizedek, Abraham received a promise from God and he believed it; the belief in God's promise alone was credited to Abraham as "*righteousness*".

> *Then Melchizedek king of Salem brought out bread and wine. He was priest of God Most High, and he blessed Abram . . . After this, the word of the LORD came to Abram in a vision . . . Abram believed the LORD, and he credited it to him as righteousness.*
>
> (Genesis 14: 18 – 15: 6)

Many of the traditional priests that came after that did not perform that rite even though many of them would have understood the meaning of what Melchizedek had done to Abraham. However, Jesus performed the rite for the sanctification of his disciples. The rite of bread and wine that Jesus made was particular to the priesthood of Melchizedek, and it might well be argued that Jesus is the one of whom David had prophesied in his Psalm that "*The LORD has sworn and would not change his mind, 'You are a priest forever, in the order of Melchizedek'*". Yet Jesus made no issue at all of the fact that Melchizedek had performed the same rite of bread and wine which ushers in a righteousness that is based upon faith (as was the righteousness of Abraham).

If we should say that Jesus was not the foretold Christ and had only gained enough insight into the prophecies concerning the expected Christ for him to deviously fulfil such prophecies, we would have to wonder why no other man before or after Jesus considered it anything important to follow the order of Melchizedek's priesthood. If Jesus was not really the Christ, it would also imply that the foretold Christ failed to come because the Christ by specific prophecies had to come at about the very time that Jesus lived on earth. Yet at that particular time, only Jesus performed the sanctification rite in the order of Melchizedek – who sanctified by bread and wine rather than the flesh and blood of animals. Considering the facts that in accordance with prophecies made in the Torah and the Proph-

if Jesus was not the Christ, who then was the Christ?

ets, the foretold Christ was to be born as Jesus was born, and to live as Jesus lived, and to die as Jesus died, within that very particular time frame; if Jesus was not the Christ, who then was the Christ?

Moreover, Daniel had prophesied that at a certain length of time after the rebuilding of Jerusalem from the destruction of the captivity, the foretold Christ shall come. He also prophesied that the Christ shall be killed. [Daniel 9: 20 – 27]. Specifically, Daniel mentioned that after the Christ is killed, the city [Jerusalem] and the Temple shall again be destroyed at a certain space of time.

> *After sixty-two 'sevens', the Anointed One will be cut off and will have nothing. The people of the ruler who will come will destroy the city and the sanctuary. The end will come like a flood: War will continue until the end, and desolations have been decreed.*

(Daniel 9: 26)

Some people have argued that Jesus was a mere opportunist who intentionally sought out and fulfilled what the prophets had said about the expected Christ. But if this were the case, how could he have fulfilled the destruction of the city and the Temple after his death? Indeed, Jerusalem and the Temple were destroyed at a set time after the killing of Jesus. The invasion of Jerusalem had no Christian connection – the invaders were not Christians, and history does not tell us that the city was invaded for any Christian or religious reason. Even if we say the soldiers that guarded the tomb of Jesus had been bribed to let go of the corpse, could Christians also have bribed the invaders to destroy Jerusalem and the Temple? How would they have found enough means to sponsor the invasion? And how could the invaders have reckoned with Christians at a time when Christians were yet counted as dung and *"sheep for slaughter"* in the world? Could the invaders have embraced Christians, when the message of Christians about Jesus being the Christ meant condemnation for even the invaders unless they also believed in the Christhood of Jesus? The invasion of Jerusalem and the destruction of the Temple were clearly independent of the making of the man Jesus and his disciples. Yet the invasion fulfilled what Daniel had foretold. If Jesus were not truly the foretold Christ, who then was the one destined to be killed at a certain length of years before the invasion of Jerusalem and destruction of the Temple?

Isaiah prophesied that a child shall be born and shall have an eternal kingdom and the child would be called *"Prince of Peace"*. [Isaiah 9: 6 – 7]. The name *"Prince of Peace"* is a variation of the name *"King of Peace"*, *"King of Perfection"* – *"Melchizedek"*.

Jesus himself had said, *"Abraham saw my day and was glad"*, yet the Bible does not inform us that Abraham had met any man called Jesus or any man called the Christ. But the Bible says Abraham met someone called Melchizedek – *"King of Peace"* – and was glad; and Jesus also called himself *"the Christ"*, whom Isaiah called *"Prince of Peace"*. And David also had prophesied that the Christ shall be an everlasting priest in order of *"King of Peace"*.

Nevertheless, the priest in order of Melchizedek that David called "Lord" was also destined to be David's son, even though Melchizedek was reckoned greater than Abraham, who in turn was reckoned greater than David. In the light of this, according to the Bible, Jesus asked the Jews, *"How could the Christ be David's son, when David himself called him Lord"*, and the Jews could not answer him. Jesus told them, *"Before Abraham was, I have been"*, but it could not make sense to them – of course, it could not have made sense to anyone that a man less than fifty years old should say he had been living before Abraham lived. [John 8: 56 – 58]. If Jesus really meant that he had been living before Abraham, he could not have lived as a human with flesh, blood and bones.

However, many of the prophets said other things about the expected Christ. Micah said the promised ruler has an origin *"from everlasting times"*:

"But you, Bethlehem Ephrathah, though you are small among the clans of Judah, out of you will come for me one who will be ruler over Israel, whose origins are from of old, from ancient times."

(Micah 5: 2)

Even though his origin is from everlasting times, as prophesied by Micah, the expected Christ was also to *"come out of Bethlehem"*. How could he be expected to *"come out of Bethlehem"* at a future date, if he already has an origin from *"everlasting times"*?

For to us a child is born, to us a son is given, and the government will be upon his shoulders. And he will be called Wonderful Counselor, Mighty God, Everlasting Father, Prince of Peace.

(Isaiah 9: 6)

In the prophecy of Isaiah again we find a contradiction in the person of the one destined to come. The very prophet [Isaiah] who called the expected Christ *"a child born to us"* also called him *"Ancient Father"*. How could he be at once *"a son born to us"* and yet also be our *"ancient father"*?

We have found the Messiah.

For those who accepted Jesus as the Christ, a whole lot of thoughtful consideration lies beyond this belief. The life and person of Jesus matched the life and person of the expected Christ that the prophets foretold. And not only his life, but his death also and what came after his death matched what should be expected of the Christ in accordance with the Law and the Prophets. Yet there was so much contradiction about Jesus; but the contradictions themselves had in fact been prophesied about he that would be the Christ. For instance, Daniel's prophecy referred to the Christ as *"Prince"*, but in the prophecy, the Prince did not rule. The Prince was just killed, and after his death, the rebuilt city and the Temple were destroyed. If Daniel's prophecy referred to the expected Christ as *"Prince"*, and yet the fact that the Prince did not rule before he was *"cut off"* did not stop him from remaining *"the Prince"*, certainly the prophecy insinuates that the concerned princedom would not be political. Jesus called himself the foretold Prince but he did not rule and after his death the rebuilt city and the Temple were destroyed. Jesus apparently matched the Prince that Daniel had prophesied. But long before everything that was foretold about the Christ were entirely fulfilled, the disciples of Jesus had begun to accept him as the Christ because they reckoned with several other prophecies.

> *Philip found Nathanael and told him, "We have found the one of whom Moses wrote about in the Law, and about whom the prophets also wrote — Jesus of Nazareth, the son of Joseph." "Nazareth! Can any good thing come from there?" Nathanael asked. "Come and see," said Philip. . . Then Nathanael declared, "Rabbi, you are the Son of God; you are the King of Israel."*
>
> (John 1: 45 – 49)

It was not much of a problem for the disciples to accept Jesus as son of Joseph and at once Son of God. Even though the doctrine of the virgin birth became popular by and by, yet the first disciples did not fail to publicly refer to Jesus as Joseph's son. It is obvious that to the disciples, the fact that Jesus was Son of Man could not preclude him from being at once Son of God, because they reckoned that having first been the Son of God, being subsequently born of a woman could not any more negate his being the Son of God. To them, and according to the prophecies of the Law and the Prophets, he who shall be the Christ has an origin that goes far back beyond his birth unto us "as a child" – Micah called his origin "***everlasting***". Summarily, Jesus was therefore not called "Son of God" on account of the "virgin birth". It was not the flesh, blood and bones that Mary gave birth to that was reckoned as having existed "*from everlasting*", rather it was the inner [spirit] being that was thus reckoned. However, when he was being charged and killed for blasphemy, the Jews reckoned with his outward (flesh and blood) being, rather than with the inward (spirit) being. Such reckoning was what Paul was used to until he ran into the unembodied *Voice* on his way to Damascus. Later on, Paul wrote a lengthy apology, the Bible's Epistle to the Hebrews, in defence of the Christhood of Jesus arguing that Jesus received the priesthood of the order of Melchizedek as prophesied by David.

Eat This Bread And Drink This Wine.

A short while before he was arrested, Jesus sat to a meal with his special twelve disciples. While they were eating, he administered bread and wine to them.

> *While they were eating, Jesus took bread, gave thanks and broke it, and gave it to his disciples, saying, "Take and eat; this is my body." Then he took the cup, gave thanks and offered it to them, saying "Drink from it, all of you. This is my blood of the covenant, which is poured out for many for the forgiveness of sins.*
>
> (Matthew 26: 26 – 28)

The Bible does not give an explanation of the bread and wine that Melchizedek had administered to Abraham. But the circumstances show that it served for cleansing from sins. Jesus explained his own bread and wine rite when he administered it to his disciples. He emphasised that the bread stood for his body that would be pierced, while the wine stood for his blood that would be poured out "*for many for the forgiveness of sins*".

That the blood of Jesus is the price paid for the forgiveness of sins is a major Christian doctrine that has met strong rebellion from non-Christians from the onset of Christianity. But prophecies made about the expected Christ long before Jesus was born implied that the Christ shall die not for his own sins but for the sins of others and to earn forgiveness for others. Indeed, Jesus was killed principally for saying that he is the Christ. But as the person, and life and death of Jesus matches what had been prophesied concerning the foretold Christ, and as he did not only die but also resurrected, Jesus is in all probability the Christ. If his claim to Christhood was therefore valid, Jesus was in essence crucified for no sin of his own. He had been killed for telling the truth about his Christhood – a truth that he had to declare in order to make the kind of righteousness that God credited to Abraham open to as many people as would believe in God as Abraham did. When we balance all the equations, we cannot but reckon that Jesus had died that many people might receive the righteousness of God by faith rather than by keeping of commandments.

He Was Wounded For Our Transgressions.

In another of the prophecies written about the expected Christ in the book of Isaiah, it is stated outright that the death of the Christ shall earn righteousness for many people. Isaiah mentions in that prophecy that it is such an "unbelievable but yet true report", for the long awaited King to be despised and even killed when eventually he comes.

See, my servant will act wisely; he will be raised and lifted up and highly exalted. Just as there were many who were appalled at him – his appearance was so disfigured beyond that of any man and his form marred beyond human likeness – so will he sprinkle many nations, and kings will shut their mouths because of him. For what they were not told, they will see, and what they have not heard, they will understand. Who has believed our message and to whom has the arm of the LORD been revealed? He grew up before him like a tender shoot, and like a root out of dry ground. He had no beauty or majesty to attract us to him, nothing in his appearance that we should desire him. He was despised and rejected by men, a man of sorrows, and familiar with suffering. Like one from whom men hide their faces he was despised, and we esteemed him not. Surely he took up our infirmities and carried our sorrows, yet we considered him stricken by God, smitten by him, and afflicted. But he was pierced for our transgressions, he was crushed for our iniquities; the punishment that brought us peace was upon him, and by his wounds we are healed. We all, like sheep, have gone astray, each of us have turned to his own way; and the LORD has laid on him the iniquity of us all. He was oppressed and afflicted, yet he did not open his mouth; he was led like a lamb to the slaughter, and as a sheep before her shearers is silent, so he did not open his mouth. By oppression and judgement he was taken away. And who can speak of his descen-

dants? For he was cut off from the land of the living; for the transgression of my people was he stricken. He was assigned a grave with the wicked and with the rich in his death, though he had done no violence, nor was any deceit in his mouth. Yet it was the LORD*'s will to crush him and cause him to suffer, and though the* LORD *makes his life a guilt offering, he will see his offspring and prolong his days, and the will of the* LORD *will prosper in his hand. After the suffering of his soul, he will see the light of life and be satisfied; by his knowledge my righteous servant will justify many, and he will bear their iniquities. Therefore I will give him a portion among the great, and he will divide the spoils with the strong, because he poured out his life unto death, and was numbered with transgressors. For he bore the sin of many, and made intercession for the transgressors.*

(Isaiah 52: 13 – 53: 12)

Even if we say that Jesus is not the Christ, over and over again many things that were prophesied concerning the expected Christ were fulfilled in Jesus and in no other person. Concerning that *"the Christ will act wisely"*, we find that even those who contend till today the Christhood of Jesus say that *"he was a very wise man"*. Concerning that the Christ would be *"exalted"*, the Bible records show that Jesus was so esteemed by many people until he told the Jews, *"I am the Son of God"*. Concerning that the Christ would be *"reproached, despised, wounded beyond measure, and killed"*, these also were reported of the arrest, torture and death of Jesus. Concerning that the Christ would not put up a defence in his trial, we find that also about Jesus, who when he was being tried simply repeated the very statement – *"I am the Christ"* – for which he had been charged, without making explanations or performing a miracle to defend that. Concerning that *"the Christ would be numbered with transgressors"*, the Bible reports that Jesus was charged for blasphemy, a thing that the Jews considered *"transgression of the highest order"* and for which they gave him a State execution of the most despicable form. Concerning that the Christ would die with the wicked and be buried with the rich, Jesus also was buried with the rich in spite of the shameful death that he died. Concerning that the LORD would forsake [completely abandon] the suffering Christ to the tortures, we find that Jesus was not miraculously rescued by God from the torture and death that followed his arrest. [Even though the Koran says that God had miraculously rescued Jesus from the torture by providing an exact lookalike, nothing else is known about this exact look-alike and the fact that the corpse of this substitute replica was not found in the guarded grave while the real Jesus was seen about gives us reasons to doubt the substitution theory].

261

Concerning that the Christ shall be *"cut off from the land of the living"*, we find it also fulfilled in Jesus – even the Koran that promulgates the substitution theory agrees **that as far as humans could know**, Jesus was **certainly crucified**. Concerning that after his sufferings, the Christ shall again *"see the results of his sufferings and be satisfied"* – which implies a resurrection – we find that Jesus was not only killed and buried in a jealously guarded tomb, he was in all probability seen alive again after the crucifixion and burial – otherwise even his own siblings could not have believed that the man who came out of their mother's womb is the Christ. And Paul who killed those who held the belief in his resurrection could also not have suddenly become willing to die for holding the same belief.

When we reconcile all the prophecies about the expected Christ from the various books in the Law and Prophets, can we realistically look any further than Jesus to find the Christ? In all probabilities, if Jesus was not the Christ, no one else was, and no one else could be, because the Christ had to come at the very time that Jesus came and had to be in every way as Jesus was, he had to die and resurrect at a certain space of time before the city and the Temple would be again invaded and destroyed, as it was in Jesus' case.

However, the import of Jesus being the Christ is not just to take the honour of that name. The import of it is that his life was a sacrifice for many, and by his suffering and death, many have yielded to God, who never would have desired the name "God". According to the Bible, Jesus had broken bread, which he gave to his disciples and told them *"my body would be pierced"*, and he had also given them the wine for his *"blood that would be poured out for many for the forgiveness of sins"*; but when he was crucified, the Jews did not charge him for the sins of other people, they charged him for his own *"blasphemy"*. That leaves us to wonder how right was the book of Isaiah to have prophesied that the Christ shall die for other people. Yet we know that as Jesus is in all probabilities the Christ, it cannot be indeed a blasphemy for him to have said that he is. He had implied, *"If I say that I am not the Christ, I would be lying. How could I be the Christ and tell you I am not?"*. [John 8: 12 – 47]. But at least he had the right to remain silent.

When picking up a suspect or accused, the police have a tradition of saying *"you have a right to remain silent, or anything you say could be used against you in the court of law"*. It was not compulsory that Jesus should say *"I am the Christ"*. He could have avoided confrontation with the

Pharisees and Sanhedrin; he could have avoided the tortures and the crucifixion if only he had kept quiet about being the Christ. He could just have kept it in his heart. But in order to preach the righteousness that comes by faith, as was the righteousness of Abraham as reported in the Torah, in order to guide people into following the path of righteousness by faith that Abraham followed, Jesus had to tell the truth about his Christhood and for that truth he was killed. In essence, he was killed for the sake of as many people as are able to obtain righteousness by faith as Abraham did.

He was a prophet.

For several years after the death and resurrection of Jesus, his teachings and reports about him were passed around by word of mouth. The Gospels, though they sound as eyewitness accounts, were not penned down at the very moments that the actions and words they report were made. Much of the Gospels as we have them today were written in retrospect, the writings were not simultaneous with the actions and speeches that they report. The disciples who wrote the Gospels put down whatever it was that they could recollect. They did not attempt to give details of everything that Jesus did and said, and neither did they intend to pass the Gospels to us as books authored by Jesus.

The four books called Gospels in the Christian Bible today have many points of agreements as well as several textual discrepancies. The discrepancies confirm that they were not written simultaneously with one another or with the actions and words that they report. The discrepancies also mean that they were not written out of collusion. If the authors had colluded between themselves to write books by which they would deceive the world, then they would have taken care of the textual discrepancies. So, the textual inconsistencies themselves suggest against the probabilities of fraudulent intentions.

The Koran teaches that the Jews have doctored the Torah that was revealed to Moses and the Christians have doctored the Gospel that was revealed to Jesus. But if the author of the Koran thus opined that Jesus was the original author of the Gospels, he must have been referring to entirely different books from what we have as the Gospels today. Authorship of the present Four Gospels in the Bible is not at all attributed to Jesus. And in all the other books of the Christian part of the Bible, no where is Jesus reckoned to have written anything. The issue about Jesus' authorship of any book is that he did not need to write any. He was teaching what had been written in the Law and the Prophets. For instance, when he taught about *"righteousness obtained by believing God"*, he was not stating an entirely new idea – Abraham has been reported in the Torah to have obtained righteousness by believing God. All that he was teaching were rooted in the existing scriptures, and therefore he did not need to write any scripture of his own. Moreover, the expected Christ had been prophesied to be one that would write his scriptures upon people's hearts rather than on tables and scrolls, and therefore, if Jesus had considered himself as the Christ, he would have avoided writing any Scriptures or epistles or gospels. But the Koran in fact wants us to believe that Jesus considered himself a prophet only and not the Christ. The Koran is not wrong to call Jesus *"a prophet"*, indeed the Bible reports that people considered Jesus a prophet in his own days, even by those who did not accept him as the Christ – and he too referred to himself as a prophet. [Matthew 13: 57; 21: 11, 46; Luke 7: 16, John 7: 52] Moreover, the Bible prophecies concerning the expected Christ stated that he would be *"a prophet"*. If Jesus had to claim the Christhood, he had to be known as a prophet – and he was thus known. But if he was just an ordinary prophet and not the Christ, for what would he have been crucified?

The Koran teaches that the Jews conspired to kill Jesus for teaching the *"truth"*, what exactly the details of those *"truths"* are, the Koran does not tell, yet it wants us to believe that the ones reported retrospectively in the Gospels have been doctored. Nevertheless, the root of all differences between Judaists and Christians is the belief in *"righteousness obtained by faith, through the priesthood of the Christ, in the order of Melchizedek"*. Because it does not give the details of the *"truths"* that Jesus was teaching, or give us the undistorted *"Gospels"* that it alleges had been revealed through Jesus, the Koran does not fully drive home the point of Jews' plot to kill Jesus. If we have the details, we would be able to compare with what the Jews believe and see where it could possibly have offended the Jews. But in the case of the Bible, it affords us the details of the teachings that could have made the Jews conspire to kill Jesus. The manner of Jesus' death, and the public support for it, his fame for miracles (which even the Koran affirms) and the fact that the people considered him a prophet and crowded after him, suggests that the claim to the Christhood and the doctrine of righteousness by faith would in all probabilities have been the offence of Jesus to the Jews.

Prophet Mohammed, who penned down the Koran, which he

claimed to have received by revelation probably was not mindful of the various prophecies that had been written in the Law and the Torah concerning *"the destined prophet that would be the Christ"*. He probably did not pay attention to the fact that it had been prophesied that at a certain number of years after the Jews would have returned from captivity and have rebuilt the city of Jerusalem and the Temple, a distinguished prophet shall be born. And that the prophet was destined to be killed at a certain number of years before the city of Jerusalem would be again invaded and the rebuilt Temple destroyed. Prophet Mohammed probably did not pay attention to the fact that Jesus was the only distinguished prophet that thus born and killed in that given time frame, and did not pay attention to the fact that the distinguished prophet thus killed at that specified time should be the designated Christ. Perhaps, if Prophet Mohammed had known all these, he would have asked the angel that (reportedly) revealed the Koran to him to explain the mysteries of the Christhood. Nevertheless, we respect the fact that Prophet Mohammed recognised the view that Jesus was a distinguished prophet, whose crucifixion was planned by the Jews on account the *"truths"* that he spoke rather than for doing any wrong, and one whom God gave *"the power to create"*. It is the balanced sum of the issues that Prophet Mohammed considered and failed to consider that is summarised at the beginning of the Gospel according to John.

In the beginning was the Word, and the Word was with God, and the Word was God. He was with God in the beginning. Through him all things were made; without him nothing was made that has been made. In him was life, and that life was the light of men. The light shines in the darkness, but the darkness has not understood it. There came a man who was sent from God, his name was John. He came as a witness to testify concerning that light, so that through him all men might believe. He himself was not the light, he came only as a witness to the light. The true light that gives light to every man was coming into the world. He was in the world, and though the world was made through him, the world did not recognize him. He came to that which was his own, but his own did not receive him. Yet to all who received him, to those who believed in his name, he gave the right to become the children of God — children not born of natural descent, nor of human decisions or a husband's will, but born of God. The Word became flesh and made his dwelling among us. We have seen his glory, the glory of the One and Only, who came from the Father, full of grace and truth. John testifies concerning him. He cries out, saying, "This was he of whom I said, 'He who comes after me has surpassed me because he was before me' ". From the fullness of his grace we have all received one blessing after another. For the law was given through Moses; grace and truth came through Jesus Christ. No one has ever seen God, but God the One and

Only, who is at the Father's side, has made him known.

(John 1: 1 – 18)

The Koran tells us that Jesus taught "truths". But one other thing that the Prophet Mohammed had failed to ask the angel that showed him the Koran is about grace. In the Bible passage that we have just read, John tells us about grace – absolutely free favour. The other prophet John the Baptist whose testimony the author of this Gospel referenced here was by physical birth older than Jesus. But he did say of Jesus *"he is coming after me, although he had been before me"*, and in this, the prophet apparently corroborates the prophecies of the earlier prophets Isaiah and Micah, who said the destined distinguished prophet *"would be born to us as a child, even though he is the everlasting Father"* and would *"come out"* of Bethlehem, even though his origin has been *"from everlasting, from eternity"*.

This abstract of the Gospel of John is one Bible passage that has met endless controversies. One fact that the passage states which cannot be disproved is that God has been from the beginning, from eternity.

Earlier in this book, we had considered the infinity of time and reckoned with the fact that when the Bible does talk of *"the beginning"*, it refers to an indefinable past. Simply, *"the beginning"* means *"before anything at all came into existence"*. Here the Bible teaches that the Christ has been before anything at all came into existence. But when it goes ahead to tell us that the Christ is Jesus, it does not mean to tell us that the flesh, blood and bones of Jesus had been before anything came into existence, rather it speaks of him as having God's nature, the spirit nature.

The Living Word.

Much earlier in this book, we reckoned that a spirit is a noumenon and may not be tangibly described. Some relative description for "spirit" as we cited from the Bible are the terms "living water" and "breath". But again we find another relative description, "living word". In the original language of the New Testament, the noun "word" [Greek: *Logos*] does not only mean "speech" – "that which is spoken", it also means "reason" – "that is which is thought". Accordingly, "word" stood for "speech" as well as for "thought" meaning "consciousness", "knowledge" or "intelligence", even when it remains unspoken.

When the Gospel of John talks of the "Word" that "has been from the beginning", it does not represent it as speech. What makes it "the word" is not that it was "spoken". What makes it "word" is that it is a "thought", a "consciousness". So it is that when John tells us, *"in the beginning was the Word, and the Word was with God"*, he does not mean *"in the beginning was the Speech, and the Speech was with God"*, rather he means *"in the beginning was the Consciousness, and the Consciousness was with God"*. Yet even this description still puts John's idea beyond our immediate comprehension because we normally do not reckon consciousness as an entity, capable of subsisting without a material body. But in the limitedness of using our mental capabilities to describe what a spirit is, we can at best reckon a spirit as a consciousness.

The Gospel of John describes the inner being of Christ as a consciousness that has been ever before the origination of the world. Yet it recognises that only God could rightly be the One and Only eternal consciousness, but the full statement of John concerning the Spirit of the Christ has generated endless controversies within and without the Christendom. John's statement paraphrases as, *"In eternity was the Consciousness, the Consciousness was with God, and the Consciousness was God"*. In the original language of the New Testament books, the articles "a", "an" and "the" were not often used as is in our English language, it is translators who fix in the articles wherever they deem fit in order to make more complete senses; only the article "the" has a variation that was sometimes joined together as one undivided word with the noun it is attached to. Thus, some English translations of the Bible puts the first verse of John as *"In the beginning was the Word, the Word was with God, and the Word was a god"*. While it is not inconsistent with the translation practices to insert the article "a" before the word "god", a more exact and word-for-word translation would be *"In beginning Word was, Word with God was, Word God was"*.

The issue is that if *"in beginning"* as used here refers to the "everlasting past", as it almost always does, then it would be less appropriate to insert the article "a" into the verse than to leave it out. As only God could be the One and Only eternal person, if the Word too were eternal, then he has to be the one and same person with God. If John had stopped just at that, it would have been a less problematic concept for many of us, but John goes ahead to say *"the Word became flesh and dwelt among us"*, and as he concludes, we see that "the flesh that dwelt among us" to which John refers is Jesus.

When that "flesh" dwelt among the Jews, they found it an intolerable idea that within the "flesh" is the *eternal Living Word*. For the Jews to have taken Jesus as the *Eternal Living Word [Consciousness]* meant that they would have needed to identify him as the one and only *Originator* of the world. What made this idea more repulsive to the Jews is the fact that Jesus was already well known among them as "the Son of Mary and Joseph, the carpenter". However, when we consider all the evidences that support the fact Jesus was in all probability the Christ, "the distinguished prophet" that was destined to be killed in Jerusalem at that specific time, and the fact that his claim to Christhood was strongly opposed by the leaders of Judaism, we are compelled to question what is so special about being the Christ.

The interesting part of it is that the prophecies that where made concerning the Christ in the Law and the Prophets are in the non-Christian part of the Bible. The Judaists were the ones to whom the Christ was promised and all the unbelievable, seemingly contradictory, descriptions of the expected Christ are in the Judaist scriptures. It was not Christians who wrote the book of Micah and put it there that the destined One *"will come out of Bethlehem even though his origin is from **everlasting**"*. It was not Christians who wrote it into Isaiah that *"a child shall be born to us"*, who would be called *"Wonderful Counsellor, Mighty God, Everlasting Father, Prince of Peace"*. It was not Christians who wrote it into the Psalm that the expected Christ shall be *"a priest forever in the order of Melchizedek"*. It was not Christians who wrote it into Daniel that the Christ shall be killed at a specified time. All that the Christians did was to recognise and testify that in Jesus the prophecies made concerning the foretold Christ were fulfilled. But when John goes further to say that the Christ is the *"eternal Living Word"*, and hence God Almighty, he further earns the indignation of Jews who found it offensive in the first place to accept Jesus as the Christ. But over the years since then, not only the Judaist Jews but many other people have found it unthinkable that God *"became flesh and dwelt among the Jews"*.

However, if the Jews had paid attention to all the prophecies made concerning the expected Christ, long before Jesus was born, they could have understood that the foretold Christ should not be an ordinary man, he was invariably described as *"King with an eternal throne"*, *"Prince who would not rule"*, *"everlasting Priest but not from the tribe of priests"*, *"Our Ancient Father, born to us as a child"*, *"Warrior who would do no violence"*, *"the one who had ever been, before he was born"*. If anyone therefore has a problem with the fact that the Christians call Jesus *"the Wonderful Counsellor"*, *"the Mighty God"*, *"the Ancient of Days"*, *"the Everlasting Father"*, *"the Living Word"*, or *"the Creator of the world"*, such a person should address his or her cause to the prophets who pointed these names at the expected Christ. It was the prophets, not the Christians, who first identified the Christ as *"the one who has been from eternity"*, and by implication, God, the Creator, the only eternal and first person. What the Christians did on their own part was recognise Jesus, the *"child that was born unto"* the Jews, as the expected Christ, and that they did without prejudice for even before their very eyes, he was killed, and they saw him alive again thereafter.

Grace and Truth Came by Jesus.

John says *"no one has ever seen God, but the Living Word has made God known"*. Even those who testify that in their dreams, visions, and trances, they have seen God cannot give us a common visual image of God, because God is a Spirit and has no material form. But humans do have material forms, and yet we seek to relate with God. Unless God has indeed put his nature within us, there is no point in us relating with him.

God, the eternal immaterial being, originated the entire material world out of absolute nothing. As much as it rises beyond human comprehension to understand how it was possible for God to create materials without using any source material at all, how God has put a replica of his own nature within us also lies beyond ordinary human comprehension. Much more, we may never understand how the *"Everlasting One"* managed to present himself as one of us, born unto us as a child, even though he is our Everlasting Father. But we know that by the death and resurrection of Jesus Christ, many non-Jews rushed to embrace the God of the Jews. Until Jesus Christ came, the proportion of non-Jews who embraced the God of the Jews was small, but after the death and resurrection of Jesus, all that changed, many more non-Jews today seek after the God of the Jews. Indeed, it had been prophesied concerning the expected Christ that he shall bring salvation unto the non-Jews. And by the fulfilment of this prophecy again is the Christhood of Jesus confirmed.

While Jesus made his claim to the Christhood, the Jews had challenged him on the breaking of some Sabbath rules and he replied that *"God justifies by mercy, not by sacrifices"*. The issue with the Jews was that they wanted to keep to the Law as given to them by Moses, and they believed that by keeping to the Law and observing some specific commandments and ordinances, a man would be made righteous in the sight of God. But they forgot that their great father, Abraham, was justified by God even before the Law was given. Abraham obtained righteousness in the sight of God long before the Ten Commandments and the entire ordinances were given through Moses. However, even the books of the Law testified that God had made a promise to Abraham, that through Abraham, God shall bless the whole world.

Abraham is the most revered ancestor of the Jews, and the Judaists of Jesus' days believed they were rightly worshipping the God that Abraham worshipped. But the Jews were bound by the ordinances of the Law. Jesus taught that Abraham was not bound by the ordinances of the Law, as in fact the Law was not yet given when Abraham lived. Jesus taught that the Jews as Abraham's descendants needed to enjoy the liberty that Abraham enjoyed with God.

The books of the Law testified that God took Abraham as a *"friend"*. God at several instances did inform Abraham of his divine plans, and Abraham was so free with God as to discuss issues with him, as though with a human friend. Such was the liberty that Abraham enjoyed with God. Even Moses through whom the Law was given to the Jews was like a friend to God. God did inform Moses of his divine plans, and Moses discussed with God as though with a human friend. But the ordinary Judaist Jew did not enjoy such personal relationship with God. They were tied to keeping rules and ordinances; they did not see the need to be intimate *"friends"* of God. But Jesus taught that everyone needs that personal relationship with God, that God wants to relate with every one personally as he did with Abraham and Moses. The Jews could not imagine enjoying such familiarity with God; they considered that personal relationship with God is a special privilege ceded only to prophets. But Jesus taught that God wishes to make every one closer to himself [God] than even prophets. To fall short of such closeness with God as Abraham and Moses enjoyed, to lack a consistent personal relationship with God as Abraham and Moses enjoyed, implies a deadness and irresponsiveness to God, and hence displeasure [sin] to God. The Judaist Jews had always thought of sin as the breaking of commandments. But Jesus taught them that even when a man does not break any commandment, in as much as he does not please God, the man is a sinner; and a man cannot please God if he lacks a one-to-one relationship with God of the kind that Abraham and Moses enjoyed. These teachings of Jesus are in consonance with the essence of the entire Law and Prophets that the Judaist treasured, but the Judaist could not understand his teachings as such.

> *To the Jews who had believed him, Jesus said, "If you hold to my teachings, you are really my disciples. Then you will know the truth, and the truth will set you free." They answered him, "We are Abraham's descendants and have never been slaves of anyone. How can you say that we shall be set free?" Jesus replied, "I tell you the truth, everyone who sins is a slave to sin. Now a slave has no permanent place in the family, but a son belongs to it forever. So if the Son sets you free, you will be free indeed" . . . "If you were Abraham's children," said Jesus, "then you would do the things Abraham did."*
>
> (John 8: 31 – 41)

According to the Bible, when Jesus had told them that they ought to follow Abraham's pattern as his true descendants, the Jews had insisted that they are following Abraham's pattern. Yet it is obvious that Abraham had a personal, one-to-one relationship with God, which they lacked, and Abraham had the witness that his righteousness was *"credited to him"* by God in exchange for faith rather than for keeping specific rules and ordinances.

The high point of Jesus' teaching is that true righteousness is obtained by faith, as was that of Abraham rather than by the keeping of commandments. If Abraham had any sins, the sins were fully forgiven by God when he credited Abraham with righteousness. The Law that was given by Moses recommended specific offerings for sin. But Abraham without making any offering received full forgiveness and righteousness from God. That was grace – absolutely free mercy.

The culmination of Jesus teaching is that as God did to Abraham, God has decided to do to every human, to give humans full forgiveness of past sins and credit every person with righteousness given by God's absolutely free mercy. Jesus taught that the righteousness now being offered requires no offering, nothing to be contributed by the sinner; all that is required is for one to have faith in God as Abraham did and one would be credited with righteousness as Abraham was. And not only would one be credited with righteousness, one would enjoy the liberty to relate with God on a one-to-one basis without any sense of guilt or fear.

However, Jesus' grace doctrine did not make much sense to the Judaist Jews. They rejected it. But a few people among the Jews embraced it and they found the personal one-to-one relationship with God that Jesus promised. Not only those few Jews, but many non-Jews who were not hindered by the Law as the Judaist Jews were, found a one-to-one relationship with the God of the Jews by having faith in God, in accordance with what Jesus Christ taught. The one-to-one personal relationship with God that many people have found by following the teachings of Jesus is not just a relationship between the outer (animal) man and the eternal Spirit God, but a relationship between the inner (spirit) man and the Spirit God. Those who refuse to take the teachings of Jesus still futilely try to relate the animal man with the Spirit God but it just does not work.

The God of Abraham, Isaac and Jacob.

Three major religions in the world – Judaism, Christianity and Islam – today lay claim to worshipping the same God that Abraham worshipped. When we examine the doctrines of these religions and the records available about Abraham, we find that whereas Abraham enjoyed a one-to-one personal relationship with God, most Judaist, Christians (so-called), and Moslems are simply going about carrying *"holy books"* and trying to keep specific laws and ordinances without having such a personal relationship with God as Abraham did. Yet they are all fighting one another, killing one another, disturbing the world peace, all the while claiming that they are rightly worshiping the God of Abraham. If we should approach issues with an independent mind, we would not be wrong to say that if Judaist, Christians and Moslems are truly worshipping the God of Abraham in the proper way that Abraham himself did, then every Judaist, Christian or Moslem should be a personal *"friend of God"*, who enjoys a one-to-one personal relationship with God as Abraham did. But how many Judaists, or Christians or Moslems, enjoy such a relationship? How many of them even consider it possible to have such a relationship with God? How many of them consider that unless they have such a relationship with God (so much that without even asking to know the mind of God, God would by himself first approach them individually to discuss issues with them as he did with Abraham), they cannot be rightly counted as true worshippers of the God of Abraham?

Let us think of it: when we read the scriptures of the Judaists, Christians, and Moslems, we find that Abraham knew God personally. But how many among even the exalted Rabbis, and Archbishops, and Chief Imams, know God personally as Abraham did? We meet them everyday and they tell us *"we speak to God in our prayers and God answers us"*. But when we pick up their scriptures and see the manner in which Abraham spoke with God, and got answers from God, is it the same with the manner in which our Rabbis, Archbishops, and Chief Imams speak with God and get answers from him? Obviously it is not. Abraham spoke with God, not just *"in prayers"*. And he got answers from God not just when the things he requested for in prayers arrived.

When it comes to relationship with God, there is a popular Bible story that we should consider. It highlights the manner in which God related with Abraham:

Then the LORD said, "Shall I hide from Abraham what I am about to do? Abraham will surely become a great and powerful nation, and all nations on earth will be blessed through him. For I have chosen him, so that he will direct his children and his household after him to keep the way of the LORD by doing what is right and just, so that the LORD will bring about for Abraham what he has promised him." Then the LORD said, "The outcry against Sodom and Gomorrah is so great and their sin so grievous that I will go down and see if what they have done is as bad as the outcry that has reached me. If not, I will know." The men turned away and went toward Sodom, but Abraham remained standing before the LORD. Then Abraham approached him and said, "Will you sweep away the righteous with the wicked? What if there are fifty righteous people in the city? Will you really sweep it away and not spare the place for the sake of the fifty righteous people in it? Far be it from you to do such a thing — to kill the righteous with the wicked, treating the righteous and the wicked alike. Far be it from you! Will not the Judge of the earth do right?" The LORD said, "If I find fifty righteous people in the city of Sodom, I will spare the whole place for their sake". . . Abraham said, "Now that I have been so bold as to speak to the Lord, what if only twenty can be found there?" He said, "For the sake of twenty, I will not destroy it." Then he said, "May the Lord not be angry, but let me speak just once more. What if only ten can be found there?" He answered, "For the sake of ten, I will not destroy it." When the LORD had finished speaking with Abraham, he left, and Abraham returned home.

(Genesis 18: 17 – 33)

That was just it. Abraham spoke to God and was spoken back to. But among the Rabbis, Archbishops, and Chief Imams, and among the millions of people that are guided by these men, how many of them speak to God and get an instant answer back from God? All that are supplied are lame excuses that Abraham and the likes were prophets. But what is it that made Abraham a prophet that we should not have? If our religions cannot afford us the religious experience of Abraham, then they are certainly not the religion of Abraham.

Islam teaches that the religion of Abraham is *"submission"*. Submission is good. But in what way was Abraham submitted to God? By

273

reading and following certain scriptures without having a personal one-to-one relationship with the God to whom he submitted? No, that is not what the *"holy books"* say about him. Christianity preaches submission as well. But more important than submission (of the outward animal human) is the need to be spiritually alive (and submissive), and have a personal one-to-one relationship with the God to whom we submit. If one must practise "submission" in the pattern of Abraham, one has to do so as Abraham did. Abraham knew God personally, and God too reckoned with Abraham. How many Chief Imams today enjoy a personal relationship with God as Abraham did? The reason why they do not enjoy such a one-to-one relationship with God is not that such a relationship is no longer possible, it is that they are ignorant of the provisions that God has made for such a relationship. Likewise are the Rabbis of Judaism and Archbishops of Christianity, and likewise are most of the followers of these three religions. They are simply ignorant of God's desire and ability to relate on a one-to-one personal basis with every human being in the world. But the desire and ability of God to do so are spelt out in the Christian scripture, although false *"broad road"* Christianity remains blind to the essence of the very scriptures that it treasures.

The forgiveness of sins.

The teaching of Jesus Christ in the Bible is that God delights to give every man the religious experience of the kind that Abraham, Moses and the other prophets enjoyed. But we should ask what it requires to become a prophet like Abraham, Moses and others. Abraham and Moses were not born as prophets. They were born as ordinary men. They had as much shortcomings and strengths as every other person. Yet God made them prophets. And Jesus taught that it as easy and pleasant to God to make every human being a prophet as much as he made Abraham and Moses.

Long before Jesus was born, Joel had prophesied that God would make many people prophets and prophetesses.

"And afterward I will pour out my Spirit on all people. Your sons and daughters will prophesy, your old men will dream dreams, your young men will see visions. Even on my servants, both men and women, I will pour out my Spirit in those days."

(Joel 2: 28 – 29).

Was Joel wrong in prophesying this, or has his prophecy been misinterpreted? Of course, the "holy books" (of Judaism, Christianity and Islam) agree that at the very onset of humankind, God spoke with the prototype humans and they too spoke with God. For Adam and Eve, it was not a matter of *"talking to God in prayer"* and *"getting his answers when what we ask for arrives"*. It was a one-to-one personal communication. They spoke and got answers immediately. They **dialogued** with God. It follows that if Adam and Eve had not by disobedience ruined that relationship, and if none of their offspring did, every human being would have continued to enjoy one-to-one personal relationship with God. Should it be an unthinkable thing then that God should want to restore every human being into that kind of relationship? At least by making Abraham and Moses examples of such a relationship, God has demonstrated that the privilege of a personal one-to-one relationship with Him that was lost in the Garden of Eden is not permanently forgone. If God could do it with Abraham, then he should be able to do it with anyone else. He could do it with you and me.

What then made it possible for Abraham and Moses to relate with God? The records from the "holy books" show that it was God who took the first step in building relationship with these men. If God had not made a fire in the bush that was not burning the bush, would Moses not have just normally tended his sheep as usual? Even when he turned aside to check out the unusual sight, if God had not spoken to him, Moses would not have known God on a personal one-to-one basis. God took the first step. And Moses yielded. Moses was not a perfect and sinless man when God spoke to him. And by the same token, the common excuse given by today's religious leaders that *"it is sin that makes us not to hear God"* is not outright. God did not mind the imperfections of Moses. He did not mind the imperfection of Abraham. He showed himself as a forgiving God.

When I read the Koran, I find the words *"In the name of God, Most Gracious, Most Merciful"*, and I wonder if Moslems understand what it really means to be *"Most Gracious, Most Merciful"*. Infinite grace and mercy means there is no sin too great for God to forgive.

Talking about forgiveness, we could borrow the term *"debt cancellation"*. Suppose you had loaned a friend two hundred and fifty thousand dollars to start a business. She starts the business and everything flourishes for a while. But then one night, fire breaks out and destroys all that she has. You had initially agreed that you would get your money back at a certain date but now you find that your friend is too ruined to repay you; she has no means at all and even depends on charity to survive. How would you get your money back? Suppose at once you are very rich, perhaps you even make a million every month, it may not so much matter to you to cancel the debts she owes you. The next morning you pick the phone and call her. *"Hey, Mary"*, you say, *"I have decided to cancel the debts you owe me"*. You would normally expect her to be pleased at that. But suppose she tells you, *"No, thanks, Meg, two hundred and fifty thousand is so much and you shouldn't cancel the debts outright, I've got some five dollars here and would send it to you. Then you can cancel the rest"*. When you hear that, would you not think she is out of her mind? So it is with trying to earn God's forgiveness. We all naturally live in sin – spiritual irresponsiveness to God. According to the Bible, God had long decided to forgive us this inherited sin, which is the root of all other sins. Forgiving us is his personal undertaking. We need not contribute any effort of ourselves in order to earn God's forgiveness. God has taken it upon himself to forgive us outright. We need not make penances for sin. In fact we cannot make such penances. Until a person becomes spiritually alive, that person cannot please God, who is a Spirit, no matter what the person does. Our spiritual irresponsive nature is itself sin, which if it were not completely overlooked (forgiven) would always prevent us from receiving the breath [spirit] of God that would make us alive and responsive towards him, and hence please him.

Spiritual irresponsiveness towards God is a condition – it is a state of our spirits, which we are not empowered to change by our own efforts. God himself is the one that can rescue us from that condition by breathing his spirit into us all over again, as he breathed it in the beginning into Adam. If he does not breathe his Spirit into us, we cannot be spiritually responsive towards him.

In order for us to receive his *"breath"* and the breath to remain in us, we have to be cleansed from all sins – spiritual irresponsiveness, because spiritual irresponsiveness would not let his spirit abide in us. We cannot by ourselves make ourselves clean in his eyes. He is the one that can cleanse us to his personal satisfaction. Thus, whatever can cleanse from our sinful nature has to be administered by him, not by ourselves.

Come and buy without money.

Here in Nigeria, people are ever advocating for free education.

President Olusegun Obasanjo responds that *"education is never completely free"*. He explains that *"even if you receive it free, someone must have paid for it"*.

Although the Bible teaches that God offers us full and free forgiveness of sin and free cleansing too, it also maintains that forgiveness is free to us that receive it but has been paid for by someone else. We are therefore required to use the opportunity judiciously bearing in mind that someone else has paid in order to make it free to us.

While prophesying concerning the expected Christ, the book of Isaiah describes the free mercy that the Christ shall make open to all men.

"Come, all who are thirsty, come to the waters; and you who have no money, come, buy wine and milk! Come, buy wine and milk without money and without cost. Why spend your money on what is not bread, and your labor on what does not satisfy? Listen, listen to me, and eat what is good, and your soul will delight in the richest fare. Give ear and come to me; hear me, that your soul may live. I will make an everlasting covenant with you, my faithful love promised to David. . . . Seek the LORD while he may be found; call on him while he is near. Let the wicked forsake his way, and the evil man his thoughts. Let him turn to the LORD, and he will have mercy on him, and to our God, for he will freely pardon.

(Isaiah 55: 1 − 7)

For us it is free pardon. But to him, it had been a cost. He asks us to *"buy without money"* and at no price. But he had himself paid the price. Jesus Christ had suffered and died. The book of Isaiah says that God had reckoned Jesus as our substitute as far as penance for sins is concerned. But in that, the prophecy makes us wonder how it could be acceptable to God, that a single man should be punished in the stead of many billion others. However, the apostles tell us that in balancing the equations, God dealt with the root of sin rather than individual sins. Adam sinned originally. It was because of Adam's one sin that the entire human race lost the otherwise natural personal one-to-one relationship with God. Consequently, all the sins that followed are routed in the singular sin of Adam:

For if, by the trespass of one man, death reigned through that one man, how much more will those who receive God's abundant provision of grace and of the gift of righteousness reign in life through the one man, Jesus Christ. Consequently, just as the result of one trespass was condemnation for all men, so also the result of one act of righteousness was justification that brings life for all men. For just as through the disobedience of the one man the many were made sinners, so also through the obedience of the one man the many will be made righteous.

(Romans 5: 17 – 19)

According to Christian doctrines therefore, as many people as possible have the opportunity to find righteousness in God through Jesus Christ. When God credited righteousness to Abraham, he simply made a promise to Abraham, which Abraham believed and was consequently credited with righteousness. This time around, God is not asking us to believe that he would give us children in our very old ages. All that he wants from us is that we should believe that Jesus died for us and had made his life the sacrifice for our sins.

The Bible teaches that God asked Moses to institute the sacrifices of animals for the forgiveness of sins.

In fact, the law requires that nearly everything be cleansed with blood, and without the shedding of blood there is no forgiveness.

(Hebrew 9: 22)

However, it was not represented that sighting the blood of animals was what pleased God. In accepting even animal sacrifices, what God accepted was not the blood of the animals but the minds of the people who brought forth the animal sacrifices. It is the obedient mind, not the blood of the sacrifice that pleased God:

Because it is impossible for the blood of bulls and goats to take away sins. Therefore, when Christ came into the world, he said: "Sacrifice and offering you did not desire, but a body you prepared for me; with burnt offerings and sin offerings you were not pleased. Then I said, 'Here I am — it is written about me in the scroll — I have come to do your will, O God.' " First he said, "Sacrifices and offerings, burnt offerings and sin offerings you did not desire, nor were you pleased with them" (although the law required them to be made). Then he said, "Here I am, I have come to do your will". He sets aside the first to establish the second.

(Hebrews 10: 4 – 9)

Again another prophet buttressed the fact that it is not the shedding of the blood that pleases God:

With what shall I come before the LORD and bow down before the exalted God? Shall I come before him with burnt offerings, with calves a year old? Will the LORD be pleased with thousands of rams, with ten thousand rivers of oil? Shall I offer my firstborn for my transgression, the fruit of my body for the sin of my soul? He has shown you, O man, what is good. And what does the LORD require of you? To act justly and to love mercy and to walk humbly with your God.

(Micah 6: 6 – 8)

Talking about sacrifices and penances for sins, although at first God had required Moses to recommend animal sacrifices involving the shedding of blood to the Jews, God subsequently sent word to the Jews that whatever the animal nature of humankind has to offer cannot appease for the disgust occasioned by the irresponsiveness of the human spirit [synedochically referred to in this passage as *"soul"*]. Rather than the shedding of blood, what God really desires is *"acting justly, loving mercy and fellowshipping with God"*. And in this is the point where the broad road Christianity differs from the narrow road Christianity. The former preaches *"acting justly and loving mercy"* but leaves out the *"fellowshipping with God"* aspect of the requirements for pleasing God. Fellowshipping with God involves being able to have a one-to-one personal relationship with God, which of course can only come when a human's spirit (the inner man) is first made alive and responsive towards God. It is the fellowship, not the shedding of blood that puts an end to sin [spiritual irresponsiveness towards God]. But the shedding of blood affected the conscience of humankind and helps the mind to overcome the sense of guilt, fear and shame that inhibits humankind's fellowship with God.

Abraham was not required to make any animal sacrifice before he had fellowship with God, because his conscience was already purified by his faith in God. For Christians, the doctrine is that because Jesus enjoyed fellowship with God being born without the irresponsive natural human spirit, he is able to extend the fellowship to as many as accept him. Although, Jesus made it clear that animal sacrifice is not required for fellowship, yet his outer animal being was sacrificed to purify the conscience of those who are still held back by the threshold of sacrifices from fellowship with God.

In all, the high point of religiousness is not in sacrifices or penances (for such do not really please God), and neither is it in *"acting justly and loving mercy"* alone, but also in *"walking humbly (that is, fellowshipping) with God"*. The only requirement for this fellowship with the Spirit God is just being spiritually alive but one cannot be spiritually alive if his or her conscience and mind is held back by any sense of guilt, or fear or ignorance. But faith – the kind of faith that Abraham had – removes all guilt, fear and ignorance. Hence, Christianity preaches "justification/salvation by faith".

Justification by faith.

On the doctrine of grace and salvation [full pardon of past sins and rescue from the sinful nature], the Bible teaches and upholds the importance of excising faith. Grace encompasses all the provisions that God has already made for humankind to be restored into fellowship with him, and faith (accepting God for whom he really is and accepting the provisions he has made for fellowshipping with him) is taught in Christianity as what gives us full access to grace.

Unless faith is reckoned with, even sacrifices and penances make no logical import. If God is deemed the Creator of the world, and of humans and animals, how does it make sense that God should require the blood of animals in order to forgive humankind? In what way is the blood pleasing to God? Is it merely sighting blood that pleases God or the agony that the animals go through while being sacrificed? If God really needs the blood of animals, does he need to consult humankind? Or in burnt offerings, as we read in the Torah, was it the *"sweet smell of the sacrifices being burnt"* that really appeased God? In his psalms, David gave us a summary answer to these questions.

> *"Hear, O my people, and I will speak, O Israel, and I will testify against you: I am God, your God. I do not rebuke you for your sacrifices or your burnt offerings, which are ever before me. I have no need of a bull from your stall or of goats from your pens, for every animal of the forest is mine, and the cattle on a thousand hills. I know every bird in the mountains, and the creatures of the field are mine. If I were hungry I would not tell you, for the world is mine, and all that is in it. Do I eat the flesh of bulls or drink the blood of goats? Sacrifice thank offerings to God, fulfill your vows to the Most High, and call upon me in the day of trouble; I will deliver you, and you will honor me".*
>
> (Psalm 50: 7 – 15)

So, where is the place for sacrifices and penances? God is less concerned about all the sacrifices, what he desires is the state of the human mind – for humankind to have fellowship with him.

In the Bible, the story is told of Cain and Abel and their sacrifices to God. Cain's sacrifice of plants was not accepted by God whereas Abel's sacrifice of animal was. But what made Abel's sacrifice acceptable was not the fact that blood or flesh was involved, it was the person of Abel that was primarily acceptable to God, and hence whatever else Abel had to offer. And for Cain, it was his person that was rejected by God and hence all he had to offer. Because the person of Cain was rejected by God, if Cain had offered animals, it would have been rejected all the same.

> *In the course of time Cain brought some of the fruits of the soil as an offering to the LORD. But Abel brought fat portions from some of the firstborn of his flock. The LORD looked with favor on Abel and his offering, but on Cain and his offering he did not look with favor. So Cain was very angry, and his face was downcast. Then the LORD said to Cain, "Why are you angry? Why is your face downcast? If you do what is right, will you not be accepted? But if you do not do what is right, sin is crouching at your door; it desires to have you, but you must master it."*
>
> (Genesis 4: 3 – 7)

That is the moral of the story. The problem was not with the sacrifice but with Cain. God could have said, *"if you do well, will* **your sacrifice** *not be accepted?"*; rather, he said, *"if you do well, will* **you** *not be accepted?"*. Hence, it was not the sacrifice that God rejected, but the person of Cain. But Abel found favour with God, not by his sacrifice but by his faith towards God.

The Bible is full of testimonies of men whose righteousness is based upon fellowshipping with God rather than in sacrifices and penances. And the Christian doctrines uphold the examples as already laid in the Torah and the Prophets. Paul argued to the Romans that justification and relationship with God is built upon faith rather than in keeping of commandments.

> *It was not through the law that Abraham and his offspring received the promise that he would be heir of the world, but through the righteousness that comes by faith . . . Against all hope, Abraham in hope believed and so became the father of many nations, just as it had been said to him, "So shall your offspring be." Without weakening in faith, he faced the fact that his body was as good as dead – since he was about a hundred years old – and that Sarah's womb was also dead. Yet he did not waver through unbelief regarding the promise of God, but was strengthened in his faith and gave glory to God, being fully persuaded that God had power to do what he had promised. This is why, "it was credited to him as righteousness." The words "it was credited to him" were written not for him alone, but also for us, to whom God will credit righteousness – for us who believe in him who raised Jesus our Lord from the dead. He was delivered over to death for our sins and was raised to life for our justification. Therefore, since we have been justified through faith, we have peace with God through our Lord Jesus Christ, through whom we*

have gained access by faith into this grace in which we now stand. And we rejoice in the hope of the glory of God.

(Romans 4: 13 – 5: 2)

Having access into God's divine nature by faith is the summation of all that the Christian gospel stands for. Once, I checked out the definition of the word "faith" in a dictionary, and found it says *"faith is a belief without evidence"*. This definition misconstrues what faith really means. The misconstruing of what faith means is one major enemy of humankind. Faith is **not** *"belief without evidence"*, as many people wrongly suppose the Christian doctrine of *"faith"* is. The Christian Bible defines faith as *"the **substance** of things hoped for, the **evidence** of things not seen"*. (Hebrews 11: 1, King James Version).

Entering into intimate fellowship with God, by his grace, through faith is therefore not a matter of trying to believe without evidence. If any faith lacks evidence, it is not the Christian faith. There are over abundant evidences that buttress the claims of the Christians in the Christhood of Jesus. To have faith is to ponder those evidences and relate them to other spheres of life.

For instance, when Abraham believed in God that he shall yet have children in his very old age, it was not that Abraham lacked evidence of the promise. The evidence of the promise was ultimately vested in the one who had made the promise, the person of God. Abraham already had a firm and intimate relationship with God, and knew that the God who made the whole world would not find it difficult to give him children. The material universe, as God's handcraft, was for Abraham an evidence of God's ability to fulfil his promise to him.

Therefore, when it comes to the evidence of the Christian gospel which teaches that righteousness is at best obtained by believing in God, *"believing in God"* is not put forth as just *"believing without evidences"*, rather it is submitted as *"carefully weighing the evidences that buttress the Christhood of Jesus, his death, his burial, his resurrection, and the fellowship with God with which those who believe in the Christhood of Jesus are endowed"*.

Fellowship with God and righteousness by faith is not forced on any person. Every human is called to consider the evidences that corroborate the report of the teachings of Jesus and of his life, death, burial, and resurrection. If you consider the evidences and you become persuaded that indeed Jesus is the Christ, and the one through whose life, death and resurrection we gain access into fellowship with God, then good luck to you. Welcome on board. But if after considering all the evidences, you still find it impossible to believe that Jesus was crucified and rose from death, and that he is the Christ, and that he is the *Living Word*, no one shall force it upon you to believe. Good luck to you too.

However, if it should be that eventually after death, you were to find that there is eternal existence for humankind after biological death, you may not then blame anyone or even God. It is you, not God, who decides whether to embrace or reject the evidences of Jesus' Christhood and his teachings on righteousness by faith and fellowship with God.

The Predestination.

At this point, one idea to question is the predestination. Many people think that God has predetermined who would obtain his free forgiveness and righteousness by faith and who would not. But predestination is not often what we think it is. Predestination is more of opportunity that programming. The Bible by telling us that God had predestined certain people to obtain righteousness by faith does not imply that God does not want some to do so.

Many of those who do not have a personal one-to-one relationship with God carry the idea that God has written the destiny of every one of us in a way that we do not have an option. If your car gets burnt, they would tell you, *"That is how God has destined it"*. But those who know God on a personal one-to-one basis testify that God says of himself that he does not plan evil for anyone:

"For I know the plans I have for you," declares the LORD, "plans to prosper you and not to harm you, plans to give you hope and a future."

(Jeremiah 29: 11)

And that it always is. God does not plan to harm anyone of us, humankind. He plans the best for us. But wherever there are consciousnesses (be it animal consciousnesses or spirit consciousnesses), the functioning of minds interfere with the plans of one another. For example, I may wake up and make plans for the things in my house — the settees, the kitchen wares, the laundries, and the pets. The settees, and pots, and clothes, cannot in anyway alter the plans that I have for them, because they are unconscious things. But the pets can alter my plans for them because they have their own minds. I can plan to pick up the bed sheets and wash them at a precise time in the morning. But if I decided to pick Andy, the dog, and wash it up at noon precisely, I may in fact be kidding myself. Because unless I had Andy chained I may spend an extra five minutes chasing it about or tricking it, before I can get to bath it.

For the things without minds, God's plans may be fixed and unchanging. But for living entities, and humankind in particular, God's plans for us are often affected by the choices we make per time, because we have our own independent minds which God does not hold bound. Our minds respond to our imaginations, experiences and environments, and these are in turn affected by our minds.

There are varied levels of reasonableness. For instance, Andy the dog cannot understand everything that I do or say. I can relate with it to a certain extent but not to all extents, because our relationship is limited by its level of abilities. Likewise, God can relate with humans to specific extents, but his relationship with us is limited by our levels of spiritual abilities. Generally, the more spiritually capable we are, the more we shall be able to relate with God. But because we have our own minds, most of our thoughts, speeches and actions, are independent of God. God does not move our feet or fingers, nor does he move our lips, we are the ones who control these things. But God responds to the choices we make, because we are in his world, just as our pets are in our homes. Andy is free to walk peacefully about in the compound and can bark at strangers. But I won't let it come into my room and urinate on my bed, or let it climb the table to eat what I have reserved for my guests. Yet if I do not control Andy, it would do just about anything.

As newborn babies, we never choose what clothes to wear, what objects to pick up or reject, or whatever. But by and by we make our own choices and reject the ones that our parents make for us, and by and by too, our parents in fact stop making choices for us.

For the Bible's submission, between humankind and God, the consciousness plays a major role. God does not decide what specific cloths we should wear at specific times. He neither chooses the specific foods we should eat at specific times. He does not put every thought in our minds, or every speech in our mouths. We choose what to say and choose the thoughts to allow. Often, our thoughts are the basic responses of our minds to the things around us and to our memories and decisions.

In the Garden of Eden, the Bible tells us that God told Adam *"you may **freely eat from any** tree in the Garden except . . ."*. That is the point where chances come into the whole picture. We never know how many thousands of species were in the Garden of Eden or in fact how large or small the area of land the Garden covered. But as many trees were in the Garden, as many would have been the possibilities of the choices of Adam and Eve. The moral of that for us is that we choose every moment from a wide range of possibilities; whilst some of us have more possibilities open to them and greater independence of choice than others. We are not all equal. There are countries in the world today that people are free to change their religions as they wish. But there are at once other countries where one dares not. To reckon that a resident of the United States, for instance, has an equal freedom of choice in religious and other matters as does a resident of Saudi Arabia, again for instance, is not correct. Here in Nigeria, a massive riot broke out just because a newspaper published an article that carried *"uncomplimentary remarks about Prophet Mohammed"*. The cars and houses of people who have no connections with the newspaper were burnt and even people who knew next to nothing about the publication or Prophet Mohammed lost their lives. But there are places in which more provocative statements do not produce any such reactions. In the light of these, it cannot be said that the ordinary Nigerian resident has the same freedom of choice as do the people in those more tolerant places. And broadly, every human being has his or her own level of freedom of choice and actions. But through and over the limits of our choices and opportunities, God can see our respective destinies (that is, futures).

Predestination is like foresight, it is more of seeing what lies ahead rather than inserting things into specific points in the future. Unlike a decree, it is not the foresight that produces an event, rather it is the (preambles to the) event that give one the foresight into it. Not too long ago, space scientists envisaged that a certain huge "rock" in space may collide with the earth in the not too distant future. They had viewed the rock from their observatories and reckoning with its orbit, speed, and other qualities, they could say *"this rock is destined to collide with the earth in February, 2019"*. If at that time, it does happen, it would not be happening because they had said so, rather they had said so because by *its course and cause* if nothing else changes, it would happen. Meteorologists tell us in weather reports when and where it would rain tomorrow and what temperatures would be somewhere tomorrow, and most of the times their predictions are just exact. But it is not the meteorologists' predictions that cause the rainfall, the sunshine or the temperatures.

Predestination, as foresight, in God's case differs from the meteorologists' foresight of weather conditions. God has his way of intervening in the courses of things whereas the human meteorologist simply observes and do not intervene. According to the Bible, concerning our everyday experiences and our ultimate destinations, God always foresees but does not always intervene. Apostle Paul wrote about the predestination to the Romans as follows:

> *And we know that in all things God works for the good of those who love him, who have been called according to his purpose. For those God foreknew he also predestined to be conformed to the likeliness of his Son, that he might be the first-born among many brothers. And those he predestined, he also called; those he called, he also justified; those he justified, he also glorified.*
>
> (Romans 8: 28 – 30)

In these verses, we see that the root of the predestination is foreknowledge. He does not foreknow them because he has predestined them; rather he predestined them because he foreknew them. It is a matter of foresights – to view the courses and causes of things and see where they normally would end up, if nothing is done to them, and to know what would happen if alternative A were applied, or else what would happen if Alternative B were applied. Choosing to use Alternative B, in stead of alternative A, is the act of predestination. Because by it, certain opportunities are closed against those that could have been favoured if the other alternative were applied.

According to the Bible, where the predestination becomes specifically applied to us is this: after humankind fell from the grace of God in the Garden of Eden and God decided to revive humankind from spiritual stupor, God was not bound to use any specific means of salvation. But he chose to bring us back into obedience and fellowship with him by making himself an example of obedience and fellowship in the person of the Christ. Making himself an example for us is to him the best means by which he could save us from our spiritual irresponsiveness towards him. Hence, he predestined that *"unto us shall be born One whose origin is from everlasting"*, to show us the way of obedience and fellowship by example. But in that, he had placed a stumbling block on the path of those who by nature shall find it offensive to reckon that God could come so close to us.

Concerning the foretold Christ, Isaiah said these:

The LORD spoke to me with his strong hand upon me, warning me not to follow the way of this people. He said: "Do not call conspiracy, everything that these people call conspiracy; do not fear what they fear, and do not dread it. The LORD Almighty is the one you are to regard as holy, he is the one you are to fear, he is the one you are to dread, and he will be a sanctuary; but for both houses of Israel he will be a stone that causes men to stumble and a rock that makes them fall. And for the people of Jerusalem he will be a trap and a snare. Many of them will stumble; they will fall and be broken, they will be snared and captured."

(Isaiah 8: 11 – 15)

Luke tells us that when Jesus was born, a Judaist prophet at that time declared in the Temple similar things concerning the child.

Then Simeon blessed them and said to Mary, his mother: "This child is destined to cause the falling and rising of many in Israel, and to be a sign that will be spoken against, so that the thoughts of many hearts will be revealed. And a sword will pierce your own soul too."

(Luke 2: 34)

Indeed, the child was destined to be a *"stone that makes men stumble, and rock that makes them fall"* , especially for his kinsmen for whom it was outrageous to accept that *"the son of the Carpenter is the Lord from heaven"*. However it may be, wherever the Christ shall be "born unto us as a child", there is no way he would not be a stumbling block for them who shall see him grow up before them as a child. Nevertheless, his being an example of obedience and fellowship with God has brought many more into spiritual aliveness and fellowship with God, and this includes many people that should have lived without knowing or loving God, but for the example of the Christ.

Even though the world of unbelief continues to wrest the witness given by the Bible, the course the world has taken corroborates the Biblical testimony of Jesus that he is the *"light that came into the world"*. The story was told of a European man in Southern Africa who once ridiculed a black woman for devoting too much attention to *"that stupid book"*, referring to Bible. The woman, looked up at him and said, *"if not for this Bible, I would have remained a cannibal and would have eaten you long ago"*. And that is just one example of many lives spared, many evils averted even long before the societies got increasingly civilised.

By choosing that the Christ should be an example for us, God had predestined many people to be spared from the dishes of cannibals, he had predestined that goods of many people should not be stolen by people who otherwise would have remained robbers, he had completely altered the way the world would have been. Yet in spite of the fact that he had by the birth, life, death and resurrection of the Christ redirected the courses of our lives, our specific moment by moment decisions still remain our responsibilities. He has given us the Christ, but has not decided whether we would believe him or not. But the manner in which the Christ came, and the aftermath of it all, affects our individual responses to God. Specifically, the birth of the Christ and the gospel of righteousness by faith are more amenable to the non-Jews than to the Jews. For the Jews, there was a set of laws and ordinances already given to them and sworn to them in perpetuity. They embraced the priesthood of the order of Aaron. But whilst they were yet keeping that, God spoke of another order of priesthood through David. Yet the tendency remains with the Jews to want to keep to the priesthood of Aaron. Jews, generally, therefore have a lesser tendency than non-Jews to become Christians because the birth of the Christ among the Jews had in fact been a stumbling block to them, preventing them from entering the way of righteousness by faith.

Like the Jews, many of us are prevented from embracing the Jesus' way of righteousness by faith by the very things that we are already used to. But God does not force it on anyone to come to the Jesus' way or force anyone to desist from it. God's clarion call is, *"whosoever will may come"*. Yet, because he know our customs, our cultures, our backgrounds, our languages, and every other thing that opposes our individual tendencies to follow the way of Christ, he can tell who would come and would not. Yet, it is not the fact that he can thus foretell that makes some come and some not.

Finally on the issue of predestination, we should consider the matter of life and death as God gave it to prophet Ezekiel in the Bible:

"But if a wicked man turns away from all the sins he has committed and keeps all my decrees and does what is just and right, he will surely live; he will not die. None of the offenses he has committed will be remembered against him. Because of the righteous things he has done, he will live. Do I take any pleasure in the death of the wicked? declares the Sovereign LORD. Rather, am I not pleased when they turn from their ways and live? But if a righteous man turns from his righteousness and commits sin and does he same detestable things the wicked man does, will he live? None of the righteous things he has done will be remembered. Because of the

unfaithfulness he is guilty of and because of the sins he had committed, he will die."

(Ezekiel 18: 21 – 24)

So, God gives room to our choices, and responds to us. For either the wicked or the righteous in the prophecy of Ezekiel, God had not assigned any unchangeable destiny. He assigns a destiny of life to the righteous only as long as the righteous keeps faithful to the righteousness and a destiny of death to the wicked just as long as the wicked keeps doing wickedly. Everyone carries a responsibility for his own choices.

However, many of us want to put all responsibilities on God, and maintain that *"if God says a thing would be, then certainly it would be, nothing would change it"* or rather, we say, *"Anything that happens has been so decided unchangeably by God"*. Such was what the Biblical prophet Jonah wanted when God sent him to Nineveh. The summary of the book of Jonah is that when God told the prophet to foretell doom against the city of Nineveh, God did not add the condition of *"if they repent, I would spare them"*. But eventually Jonah gave his message to the city and they repented, and God sent the prophet again to tell them *"no more doom"*. But the prophet was not pleased, because he wanted to see his prophecy fulfilled without question. However, God would tell him that is not the way it is.

Now, there are millions of so-called Christians out there who say that God has decided who would follow the way of righteousness by faith and who would not. But the Bible shows us that God does not do that. God **foresees** but does **not decide** our destinies until we ourselves have decided.

Chapter Ten

NOT OF WORKS

"Born of the Spirit".

You must be born again!

On the night that Nicodemus visited Jesus and discussed with him about the kingdom of God, Jesus Christ used the term *"born again"*, which has found many varied meanings in the world ever since.

Nicodemus himself had asked the question, *"How can one be born again?"* or, *"What does it mean to be born again?"*. (John 3: 4). But when we ask many so-called Christians in the world today, the answer we get is often different from the one that Jesus Christ had given Nicodemus.

The Bible's principles suffered through the poor illumination of the Dark and Middle ages, and during those times the term *"born again"* was pushed into obscurity. And when it would be rediscovered, it is applied as just *"a term popularly used by the evangelistic/charismatic movement of the church"*. For even this movement, the term *"born again"* is often misapplied.

If on any evening you are invited to a meeting of an evangelistic or charismatic group, the odds are that you would sit in the audience and listen to some rhythmic music from the ultra-modern choir – guitars, jazz sets, drums, cymbals, and rock music. Then the preacher comes on stage, reads a Bible passage or two and begins to tell you stories of how some people had been in low financial situations and after they began to pay tithes regularly have come to have a very prosperous business. Then as he rounds up his "message", he would say, *"If you want to be born again, please come forward to the podium here"*. Then you step forward, with smiles and grin, while being clapped for by the church, and go to the podium to recite a "sinner's prayer", and the pastor would say, *"Congratulations! You are now born again. As long as you believe it, you are"*.

The other common method is that the choir renders some slow and soulful music, the preacher hammers upon the "wicked things" that you have been doing, and your eyes fill with tears, the preacher may in fact encourage you to weep, and then asks the rest of the church to close their eyes, while he invites you to *"come forward to the altar"*, and quietly, he leads you through a repeat-after-me-please prayer of repentance. Then he tells you, *"Congratulations, you are now born again"*.

There are several other typical methods, but the bottom line is that being born again as Jesus told Nicodemus in the Bible differs from all these, in fact it is not methodical. It is not a matter of repeating a sinners' prayer after a preacher, nor is it a matter of claiming it by faith. Jesus had told Nicodemus that an actual birth process is involved in being born again. In further explanation of the term *"born again"*, the Bible uses the more explicit term, *"born of the Spirit"*.

> *"How can a man be born when he is old?" Nicodemus asked. "Surely he cannot enter a second time into his mother's womb to be born!" Jesus answered, "I tell you the truth, no one can enter the kingdom of God unless he is born of water and the Spirit. Flesh gives birth to flesh, but the Spirit gives birth to spirit. You should not be surprised at my saying, 'You must be born again.' The wind blows wherever it pleases. You hear its sounds, but you cannot tell where it comes from or where it is going. So it is with everyone born of the Spirit."*
>
> (John 3: 4 – 8)

In the human birth process, the woman feels an urge and is encouraged to "push". The baby does not come out by its own efforts. Of course, by the course of nature, the baby already makes some movements in the womb and is positioned to come out from it, yet the mother's "pushes" are what ultimately brings out the baby.

When it comes to the paternity of a child, the involvement of the child in the birth process is absolute zero. Nothing is contributed by the child to the father's involvement in its birth. In like manner, when a human is "born again" by God, in accordance with the teachings of Jesus, it is the entire working of God, and not of the human, it is an actual birth process – God breathes his spirit into the human again, as he breathed it into Adam, in the beginning.

Jesus had made it frankly clear that a person that is not *"born of the spirit"* cannot be part of the kingdom of God, that is, cannot have fellowship with God. Having fellowship with God is the test of the acceptability of one's worship. Some religions preach worship alone because they do not know what it means to fellowship with God. But the Bible gives us an example in the story of Cain and Abel of people who wish to worship God when in fact they have no fellowship with God. Abel's worship was acceptable to God because Abel enjoyed a fellowship with God, but Cain's worship was rejected because he did not fellowship with God.

Fellowship with God is possible only after a person has received the enlivening breath of God. No matter how many times a person answers "the altar call", or confesses to "the sinner's prayer of repentance" or "claims by faith" to be born again, he remains spiritually dead towards God until he or she has received the *"breath"* of God, as Adam was said to have received in the Garden and by that breath can have fellowship with God. Receiving the spirit of God anew is what it simply means, in the light of Christian scriptures, to be "born again", and anyone who has not received the spirit of God is not born again and is not an acceptable member of God's kingdom.

It is the gift of God.

The apostle Paul wrote in his lengthy epistle to the Christian community in Rome, to further enlighten them on what it means in practical terms to be "born again":

*Those who live according to the sinful nature have their minds set on what that nature desires; but those who live in accordance with the Spirit have their minds set on what the Spirit desires. The mind of sinful man is death, but the mind controlled by the Spirit is life and peace; the sinful mind is hostile to God. It does not submit to God's law, nor can it do so. Those controlled by the sinful nature cannot please God. You, however, are controlled not by the sinful nature but by the Spirit, if the Spirit of God lives in you. **And if anyone does not have the Spirit of Christ, he does not belong to Christ.** But if Christ is in you, your body is dead because of sin, yet your spirit is alive because of righteousness. And if the Spirit of him who raised Jesus from the dead is living in you, he who raised Christ from the dead will also give life to your mortal bodies through his Spirit, who lives in you. Therefore, brothers, we have an obligation — but it is not to the sinful nature, to live according to it. For if you live according to the sinful nature, you will die; but if by the Spirit you put to death the misdeeds of the body, you will live, **because those who are led by the Spirit of God are sons of God.** For you did not receive a spirit that makes you a slave again to fear, but* *you received the Spirit of sonship.* **And by him we cry, "Abba, Father." The Spirit himself testifies with our spirit that we are God's children.** *Now if we are children, then we are heirs –* **heirs of God and co-heirs with Christ,** *if indeed we share in his sufferings in order that we may also share in his glory.*

(Romans 8: 5 – 17)

The non-Christian world has been confused about the Christian message till today, and the church herself is despised all because many people have been professing to be "born again" or "become Christians" without having received the Spirit of God. People count them as Christians, but to God, and according to the Bible, in fact those who do not have the Spirit of God "have no part nor share" in the true "narrow way" Christianity.

The Holy Spirit of God is the seal of the Christian faith, the one without which a person cannot be counted as true Christian no matter how pious in thoughts, words, and actions the person is. That is why the Bible warns even those who have received the spiritually enlivening Spirit of God to avoid grieving the Holy Spirit.

And do not grieve the Holy Spirit of God, with whom you were sealed for the day of redemption.

(Ephesians 4: 30)

Everyone who believes in the Christian gospel is recognised as a "believer". But not every believer is automatically born again. It is the believer who has received the Holy Spirit that is saved from the control of the ordinary animal mind of humans, and has a renewed spiritual mind.

For it is by grace you have been saved, through faith – and this not from your-selves, it is the gift of God – not by works, so that no one can boast.

(Ephesians 2: 8 – 9)

In the process of transition from spiritual death to spiritual life, what follows grace and faith is the gift of God, which is his Holy Spirit. It is the Spirit that completes the work of restoration, and until one has received the Holy Spirit the work of restoration from the sinful nature into the nature that pleases God remains incomplete.

The Bible submits that every human has a spirit within, which is born by our parents as part of our complete nature. But the natural spirit in us is irresponsive and inactive towards God and we experience only the consciousness of our outward animal nature. But when a person comes into the understanding of the fact that human nature has animal as well as spirit nature, and that God by grace has made provision to restore every one of us into full spiritual aliveness, then the person has just begun. Understanding the fact that God is not holding our sinful nature and our sins against us, because of the death, burial and resurrection of Jesus Christ is faith. But that understanding alone does not change our spirit, because it is a mental understanding. Faith in God's redemptive grace alone does not make us spiritually alive. What can revive and restore our non-material nature cannot be received from the material realm; it has to come from the non-material spirit realm, from the original source himself. And it is a **gift** – there is no service or penance that we can render in the material realm that can draw it into us. As a dead body cannot draw in a reviving physical breath from a living person, so can our spiritually dead nature not draw in spiritual breath from God – God is the one who can breathe into us. No action taken by us can yield spiritual live in us – the reviving spiritual breath comes from God, "it is not of works, so no one can boast".

Where our outward nature is involved in this matter is that if the outward nature is not itself inclined towards God, there is no way it would not grieve the Spirit of God if God should by any means breathe into us. To receive the Spirit of God, therefore, one's outward animal nature itself must be made ready to yield towards God. But making ready does not guarantee that one would automatically receive the Holy Spirit. Nevertheless, if even those who remain pious in all aspects of the animal nature – thoughts, words, and actions – and seek after God, still may not receive the enlivening Spirit of God, how shall those who continually reject the knowledge of God, and even hate God, receive the Spirit?

And, "If it is hard for the righteous to be saved, what will become of the ungodly and the sinner?"

(1 Peter 4: 18)

Every bird makes its nest upon the tree where it feels comfortable. Like a dove, the Holy Spirit would not nest himself into the person that would perpetually grieve him. The Spirit can only be received by those who are clean in the outward man. Even humans store their pure drinks in clean vessels; you cannot store up your drinking water in a maggot infested cistern, otherwise the pureness of the water would be marred by the filth of the vessel. How much more would God pour the "Living Water" into us if our animal natures remain wayward? Of course, unlike physical water, the Living Water would not mix with the filth of the vessel into which he is poured, if by any chance he is poured into such, it would simply depart from there for not being at home there. Yet the mere fact that a cistern is clean does not mean that one would automatically fill it with one's drinking water, however, for a person who is eagerly looking about for vessels to pour the Living Water into, every clean cistern would be considered, but not every clean cistern would be filled. (How much more the filthy ones?) The Living Water is the gift of God.

When he is come.

There is the issue that must be understood about the Holy Spirit and our human spirits. It is important to note that Christianity is the only religion that teaches the baptism of the Holy Spirit. Islam teaches submission of the animal nature to a Spirit God but does not teach the revival and restoration of the human spirit, but can we indeed please God if the nature that we share with him (the spirit nature, not the animal nature) remains irresponsive towards him? Judaism teaches the commandments of God, but if our animal nature continues to keep the word of God until death, then what shall become of our spirit natures after the death of the animal nature? Can the spirit nature that has ever remained dead to God automatically be made responsive to the God that it has never been in fellowship with? If it could, then what is the point in keeping the commandments in our animal natures, if our spirit natures would be automatically saved irrespective of whether it has been in fellowship with God or not? For the New Age religions that teach the spirituality of humankind, and encourage astral projections, where the human spirit nature is brought into fellowship with the angels that sinned, how is it expected that by fellowshipping with the spirits that have been excommunicated from fellowship with God, our human spirits would be made acceptable to God? Or yet for the religions that teach that *"God is the sum of all things, and is not a person"*, what is the use of their religious principles, if God is supposed to be the sum of good and evil, why choose good, what advantage does good have over evil, when it all adds up together to one whole?

When we consider what each religion teaches about God's nature and the human nature, and weigh the practices prescribed by the religion in balance with its purpose and principles, there is often no point to many religious practices, because the purpose of many religions are negated by their principles. For Islam, submission without spirituality is meaningless. For Judaism, obeying the commandments, without being spiritually responsive to God is pointless. For the religions that teach that God is not a person but just the sum of all things, there is no point in choosing to do good rather than evil so long as evil is deemed as useful as good; if *"it all adds to a perfect whole"*, as they say, then let everyone simply be as bad as he or she wants to be, since it will still add to a perfect whole – let us steal, kill and destroy one another, it will yet add to a perfect whole. Really? How could it?

However, for Christianity (and this I say not for being a part of it), there is a justified correlation between the principles of the religion and its submission on the nature and purpose of human life in the world. Its doctrine on the nature of God and the way to please God do not negate its principles as do those of the other religions. And the ultimate submission of Christianity is that there is a Spirit God, and Originator of the world, a living person and NOT "just the sum of all things that exist", whose offspring we are, not by our animal nature but by our spirit nature. In furtherance of this submission is the principle that unless the Creator breathes again into our spirits, so that our spirits are brought alive towards him once more, to fellowship with him, and NOT with the angels that sinned, then we cannot in anyway enter into eternal fellowship with him. If religion is not in the way that the Christian faith teaches, the whole issue about religion would be utterly useless.

Nevertheless, when it teaches that God revives us by breathing his Holy Spirit into us, Christianity does not represent that without it we are animals only. A person who is not born again, still has an inner spirit nature – the image and likeness of God – but the natural human spirit, by the sin of Adam is irresponsive towards God.

When a person receives the Holy Spirit of God again to become born again, the new breath from God does not replace the natural human spirit that is already in the person. Rather, the coming in of the Holy Spirit can be likened to refuelling an engine. The whole engine is there and ready to go, but remains inactive because there is no fuel in it. Again, the coming in of the Holy Spirit can be likened to rekindling the fire of charcoals. An ordinary black charcoal cannot give heat or light. It is dead, yet it is charcoal all the same. And no matter how much you fan it, it would remain dead. But you can take a small spark of red-hot burning charcoal from the Big Source and attach it to the black dormant charcoal, and then begin to fan it. As you fan, the black dead charcoal itself comes alive, turns red and burns, giving heat and light, like the Big Source red burning charcoal from which it was originally grafted. The small spark of red burning charcoal does not replace the black dead one; rather it comes to enliven it. The Big Source is the Spirit God, the Almighty, the Originator, the only first person, who has ever been. The natural human spirit is the black dead charcoal. Fanning the black dead charcoal without adding fire to it is what religion does to a human that has not received the Holy Spirit. The Holy Spirit is the spark of red burning charcoal coming in from the Big Source and attaching itself to the dead black charcoal. The transformation from being a black dead charcoal into a hot glowing red one is what it means to be born again.

What can one do to be born again?

When the apostles were asked a similar question on the day that the Holy Spirit was poured on the Church, according to the Bible, Peter gave them a prescription that still remains valid till today.

*Then Peter stood up with the Eleven, raised his voice and addressed the crowd: "Fellow Jews and all of you who live in Jerusalem, let me explain this to you; listen carefully to what I say. These men are not drunk, as you suppose. It's only nine in the morning! No, this is what was spoken by the prophet Joel: " 'In the last day, God says, I will pour out my Spirit on all people. Your sons and daughters will prophesy, your young men will see visions, your old men will dream dreams . . . ,". . . "Therefore let all Israel be assured of this: God has made this Jesus, whom you crucified, both Lord and Christ." When the people heard this, they were cut to the heart and said to Peter and the other apostles, "**Brothers, what shall we do?**" Peter replied, "Repent and be baptized, every one of you, in the name of Jesus Christ for the forgiveness of your sins. And you will receive the gift of the Holy Spirit. The promise is for you and your children and for all who are afar off – for all whom the Lord our God will call." With many other words he warned them; and he pleaded with them, "Save yourselves from this corrupt generation." Those who accepted his message were baptized, and about three thousand were added to their number that day.*

(Acts 2: 14 – 41)

So, we have the answer from the passage – to be born again a person should "repent and be baptized and receive the Holy Spirit". The three are important.

Repentance is not exactly sorrow, but change of mind and attitude. There are churches of the broad road (false) Christianity that would say, *"Hey, you must weep and beat upon your chest"* in order to be forgiven. But in truth, the narrow road (authentic) Christianity teaches that in the cross of Jesus Christ, God has already forgiven you. You are not invited to feel sorry and weep for your sinful nature and your sins, since they are already forgiven. What is pathetic is the fact that you have been ignorant of the overabundant grace of God and the limitlessness of his mercies, and that for which you should be sorry is the fact that you have continually resisted the saving gospel of Jesus Christ. But God is not interested in your sadness and tears, God is interested in our joyful acceptance of the provisions of his grace, although indeed you may not be able to joyfully accept the grace and gift of God, if you do not first admit the simple fact that you have ignorantly, or rebelliously, erred from his way of salvation.

Having taken the first step of realising that Jesus indeed was crucified and raised again from dead, and is the Christ; and having recognised that whatever religion or belief that you have embraced, which does not preach the free forgiveness of sins as sealed by the sufferings and death of Jesus, and does teach the free gift of the Holy Spirit, is a path of error, the next thing required in order to be born again is to admit your error and joyfully embrace God's grace and way of salvation. And while doing that, you must also recognise that turning around from whatever you have believed to embrace the narrow road Christianity would put a lot of pressure on your lifestyle, and your relationship with other people, and yet know that the eventual cost in terms of eternal excommunication from God and torments is greater than whatever the cost of coping with the pressures from the new faith.

Then comes the next major step, you must practically **submit** yourself to be committed to the narrow road Christianity. The practical submission begins with baptism in water. Baptism by immersion in water is a rite that confirms that you accept the death and resurrection of Jesus Christ as undeniable truths, and are prepared to be committed to the narrow road Christianity even in the face of death. Indeed, a person who does not understand what water baptism stands for may be baptised without this conviction and preparedness of mind, but such baptism is void. And at once, if God already finds this conviction and preparedness of mind in a person, God can endow the person with the Holy Spirit. And hence, not having been baptised in water may not prevent a person from being born again because in the rite of water baptism, the most essential thing is not the water but the conviction. But this does not mean that a person who has already received the Holy Spirit should no longer be baptised in water. By Christian principles, as long as there is a born again person available to administer the rite of water baptism to you, and as long as water is available for the immersion, you have to be baptised because the water aspect of it is also important, which if there is an opportunity to do becomes **essential**. The further reason is that the immersion in water is a token, a proof, a seal, an open acknowledgement (confession) of your conviction in the redemptive work achieved by the death, burial and resurrection of Jesus and of your preparedness to follow the way of Christ even in the face of physical death. As much as the opportunity for that confession exists, it becomes required.

> *"Do not be afraid of those who kill the body but cannot kill the soul. Rather, be afraid of the One who can destroy both soul and body in hell. . . . Whoever acknowledges me before men, I will also acknowledge him before my Father in heaven. But whoever disowns me before men, I will disown him before my Father in heaven."*
>
> (Matthew 10: 28 – 33)

The Christendom is full of many arguments about water baptism. However it may be, anyway, Christian baptism by immersion in water is an act of confession – and confession is not an option, but a requirement, as much as the opportunity arises. Water baptism may come before or after one has received the Holy Spirit, but by the principles of the Bible, it is required to be done at the earliest opportunity and administered by a born again person, and not unless the person being baptised has conviction in the death, burial and resurrection of Jesus Christ and is prepared to pay the cost of following the way of Christ to the end.

Receiving the spiritually enlivening Holy Spirit from God, which the Bible variously describes as "Holy Ghost baptism", "being filled with the Holy Spirit", is an instant act of God. One can gradually believe the gospel of Jesus but one cannot gradually receive the Holy Spirit.

There are branches of the broad road Christianity that teach that it is no longer possible to receive the Holy Spirit or that only leaders of the church or selected people can receive the Holy Spirit. Such doctrines are not in accordance with the principles of the Bible and original Christianity. The Holy Spirit is still being received by people in the world today. While there is no automatic thing to do in order to receive Holy Spirit, it has already been explained that God cannot fill you with his Holy Spirit if you have a tendency to grieve the Holy Spirit. The things that can be done in order not to grieve the Holy Spirit are highlighted in the next chapter of this book. While doing those things, you have to desire the baptism of the Holy Spirit and pray for it until you have it. And when you have it, you would know. You cannot reckon yourself by faith to already have it, you can only pray for it expectantly and ask people who are born again to pray with you and for you. Then when the Holy Spirit comes, the evidence would be that He would communicate with you.

The Voice of God.

I lived in a bungalow. Behind my bedroom window, a hen made its nest in a corner where two walls join in a right angle. It sat on those eggs for days, and was usually silent even when I move near it. Occasionally, it made some sounds. But the chicks in their shells were not yet fully formed, I could not hear any response from them to the sounds of their mother, and it is likely they had not even developed any sense of hearing yet. But their lives dawned one beautiful morning – they hatched into the world. The mother hen makes sounds to them, and they make theirs too. They are alive.

When it comes to spiritual aliveness and being born again, as the Bible teaches, coming alive in God is much like the way the chicks are hatched. When you are yet to be born again, your spirit does not hear what the Father Spirit, the eternal God, says. But as you wait to be hatched into spiritual vitality by the Holy Spirit of God, it just comes to you suddenly that you hear and recognise the voice of God.

Yesterday someone asked me, *"how does one know the voice of God?"*. Indeed, many people want to have a pre-knowledge of the voice of God, so that they would not mistake another voice for God's. However, the voice of God is one thing that nobody can describe to you. If someone who had answered a phone call on your behalf reports to you that a "lady with a high-pitched, soprano voice" has left a message for you, how would you tell if it was your friend, or your cousin, when the brief description fits the voices of both ladies? However, if you had been the one who answered the call, there is the likelihood that you would be able to tell the voice of the one apart that of the other. Likewise, as children we grow to recognise the voice of our mothers and distinguish between it and other voices. As for the voice of God your spirit by its nature as God's offspring would recognise it when the Holy Spirit begins to speak with your spirit. As no one coaches the chicks to distinguish between the voice of their own mother and those of other mother hens, you need no one to coach you ahead on how to recognise the voice of God. Nevertheless, because the Holy Spirit is the Spirit of the Christ, the voice of God would not speak to you things that contradict the doctrines of Jesus Christ, the bulk of which are taught to you by the Bible and born again persons around you. Yet you would in time get accustomed to the voice of God and would be able to recognise when the divine inspiration – voice of God – springs up from beneath your mind. Then you can speak forth with unwavering assurance, "thus says the Lord", like the prophets.

Concerning the voice of the Holy Spirit, here are a few Bible guidelines:

"I tell you the truth, the man who does not enter the sheep pen by the gate, but climbs in by some other way, is a thief and a robber. The man who enters by the gate is the shepherd of his sheep. The watchman opens the gate for him, and the sheep listen to his voice. He calls his own sheep by name and leads them out. When he has brought out all his own, he goes ahead of them, and his sheep follow him because they know his voice. But they will never follow a stranger; in fact, they will run away from him because they do not recognize a stranger's voice." Jesus used this figure of speech, but they did not understand what he was telling them.

(John 10: 1 – 6)

"I have much to say to you, more than you can now bear. But when he, the Spirit of truth, comes, he will guide you into all truth. He will not speak on his own; he will speak only what he hears, and he will tell you what is yet to come.

(John 16: 12 – 13)

This is how you can recognise the Spirit of God: Every spirit that acknowledges that Jesus Christ has come in the flesh is from God, but every spirit that does not acknowledge Jesus is not from God . . ..

(1 John 4: 2 – 3)

Summarily, when the prophetic inspiration comes to you; you would know it is the Spirit of God. But any prophetic inspiration that is against Jesus Christ is ungodly.

Chapter Eleven

FAITH WITHOUT WORKS

"The Value of Good Works".

You are saved by faith.

The Bible talks of being born again as being "saved". Invariably, when the word "salvation", is used in the Christian part of the Bible, it implies *"being saved from the sinful nature of spiritual irresponsiveness towards God"*. While it maintains that it is by his grace that God saves us, the Bible teaches that it is by faith that we enjoy the provisions of this grace, yet having faith alone in God's saving grace is not the totality of what a person needs in order to be born again. The Holy Spirit would only rest upon the person that would not grieve him. In addition to faith, therefore, there are quite several other things that one must endeavour to keep, so as not to grieve the Holy Spirit.

Of course, it is possible that one should receive the Holy Spirit even before one has fully developed all the "additional things" or *"good works"*, yet that would not negate the need to add them to one's faith, because in fact the Holy Spirit can depart from one again even after one has become spiritually alive and can recognise the voice of God. The "good works" or "virtues", therefore, are things that those who aspire to the kingdom of God must add to their faith whether or not they have received the Holy Spirit. Faith alone, without the added virtues cannot keep one spiritually alive in God.

In the same way, faith by itself, if it is not accompanied by action, is dead.

(James 2: 17)

So, if a man is saved from the sinful nature by faith in God's grace, what are the actions or virtues that one must add to one's faith in order not to lose one's salvation? The Bible's answer is given in a brief epistle written *"to those who through the righteousness of our God and Saviour Jesus Christ have received a faith as precious as ours [the apostles]"*. (2 Peter 1: 1). In that epistle, the importance of the "additional virtues" is highlighted as a security against falling back into the paths of error:

> *For this very reason, make every effort to add to your faith goodness; and to goodness, knowledge; and to knowledge, self-control; and to self-control, perseverance; and to perseverance, godliness; and to godliness, brotherly kindness, and to brotherly kindness, love. For if you possess these qualities in increasing measure, they will keep you from being ineffective and unproductive in your knowledge of our Lord Jesus Christ. . . . Therefore, my brothers, be all the more eager to make your calling and election sure. For if you do these things, you will never fall,*
>
> (2 Peter 1: 5 – 10)

Indeed, nothing setbacks the backsliding of Christians from the narrow road, and nothing mortifies spiritual death more than these virtues.

Add to your faith goodness.

There is a saying that *"vision is in the eye of the beholder"*, and many people have perverted it to mean that *"nothing is in fact visible, it is only visible to you who see it; and nothing is in fact invisible, it is only invisible to you who cannot see it"*. How so? How logical is it to think that *"a thing is neither visible nor invisible, if you think it is visible then it is, and if you think it invisible, then it is invisible"*? In that same class of deliberate babbles is the idea that *"a thing is neither good nor bad, if you think it is good, then it is good, and if you think it is bad, then it is bad"*, and yet it goes down well with many people. In reality and fact, *"what is good is good, irrespective of what you think of it, and what is bad is bad, irrespective of what you think of it"*.

Life is good, death is bad. Why? There are listless reasons, but primarily life brings joy, gladness, laughter and unity, whereas death brings sadness, sorrow, mourning and separation. Life heals, death hurts. Life causes increase, but death causes decrease. To increase is a *plus* sign, life is positive; to decrease is a *minus* sign, death is negative. To be frank, life is good, no matter what anyone thinks of it, and life is not the same as death.

Because life is good, spiritual goodness consists in being spiritually alive. And when the Bible thus admonishes that those who have faith in God should *"add to faith goodness"*, it directly implies that besides believing in the limitless grace of God and the mercifulness of the redemption effected by the cross and resurrection of Jesus, those who seek for spiritual aliveness must *"love and appreciate **life**"* – spiritual life in particular. Because the way of spiritual life is the way of Christ, which is confirmed as indeed belonging to Christ in his death, burial and resurrection, to love spiritual life is also to love the Spirit of Jesus.

Like a virgin being wedded, a believer who would not grieve the Holy Spirit says to himself or herself, *"I take Jesus Christ, to be my Lord and Saviour, to have and to hold, from this day forward, for better, for worse, for richer, for poorer, in sickness and in health, to love and to cherish, lest death (the sinful nature) do us apart, according to God's ordinance of grace, and thereto I give Christ my troth"*.

In certain Nigerian evangelical churches, it is becoming the vogue to wed only *"for better, for best, for richer, for richest, . . ."* but this is not the pattern of love. The one who truly loves you will stick to you *"for better, for worse, for richer, for poorer . . ."* and so must everyone who embraces the righteousness that comes by having faith in God (the righteousness of the kind that God credited to Abraham, which Jesus preached) be prepared to stick to fellowship with God, notwithstanding the changes in material circumstances. In the Bible the story is told of a faithful bride who espoused herself with these poetic words:

. . . "Do not urge me to leave you or turn back from you. Where you go I will go, and where you stay I will stay. Your people will be my people and your God my God. Where you die I will die, and there I will be buried. May the LORD deal with me, be it ever so severely if anything but death separates you and me."

(Ruth 1: 16 – 17)

That is goodness, which once a person believes in God and in the death burial and resurrection of Jesus Christ, and in the gift of the Holy Spirit, must add to his or her faith.

There is a Christian song that every new believer should master:

I have decided to follow Jesus,
I have decided to follow Jesus,
I have decided to follow Jesus;
No turning back, no turning back.

Though none go with me,
I still will follow;
No turning back, no turning back.

O take the whole world,
But give me Jesus;
No turning back, no turning back.

Indeed, that was what the apostles added to their faith, as they said:

Who shall separate us from the love of Christ? Shall trouble or hardship or perse-
cutions or famine or nakedness or danger or sword? As it is written: "For your
sake we face death all day long: we are considered as sheep to be slaughtered." No,
in all these things we are more than conquerors through him that who loved us.
For I am convinced *that neither death nor life, neither angels nor demons,*
neither the present nor the future, nor any powers, neither height nor depth, nor
anything else in all creation, will be able to separate us from the love of God that is
in ***Christ Jesus our Lord****.*

(Romans 8: 35 – 39)

And to goodness, knowledge.

Is it not pathetic that our generation does not afford us so many endowed persons, called *"thinkers"*, whose illuminated minds provide guidance for both themselves and for their contemporaries? The pity is not that there are no endowed minds, the pity is that we are all endowed with the thinking faculty but not many of us spend quality time thinking.

The ability to think is God's greatest bequest to the animal called humankind, but even then not many of us think any wiser than chickens do. But the authentic faith is a fellowship for great thinkers, people who take time away from the world around them, away from books and videos, away from television and pleasure to think on issues past, present and future. In fact, if you fail to set apart a time and place for thinking (analytically and creatively), you cannot but grieve the Holy Spirit of the Judge and Creator of the world. Reading sifts knowledge, but thinking creates knowledge.

When Moses handed over the leadership of the ancient Jewish nation to Joshua, according to the Bible, he charged Joshua to ***"con-***

stantly think on the scriptures" that he passed on to him:

> *"Do not let this Book of the Law depart from your mouth;* **meditate** *on it day and night, so that you may be careful to do everything written in it. Then you will be prosperous and successful.*
>
> (Joshua 1: 8)

Many people simply read the "holy books" of their religions without taking time to think critically and analytically at what is written in those books, how much less, finding time to pick up books from other religions to analyse critically and comparatively. And how so much less to analyse books and speeches on other issues – the cosmos, evolution, society – *et cetera*. But the Christian faith encourages one to think and compare.

The Christian scriptures are not passed to us as teachings to be imbibed without thought, question or reason.

> *Finally, brothers, whatever is true, whatever is noble, whatever is right, whatever is pure, whatever is lovely, whatever is admirable – if anything is excellent or praiseworthy –* **think** *about such things.*
>
> (Philippians 4: 8)

That sums it up, in authentic Christianity, the mere fact that a doctrine is presented to us as "*true, noble, right, pure, admirable, lovely, excellent or praiseworthy*" does not stop us from thinking critically and analytically on it, much less anything else. If you would not grieve the Holy Spirit, then add to goodness, knowledge by **meditating** on the scriptures and by seeking clarity wherever needed.

And to knowledge, self-control.

I have had bouts of anger, even rage. But over time I have learnt that the enlightened person submits control of the animal passions to what is *known* rather than what is *felt*. Of course, anger like fire does find its use as a tool in some circumstances. But what a good servant and a bad master it is.

In the Bible, God used his anger. Jesus Christ also used his anger. But it takes one who has mastered the use of anger to positively stir this beautiful passion (beautiful when it is the only means by which a quick correction can be effected). The ability to control one's passions (anger and affection inclusive) is self-control, which cannot be employed without sound knowledge. For instance, once a person understands that it is **not** Satan that effects **every** temptation, the person can learn to curb his desires, and nip the inordinate ones in the bud. If you totally avoid tempting yourself, you would be tempted less often.

Self-control is to say to oneself, *"although I feel like doing otherwise, this is the right and good thing for me to do, and it is what I shall do"*.

And to self-control, perseverance.

Perseverance, or patience, or endurance is one thing without which self-control would easily give way. All manners of challenges surge up from time to time, but only a patient person can hold on under constant pressure. Sometimes I have had to wonder what patience really entails. Is it really patience, when a person waits for nothing definite? Is it really patience to keep waiting and not knowing what exactly one is waiting for?

In deed and in truth, one cannot realistically wait indefinitely, without losing patience, unless one is certain of what he or she is waiting for. Learning to fellowship with God is a tortuous, and perhaps also torturous, journey – one cannot simply sprint it through. There would be times when one prays, and do not get what one desires, and for the believer who has not received the gift of the Holy Spirit by which the voice of God is heard, it could be a most discouraging time. But right there is where perseverance helps. Perseverance entails constantly remaining conscious of the fact that the gift of the Holy Spirit is a promise of God to humankind, and it is God's pleasure to endow each of us with his prophetic spirit, and no matter how long the wait, it is a promise he has ever fulfilled to all those who wait for it.

For those who already have the Holy Spirit, there is not much cause to ever be impatient because often times the Holy Spirit speaks in precise terms of things that lie ahead. But there are times when he does not. Above, all there remains the promise concerning the return of Jesus Christ to the world for the final judgement of the world, which every Christian believer looks forth to as a time to enter into perfect fellowship with Christ. In this promise, what causes impatience is the fact that God has not announced a definite time to anyone in this respect and at once the Holy Spirit would ever prompt a person to keep working as though the return of Christ into the world would happen today, in a few hours time. It is not very easy to keep that kind of a mindset of always looking forward to the appearance of Jesus – that *"he would come any moment from now"*, yet the Holy Spirit and the Bible would ever enjoin a person to do so. In this again, the value of perseverance cannot be overemphasised.

You need to persevere so that when you have done the will of God, you will receive what he has promised.

(Hebrews 10: 36)

And to perseverance, godliness.

For the grace of God that brings salvation has appeared to all men. It teaches us to say "No" to ungodliness and worldly passions, and to live self-controlled, upright and godly lives in this present age, while we wait for the blessed hope — the glorious appearing of our great God and Saviour, Jesus Christ, who gave himself for us to redeem us from all wickedness and to purify for himself a people that are his very own, eager to do what is good.

(Titus 2: 11 – 14)

The *"eagerness to do good"* must be consummated by the very acts of godliness and peacemaking. Godliness and worldliness are two things that will never blend. Worldliness is focused on the material world, whereas godliness, even while it considers the material things of this world, look beyond them into spirituality. Worldliness does things towards a material and temporal profit, whereas, godliness does things towards spiritual and eternal gain.

And to godliness, brotherly kindness.

This is how we know what love is: Jesus Christ laid down his life for us . . . If anyone has material possessions and sees his brother in need but has no pity on him, how can the love of God be in him?

(1 John 3: 16 – 17)

The broad road Christianity teaches people to treat as *"brethren"* only those who belong to the same local church congregation or denomination with them. However, authentic Christianity encourages one to embrace as *"brethren"* all who are named by the name of Christ in every place, irrespective of the denomination or sect or local assembly to which they are joined. And this brotherly kindness is not limited to the empty verbal expression *"I love you in the Lord"*. Indeed, it goes further to treating all Christians everywhere to the material possessions that God has put in your care as much you would have treated your own biological siblings, and even more.

And to brotherly kindness, love.

In his famous sermon on the mount, Jesus taught about loving even those who do not deserve love. This is the point where love differs from brotherly kindness. Brotherly kindness is a reciprocal bond – shared and returned between close friends, especially those who belong to the same religion or sect of a religion, or to the same local congregation. But love – pure and unfeigned – as Jesus taught is expended without being replenished yet it never diminishes, because true love once planted is eternal.

> *"You have heard that it was said, 'Love your neighbor and hate your enemy.' But I tell you: Love your enemies and pray for those who persecute you, that you may be sons of your Father in heaven. He causes his sun to rise on the evil and the good, and sends rain on the righteous and the unrighteous. If you love those who love you, what reward will you get? Are not even the tax collectors doing that? And if you greet only your brothers, what are you doing more than others? Do not even pagans do that? Be perfect, therefore, as your heavenly Father is perfect.*
>
> (Matthew 5: 43 – 48)

The perfection of love is being able to love even those who hate you. Until a person has grown to this peak of virtues, in which one blesses even those who curse one, and work out the well-being of those who plot to destroy one, one cannot but grieve God's Holy Spirit.

Chapter Twelve

SIT AT MY RIGHT HAND

"*Your God Shall Fight for You*".

The fruit of the Spirit is love . . .

The most important lesson in all that has been said about the "good works" or "virtues" that a Christian believer must add to his or her faith is NOT that once a person has added all the identified virtues to once faith, one has automatically become born again. Rather, it is indeed possible for one to have all these things and yet remain spiritually irresponsive towards God. But anyone who is alive towards God, having had his or her spirit reawakened by God's gift of the Holy Spirit, cannot lack any of these things.

Paul while he wrote to the Christian believers of Galatia to educate them on the difference between righteousness as obtained by efforts under the Law and the Prophets and righteous as freely obtained by faith in Christ, summed up the manifestation of a regenerated spirit in the life of a Christian believer as such that the Law cannot negate:

> *But the fruit of the Spirit is love, joy, peace, patience, kindness, goodness, faithfulness, gentleness and self-control. Against such things there is no law.*
>
> (Galatians 5: 22 – 23)

Jesus himself has said in his sermon on the mount, that "*A city on a hill cannot be hidden*", [Matthew 5: 14], with the further clarification that those to whom God inputs righteousness by faith must demonstrate "good works" openly and without guise. But the "fruits of the Spirit" as Paul called the "good works" do not begin to manifest immediately the tree is planted, just as much as the fruit of any other tree. As there is invariably a time lag between the planting and fruiting of a physical tree, there is always a time lag between the time a Christian believer embraces the faith and/or becomes born again, and the time at which the person begins to demonstrate all the good works. Most Christian believer, in fact, do not begin to fruit until they have passed through periods of trials and tests.

Have you considered my servant, Job?

The story is told in the Bible of a most virtuous man, Job, who was so good that God boasted about him to Satan.

According to the story, Satan protested to God that Job only served God because Job was blessed and protected on all sides. But God insisted that with or without blessings and protections, Job would maintain his faith and righteousness in him. Then God agreed to put Job to trial in order to make him openly demonstrate his "good works" without guise and prove to Satan that Job's faith and faithfulness were unconditional and unflinching.

So it was that all the material greatness of Job was wrecked and he lost everything, including his ten children. Yet Job remained faithful to God and continued in his religious convictions against all the odds. Even at that, Satan was not satisfied. Satan protested to God that at least, Job's life was not being threatened and that Job could even have willingly sacrificed all he had lost in order to remain alive:

Then the LORD said to Satan, "Have you considered my servant Job? There is no one on earth like him; he is blameless and upright, a man who fears God and shuns evil. And he still maintains his integrity, though you incited me against him to ruin him without any reason." "Skin for skin!" Satan replied. "A man will give all he has for his own life. But stretch out your hand and strike his flesh and bones, and he will surely curse you to your face." The LORD said to Satan, "Very well, then, he is in your hands; but you must spare his life." So Satan went out from the presence of the LORD and afflicted Job with painful sores from the soles of his feet to the top of his head. Then Job took a piece of broken pottery and scraped himself with it as he sat among the ashes. His wife said to him, "Are you still holding on to your integrity? Curse God and die!" He replied, "You are talking like a foolish woman. Shall we accept good from God, and not trouble?" In all this, Job did not sin in what he said.

(Job 2: 3 – 10)

There is the argument that the story of Job as recorded in the Bible is mere fictional poetry. But here we are not after proving whether it was fact or fiction as that would unduly lengthen this book and take us away from the focus of our arguments. However, we shall sift the moral of the story, which culminates in the submission that even when Job's health failed so much that his life was at risk, Job yet trusted and also loved the LORD. The salient point is that Job's wife advised him to *"curse God and die"*, probably supposing that a person's existence ceases at biological death. But Job, obviously because he believed that biological death does not put an end to a person's existence, retorted that his wife's suggestion was *"foolish"*.

Nevertheless, as it happened to Job, so it pleases God to happen to anyone who would believe on the name of the same God that Job served: God invariably allows everyone who would follow the narrow road religion to be tried and tested in one way or another – in multiple ways, in fact. It is in these various tests and trials, and through them, that a Christian believer practically affirms his faith in God and adds the *"good works"* – *"fruits of the Spirit"* to his or her faith. Without trials, the fruits of the spirit are not likely to ripen. For instance, how can a man or woman who is not hated by anyone *"love those who hate"* him or her?

Consider it pure joy, whenever you face trials

The apostles encouraged themselves and all those who share the faith in Christ for the imputed righteousness to joyfully embrace various trials:

> *Consider it pure joy, my brothers, whenever you face trials of many kinds, because you know that the testing of your faith develops perseverance. Perseverance must finish its work so that you may be mature and complete, not lacking anything.*
>
> (James 1: 2 – 4)

The depth and length of the trials and tests that a Christian believer faces is often proportional to the extent that Christianity has gained ground in the community in which he finds himself or herself. Generally, new Christian believers living in predominantly Christian communities face less trials and persecutions than people who live in non-Christian communities. And the people of the false, but popular, broad road Christianity often persecutes the people of the authentic faith. However, even where the people in the person's community do not directly oppose a person's Christian faith, tests and trials come in various other ways. For instance, how easy was it for Job to continue with his faith in "the giver of life", who calls himself "the resurrection and the life", when in fact all his ten children died in one day and did not resurrect? How easy is it for Christian believers to trust in the "the Creator and provider" when many millions of them live in abject poverty? How easy is it for Christians who are terribly sick to continue their faith in the "Almighty healer" and "Great Physician" when many of them are afflicted with terrible sickness and diseases without cure?

Having lost two very close Christian friends to sickle cell anaemia, including one who died while his father, a Christian pastor, and myself, held his hands praying for him to recover and live, I am able to identify with the challenges that Christians face in their health conditions. Under the very trying circumstances, how easy is it for a new Christian believer to cling to faith in the "eternal miracle worker", when the miracle or healing that he or she expects fail to come?

Though he kills me, yet will I trust in him.

When his faith was being tested and tried, Job staunchly affirmed that he would maintain his faith in God even in the face of death.

Though he slay me, yet will I hope in him; I will surely defend my ways to his face.
(Job 13: 15)

Like Job, every Christian invariably must reach the point in life, when he or she would have to decide that *"even if it comes to death"*, they shall remain committed to the way of Christ. Indeed, many Christians have died for their convictions in the name of Christ to prove their love for God and the certainty of their convictions in human existence after death.

Christian martyrdom is not such that should come by suicide, though some other religions lay claim to martyrdom by killing themselves in suicide attacks on other people. While I may not perfectly understand from their own point of view why they should do that, at least I understand that Christians believe that the ultimate Judge and Avenger is God. A true Christian must prove his love to God and his love to humankind by submitting himself or herself to death if it comes, whilst remaining conscious of the fact that the hallmark of love is to love one's enemies. I do not know how to argue in defence of the "love" that a suicide killer has for the people he or she kills because suicide killing often springs from a motive of anger and vengeance, rather than compassion for the people that one kills in the attack. Unlike a suicide bomber, however, the Christian martyr must prove that *"God is Most Gracious and Most Merciful"* by having compassion on the people at whose hands he or she is killed for the faith.

Your God shall fight for you!

The story is also told in the Bible of a Hebrew fellow, Gideon, who had destroyed the idols of some non-Hebrews. When the issue was reported to his father, the father said to the people who worship that idol to let the god fight for himself.

In the morning when the men of the town got up, there was Baal's altar, demolished, with the Asherah pole beside it cut down and the second bull sacrificed on the newly built altar! They asked each other, "Who did this?" When they carefully investigated, they were told, "Gideon son of Joash did it." The men of the town demanded of Joash, "Bring out your son. He must die, because he has broken down Baal's altar and cut down the Asherah pole beside it." But Joash replied to the hostile crowd around him, "Are you going to plead Baal's cause? Are you trying to save him? Whoever fights for him shall be put to death by morning! If Baal really is a god, he can defend himself when someone breaks down his altar. So that day they called Gideon "Jerub-Baal," saying, "Let Baal contend with him," because he broke down Baal's altar.

(Judges 6: 28 – 32)

Letting God fight for himself is a fundamental Christian principle. Indeed, there are so many bloodsheds occasioned by the claims and counter-claims of various religions, and this is very unfortunate. In Nigeria, we have witnessed many such simply because the Moslem community, for instance, may consider the statements made by a Christian to be blasphemous, or vice versa. But the factor of blasphemy is deep and inherent. Moslems should know that it is as much blasphemy to Christians when Moslems say that Jesus is not the Christ or the Son of God as when Christians too make statements that Moslems consider offensive in reference to Prophet Mohammed. We rationally cannot afford to continually kill ourselves over issues that we cannot change. The disagreement on the person of Jesus Christ is rooted in the mutually exclusive claims already recorded about him in both the Bible and the Koran. Christians, because they consider the Bible sacred would not re-write it, and neither would Moslems re-write the Koran, for the same reason. Thus, the dispute cannot be changed. But what can be changed, and should be changed, are our attitudes and reactions to so-called blasphemies. If blasphemies are indeed "statements that are wrongly made against God", then God if he is truly God should be able to fight for himself.

If a thirty-year-old man and his six-month old baby should come under attack, we normally do not expect the baby to fight in defence of both himself and his father. It is the stronger person that should defend the duo. Likewise is this issue: those who worship God can only rationally fight in defence of both themselves and God if they consider themselves stronger than God, in which case such a God as they defend would be a false God – an impostor. But as God or Allah is reckoned to be stronger than humans, he should be allowed to fight in his own defence and in defence of those who trust in him. That is the more reason why Christian principles uphold that *"Christians should not avenge themselves"*. (Romans 12: 19).

All religions teach that at the end of a human's life on earth, God makes an evaluation and judgment of that person's life. However, if all who embrace these religions truly believe this, why should there be found anyone who fights to defend God? A person who blasphemes the name of God has not sinned against humans but against God, and if anyone believes that no blasphemer would escape the judgment of God, or that God is the wisest, then such a one should leave the judgement and punishment of the blasphemer to God. Otherwise, how else can one prove that one is living in conformity with the mind of the God that is deemed *"Most Gracious, Most Merciful"*? Indeed, the greatest grace one could bestow and the greatest mercy that one could show is to love even those who hate one. If God demonstrates by himself that he loves even those who blaspheme against him, and thinks it is best to give them a long opportunity to repent, then those who worship God should consider God's approach as the best. This is what true Christianity teaches and upholds.

Every new Christian must come to God with the preparedness to love, tolerate and be most merciful and most gracious to even those who hate him or her, and those who hate and blaspheme against God. Anything less than this cannot but grieve the Holy Spirit of God, which is what makes a human born again and spiritually responsive towards God. This preparedness is always learned and demonstrated in the trials and tests that come the way of a Christian believer.

Chapter Thirteen

HE TEACHES MY HANDS TO WAR

"Fight the Good Fight of Faith".

Now I know that you fear God.

The Bible is full of many stories, many of which sound quite incredulous. One such story is that told about how God tried Abraham by asking him to sacrifice his son. According to the story, Abraham had waited so many years to receive the promised child, and just when everything seemed to be going perfectly aright, God asked Abraham to sacrifice the child. Abraham demonstrated his love for God, and his respect for the wisdom of God, by taking the child with him to the place of sacrifice and preparing to kill him in sacrifice to God. Indeed, he could have wondered why God chose to have the child sacrificed rather than any of his numerous animals. Yet, he refused to question God's wisdom and decision. He simply yielded in obedience. Then, just a slight moment before Abraham would kill the child; God stopped him and gave a ram as ransom for the life of the young man. In approving Abraham's faithful devotion as demonstrated by his willingness to obey the *Everlasting Father* even when it seemed most stupid to do so, God said to Abraham, *"Now I know that you fear God"*.

Times of trial do not persist forever, although a Christian constantly faces tests all through from the very moment that he or she decides to become a Christian to the instance of his or her biological death. But trials do not last forever. Indeed there comes a time of refreshing, when the strength and conviction of the Christian is replenished.

"For a brief moment I abandoned you, but with deep compassion I will bring you back. In a surge of anger I hid my face from you for a moment, but with everlasting kindness I will have compassion on you," says the LORD your Redeemer. "To me this is like the days of Noah, when I swore that the waters of Noah would never again cover the earth. So now I have sworn not to be angry with you, never to rebuke you again. Though the mountains be shaken and the hills be removed, yet my unfailing love for you will not be shaken nor my covenant of peace be removed," says the LORD, who has compassion on you. "O afflicted city, lashed by storms and not comforted, I will build you with stones of turquoise, your foundations with sapphires."

(Isaiah 54: 7 – 11)

The trials that a Christian faces always strengthen the faith of the Christian if the Christian does not recoil from them. The trials, and the *"good works"* that they bring into the life of the Christian, are a foundation for a time that the Christian is able to *"fight the good fight of faith"*. Lest *"fighting the good fight of faith"* should appear a contradiction of the principle of *"letting God do the fighting"*, it should be further clarified that what is termed as *"good fight"* differs from a fight that is rooted in strife and clamour.

With Christianity, there are no hard and fast rules as per the strata of progress that one passes through in the faith, and this particularly applies to how soon a Christian recognises what *"the good fight of faith"* means and how soon he or she actually begins to do *"martial exploits"* accordingly.

We do not fight against flesh and blood!

The *"good fight of faith"* to which Christians are called to actively engage in, and for which the various trials and tests prepare them, is not such as is waged against outward human forms, or indeed anything in the material world.

Finally, be strong in the Lord and in his mighty power. Put on the full armor of God so that you can take your stand against the devil's schemes. For our struggle is not against flesh and blood, but against the rulers, against the authorities, against the powers of this dark world and against the spiritual forces of evil in the heavenly realms. Therefore put on the full armor of God, so that when the day of evil comes, you may be able to stand your ground, and after you have done everything, to stand. Stand firm then, with the belt of truth buckled around your waist, with the breastplate of righteousness in place, and with your feet fitted with the readiness that comes from the gospel of peace. In addition to all this, take up the shield of faith, with which you can extinguish all the flaming arrows of the evil one. Take the helmet of salvation and the sword of the Spirit, which is the word of God. And pray in the Spirit on all occasions with all kinds of prayers and requests. With this in mind, be alert and always keep on praying for all the saints.

(Ephesians 6: 10 – 18)

The good fight of faith is not fought by swords, or guns, or bombs. It is not executed by schemes of murder attacks or suicide attacks. To the Christian, fights in the material realm are evil fights. Instead of a belt of explosives, a Christian's warfare belt is simply the truth; instead of warfare boots, a Christian's feet are ever ready to go about spreading messages of peace; and instead of swords and guns, a Christian's offensive weapons is simply the knowledge and wisdom of God.

Although the narrow road Christianity is often vehemently opposed by the followers of the other roads, a Christian does not count as enemies the humans who fight against Christianity, yet he or she must recognise that anyone who wages war against Christianity follows after the pattern of the archenemy of Christianity, Satan. Even though Christianity teaches that *"whoever is not for Christ is against Christ"*, yet its message of love, joy and peace negates waging war against human beings.

The belt of truth.

For the ancient Roman soldier, the configuration of whose armour the Apostle Paul uses to demonstrate a Christian's armour for *"the good fight of faith"*, the belt served as both a girdle and a holster for darts and some other weapons of attack.

Like that girdle and holster, it is the truth that a Christian uses to hold himself or herself in place and as well hold the *"weapons"* by which he or she attacks Satan and the evil spiritual cohorts of the devil. However, truth is not often what most people suppose it is. Many people think that the truth has a mere a linear logic value (a + b = c) but the truth, when it comes to spiritual issues and the rudiments of life, is not linear but spherical. As such, therefore, anyone who would totally grasp the knowledge of the truth must view it **circumspectly**, looking at things from all sides and not rushing into conclusions.

Test everything. *Hold on to the good.*

(1 Thessalonians 5: 21)

Testing and researching everything and sifting out only what is good is the way that a Christian holds his or her faith together and as well provides a holster of knowledge upon which he hangs the sharpened reasons, words and strategies that he or she directs against the plots of Satan.

The breastplate of righteousness.

Like the modern-day bullet-proof vest, the breastplate was what protected the soldier's thorax from the enemies' weapons of attack. Arguably, apart from the head region, the part of the human body most vulnerable under attack is the thorax. It is this region of the body that encloses the next two most important organs of the body, after the brain, which are the heart and the lungs. Anything that terminates the functions of the brain, or the heart, or the lungs, would invariably terminate human life. Hence, in warfare, the role of the breastplate cannot be over-emphasised. However, a Christian's breastplate is not the physical bullet-proof vest, or metal breastplate, but the righteousness that God inputs for faith.

Righteousness is not simply a matter of doing what is *"right"* or *"required"*. Rather, righteousness simply consists of yielding continually and increasingly to the voice of the Holy Spirit and taking delight in what is good and beneficial to humankind, and indeed to the entire creation. What would benefit humanity and the environment may not always be expressly *"required"* by law or commandments, but where true righteousness excels man-made righteousness is that it does well for the simple sake of the benefit it would be to the ones on whom the benevolence is bestowed, as though it were required. Righteousness in the inner human always prevents the gift of the *"Holy Breath"* that God gives a believer from being exhaled.

The armoured boots of the gospel of peace.

A soldier's boot is normally for defence, although for the ancient Roman soldier who wore a metallic boot, the boot could enhance a kick in man-to-man combat. Aside for this occasional use in kicking an enemy, a boot is not much more useful than for protection of the soldier's feet.

In the Trojan War, perhaps the greatest of the Greeks that fought was Achilles, the son of Peleus and Thetis – so the story is told. It was said that when Achilles was a child his mother had held him by a heel and dipped him in the river Styx so that every part of him would be invulnerable. However, the heel that was covered by the mother's hand remained vulnerable and was ultimately responsible for his death.

Christians more often seek knowledge and wisdom from the scriptures of the Bible than from Greek stories, yet *"testing everything and upholding the good"* implies that Christians also sift wisdom from even the Greek stories. As with the Bible stories, we are not pursuing whether it was fact or fiction that Achilles became invulnerable after he was dipped into the Styx, or whether there is indeed any such river that separates the world of the living from the world of the dead. However, the moral import of the story, for a Christian believer is that though a person were armed from head downwards and all over, he or she would still remain vulnerable if only an heel remains unprotected. The salient point is to be armed every whole without exception, for once the heel is badly wounded, the soldier can no longer run, or stand firmly to deal with the enemy.

For Christians the readiness to preach the gospel of peace is likened to guarding one's feet. Every Christian is charged to preach **peace** in the world. In his Sermon on the Mount, Jesus Christ taught that *"the peacemakers shall be called the sons of God"* (Matthew 5: 9). And indeed the call to Christianity is call to the *"renewed sonship of God"*, which implies that the one who would be a Christian must also be a peacemaker.

Preaching peace to the world works for the individual Christian and as well for the Church as a whole, serving for what the armoury boot means to the soldier – preaching peace helps a Christian, and indeed the Church to keep on standing firm in the faith. Every true Christian, without exception, whether they carry the name tag "evangelist" or not, has the commission of reconciliation and peace.

Since, then, we know what it is to fear the Lord, we try to persuade men. What we are is plain to God, and I hope it is also plain to your conscience. We are not trying to commend ourselves to you again, but are giving you an opportunity to take pride in us, so that you can answer those who take pride in what is seen rather than in what is in the heart. If we are out of our mind, it is for the sake of God; if we are in our right mind, it is for you. **For Christ's love compels us***, because we are convinced that one died for all, and therefore all died. And he died for all, that those who live should no longer live for themselves but for him who died for them and was raised again. So from now on we regard no one from a worldly point of view. Though we once regarded Christ in this way, we do so no* *longer. Therefore, if anyone is in Christ, he is a new creation; the old has gone, the new has come!* **All this is from God, who reconciled us to himself through Christ and gave us the ministry of reconciliation: that God was reconciling the world to himself in Christ, not counting men's sins against them.** *And he has committed to us the message of reconciliation. We are therefore Christ's ambassadors, as though God were making his appeal through us. We implore you on Christ's behalf: Be reconciled to God.*

(2 Corinthians 5: 11 – 20)

So, that is just what it is. Christians are not out to preach that God is angry with the world and looking down with volcanic nostrils that steam with fire and brimstone, at the sins of humankind. All we are saying is that God has used Jesus Christ to provide the means of reconciliation between himself and humankind, not counting sins against humankind, but reaching out to us in love and mercy. The armoury boot of the Christian is the eager preparedness to always share this knowledge with everyone that would listen.

Christians as ambassadors of Christ stand to carry on the commission of reconciliation, which Christ instituted, between humankind and God. Being peacemakers therefore is not just a matter of brokering peace between humans and humans alone, but also that of brokering peace between God and humankind. Ideally, the sole objective of Christians' preaching of the gospel is to broker peace.

The shield of faith.

The shield of the ancient Roman soldier does not have a modern-day replacement in wars, unlike the breastplate for which bullet-proof vests now stand. However, the modern soldier is often shielded in battle by armoured vehicles which provide greater security than just an arm-held shield.

For the Christian waging war against Satan and the evil spirits in order to liberate the humans that are held bound by these under the yokes of ignorance, faith provides a shield from the various spiritual attacks of the enemy. Yet faith, like monetary currencies, is not an end in itself. Money buys food, but no sane person would normally chew up currency notes to quench hunger. In like manner, faith is not an inherent power that a human could always use at will without recourse to God. Contrary to a watered-down definition of faith, as mere confidence, the Christian protective faith is **recourse** to God. God by his awesome power, not our mere confidence, is what shields us.

Indeed, in the Bible Jesus Christ specifically stated that *"if one has faith, all things are possible to the one who believes"*. (Mark 9: 23). But the word *"believe"* is always a transitive verse; its meaning is not complete unless there is an object of belief. And "having faith" too is transitive – Jesus Christ did not say we should just *"have faith"*; he specifically clarified that we should *"have faith in God"*. (Mark 11: 22). This marks apart the true Christian faith from that which is preached by the false and popular Christianity. It is not the Christian faith, when one says *"I believe I can fly, and because I believe, therefore I would fly and touch the skies"*. Rather, the Christian faith says, *"I believe that God can make me fly, and because God enables me, therefore I would fly"*.

Paul stated that he *"could do all things,* **through Christ who strengthens**" him (Philippians 4: 13). As every work done requires strength, when Paul did whatever he did, it was **the strength** that Christ gave him that was employed, not just **the confidence** that Paul reposed in Christ. The confidence linked Paul to Christ's strength but it was not the confidence that did the works, but God.

In the psalms, a comparison was made between two people who both had faith. One people had faith in their own horses and chariots, while the other people had faith in God. There is good reason to believe that both people have commensurate confidence. However, the faith of those who trusted in horses and chariots could not save them, whereas the faith of those who trusted in God worked. In fairness of judgment therefore, it was not simply the faith that worked – what worked was the power and strength of God, which excelled the powers and strengths of horses and chariots.

Now I know that the LORD saves his anointed; he answers him from his holy heaven with the saving power of his right hand. Some trust in chariots and some in horses, but we trust in the name of the LORD our God. They are brought to their knees and fall, but we rise up and stand firm.

(Psalms 20: 6 – 8)

The helmet of salvation.

Salvation implies being saved. And being saved implies that there is a situation or danger from which one has been rescued. The helmet of salvation, as it were in Paul's epistle represents salvation from the sinful nature, which is enmity with God.

Although as a shooting target, the head is not always the best part of the body to target in warfare much more that it is easily shifted and has a smaller surface area in comparison to the thorax, yet the fact that the head is not so easy to target does not negate the importance of covering it with an helmet. Since the head houses the most important organ of the body, the brain, which coordinates and controls every other member of the body, it is compulsory to protect the head in every possible way.

Like the helmet, salvation by being born again ensures that a Christian believer does not lose control over every other aspect of his spirituality and faith.

The sword of the spirit, which is the word of God.

When I was newly converted to Christianity, I was given a small booklet by a friend. The booklet has the title *"A Letter for You"*. The booklet taught that *the Bible is God's Word, which can be taken as a boss' letter dictated to his secretary for typing out.* The overall idea of the booklet is that God is the real author of the Bible and the human writers of the various books of the Bible were just like secretaries to God. The booklet further teaches that *"every time a person reads the Bible, God is directly speaking to the person"*. Growing up in the Christian faith after reading that book, I found that the Bible is not as simple as just a letter from God to me.

Indeed, most Christians hold that because the Bible is written by men that were inspired by God's Holy Spirit, the Bible is therefore God's Word. I personally do not have any problems with that, although I very much sympathise with the concerns of many people who find it hard to take it this way. And that is much more because I have read the Bible itself and found out firsthand that the Bible is presented by its human writers more as *"God's Witness"*, or *"God's Wisdom"* than as *"God's Sayings"*. I have explained earlier that in the original languages of the Bible, what is called "word" is not always that which is spoken, but also that which is known. Hence, when the Bible is referred to as *"the word of God"*, it is represented as *"the mind [reason, thought, knowledge] of God"* rather than as *"the speeches of God"*.

The last time I spoke extensively on this point with a younger Christian, he seemed to get all the more confused, and perhaps, for that reason, I should refrain from speaking extensively on it in this book. However, I did have another experience with another Christian friend who said, *"The Bible is the Word of God, Jesus is the Word of God, therefore the Bible is Jesus; and since Jesus also said 'I and my Father are one', then the Bible is God*". Indeed, many Christians know the Bible more than they know God as a person, and quite many of them do not even want to know God personally so far they know the Bible thoroughly. Alas, they worship the Bible rather than the God to whom the Bible was intended to direct them.

For many worshipers of the Bible, all they care to know about any idea is the label *"it is written"*, and they find that there is at least one Bible verse that supports an idea, they are ready to go with the idea. All they remember is that when Jesus would overcome the temptations as recorded in the Bible, he used the scriptures, saying *"it is written"*, but they in fact forget that the tempter had also used the scriptures to tempt Jesus, also saying *"it is written"*. (Matthew 4: 6). Indeed many people who seek guidance for Christian living today and look to the Bible for help and guidance are easily misled by the Bible! Not because the Bible mislead, but because many Bible readers fail to realise that Satan sought to mislead even Jesus Christ by use of the scriptures. There is no contention that what is written in the Bible has been written with intentions towards the good of the reader; but quite many things written in the Bible are respectively true in the linear logic of it: whereas the comprehensive truth is spherical and circumspective, taking into consideration a balanced and proportionate mix of all that is linearly true. Quite many biblical directions are negated and overridden or otherwise modified by other biblical directions such that the person that would embrace a doctrine simply because it is biblical must first recognise that being biblical is not so simple. And we have not even mentioned the fact that quite many versions of the Bible are **interpretations** rather than **translations** of the original text and as such are products of made-up minds. Even though it is commendable that the various editions of the Bible's interpretations compare favourably with one another in their overall submission, yet there is the fact that many **details** do not exactly tally.

When the Bible does say that the *Word of God* is the *"sword of the Spirit"* for the Christian believer, it does not represent that the Bible is the sword. What is unquestionably the sword of the spirit is in fact to be found in the spiritual realm rather than in the material, and it is nothing else but the constant directional voice of God's Holy Spirit.

To the ancient Jewish nation, God had said that he would give them guidance continually by *"**the voice**"*, although at that time the Law already existed as *"scriptures"*.

*Whether you turn to the right or to the left, your ears will hear **a voice** behind you, saying, "This is the way; walk in it."*

(Isaiah 30:20 - 22)

For Christians, the Bible does not say that *"as many as are led by what is written are the children of God"*, rather, the Bible says *"as many as are led by **the Spirit of God** are sons of God"*. [Romans 8: 14]. The guiding inner voice which tells a person *"thus says the Lord"* is exactly what the sword of the Spirit is for a Christian believer, and the only major means by which the believer attacks the spiritual forces of Satan. The **inspiration** of God's Holy Spirit is the sword of the Spirit.

Praying in the Spirit.

Many times when people pray, they seem to forget that God is Spirit, and the mouths with which humans voice out prayers are physical – animal to be exact – and so also is the brain in which the thoughts expressed in prayers are conceived. With this fact in mind, can we really say that God hears the prayers made by humans?

Solomon, the wise king of the ancient Jews, wrote about communing with God – giving an advice which implied that prayer is not just a matter of "teaching God" what we wish should be done for us:

Do not be quick with your mouth, do not be hasty in your heart to utter anything before God. God is in heaven and you are on earth, so let your words be few.

(Ecclesiastes 5: 2)

The statement *"God is in heaven and you are on earth, so let your words be few"* makes us wonder if and how God hears us at all. When people kneel to pray, other people nearby (say, living in the next street) may not hear any sound at all, yet the person who prayed would believe that God who *"is in heaven"*, so very far away, hears the words of the prayers. How does God hear? If God hears, does he hear because he is omnipresent or because he is Spirit? If it is because he is Spirit, does it mean that every spirit hears everything we say with our animal lips?

For Christians, the sense in prayer is not that God reckons with the exact words that are used in prayer; rather Christians believe that God in his omniscience knows and reckons with our minds and spirits and answers our yearnings even when they are not yet voiced out. Nevertheless, the founding pillars of Christianity advocated that we pray by the employ of both our minds and spirits.

For this reason anyone who speaks in a tongue should pray that he may interpret what he says. For if I pray in a tongue, my spirit prays, but my mind is unfruitful. So what shall I do? I will pray with my spirit, but I will also pray with my mind; I will sing with my spirit, but I will also sing with my mind.

(1 Corinthians 14: 13 – 15)

Because the physical world is borne out of the spiritual, and remains a dimension and shadow of the spiritual, God although he is Spirit reckons with what is thought, said and done, in the physical world. However, life in the physical world is temporal and cannot continue eternally. Therefore, if any human does pray in the outer (animal) nature, God still reckons with such prayers but he is not utterly pleased with such because the animal nature is a mere shadow of the spiritual nature.

In his bestseller book, *Getting Through Customs*, Chua Wee Hian tells us how his name *"Chua"* means *"Rat"* in one language, and also means *"Lord"* in another language. There are myriads of languages and dialects on earth in which people pray to God. When they do, God reckons with what the mind and spirit desires, and so when a man or woman says *"Chua"* to God, God knows from the person's mind whether it means *"Rat"* or *"Lord"*. So, shouting at the top of ones voice does NOT make God hear more clearly than when one whispers. Likewise, a person may kneel in prayer and may not so much adore God as the other person who remains *"standing in awe"*, the sitting, or bowing, or kneeling, or standing, or whatever other bodily position is maintained while one prays is not what matters to God. It is the minds of our spirits that God reckons with, primarily; and then the minds of our bodies, secondarily. However, as when we touch the flames of two candles and the two flames burn together as a single flame; so it is that the minds of our bodies and the minds of our spirits work in synchrony while we remain alive bodily. By the Bible, our respective outward (animal) persons and our respective inward (spirit) persons, though they are distinct and separate *"consciousnesses"* combine in each of us as one flame from two candles, while the flame of our material lives still burns.

In many churches, speaking in tongues or expressing undecipherable sentences is often taken as praying in the spirit. But in reality, it is very possible to deliberately say meaningless words [if we might so say, though no sound is utterly without meaning – what makes no meaning in your language, might well make a meaning in mine] and claim to be speaking in tongues, while at once those who really pray in the spirit would indeed speak in tongues. Yet speaking in tongues (so-called) is not necessarily praying in the spirit.

Praying in the spirit implies communicating extra-mentally with God – letting our spirit persons communicate with the eternal Spirit Father. Only people who have the enlivening Holy Breath of God in them, and whose spirits have thus been made responsive towards God can pray in the Spirit.

When a person prays in the spirit, his or her inner person communes with God and the outward person (consisting of the body and its brain) may not understand what is really communicated between the spirit and the Spirit Father. However, it is also possible to have an understanding of the sounds that comes from the mouth of such a person at such times.

Communing with God by our inner persons means that we can reach him in ways that are much purer and spiritual than our outward attachments to materiality. It is the person who has reached God in the spirit that has the best communion with God, because God is primarily in the spiritual realm, even though the physical realm is a shadow and dimension of the spiritual.

Having Done All, Stand Firm.

For the Christian that has put in place all the various spiritual armour pieces, the most important thing is not just to put them on but to also use them and continually stand firm in them.

There is a profit motive that is associated with the spiritual armours – and that is the singular objective to "gain" as many souls as possible into the Kingdom of God and to ensure that every possible thing is done to establish the peace of God, and peace with God, on earth. The more people are brought into the Kingdom of God, the fewer the people that are left on Satan's side and the weaker Satan's army becomes.

For some other religions, evangelism by Christians is deemed as mere proselytising with a view to gaining material profits and glory. But far from this, the point of view for the true Christian is that because a human that is not spiritually responsive towards God is at risk of eternal torments, every possible thing must be done to rescue as many people as possible from spiritual death.

A Christian must increasingly recognise that all humans are in fact blood relatives. And as much as it is undesirable for anyone to watch his blood brother perish irrevocably, albeit ignorantly, the Christian heart cannot watch idly while any single soul follows the paths of eternal doom without making effort to rescue such a one. For Christian, evangelism is a matter of life and death, and the struggle to win over people into spiritual aliveness towards God is more important than any medical doctor's efforts to rescue the life of a dying wounded person.

Among Christians there are people who excel in the gift and ministry of evangelism, because they are so effectively endowed by the urge of the Holy Spirit in them, yet this does not translate that unless one is an evangelist one cannot preach the gospels. Since it is a matter of rescuing the perishing, it is more like having escaped death in a ship wreck and fully recovered, to join in the effort to rescue those that are still unfound in the wreck.

The utmost and wisest Christian is the soul-winning one. And any Christian who does not labour towards bringing as many people as possible into the knowledge of God and peace with God, cannot but fall away from the true Christian faith. Every moment, as a Christian born-again believer goes about his or her daily activities, he or she hears in a tone soft but horrid the footsteps of time as it hurries past us; warning us [of the non-recoverability of the time spent] and urging us to always work for the salvation of souls as long time endures.

The fruit of the righteous is a tree of life, and **he who wins souls is wise.**
(Proverbs 11: 30)

Walk while you have the light with you,
The night comes when no man can work,
Walk while you have the light with you,
There may be no more time to work.

Christ Jesus worked when there was light,
He never failed to do the chores,
He toiled through all the days and nights,
The night came that he worked no more.

Saint Peter worked when there was light,
He stood and spoke at Pentecost,
Trudging the Lord's Path which is bright,
The night came that he paid the cost.

Walk while you have the light with you,
The night comes when no man remains,
Work while you have the light with you,
You may not walk this path again.

Praying in the Spirit, and spreading the good news of free reconciliation with God, is the ultimate way that a Christian (and indeed the church as a whole) wages war against Satan and the evil spirits.

There is more about prayer and evangelism than can be discussed in this book, *Does God Truly Exist?*, as such extensive review of these issues fall outside our objective. Yet it is important to mention here that true Christians pray and preach from a pure motive. And the overriding objective is to save as many as could be saved from ignorance and eternal loss, and to bring them into the knowledge of everlasting life that God bestows upon humankind by his Holy Spirit.

Chapter Fourteen

THE HOPE OF GLORY

"Everlasting Life".

Our Father, who is in Heaven.

Of that all been considered, it still behoves us to recognise that the summary reason why people embrace religion is just because they wish to go to Heaven after their earthly life is over. But where exactly is Heaven? And how does Heaven look like?

According to the Bible, Jesus Christ did teach his disciples to pray to *"our Father in Heaven"*, and after his resurrection from the dead, he was lifted up from the earth higher and higher until he was received into the clouds – so the Bible says. Christianity accordingly maintains that he went to Heaven. But is Heaven just a beautiful land beyond the skies or an undefined place beyond the clouds?

At the time that the Bible books were written, it was possible to believe that just beyond the skies is the dwelling place of God, for then the earth was widely thought to be a flat plane. But today, it is no longer the same. The person on the South Pole and the one on the North Pole in fact have their respective heads pointing *"upwards"* in opposite directions.

However, when Christians *"lift up their hands towards Heaven"*, irrespective of the location on the surface of the earth that they respectively do so, they consider themselves as pointing to the same direction. For one thing, it remains the same direction whether or not one is standing on the South Pole or the North Pole, because the direction of Heaven is not in fact as literal as it is supposed.

I came down from heaven.

One of Jesus Christ's controversial doctrines, according to the Bible, is the declaration that he had been in *"Heaven above"* and had *"come down"* to the earth. Indeed, it may be argued that anything that is not located on the surface of the earth, or beneath the surface of the earth, is in fact *"above"* the earth, irrespective of the point on the surface of the earth that one is located. A good example is the moon.

The man on the South Pole perceives the moon as *"up above"* him, just as much as the woman on the North Pole perceives the moon as *"up above"* her, although the position of the moon remains the same whether one is on the South Pole or the North, whereas whatever points *"up"* on the North Pole is not pointing in the same direction with any other thing pointing *"up"* on the South Pole. If a rocket takes off from the South Pole and aims for the moon, it would go *"upward"* from the earth, and likewise would another rocket setting off from the North Pole go *"upward"* from the earth – as though *"upward"* on the North Pole is exactly the same as *"upward"* on the South Pole. Nevertheless, whether a rocket sets out from the North Pole or South Pole, it would eventually reach the moon (if the moon were its destination) because in real terms, the moon is *"beyond"* the earth, not exactly *"above"* it, but whoever would reach that *"beyond"* from anywhere on earth must go *"upward"* as though the *"beyond"* is really *"above"*. It is only *"above"* in perspectives – viewed from earth here – but indeed just *"beyond"*.

As for Heaven, when we read the Bible, it is presented to us as though it just lies *"above"* the clouds, *"above"* the stars, *"above"* the entire material atmosphere, whereas it is indeed represented as *"beyond"* the material world.

Can you by searching find out God?

In the book of Job, we read this thought-provoking question:

Can you fathom the mysteries of God? Can you probe the limits of the Almighty?
(Job 7: 11)

Physical travel into space originated from various interests, not the least of which is the curiosity that makes us want to find out if there are any other living things in places beyond the earth, and perhaps also our curiosity to discover God's Heaven.

Perhaps, if there were balloons or aircrafts on the day that (according to the Bible) Jesus ascended into Heaven, some people would have used this means to follow him and so discovered how humans can physically get to Heaven. However, Heaven as the Bible presents to us is not such that could be entered into with bodies of blood, flesh, and bones.

I declare to you, brothers, that flesh and blood cannot inherit the kingdom of God, nor does the perishable inherit the imperishable.

(1 Corinthians 15: 50)

When the resurrected Jesus Christ ascended into Heaven, the picture that the Bible gives us in the linear truth is that he has gone bodily into Heaven; whereas, the Bible in its circumspective knowledge informs us that he could not have gone into Heaven with flesh, blood and bones. Heaven is not a place in the material dimension and cannot be reached by travels and transport in the material dimensions, even though the material dimension is a shadow and subset of the spiritual. If Heaven cannot be geographically located, or spotted by telescopes, then, how can we be sure that such a place exists?

Christians believe in Heaven, not only because the Bible speaks of such a place, but also because the prayer and prophecy cycle proves the existence of the spiritual world. When God speaks in prophecy, there are often no sounds in the material realm yet the prophets hear God. From where do the messages of the prophecies come from? Since the precise fulfilments of prophecies often confirm their authenticities, are prophecies not indications that there are speeches in the nonmaterial realm which can be translated into the material minds of humans?

The translation from the material dimension into the spiritual dimension or vice versa is such that we may not be able to definitely comprehend with uninspired minds. However, the Bible represents to us that Jesus Christ is not having any more that perishable body (of blood, flesh, and bones) into which Thomas had dipped his finger and hand after the resurrection. In fact, the apostles looked forward to seeing the beauty of that "*spiritual body*" into which Christ's body must of necessity have been translated before his re-entrance into the spiritual dimension:

Dear friends, now we are children of God, and what will be has not yet been made known. But we know that when he appears, we shall be like him, for we shall see him as he is.

(1 John 3: 2)

Apostle John here recognises that the nature of the *"spiritual body"* remains indescribable relative to our material dimension, yet he submits that a set time approaches at which those who have the Spirit and mind of the Christ shall also be translated into the kind of the *"spiritual body"*, which the Christ now has, as his children.

Shall we be here forever?

Three mysteries that the ordinary animal minds of humankind will ever probe but never fully comprehend are time, space, and *The Originator*, God – the three of which are eternal.

When as scientists and cosmologists we say *"ten billion years ago"*, we quite forget that the word *"year"* to us means *"365 days"*, averagely; being the duration of time that it normally takes the earth to revolve round the sun. And at that, when there was no earth, there were practically no *"years"*. So, ten billion years ago, there were in fact no *"years"* – for the earth was not yet existing – but there was time, notwithstanding. If at any time in the future the earth explodes and vanishes, there would be no more *"years"*, but time shall endure, and lengths of time equivalent to the length of a year on earth shall yet endure.

It surprises us, humans, that our tiny speck of dusts and water is so distinct and unique among all the planets and stars in the entire material universe. Our planet – the earth – is special. We are special. But the earth is not eternal; it has a beginning and will as a matter of course have an end. We cannot tell precisely when and how it will end, but we know that it shall definitely end – whether we like it or not.

However, the interesting point is not that our earth is simply special to us – it is in fact special to *Nature* and to *The Originator* of the world so much that we might well call the planet Earth *"the Capital of the material universe"*, even though it is not located at the geographic centre of the universe. Geographic centrality does not really count even among the nations of men – Washington DC, for instance is at the edge of the United States; Cairo is not at the very centre of Egypt; Moscow is not at the very centre of Russia. Although there are countries like Nigeria that relocated their capitals geographically from the edge to the centre, yet most capital cities of world are not at the centre but at the edge. And as such too, the fact that our planet is not at the centre of our solar system or of the universe does not stop it from being reckoned as the capital of the universe. Our planet among all the countless many planets and stars in the material universe is so special – it is the only planet where *"dusts"* are alive and where living *"dusts"* have minds of their own and also produce offspring after their own kinds.

For its speciality to *The Originator*, we know spiritually that we are God's children. Our planet, among all others, is God's nest in the material universe and as such the sun is *"our sun"*, the galaxies are *"our galaxies"*, the stars are *"ours stars"*. All the things in the material universe are ours in God, through God, and for God. Let us take the moon for example, it goes with earth wherever the earth goes, it gives light at night to the earth, but what does it get from the earth in return? The sun gives light and heat and food to the earth, but what does it get back from the earth? All things are for us, and we are for God.

It is by our interactions in prayers and prophecies – when our spirits fellowship with the *Spirit*, the *Everlasting Father* – that we know that God exists and that we are his offspring. Nevertheless, it has also been prophesied that the earth shall come to an end. Of course, among humans – as animals – we know that the crib does not endure forever. The earth is to God what a baby cot is to a woman – we do not keep our children in the crib forever, there always comes a time when the crib is done away with. So it has pleased God to purpose that when his offspring mature in the earth, and have attained in the unity of faith and knowledge to *"the whole measure of the fullness of Christ"*, this earth, our crib, shall be done away with.

> *But the day of the Lord will come like a thief. The heavens will disappear with a roar; the elements will be destroyed by fire, and the earth and everything in it will be laid bare. Since everything will be destroyed in this way, what kind of people ought you to be? You ought to live holy and godly lives as you look forward to the day of God and speed its coming. That day will bring about the destruction of the heavens by fire, and the elements will melt in the heat.*
>
> (2 Peter 3: 10 – 12)

Christians believe and look forward to that time at which everything on earth here would come to an end – a time at which the harvest of the earth would be fully due and perfected. It is in prophecies by God's Holy Spirit that we come to know this, and not by mere mental reckonings. And in as much as the Spirit foretold the birth of the Christ unto us as a child, and that prophecy did not fail, we can, and should, believe that the Spirit's prophecy concerning the return of the Christ in his spiritual body shall not fail. It does not baffle Christians to believe that God would so much care for our very tiny planet and for us humans because Christians understand that here is the centre of God's affection, because he is the Father of our inward (spirit) nature.

The Dead in Christ shall rise first.

As for the abode of God, Heaven, which all Christians look forward to entering, when this earth shall be destroyed it is not reckoned as a place that has been visited by humans. Christians only hope in it because of the promise that has been given to us by God's Holy Spirit.

In my Father's house are many rooms; if it were not so, I would have told you. I am going there to prepare a place for you. And if I go and prepare a place for you, I will come back and take you to be with me that you also may be where I am.
(John 4: 2 – 3)

However, as it is written: "No eye has seen, no ear has heard, no mind has conceived what God has prepared for those who love him" but God has revealed it to us by his Spirit. The Spirit searches all things, even the deep things of God.
(1 Corinthians 2: 9 – 10)

There is a popular and wide-spread sect of "Christians" – as called – who go about teaching that this earth shall endure for ever and that God would change it into a paradise on which resurrected humans would live forever. However, such a doctrine departs from what the Holy Spirit reveals, and from the written Christian scriptures, and from what has been handled down from mouth to mouth over the ages by those who know the Lord. The Bible reiterates that our form of bodies cannot endure forever and that if we must live eternal life, we must of necessity be translated from the material dimension to the spiritual. And when it does speak of the resurrection of those who have died and decayed, begging the fact of the resurrection of Jesus Christ as proof that resurrection takes place, the Bible does not imply that those who have died and decayed and have been absorbed as soil nutrients into trees to become part of your office desk would come back to life to again eat apples and apricots on this earth in the manner that Jesus ate fish and bread after his resurrection. Rather, the Bible submits that when the dead would be raised, they would come with a *"spiritual body"*, the nature of which we may not fully comprehend now. And for those who remain physically alive at that set time, there would be a translation from this material body into the *"spiritual body"*. So the promise of the resurrection is not towards *"living forever in the paradise on earth"*, rather it is about going into the prepared place, which eyes have not seen, nor ears heard, nor minds conceived.

> *According to the Lord's own word, we tell you that we who are still alive, who are left till the coming of the Lord, will certainly not precede those who have fallen asleep. For the Lord himself will come down from heaven, with a loud command, with the voice of the archangel and with the trumpet call of God, and* **the dead in Christ will rise first**. *After that, we who are still alive and are left will be caught up together with them in the clouds to meet the Lord in the air. And so we will be with the Lord forever.*
>
> (1 Thessalonians 4: 15 – 17)

That the dead and decayed would yet live again is unbelievable to those who do not understand the limitlessness of the power and wisdom of *The Originator*, but Christians believe in the resurrection – as unbelievable as it is. This we believe not only because Jesus lives, which we are sure of because of the Holy Spirit given to us, but also because we reckon that the power and wisdom that created the entire magnificent universe out of absolute nothing is capable of anything at all.

Christians do not, however, look forward to resurrecting into this kind of bodies that is composed of *"dusts"*. And neither is it believed that once a human dies, his or her inner spirit person has *"entered the cycle births and deaths"* to be reincarnated into another form. Rather, Christians by prophecies have received that God has set a day of judgment in which to judge the living and the dead and has therefore pronounced any judgment on those humans that have died thus far. Even though at death, the stock is taken of the human life, yet the judgment is not yet pronounced because the Day of Judgment has not yet come. And because the Day of Judgment has not come, Christians believe that when humans dies, their inward (spirit) persons are laid to rest by God, and kept against the Day of Judgment. And as such when a person dies bodily, the two candles are snuffed out – the bodily consciousness ceases to be, and the inward consciousness that shall never cease is laid to rest – preserved by God against the judgment. So until that day, the dead remain utterly unconscious: they neither proceed immediately to Heaven or to the Lake of Fire, and neither are they reincarnated – because their judgments have not yet been pronounced, and shall not be until the Day of Judgment.

When we sleep physically, our animal consciousnesses are at rest, they do not cease. Our animal consciousnesses are preserved through our biological sleeps until we are awakened again. In the like manner, when our animal consciousnesses finally cease at death, the inward (spirit) consciousnesses are laid to rest by God, as though like a sleep. It is that inward (spirit) consciousness that God would awake at the last day for the judgment.

When that day comes, according to the Bible, God would rouse the inward (spirit) persons of those that have received his Holy Spirit and he would translate them together with those who have the Holy Spirit among those who remain physically alive at that time: thus, the *"dead in Christ will rise first"*, on the day that Christ returns to take with him those who have become spiritually responsive towards God. The rest of the dead shall remain dead until their own turn to be raised towards their sentence into the lake of fire.

What we cannot tell.

Every time we speak on the resurrection and the Day of Judgment, and about existence after death, Christians are invariably prompted to disclose more about it than we have already mentioned in this book thus far, and to also prove them. Even though it is such a desirable thing to submit such disclosures and proofs, there are limits to what can be revealed and what can be discussed about these issues much more that spiritual truths are more often known than told. You come into cognisance of it, but really cannot tell. Not so much because it is difficult to fully explain spiritual phenomena with the physical, but more because even when told, the uninspired minds still cannot fully grasp what is spiritual.

Concerning Heaven, how it is, how we shall live there, and whatever else our questions about it are, they are things revealed by the Spirit to those who have the Holy Spirit in them. The other night that Nicodemus came to Jesus, he wanted explanations of spiritual phenomena just as much as many of us want today, but Jesus had simply told him the most rudimentary thing about the *"Kingdom of Heaven"* and that first rudiment, being born again, was too difficult for Nicodemus to grasp.

"How can this be?" Nicodemus asked. "You are Israel's teacher," said Jesus,

"and do you not understand these things? I tell you the truth, we speak of what we know, and testify to what we have seen, but still you people do not accept our testimony. I have spoken to you of earthly things and you do not believe; how then will you believe if I speak of heavenly things?

(John 3: 9 – 12)

Much earlier in this book, I had written about the Big Bang, evolution, and the origin of the world, and about spheres and circles, which are issues about the physical world. My summary, then, that the universe could not have originated by itself unless there is an eternal *Spirit* who used his power and wisdom to create the entire universe is the same submission that Christianity has ever preached to the world in more succinct ways, but the world has ever failed to grasp. Considering that the world has not understood such a simple issue as the creation of our material universe, and of the birth of our spirits, does it make any sense that we should further discuss the spiritual dimensions? If the simpler and immediate dimension, the physical, is not fully comprehensible to many, we shall unduly torture their immature minds by bringing to them the *"harder meats"* of the spiritual.

Beyond that, there is a tradition in Christianity that I must build upon. For the Apostles, the invitation to those who wish to comprehend the spiritual dimension is *"Come and see"*:

I must go on boasting. Although there is nothing to be gained, I will go on to visions and revelations from the Lord. . . . And I know that this man – whether in the body or apart from the body I do not know, but God knows – was caught up to paradise. He heard inexpressible things, things that man is not permitted to tell.

(2 Corinthians 12: 1 – 4)

According to the Bible, and as we have read, when Philip found his brother Nathaniel whom he told, *"We have found the Messiah"*, Nathaniel could not believe and Philip said, *"Come and see"*. In like manner, the things that are made known by God's Spirit about the dimension of the spiritual by *"visions and revelations"* are not such that are to be proved by mere words. We can only **tell that they exist** but as for **proving** that they exist, whoever would pursue such proofs must come in by being born again and see for himself or herself the realities of the Kingdom of Heaven. However, as per the resurrection of the dead in Christ, it is a promise, in which all Christians hope. And Christians are sure of it, because God never breaks his promises.

PART III
MAKE A WISE CHOICE

Sometimes ago, I ran into a senior friend whom I had not seen for a long while. We greeted each other so warmly and after a brief chat, we had to part. While parting, he said something, which I did not hear very clearly: I thought I heard him say, "*Make a future*". I replied, "*There is no problem about the future. The future will make itself*". But he turned back to tell me, "*I didn't say 'make a future', I said, 'make a wise choice'*".

That brief encounter is my motivation for this last part of *Does God Truly Exist?*. I should thank you for your time and attention thus far, but as we now part, I should give you the same complement that I have kept for many years, "*make a wise choice*".

Chapter Fifteen

CHOICE AND CONTINUANCE

"Let the vile be vile still, and let the holy by holy still".

A blessing and a curse.

After writing this whole book, I decided to read it through for myself. Reading through now, not as the author, but as a reader, I might well wonder what is the point of it all. The simple point, I would say, is about the choices we make.

What really concern me if you know nothing at all, or rather all that could be known, about cosmology and the Big Bang? What really concerns me if you have never read the Bible and would never do? What is my business if you wake up to curse God every morning? Your life is yours and not mine; I have my own life to live and with my own concerns. Nevertheless, I have a duty towards you. And my duty is to in form you and draw your attention to the issues that concern your personal one-to-one relationship with God – your *Father*, your *Maker*. That is a duty assigned me by God to whom I owe the responsibility of discharging the duty. But having discharged my duty, the responsibility shifts to you as per what you decide to do with the information that I have passed to you.

In the Bible, we read of Moses and how he led the ancient Jewish nation out of Egypt towards *"the promised land"*. When he could no longer continue with them and had to depart, he recounted to them the options that were open to them. And like Moses, Joshua who took over the leadership of the Jews from Moses, also urged them to make a choice when he too was to depart.

See, I am setting before you today a blessing and a curse – the blessing if you obey the commands of the LORD your God that I am giving you today; the curse if you disobey the commands of the LORD your God and turn from the way that I command you today by following other gods, . . .

(Deuteronomy 11: 26 – 28)

But if serving the LORD seems undesirable to you, then choose for yourselves this day whom you will serve . . . but as for me and my household, we will serve the LORD.

(Joshua 24: 15)

Like Joshua, I have made my own personal choice. You are left to choose for your own self. In the first chapter of this book, I had informed you that the material world could not have originated by itself – there is someone in particular, *The LORD God*, the *One and Only*, who is **the Creator**. In the second chapter, I have informed you that it is not in our outward (animal) forms that we are God's image and likeness but in our inward (spirit) forms. In the third chapter, I submitted that unless a human being is spiritually responsive towards God, the life of such a person is meaningless. In Chapter Four, I talked about Satan and how he is not always responsible for the bad decisions you make. In Chapter Five the submission was on evil spirits and why humankind should not fellowship with the angels that sinned. In Chapter Six, I told you of the false but popular form of Christianity *"the broad road"*, which many people mistake for genuine Christianity. Also in Chapter Six, I told you that secularity is not as harmless as it appears to be. In the seventh chapter, we considered the possibility that if people depart from true Christianity, it may well be because the religion failed to satisfy them; yet, by the examples of Judas and Demas we see that backsliding is not a problem with the religion but with the backsliders. And in the last chapter of the first part of this book, we examined questions about death and the eternal torment of which the Bible warns us.

In the second part of this book, I began by telling you about Jesus and his death, burial and resurrection, and about how the prophecies that were made concerning the destined Christ were fulfilled in his person. In Chapter Ten, the second chapter in *Part II*, I told you what it means to be born again and to have a personal one-to-one relationship with God. The eleventh chapter was about the things that must be added to your faith in case you wish to be born again. Chapter Twelve talks about waiting for God's promise against the odds – which you would by any means get used to if you would walk with God. Chapter Thirteen was about *"fighting the good fight of faith"*, that is *"waging peace"* rather than *"waging war"* on the world, and employing the use of prayer and evangelism above all towards establishing peace between humans and God. In the fourteenth chapter, we reviewed the promise that Christ has made concerning his return to separate those who are spiritually alive from those who are not. That is one promise he reiterated in the concluding part of the book of Revelations:

> *Let him who does wrong continue to do wrong; let him who is vile continue to be vile; let him who does right continue to do right; and let him who is holy continue to be holy.* **Behold, I am coming soon! My reward is with me**, *and I will give to everyone according to what he has done. I am the Alpha and the Omega, the First and the Last, the Beginning and the End."*
>
> (Revelations 22: 11 – 13)

Therefore, choose life.

I could keep on writing on many issues associated with the question *Does God Truly Exist?* but just as the Preacher rightly submitted in his own case, *"Of making many books there is no end, and much study wearies the body"*. [Ecclesiastes 12: 12]. So, adding more and more arguments, analogies, and examples would further lengthen this book beyond what can be conveniently handled and read. In all that has been said anyway, the conclusion we pursue as per our questions would be individually reached. Since choosing to be born again or otherwise is a personal decision that is deemed to have eternal import, you cannot afford to simply jump to a decision – you would of course want to take your time to reflect on all that you have read in this book and may as well re-read several portions of the book while you think on the issues discussed. But the salient point is that you have to actively take the decision to be born again – and have a personal one-to-one relationship with God or not. You would of necessity bear in mind that whatever you decided affects you most importantly. My **well-thought** counsel to you is that **you should choose to be born again**. It will pay you better, in the long run. Whether you do or not, however, you are aware of the consequences of your decision.

This day I call heaven and earth as witness against you that I have set before you life and death, blessings and curses. **Now choose life**, *so that you and your children may live and* **that you may love the LORD your God, listen to his voice**, *and hold fast to him. For the* **LORD is your life** . . .

(Deuteronomy 30: 19 – 20)

APPENDIX

So, what next?

Once more, I should thank you for taking your time to read *Does God Truly Exist?* and to think analytically on the entire discussion and the specific issues in it. Should you have any questions, comments, or response whatsoever, I shall be glad to hear from you. You can input your reactions online at www.doesgodtrulyexist.com/whatnext.htm

In particular, if you decide to have a personal one-to-one relationship with God by becoming born again, or if you are already born again but need any support in enhancement of your present relation ship with God, I should like to hear from you too. The link www.doesgodtrulyexist.com/whatnext.htm contains information for you as well.

LOOKING FORWARD TO HEAR FROM YOU!
Yours sincerely,

Temitope O. Oyetomi, (Email author@doesgodtrulyexist.com)
c/o Baal Hamon Publishers,
P. O. Box 2338, Akure,
Ondo State, Nigeria.

INDEX

You can order additional copies of this book from the following sources:

www.amazon.com

www.baalhamon.com

www.bn.com

www.doesgodtrulyexist.com

www.joyandtruth.org

and at many other bookstores worldwide.

Printed in the United States
132198LV00004B/34/A

9 789780 756826